The Case for the Prosecution

IN THE

Ciceronian Era

The Case for the Prosecution

IN THE

Ciceronian Era

MICHAEL C. ALEXANDER

THE UNIVERSITY OF MICHIGAN PRESS
Ann Arbor

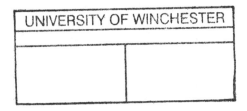

A CIP catalog record for this book is available from the British Library.

Library of Congress Cataloging-in-Publication Data

Alexander, Michael Charles, 1947–
    The case for the prosecution in the Ciceronian era / Michael C.
Alexander.
        p.   cm.
    Includes bibliographical references and index.
    ISBN 0-472-11261-9 (cloth : alk. paper)
    1. Trials—Rome.   2. Prosecution—Rome—History—Sources.
3. Criminal justice, Administration of—Rome—History—Sources.
I. Title.
KJA127.A42   2002
345.45'63205042—dc21   2002003604
    ISBN13 978-0-472-11261-6 (cloth)
    ISBN13 978-0-472-02584-8 (electronic)

TO JEAN

Acknowledgments

I wish to acknowledge the generous assistance that I have received from the University of Illinois at Chicago: to begin the project, a Short Research Leave funded by the Campus Research Board for the fall semester of 1993 and a sabbatical leave granted by the Department of History and the College of Liberal Arts and Sciences for the spring semester of 1994; and to finish the first draft, a sabbatical leave granted by the Department of History and the College of Liberal Arts and Sciences for the fall semester of 1998. In addition, in 1998 the Office of the Vice Chancellor for Research awarded me an Arts, Architecture, and Humanities Equipment Award to purchase a laptop computer.

I am indebted to three libraries in particular for the use of their collections: the Richard J. Daley Library of the University of Illinois at Chicago, the Hillman Library of the University of Pittsburgh, and the John Miller Burnam Classical Library of the University of Cincinnati.

I am also grateful to two editors of the University of Michigan Press, Dr. Ellen Bauerle and her successor Collin Ganio, who have encouraged me and facilitated the publication of this volume, and to the Press readers. I am also indebted to the perspicacious copyediting performed by Jill Butler Wilson, who has substantially improved my manuscript. Any errors that remain are, of course, my responsibility.

Contents

x   *Contents*

Abbreviations

Austin, *Pro Caelio*³	Marcus Tullius Cicero. *Pro M. Caelio Oratio*. Ed. R. G. Austin. 3d ed. Oxford: Clarendon, 1960.
Berry	Marcus Tullius Cicero. *Pro P. Sulla Oratio*. Ed. D. H. Berry. Cambridge Classical Texts and Commentaries 30. Cambridge: Cambridge University Press, 1996.
D.-G.	W. Drumann. *Geschichte Roms in seinem Übergange von der republikanischen zur monarchischen Verfassung, oder Pompeius, Caesar, Cicero und ihre Zeitgenossen nach Geschlechtern und mit genealogischen Tabellen*. Revised by P. Groebe. 2d ed. 6 vols. Berlin and Leipzig: Gebrüder Bortraeger, 1899–1929.
Douglas, *Brutus*	Marcus Tullius Cicero. *Brutus*. Ed. A. E. Douglas. Oxford: Clarendon, 1966.
Du Mesnil	Marcus Tullius Cicero. *Ciceros Rede für L. Flaccus*. Ed. Adolf Du Mesnil. Leipzig: Teubner, 1883.
FIRA	Salvatore Riccobono, ed. *Fontes Iuris Romani Antejustiniani*. 3 vols. Florence: Barbera, 1968–72.
Landgraf	Gustav Landgraf, ed. *Kommentar zu Ciceros Rede pro Sex. Roscio Amerino*. 2d ed. Leipzig: Teubner, 1914.
MRR	T. Robert S. Broughton. *The Magistrates of the Roman Republic*. 2 vols. Philological Monographs of the American Philological Association 15. Cleveland, 1952.

MRR Suppl.	T. Robert S. Broughton. *The Magistrates of the Roman Republic*. Vol. 3. Supplement. Atlanta: Scholars, 1986.
*OCD*³	Simon Hornblower and Antony Spawforth, eds. *The Oxford Classical Dictionary*. 3d ed. Oxford: Oxford University Press, 1996.
ORF	H. Malcovati, ed. *Oratorum Romanorum Fragmenta Liberae Rei Publicae*. 4th ed. Turin: Paravia, 1976.
Pocock	Marcus Tullius Cicero. *A Commentary on Cicero* In Vatinium, *with an Historical Introduction and Appendices*. Ed. L. G. Pocock. London: University of London Press, 1926.
RE	*Real-Encyclopädie der klassischen Altertumswissenschaft*. 70 vols. Stuttgart: J. B. Metzler, 1893–.
Schanz-Hosius	Martin Schanz. *Geschichte der Römischen Literatur bis zum Gesetzgebungswerk des Kaisers Justinian*. Revised by Carl Hosius. 4th ed. 4 vols. Munich: C. H. Beck, 1927–59.
Shackleton Bailey, *CLA*	Marcus Tullius Cicero. *Cicero's Letters to Atticus*. Ed. D. R. Shackleton Bailey. 7 vols. Cambridge: Cambridge University Press, 1965–70.
Shackleton Bailey, *CLF*	Marcus Tullius Cicero. *Epistulae ad Familiares*. Ed. D. R. Shackleton Bailey. 2 vols. Cambridge: Cambridge University Press, 1977.
Shackleton Bailey, *CLQf*	Marcus Tullius Cicero. *Epistulae ad Quintum fratrem et M. Brutum*. Ed. D. R. Shackleton Bailey. Cambridge: Cambridge University Press, 1980.
Statutes	Michael H. Crawford, ed. *Roman Statutes*. Bulletin of the Institute of Classical Studies Supplement 64. 2 vols. London: Institute of Classical Studies, 1996.
TLRR	Michael C. Alexander. *Trials in the Late Roman Republic, 149 B.C. to 50 B.C. Phoenix* Supplement 26. Toronto: University of Toronto Press, 1990.
Webster, *Pro Flacco*	Marcus Tullius Cicero. *Pro L. Flacco Oratio*. Ed. T. B. L. Webster. Oxford: Clarendon, 1931.

CHAPTER ONE

Introduction

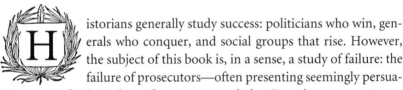istorians generally study success: politicians who win, generals who conquer, and social groups that rise. However, the subject of this book is, in a sense, a study of failure: the failure of prosecutors—often presenting seemingly persuasive cases of criminal conduct—to overwhelm Rome's greatest orator, despite weaknesses in his brief. Of the eleven trials analyzed in this volume, none definitely resulted in condemnation, eight definitely ended with acquittal, and two—or possibly three, if we opt for extreme caution in saying that we do not know the outcome of the trial of Roscius of Ameria (see chap. 8)—have uncertain outcomes. The failure of most or perhaps all of these eleven prosecutions is all the more remarkable because prosecutors must usually have believed that they had a real chance to win their cases.

Criminal prosecutors at Rome were private individuals who applied to a court for the right to indict a citizen. They held no office that obligated them to bring wrongdoers to justice. The rewards for victory were glory primarily, the satisfaction of having ruined an enemy, and, under some laws, official *praemia* (rewards). There were no official rewards for the defeated prosecutor. To be sure, it was praiseworthy to be a *bonus orator* (as Cicero argues throughout the *De oratore;* see also Plin. *HN* 7.139 and Livy 30.1.5) and to defend victims of crimes by prosecuting the perpetrators;

electoral opponents might be deterred from illegal acts by threats of impending prosecution (see [Q. Cicero?], *Comment. pet.* 57); and perhaps in a few cases, someone would set about a hopeless prosecution just to cause a nuisance to an enemy. But there were few kudos to be won by mounting prosecutions that had little or no chance of success. A prosecution that persuaded almost no jurors would bring an orator little respect (as well as making him vulnerable to a charge of *calumnia;* see "The Role of the Prosecutor" later in this chapter), and an orator would gain little psychic satisfaction from seeing the trial of a personal enemy end in a sea of votes for acquittal. So prosecutors must have generally thought that they had a good chance of winning their cases; otherwise, they would not have brought them forward in the first place. The exegesis of the eleven prosecutions in this book is intended partly to explain why the prosecutors involved believed they could win and, where we know they lost, why they were mistaken in that belief.

Seneca the Elder (*Controv.* 3 pr. 16–17) tells the story that he once heard L. Cestius Pius, an eminent and conceited declaimer, boasting as he was about to deliver a speech in an imaginary prosecution of Milo in opposition to Cicero's speech for the defense. Seneca humiliated Cestius in public and left him speechless, without a response, although, as Seneca remarks, Cestius thought that he could respond to Cicero. When Cestius told Seneca to leave, Seneca refused and even threatened Cestius with legal actions, first by a so-called law of an unspecified offense ("lege inscripti maleficii"),[1] then for ingratitude ("ingrati"); finally, Seneca sought a *curator* (caretaker) for Cestius, charging that Cestius was insane. Seneca said that he would drop the charges only when Cestius took an oath that Cicero was more eloquent ("disertus") than he. Cestius refused to take this oath, but Seneca (*Suas.* 7.13) reports that Cestius got his comeuppance later. When Marcus Cicero, the orator's son and the governor of Asia in the mid- or late twenties B.C. or thereafter, learned that Cestius (a native of Smyrna), a guest at his table, had said that Cicero was illiterate ("hic est Cestius, qui patrem tuum negabat litteras scisse" [This man is Cestius, who said that your father was uneducated]),[2] the governor had his guest flogged.[3] I begin this book with this anecdote to emphasize that I consider it a cautionary tale for me to keep in mind. My intention is not to outdo Cicero, to prove that his speeches were defective, or to refute him—and it is certainly not to challenge him by composing a speech, in any language.

Less easy to dismiss is the challenge presented by the censure that Quintilian (*Inst.* 10.5.20) aimed at Cestius with regard to his speech *In Milonem.* He contrasts this speech with a *Pro Milone* written by Brutus.[4] Quintilian criticizes Cestius for attempting to write such a speech when his own source was Cicero's speech for the defense.

> Melius hoc quam rescribere veteribus orationibus, ut fecit Cestius contra Ciceronis actionem habitam pro eodem [i.e., Milo] cum alteram partem satis nosse non posset ex sola defensione.

> [This [such a literary exercise as Brutus wrote] is better than writing speeches in refutation of old speeches, as Cestius did against the speech of Cicero delivered on behalf of the same person [Milo], since from the defense alone he could not sufficiently know the opposing side.]

Quintilian thus denies that a prosecution speech can be reconstructed from the speech for the defense. He is certainly right that a speech of Cicero for the defense does not reveal enough to allow us to write a complete speech for the prosecution. But it does contain some useful information about the case for the prosecution, and discovering as much of that information as possible is the more modest aim of this book.

In so doing, I am trying to act in the spirit of another piece of advice from the great master of rhetoric. Quintilian (*Inst.* 10.1.22–23) advocates studying both sides of the case when possible, strongly recommending a reading of both speeches in a case when they are available; he argues that even if the speeches are unequal in rhetorical artistry, the reader will understand the case better by doing so. We can agree with Quintilian that it would be fruitless to try to re-create a prosecution speech on the basis of the defense speech. But I hope to show that we can learn something of value about a prosecution case even when our main and sometimes only source for it is the speech for the defense. So one intended goal of this book is to understand these trials from the point of view of the prosecutors.

That is not to say that the prosecutors were right and Cicero was wrong. When I state that the prosecution made or probably made a certain argument, I am simply stating a fact or a guess, as the case may be, that a prosecutor did say something like that. It may well be the case that a prosecutor's argument was weak and that Cicero's refutation of that argument was sufficient. When I venture an opinion on the prosecution's response to

Cicero's rebuttal, again I am not claiming that Cicero's rebuttal is inferior to the prosecutor's counterrebuttal. Moreover, even if Cicero's defense does on occasion seem inferior to the prosecution side of the case, that is no reason to disparage his efforts, for to the extent that the prosecutor had the stronger argument and Cicero the weaker, we must admire Cicero all the more for playing the weak hand dealt him as well as he does. Ultimately, in fact, the process of reconstructing the case for the prosecution leads us not only to a better understanding of that case but also, as a by-product, to a greater appreciation of and respect for Cicero's skill as an advocate.

In this book, I examine the prosecution of eleven defendants. There are two common features of these trials: all of them were tried at Rome in the standing criminal courts (*quaestiones perpetuae*) of the late Republic;[5] and in all of them, Cicero delivered an extant speech for the defense. A similar study, albeit with a smaller scope, has been attempted once before. In his doctoral dissertation, Ayers tries to reconstruct the contents of the prosecutors' speeches for Roscius of Ameria and for Murena (as I do in this book) and also the defense case for Verres.[6] In his introduction, Ayers recognizes the problem of depending on Cicero to determine what his opponents had said or would say, but he makes three sound arguments for the validity of his project.[7] First, the process of reconstructing the case against which Cicero was arguing reminds us that he was not speaking in a vacuum and helps us better understand some of the seemingly peculiar points he makes. Second, the study of the opposing side helps us arrive at a clearer view of the background to the speech, for example, the issues in the case. Third, by conceptualizing the opposing case, we are less likely to take Cicero's victories for granted; we see the difficulties that he faced in achieving them. These three points are well taken by Ayers and help justify both his dissertation and the present, more extensive study (of eleven prosecutions as compared to two).

This book is not a study of Cicero's *Pro Fonteio, Pro Flacco,* and so forth, though each chapter within the book's three parts is closely associated with one particular Ciceronian defense speech.[8] Nor, as I have said, is this a re-creation or study of the speeches *In Fonteium, In Flaccum,* and so forth; it is a study of the arguments presented in those prosecution speeches—arguments to which Cicero responds in his orations—and also of the ways that the prosecution might have tried to undermine Cicero's defense. In other words, I deal only with the *inventio,* the discovery of arguments, not with all the other aspects of composing, arranging, and presenting an oration.

The primary goals of this study are threefold: to gain a fuller appreciation of the case for the prosecution in each of these eleven trials, more generally to understand better what was involved in presenting a prosecution before a *quaestio perpetua,* and finally to gain a better understanding of the trials themselves. If we are to redress, as much as we can, the balance between prosecution and defense, and to understand the whole trial more fully, it is helpful temporarily to avert our gaze from the glare of Cicero's speech. The process of ascertaining the strengths and weaknesses in the prosecution case requires an understanding of the corresponding strengths and weaknesses in the defense case and thereby can lead to an enhanced respect for Cicero's handling of cases that often contained substantial difficulties for the defense. The one element of each of these trials for which we have direct knowledge, Cicero's speech, was only a small part of the whole trial. It was often only one of the speeches for the defense; the defense speech or speeches were the counterpart to a prosecution speech or speeches; and the trial had many elements other than speeches, most notably testimony from witnesses. By focusing on the prosecution rather than the defense, I hope to move closer to portraying the whole trial as a historical event, rather than letting Cicero's text alone represent the trial.

Cicero emerged as the victor in most or all of these eleven trials. That is not to say that in reality Cicero was the victor in every trial in which he appeared. Of the sixty-two such trials known to us, he won thirty-five and lost ten; for seventeen, we do not know the outcome for sure. Even if we suppose that he lost every trial for which we are not sure of the outcome, his winning percentage would be 56 percent, and if we leave out the unknown outcomes, that percentage rises to 78 percent.[9] Cicero's success as a defense speaker is all the more remarkable in view of the fact that, to judge by the evidence that we have, Roman criminal trials generally ended in conviction about as often as in acquittal.[10]

Admittedly, our evidence is strongly biased by the fact that so much of it comes from Cicero himself, either from his published forensic speeches or from *testimonia* about the trials in his writings. He was undoubtedly more likely to publish speeches from forensic victories than from defeats—though he did publish the *Pro Milone,* in which we know his client lost (see Asc. 53–54C)[11]—and it may well be that he inclined to emphasize his victories in his other writings as well. Nevertheless, there is no disputing that he was a remarkably successful orator. By focusing on the attempts launched by prosecutors to convict defendants who had the good fortune to acquire him as their advocate or as one of their advocates, I hope to clarify some of the reasons for his success.

This book grows out of a conviction that forensic speeches need to be seen in their context. This aim is nothing new. The attempt of the so-called prosopographical school to analyze trials as expressions of political forces in the Roman Republic was an attempt to explain the context of trials. But this method perceived context in a rather narrow sense—that is, within traditional political history—and foundered on some of its premises about Roman politics, especially the belief that Romans allowed themselves to be controlled by the dictates of some faction to which they belonged.[12] Its passing as a method of judicial analysis has left a vacuum, which scholars are beginning to fill.[13] Here, I try to understand the trials with which I deal in their full context, partly a political context, but also a judicial and rhetorical one—*Recht, Rhetorik,* and *Politik,* in Classen's (1985) triad, which, I would suggest, he has put in the right (descending) order of importance. I have tried to describe the legal issues, the rhetorical strategies, and the people who participated in each trial, particularly the prosecutors, all as factors contributing to the dynamics of each trial.

The result reveals, I hope, neither the rule of men as distinct from the rule of laws nor the rule of laws as distinct from the rule of men but the rule of laws and men, mediated by the highly developed form of language called rhetoric, the language in which people conceived and communicated their ideas about justice in particular cases. The teachings of rhetoric do not always conform to modern ideas of logical argument; it was, after all, a discipline that encouraged people to be able to argue both "X, therefore Y," and "X, therefore the opposite of Y."[14] But we cannot dismiss this kind of reasoning with the label "rhetorical." As Crook writes (in a book that does much to move us away from patronizing the ancients for their advocates' use of rhetoric),

> The advocate belonged to a culture, as much in Rome as in Greece, in which the word, the *argumentum* (not necessarily logical argument, it might just as well be emotional) was the most highly developed tool of communication, and persuasion by means of the word the most fully worked-out technology.[15]

To evaluate the strength of a prosecution case, we need to take into account both the "technology" through which it was expressed and the facility with which individual prosecutors were able to make use of that technology.

After the following descriptions of the role of the Roman prosecutor and its treatment in the rhetorical literature, the rest of this introductory chapter handles three types of problem relating to the study of Roman prosecution in general. First, I deal with three source problems. First is the often debated question of the reliability of our texts of Cicero's forensic orations as reflections of what he actually said in the trials. Second is the extent to which Cicero's second *Verrines* reliably reflects what occurred in the first *actio* (hearing) of that trial. Third is a section on method that outlines criteria for evaluating the credibility of statements made in a forensic speech. Next follows a section on the importance of law in these trials—a point of view that is much less self-evident than it sounds. Finally, in two sections, I compare the inherent advantages and disadvantages of serving as prosecutor as compared to defense speaker.

THE ROLE OF THE PROSECUTOR

The Roman prosecutor was a citizen who chose to initiate a trial against another citizen.[16] In the primary courts of the post-Sullan Republic, the *quaestiones perpetuae* (or standing criminal courts), he was not a magistrate, although he did have the power to compel a limited number of witnesses to testify. The prosecutor was not required to possess any special qualifications, except that anyone who was *infamis* could not prosecute. A prosecutor received no pay for his work, although under some criminal laws, if he was successful, he was eligible for *praemia,* or rewards. There were risks involved. A prosecutor was responsible for avoiding two offenses: *calumnia,* launching a prosecution that one knows to be unfounded; and *praevaricatio,* collusion with the defendant for the defendant's benefit (Marcianus *Dig.* 48.16.1.1–3; Ulp. *Dig.* 50.16.212). A prosecutor could be assisted by others, called *subscriptores.*

One or more of several motives could lead someone to launch a prosecution. Cicero (*Off.* 2.49–50) lists four: the desire to make a name for oneself; the public good; revenge against an enemy, often one inherited as part of a family feud; and the protection of provincials. It was considered improper to make a habit of prosecution (Cic. *Off.* 2.50; *Brut.* 130), and this stricture, combined with the motives of making a name or seeking revenge against a family enemy, explains why prosecutors were often junior to the *patroni* (advocates) of the people whom they were prosecuting.[17]

The first step in initiating a prosecution was to go to the magistrate who presided over the appropriate court—generally a praetor, but sometimes a more junior official called a *iudex quaestionis*—and seek permission to bring the charge (*postulare*). The would-be prosecutor swore an oath to conduct the prosecution in good faith. If more than one person requested permission to conduct the same prosecution, a *divinatio* was held to determine who would be awarded the right;[18] in this way, Cicero defeated Q. Caecilius for the right to prosecute Verres in 70 B.C. (see Cic. *Div. Caec.*). The next step was the *nominis delatio* (institution of the charge) before the magistrate in the presence of the defendant. The magistrate conducted a *legibus interrogatio* (interrogation according to the laws) to determine whether the case could be properly brought. It is debated as to how specific the prosecutor had to be at this point about the particular charges he would bring and to what extent he was legally bound in the future to stay within those charges.[19] At this point, at least in the extortion court, the defendant could admit his guilt, and proceedings to determine punishment would commence (Ps.-Asc. 207St). If the defendant did not yield, an *inscriptio* was drawn up and was signed by the *nominis delator* (the chief prosecutor) and any assistant prosecutors (*subscriptores*) who were acceptable to him. The praetor gave the prosecutor a fixed period of time in which to gather evidence and prepare his case. When the parties returned to court, jurors were chosen, and the trial began. The prosecutor or prosecutors spoke first, also presenting any written evidence, and then the defense *patroni* spoke; after these speeches, the two sides brought out their witnesses. Thereafter, there could be an *altercatio,* a series of questions and answers between the two sides.[20] Under some statutes, more than one *actio,* or hearing, took place. Then, the jurors voted on a verdict. If a majority of the votes were for condemnation, the defendant was convicted and punished according to the law. If the charge was capital, he generally lost his status as a Roman citizen and went into exile, sparing himself actual execution.[21] The extortion and embezzlement statutes required a *litis aestimatio,* or calculation of damages, adjudicated by the same jurors. The damages in an extortion case were distributed to the injured parties.

PROSECUTION IN RHETORICAL WORKS

Despite the fact that, roughly speaking, half of forensic speeches must have been delivered by an *accusator* for the prosecution or by an advocate for the *petitor* (plaintiff) in a civil suit, the rhetorical literature contains relatively little advice specifically for the prosecutor or plaintiff's speaker. Most of the information provided by such rhetorical writers as Cicero and Quintilian pertains to both the prosecution and the defense. But there are some exceptions.

It is commonly accepted among criminal lawyers today that prosecution and defense require quite different styles of advocacy and personalities to fit those styles. Prosecutors must relentlessly tell a clear and coherent story, so that their audiences will easily grasp what the defendant is supposed to have done. Defense lawyers try to destroy the clarity of the story by casting doubt on various pieces of it, picking here and pulling there until it falls apart.[22] In a modern legal system with a clearly enunciated principle of the presumption of the defendant's innocence, it is clear why the two roles are so different, since the defense attorney is not required to tell a story explaining what really happened, only to undermine the prosecution story. But even if the presumption of innocence was not a formal principle in Roman law, juries must have felt that the prosecutor had to present to them a clear and coherent story of what the defendant was supposed to have done, in the absence of which they would not be inclined to convict.[23] If one compares Cicero's *Verrines* to his defense speeches, the dichotomy becomes apparent; in the former, the prosecutor hammers home time and again his basic points about the defendant's tyrannical conduct, whether in his administration of justice, collection of tithes, art collecting, or military maneuvers. As a defense speaker, however, he constantly raises questions and doubts about what the prosecution has alleged, pursuing multiple lines of attack against the charges, even if these lines do not entirely cohere with each other. The reason for the difference lies not in the criminality of Verres in contrast to the other defendants, even if one is convinced that Verres was especially wicked, but in the two different roles played by the same advocate.

It clearly was debated among the ancient rhetoricians whether the task of the prosecutor or that of the defense speaker was the most demanding (see "Advantages for the Prosecution" and "The Difficulties of the Prosecutor" later in this chapter). Quintilian (*Inst.* 4.1.36) makes the obvious but sensible point that the fact that the prosecutor spoke first put a special demand on him:[24] in his exordium, the prosecutor had to instruct (*docere*) the judge, whereas the defense, in its response, had only to remind (*admonere*) the judge of what had already been said.[25] For the same reason, the defense has an advantage when it comes to the cross-examination of

witnesses, in that it knows what they have already said, whereas the prosecutor cannot always predict what the witnesses will say. Moreover, one
piece of evidence shows that when prosecutors delivered their speeches (at
least in the *quaestio de sicariis et de veneficiis* [court for homicide and poi-
soning]), they did not necessarily know who the opposing defense speaker
or speakers would be (see Cic. *Rosc. Am.* 59). Quintilian maintains that the
prosecutor has the advantage that the defense did not know what the witnesses would say (5.7.22). Quintilian is clearly thinking of witnesses called
by the prosecution,[26] but while it is true that only the prosecution could
compel witnesses to appear, the defense could present voluntary witnesses.
This option might have meant little in practice, however, if I am right that
the defense did not have a specific idea of the charges. Apart from lining up
character witnesses, the hands of the defense might have been tied in terms
of knowing what witnesses would help its side of the case.

Overall, Quintilian is of the opinion—which he also ascribes to
Cicero[27]—that it is harder to speak for the defense than for the prosecution
(see *Inst.* 5.13.2–3, quoted in full under "Advantages for the Prosecution"
later in this chapter). The prosecutor has only to make a case, which he can
plan at home. Moreover, his charges naturally excite *invidia* against the
kind of crime he is alleging, even if these allegations are untrue. In comparison, the defense must be ready to respond in court to the prosecution case
with a variety of tactics, without any foreknowledge of what is to come, and
cannot deny the evil inherent in the crime (parricide, sacrilege, treason, or
whatever offense is involved). For that reason, speakers of modest ability
can function for the prosecution, but only a master orator can present a
good defense.

At various points in the *Institutio oratoria,* Quintilian offers a few bits of
advice that vary according to the role of the speaker. The two roles generally require a different effect on the emotions of the jurors—the accuser
must arouse the emotions (*concitare*), while the defense must turn them
aside (*flectere*)—though Quintilian points out that this is not an invariable
rule (6.1.9). The arrangement of arguments is somewhat different for prosecutor and defense. Generally, the prosecutor begins with a strong argument but saves his best argument for the end and puts the weaker arguments in the middle, whereas the defense should attempt to refute the
strongest argument right away. Quintilian (7.1.10–11) says that he does not
endorse this policy as dogmatically as did Celsus. Quintilian maintains that
each side wants to present the defendant's character in a way that is advan-

tageous to his case: the prosecutor should try to find vices in the defendant that are consistent with the case, such as cruelty in someone accused of homicide; the defense will try to deny or diminish the effect of these character attacks, argue their irrelevance to the charge, or show that they are actually inconsistent with it (7.2.28–30).

At the other end of the intellectual spectrum, we have the pedestrian and, for that reason, very useful rhetorical handbook called the *Rhetorica ad Herennium*.[28] Its anonymous author sometimes divides advice on a topic into two parts, one for the prosecutor and one for the defendant. The author argues (1.18) that in a case where the issue is conjectural, that is, where it turns on a question of fact, the prosecutor should use a different strategy in his *narratio* from the defense speaker: whereas the latter presents a clear and straightforward account of what happened, the former should intersperse his telling of the facts with insinuations of foul motives (*Rhet. Her.* 2.3), portraying the defendant as motivated by desire to obtain some benefit or to avoid some disadvantage. The author suggests that the prosecutor seek corroboration in three areas defined by time: the past, present, and future. In the past, the prosecutor should seek anything suggestive of guilt, such as where the defendant was, with whom he was, any preparations he made, or anything out of the ordinary in comparison with his usual conduct. In the present (i.e., the time of the crime), the prosecutor should look for any perception at the time (through one or more of the five senses) that relates to the crime. In the future (following the crime), he should look for any evidence that suggests that a crime was committed or by whom it was committed, such as, in a homicide case, the state of the body, a weapon, a footprint, or blood on someone's clothing—in other words, what we would call physical evidence. According to the author of the *Rhetorica ad Herennium* (2.8), the prosecution should claim that the accused afterward showed signs of guilt (e.g., he blushed, stumbled, or made some offer) or, conversely, that his shameful calm shows the premeditation of the crime and his audacity ("confidentia").

At *Rhetorica ad Herennium* 1.24, the author has special advice for the prosecutor on dealing with an assumptive juridical issue where the defense draws on extraneous matter, such as *concessio* (acknowledgment of the charge), *remotio criminis* (rejection of the responsibility), *translatio criminis* (shifting of the question of guilt), and *comparatio* (comparison with the alternative course). The author of the *Rhetorica ad Herennium* argues that if the defense claims that the defendant's actions were honorable, the prosecutor should suggest that the defendant was not attempting to let honor guide his or her actions but had merely used honor as a cover (2.21). A *locus communis* that the author says a prosecutor can use against a defendant who has acted to his own disadvantage is that the defendant lacked the power to make that decision. The author says that if the defense argues that the defendant was only reacting to a greater crime committed by someone else, the prosecutor should argue against taking the law into one's own hands (2.22). The author maintains that the prosecutor can undermine a defendant's plea for exculpation that his mistake was due to ignorance by asking whether the defendant should not have informed himself better. If the defendant claims that he acted under the influence of wine, sexual passion, or anger, the prosecution should say that the defendant, by admitting to a fault of character, has incriminated himself (*Rhet. Her.* 2.23–24). Finally, the author of the *Rhetorica ad Herennium* recommends that when the prosecutor has no single telling point to make, he should combine a number of points that would be unconvincing by themselves but, when taken together, have such a strong cumulative effect that the verdict must be guilty (4.53). These passages from the *Rhetorica ad Herennium* provide some step-by-step instructions as to how to build a prosecution.

The richest source for advice on how to conduct a prosecution comes from the young Cicero's *De inventione rhetorica,* written during the same period as the *Rhetorica ad Herennium.*[29] Although Cicero there says that he cannot analyze every kind of argument, one by one, in terms of how it can be used by the defense or by the prosecution (2.44–45), he does provide many specific pieces of advice to would-be prosecutors. He advises that both the defense and the prosecution can make use of *remotio criminis* to shift responsibility from one person to another; for example, the prosecutor might claim that a praetor acted improperly in summoning the people to arms when there were consuls with that responsibility (2.93). Cicero argues that to make his case plausible, the prosecutor must show why the defendant did the deed that forms the basis of the accusation. Either the prosecutor must argue that the defendant acted on the basis of a reasoned decision to acquire an advantage or avoid a disadvantage and that advantage or disadvantage led the defendant to the crime (e.g., glory, power, money, friendship, and hatred), or he must argue that the defendant acted on some irrational impulse, such as love or anger. Cicero argues that the prosecutor may show that no one else had a motive or as likely a motive to commit the act or that no one else had the means or opportunity or desire

(2.24). Cicero maintains that to make the motive plausible, the prosecutor must show that the defendant possesses the appropriate vices for the case and, as much as possible, that the defendant has been convicted or suspected of having committed a similar crime before (2.32).[30] According to Cicero (2.53), the prosecutor must define the crime that forms the basis of the charge, such as *maiestas*. Cicero later on provides some advice on how to undercut various lines of defense (2.77–82). He maintains that if the defense argues that although the defendant did commit a blameworthy act, his conduct can be justified for some external reason (e.g., as a response to someone else's misdeed), the prosecutor should attempt to show that this prior misdeed was not as serious as the crime with which the defendant has been charged. He should accentuate the baseness of the deed or argue that the defendant, to be taken seriously, should be expected to bring this supposed crime before a court of law, maintaining that the jury should pay attention only to those crimes that have been confirmed by the decision of a court of law. Cicero argues that in general, in such a situation, the prosecution should expatiate on the necessity to follow due process. He should either defend the "alternative defendant" proposed by the real defendant or urge the court to focus only on the real defendant and the crimes with which he has been charged (2.88). He should undercut excuses based on the involuntary nature of the alleged offense, arguing that excusing people for crimes because they did not intend to commit them will result in a license for bad behavior (2.99–100). All in all, according to Cicero, the prosecution should argue that the defendant is a wicked person to whom these alleged crimes came naturally and that any good deeds ever committed by him should not enter into the decision facing the jurors, that pardon is wrong, and that the jurors should seize the opportunity granted to them to punish the wicked (2.108–9).

Given the large body of Latin rhetorical literature, the relative paucity of material devoted specifically to presenting the case for the prosecution calls for some explanation. Two possible explanations come to mind, the second of which seems more convincing than the first.

Prosecution was regarded as a necessary evil.[31] That attitude is implied by Cicero's apology for applying to obtain that role in the prosecution of Verres (*Div. Caec.* 1), and Cicero makes it explicit in his defense of Roscius of Ameria, where he compares prosecutors to the geese and guard dogs on the Capitoline (*Rosc. Am.* 56–57). He also expresses this attitude in his remarks, ranging from the dismissive to the scathing, on the orators described in the *Brutus* as specializing in prosecution. He reports that an "accusator vetus"[32] like C. Rusius is completely unknown to Brutus, even though Rusius was a contemporary of Sisenna, who died in 67 B.C. To L. Caesulenus, Cicero gives the backhanded compliment, "Non fecissem hominis paene infimi mentionem, nisi iudicarem qui suspiciosius aut criminosius diceret audivisse me neminem" [I would not have mentioned this man who was almost the least distinguished if I did not judge that I had heard no one speak *in a manner more calculated to create suspicion or conviction of guilt*][33] (*Brut.* 131). Cicero's strongest scorn goes to M. Iunius Brutus, the ancestor of Cicero's interlocutor, who made a habit of prosecution ("accusationem factitaverit"); Cicero calls him an "accusator vehemens et molestus" [forceful and vexing prosecutor] and a disgrace to his family (*Brut.* 130). It is not hard to see why prosecutors created such antagonism: not only were they a possible source of substantial anxiety for any defendant and of total ruin for a convicted defendant, but they could be anyone, *quidam e populo*, ὁ βουλόμενος in Greek terms; they were certainly not specific, identifiable government officials. The best that can be said for the kind of prosecutor described in the *Brutus* comes from Cicero's description of M. Calidius's unsuccessful speech for the prosecution against Q. Gallius (*TLRR* no. 214), where Cicero was able to show that the prosecutor's claim that Gallius had tried to poison him was rendered implausible by Calidius's calm demeanor. Cicero there maintains (*Brut.* 276–77) that Calidius was able to instruct (*docere*) and please (*delectare*) his listeners but not to arouse in them the necessary emotion (*movere*). This might be construed as a grudging admission that prosecution does call for some special talent, but generally Cicero accepts the view that defense requires greater flexibility than prosecuting. As Cicero explains (*Part. or.* 14–15), the prosecutor marshals his arguments and evidence, holding to a preconceived plan, whereas the defense speaker has to be prepared to modify, rearrange, and abbreviate his oration to stay in the good graces of the jury.

It is understandable that no writer on rhetoric would want to aim all or a major part of his work only at the would-be prosecutor. But it can also be said that about the same amount of the rhetorical literature deals solely with the defense role, although it is treated as the more honorable of the two.

The more persuasive reason for the scarcity of rhetorical advice specifically on prosecution is that the ancient orator had to be trained to handle both prosecution and defense. Consider the many vituperative passages uttered by Cicero as a spokesman for the defense and the many ways in which he fashions a defense by mounting an attack against someone other than the defendant. The rhetorical manuals needed to cover the whole range of rhetorical techniques, since any orator had to be prepared to use all of them, no matter which side of the case he was representing.

THE DELIVERED SPEECH AND THE
PUBLISHED SPEECH

The main source we possess for the prosecution speeches to which Cicero replied for the defense is the published text of these defense speeches. But does this text preserve the speeches that Cicero actually delivered in the Roman Forum? The problem of publication, that is, the relationship between the speech as delivered and the speech as published, has been debated at least since Humbert (1925) issued a challenge to any claim of similarity—a challenge that has recently been revived by Zetzel. The questions raised by Humbert have been enduring; it is hard to believe that his answers to these questions have proved to be so, after one reads Clark's (1927) negative review of this work and of another work on which it is based, as well as Stroh's demolition of Humbert's thesis.[34]

Unlike two recent authors, I need to confront this question directly. Riggsby takes the stance that, for his purposes, even if the written speeches we have bore little resemblance to the delivered version, they would still represent court proceedings and therefore would still constitute suitable evidence.[35] Vasaly takes a similar position.

> Therefore, even if we can never know for sure whether the words of a Ciceronian oration were identical with those that the orator actually spoke, we can nevertheless feel assured that the text is a plausible recreation of the sort of speech that he gave (or would have given) in a particular occasion.[36]

But in this work, whose purpose is to determine the gist of what the prosecutors in eleven real trials actually said, I cannot follow the same path. If the defense speeches we read today bear no relationship to the speeches as delivered, it is entirely possible that they respond to imaginary charges made by an imaginary prosecution and therefore that they have no historical value as records of specific trials. If we are sure that this is the situation, this study, for which the defense speeches of Cicero are my main source, will have no claim to historical truth about the trials, even though they might convey an idea of what a typical trial was like. But it is not fair to hold that any discrepancy between the speech as delivered and the speech as published renders nugatory the entire enterprise. It is even possible, as I will show later in this section, that in some cases the written text includes additional or more accurate historical evidence, precisely because it was edited after delivery. I believe that the available evidence fails to support the position of radical skepticism (i.e., that there was no relationship between the delivered and published speeches) and that in the absence of such evidence, we should accept as a definite possibility, though not as a proven fact, substantial congruence between the speeches as delivered and the speeches as published.

Humbert attempted to demonstrate that Cicero's "plaidoyer écrit" (written speech) constituted a combination of various "plaidoiries réelles" (real pleadings) taken from utterances made by Cicero during various parts of a trial. Stroh, however, demonstrates that what we read as one speech was in fact a speech, often delivered at the second *actio* of an extortion trial.[37] But how did a speech of Cicero transmute from a series of words descending on the Forum to a written and published text?

It is important to distinguish between three different routes by which the published version could be the same as or at least could closely resemble the delivered version: (1) Cicero might have read from a text, which was preserved and later published; (2) someone else might have recorded Cicero's speech as he delivered it; or (3) Cicero could have reconstructed the speech after the fact, using his notes and/or memory. I will here argue against the first two vehicles of transmission and for the third.

The evidence firmly contradicts the idea that Cicero read his speeches from a prepared text, which could then have been published after the trial. Different orators differed in the way that they would make use of written material that they had prepared in advance, as we shall see, but it is important for us to keep in mind that for the purposes of this discussion, we need look at the practice of Cicero alone, since only his defense speeches have survived from this period and since those speeches alone form the foundation for this study of the prosecution speeches. In court, Cicero did not speak from a written text throughout an oration. Quintilian (*Inst.* 10.7.30) describes the general practice of forensic orators with many cases to plead, and he specifically cites Cicero as one of these orators: they wrote out vital portions and especially the opening passages, they planned as much as possible for the rest, and they stood ready to improvise to deal with whatever came up unexpectedly. Asconius (87C) confirms Quintilian's understanding of Ciceronian procedure when he makes the point, as an argument to show that Cicero did not defend Catiline, that he (Asconius) did not find *commentarii*[38] (notes) or a *principium*[39] (introduction) for such a speech. Although Quintilian was not an eyewitness to Cicero's delivery, he cites *commentarii* of Cicero that existed in his day, the edition of which modern scholars have credited to Cicero's freedman Tiro.[40] Cicero himself makes it clear that the written speech was created after the fact. Using himself as an example, Cicero says that an orator does not actually feel anger when he writes his orations after the trial has already been conducted.[41] He writes in the *Brutus* (91), "most speeches are written when they have already been delivered, not so they may be delivered."[42] For various reasons, says Cicero, some other orators do not choose to take the trouble to write out their speeches afterward, either because they are too lazy to do this, because they think that their reputation will be better served if no written orations survive, or because they lack the erudition to perform this task. A strong contrast with Cicero's own practice is implied.

On the subject of shorthand, the Ciceronian era did see a growing interest in finding some way of writing more quickly. The senatorial proceedings of 3 December 63, containing the evidence of the Allobroges and the arrested conspirators, were recorded by four senators whom the consul Cicero selected (see Cic. *Sull.* 42) as capable of performing this function by their *memoria* (memory), *scientia* (knowledge), and *celeritas scribendi* (speed of writing), and two days later, as Plutarch reports (*Cat. Min.* 23), Cato's speech was taken down by exceptionally rapid writers, by means of a system of shorthand that Cicero provided for them, in which one sign stood for many letters. Plutarch claims this is the first time that any shorthand was ever used. If he is right and if this shorthand explained the origin of our written texts, it would do so only for speeches dating from the end of 63 and thereafter. Shackleton Bailey suggests that Plutarch is probably exaggerating the extent of what was just a series of abbreviations, on the false assumption that something that existed in his (Plutarch's) own time was already available in the first century B.C.[43] The fact that *memoria* was one of the qualities Cicero wanted in the senators whom he chose suggests that they were not using a true shorthand, as does the fact that Cicero needed four of them; presumably, they functioned as a kind of relay team, with one writing down one sentence or section while another listened and got ready to write down the next and so on.[44] Moreover, it is somewhat surprising that a senator could be described as a γραφεύς; that functionary would more naturally be equated with *scribae mei* (see Cic. *Sull.* 44). It is not inconceivable that Cicero used both senators and scribes to take down dictation on this occasion—the senators possessing more independent authority, the scribes more skill.[45]

It is tempting to connect this development in 63 B.C. with the report that Cicero's freedman Tiro invented a kind of shorthand. According to Isidorus (*Origines* 1.22.1), Tiro was the first to invent an extensive system of abbreviations, but these were only for *praepositiones,* which Mentz explains as prepositions, conjunctions, adverbs, and pronouns.[46] If one believes that Tiro was almost as old as Cicero, it is possible that the development of Tironian tachygraphy occurred early enough that a stenographic redaction of Cicero's forensic oratory was possible throughout his career as a speaker, but if he was considerably younger than his patron, this tachygraphic method would have developed only when Cicero had already delivered many of his speeches or even after Cicero's death.[47] If the method was known only to Tiro, if his shorthand was the vehicle by which speeches have been preserved, and if Cicero controlled his freedman's activities, only Cicero would have been in a position to decide whether to have a record made of his actual speech. But in any case, even though Cicero's freedman Tiro was responsible for the invention of some abbreviations that later developed into what we call the *notae Tironianae,* it was probably only later, in the early empire, that it became possible to write down a speech as it was delivered.[48] All in all, it would be unwise to assert that by the time of Cicero, shorthand had developed to the point where it could explain the preservation of Cicero's speeches (especially the earlier ones) in a form close to the words with which they were actually delivered, like a modern court transcript.

We know that the speeches we possess are, at least in part, the product of Cicero's editorial efforts after the trial was over. In his *Letters,* we see Cicero the editor at work. He adds two topographical descriptions to a speech and comments on a chronological error (*Att.* 1.13.5), and Brutus asks Cicero for his corrections on a speech that Brutus intends to publish (*Att.* 15.1a.2). On two occasions, Cicero says in a letter that he will make a change in his published speech, but to judge by the extant text, he was not able to effect these changes. He writes to Atticus (*Att.* 13.44.3) that, following the advice of Brutus, he will delete a mention of L. Corfidius from the *Pro Ligario* (33). The text of the speech included this person in a list of those present at the trial, but Brutus pointed out to him that this must have been a lapse of memory, because Corfidius, although a friend of Ligarius, was already dead before the trial. Curiously, the name still survives in our text, so Cicero was unable to effect the change. (The same process occurs at *Orationes Philippicae* 2.103, where Cicero decided to make a change [see *Att.* 16.11.2] and did so.)[49] Since the point of this analysis is primarily to determine how historically accurate the extant texts are, it is worth pointing out that the process of editing the *Pro Ligario* was going to render it more accurate, not less so, in the sense of bringing it back to something closer to the speech as it might have been when it was actually delivered. As he delivered his speech for Ligarius, Cicero had listed supporters of the defendant who were present at the trial. It is very likely that he did so extemporaneously, since he would not have known in advance who would appear. But when he edited the speech for publication, his memory played a trick on him, and he put down the name of someone who, although he would have been a logical person to be present as a supporter, was in fact dead. Brutus caught this error and persuaded Cicero to make the change; clearly, Brutus thought that the written speech should possess as much historical verisimilitude as possible. However, Cicero was apparently unable to get to the scribes in time to get them to erase the name in the copies they had made.[50]

The incident illustrates two points. On the one hand, the text we have may not be an entirely accurate rendition of Cicero's spoken words, as Cicero is reconstructing the speech from memory. On the other hand, the process of editing does not necessarily involve diluting the text's historical value and may actually increase it.[51]

Cicero's *Letters* provide us with other insights into the "publication" process. From Cicero's perspective, the edited text could be a small gift that formed one of the media of social interaction (*Att.* 2.7.1, 15.1a.2; *Fam.* 9.12.2), as was the acknowledgment of comments and suggestions (*Att.* 1.13.5).[52] Cicero clearly took some care over editing the "consular speeches" (*Att.* 2.1.3). He says that Atticus should rest assured—and feel flattered—that he is almost always the first to receive a copy (*Att.* 4.5.1), though Pompey got first crack at Cicero's "palinode" in 56.[53] Cicero sent some orations to Lentulus in 54, as part of his effort to ingratiate himself with him (*Fam.* 1.9.23). His brother, Quintus, received the *Pro Scauro* and the *Pro Plancio* at Quintus's urgent request (*Q Fr.* 3.1.11).

It is reasonable to believe that Cicero typically wrote out several sections of his defense speeches and made notes (*commentarii*) for other sections by way of preparation. After delivering some speeches, he created a continuous, written version of them, which he circulated to friends for their suggestions and corrections. The result is what we read today. But leaving the subject of Cicero's general practice, we should look at two examples that may indicate its extremes: one in which the oral and written speeches may have been almost identical and one in which they may have been different.

A fragment of Cornelius Nepos's life of Cicero, preserved by Jerome (Peter, *HRRel.* 23.365M = frag. 2, vol. 2, p. 34), contains the information that the trial of C. Cornelius (tribune of the plebs in 67) was delivered in his presence ("se praesente") in almost exactly the same words ("iisdem paene verbis") as it was published. Clearly, this anecdote is supposed to be relating something unusual, and unlike Riggsby,[54] I take as surprising the exact correspondence, not the fact that Nepos was there, which in my opinion Nepos adds to establish that this is an eyewitness report. Marshall argues that this information is contradicted by Pliny at *Epistulae* 1.20.8, where Pliny says that the *Pro Cornelio* as published must be an abbreviated version of the four-day-long speech that Cicero actually delivered, condensed into one book, albeit a long one.[55] But Riggsby is correct to point out that Pliny is making an inference from the text of those speeches, so the question seems to be whether one large book could have contained a four-day-long speech.[56] Kumaniecki, following Humbert, argues that there is no contradiction between the statements of Nepos and Pliny.[57] Kumaniecki explains that Cicero published two speeches, the first being the continuous defense of Cornelius, which Nepos compared to the delivered version and found to be almost identical, and the second being an adaptation of his interrogation of witnesses. Thus, Kumaniecki maintains both that Pliny could be right to say that the published corpus represents a digested and compressed version of four days of proceedings and that Nepos could be right about Cicero's *oratio pro Cornelio*. But Stroh presents the simplest solution: the defense lasted four days (including testimony), during which Cicero made two speeches in each of two *actiones* (Asc. 62C), and these two speeches are what Pliny read.[58]

The case of the *Pro Milone* is even more vexed. Even though the present study does not contain a study of this trial of Milo in 52, any discussion of the relationship between Cicero's delivered and published speeches has to take account of reports that the delivered and published speeches were substantially different in this instance. The fact that sources comment on the discrepancy suggests that it was not the norm. Asconius reports that an *excepta oratio* actually survived to his day, but nevertheless he chooses to comment on a speech that we can read, since it was considered so outstanding (41–42C). Marshall has refuted the idea that Asconius testifies to the existence of a verbatim transcript of the speech taken down in shorthand.[59] Asconius tells us that when Cicero began to speak, he was received ("exceptus") by the shouting of Clodius's followers. (Settle has rightly called attention to the weakness of the proposition that Cicero was entirely unnerved by Clodian hecklers.)[60] As a result, he did not speak with his customary firmness. This *excepta oratio* (i.e., the one that was received [with shouting], although the verb *excipere* can also refer to taking down in shorthand) still existed in Asconius's time. Quintilian (*Inst.* 4.3.17) testifies to the fact that Cicero had to break away from the exordium that he had prepared for his speech for Milo because of the interruption, "ut ipsa oratiuncula qua usus est patet" [as is clear from the short speech that he made].[61] Can the delivered speech be described as an *oratiuncula,* which would be much less substantial than what we now possess?[62]

The evidence provided by other ancient authors is somewhat contradictory. Plutarch (*Cic.* 35) writes that Milo took precautions so that Cicero would not be cowed by the sight of the soldiers whom Pompey had stationed around the Forum, since Cicero was prone, in many trials, to tremble when he reached the heights of oratory. But Plutarch does not say that Cicero failed to deliver a speech for Milo. Dio Cassius (40.54) elaborates this picture of confusion by claiming that Cicero ceased to speak after uttering a few words, and he portrays Cicero as totally undone by the Clodian commotion, but his discussion of the trial may reflect his anti-Ciceronian bias.[63] For his part, Cicero expresses or at least feigns some pride in his performance on this occasion (*De optimo genere oratorum* 10). Dio specifically says that the speech we read was written later and that Milo made a famous joke that he would have been denied the pleasure of eating Massilian mullets if Cicero had really delivered that speech. The argument of the Bobbian scholiast (112St) tells the same story as Dio. Remnants of the original speech survive, quoted by Quintilian (9.2.54) and the Bobbian scholiast (173St).[64] The source may have been the *Acta Diurna.*[65]

As Marshall demonstrates, Cicero had shown himself able to stand up to hecklers in the first days of the trial, and there is no reason to believe that he failed to use his full share of time on the final day of the trial.[66] Stone has argued persuasively that what we see in the published *Pro Milone* is not a drastically altered version of the original speech but rather an intact original speech, with minor alterations, expanded by the addition of two major sections (an *extra causam* [72–91; the phrase is Cicero's own at 92] and a large section on Pompey [65–71]) after the trial, when political conditions had changed—probably, according to Stone, in early 51.[67] The original oration, without these additions, delivered within the tight constraints of time contained in the *lex Pompeia de vi,* could have then been much closer in length to an *oratiuncula.*

As Kennedy says, Cicero's conduct varied in regard to the relationship between the delivered speech and the published speech.[68] Cicero himself says that he read his *Post reditum in senatu* oration "de scripto" [from a text] (*Planc.* 74). At least one of the speeches delivered by Cicero in defense of Cornelius may have been very close to the published speech. At the other extreme, Cicero may have altered the *Pro Milone,* but, if Stone is right, Cicero would have done so much more through additions than through rewriting.

Since all the speeches that form the basis of this study are Cicero's, we do not have to attempt to determine for other orators what the relationship between their delivered and published speeches was. Nevertheless, it is useful to survey this question briefly, to corroborate the foregoing understanding of Ciceronian practice. In other words, if Cicero appears to have behaved in a totally different fashion from other orators, that might be a reason either to question this account or at least to see Cicero as an isolated example.

Quintilian makes it clear that he assumes that a speaker engages in some improvisation. He recommends, in connection with the subject of *partitio* (division), that a speaker ought to have thought out clearly, in advance, what points he will make. But he maintains that the appearance of spontaneity must be preserved: "pleraque gratiora sunt si inventa subito nec domo adlata, sed inter dicendum ex re ipsa nata videantur" [very many things are more pleasing if they seem to have been invented on the spot and not brought along from home but rather to have come into being in the act of speaking from the matter at hand itself] (*Inst.* 4.5.4). This precludes reading from a text, as is shown by the ridicule that C. Cassius Severus, an orator of the Augustan era, poured on a young speaker who asked him why he was looking at him "torvo vultu" [with a fierce expression]. He answered that he was not doing so but that he would do so if that was what was written in the young speaker's text ("sic scripsisti" [so you wrote it], 6.1.43). Yet Cassius himself probably represents the extreme of careful preparation. During his speech, he needed notes (*commentarii*) providing not a bare outline but most of the speech written out. He would mark opportunities for jokes, though he clearly realized that his jokes would fall flat if he recited them from a text. But as Seneca the Elder reports (*Controv.* 3 pr. 6), even Cassius would set his text aside and extemporize effectively. In the passage where Quintilian describes Cicero's practice with regard to his notes (10.7.30, discussed earlier in this section), he comments that in some cases the notes of orators have been found by chance and circulated; it is not clear from this passage whether these notes were just a part of the process of preparing for a trial or whether the author actually referred to them while speaking. Ser. Sulpicius, a contemporary of Cicero, published his *commentarii* in book form; to Quintilian, they seem to have been composed with a view to publication. Quintilian implies that these belong to a larger forensic corpus than the three speeches of Sulpicius that survived in his time. Yet spontaneity was not just an appearance, and Quintilian even advises the speaker to memorize passages from the same wax tablets on which he wrote them, so that the various erasures and connections will serve as a mnemonic device. Quintilian then discusses the advantages and disadvantages of memorizing a speech by reading it silently to oneself, as opposed to learning it from hearing someone else read it aloud (11.2.32–37). Overall, we can conclude that it would have been unlikely that the draft of the speech would have been delivered exactly as written and unlikely that this draft, if subsequently published, would have constituted a verbatim text of the delivered speech.

Quintilian's *Institutio oratoria* contains quite a long passage, a kind of internal debate, on the relationship between the written and spoken versions of speeches (12.10.49–57). Quintilian takes the position that equivalence is desirable; the *oratio scripta* should be a "monumentum actionis habitae" [record of a speech as delivered] (12.10.51). He admits that to please the jurors, the orator must say many things that ideally would not be necessary. But Quintilian is clearly most strongly swayed by the educational purpose of publishing speeches: he argues that students need to see how the oration works, "si modo ideo scribimus ut doceamus quo modo dici oporteat" [if at least we write with the purpose of teaching how it should be spoken] (12.10.53). He admits that at the trial, the speaker may have to omit prepared sections for reasons of time, but he recommends that the orator later publish these passages omitted from the actual speech. He grants the orator the privilege of omitting from the written speech those points made as a concession to the nature of the jurors, with the result that these points do not appear in the published text. If a defense speech was edited according to these principles set out by Quintilian, it would not necessarily misrepresent the prosecution case to which the defense had responded, although it might.[69]

I have saved the locus classicus, Pliny's *Epistulae* 1.20.6–10, for last. There, Pliny the Younger comments directly on the relationship between the delivered speech and the published text. He presents the argument that whereas some of his contemporaries believed that the speeches were expanded in the process of publication, they were actually shortened. His evidence is that legal arguments especially are sometimes summarized by a mere rubric. How reliable is his testimony?

There is no question that the factual basis on which Pliny formed his conclusion is correct. One of the examples presented by him, from Cicero's *Pro Murena* 57, still survives ("DE POSTUMI CRIMINIBUS,"[70] "DE SERVI ADULESCENTIS"); the other, from the lost *Pro Vareno*,[71] does not. Although Pliny does not cite them, we possess at least one other example and possibly two: Cicero's *Pro Fonteio* 20 ("DE CRIMINE VINARIO. DE BELLO VOCONTIORUM. DE DISPOSITIONE HIBERNORUM") and possibly Cicero's *Pro Caelio* 19 ("DE TESTE FUFIO"), although this may be the work of a later editor.[72] Pliny's analysis shows that by the end of the first century A.D., scholars were already debating the relationship between the published texts of speeches and the speeches as delivered. As Riggsby rightly argues (see discussion earlier in this section), Pliny is making an inference on the basis of the Ciceronian text in front of him, nothing else, so he is in the same position as we are, although he may have had available to him a somewhat larger corpus of Cicero's forensic rhetoric than we have, as is shown by his knowledge of the *Pro Vareno*. Pliny's inference seems reasonable with regard to legalistic sections, but it would be rash to agree with Pliny that a speech as delivered was necessarily longer than its published version. At least, the practice of placing rubrics in the published texts as a marker for excisions suggests that ancient editors felt some allegiance to the spoken text and thus felt obliged to provide their readers with some indication of their departures from it.[73]

In conclusion, it seems clear that speeches typically went through three stages. First, the orator prepared notes (which were sometimes published later) and also wrote out and memorized some passages. Second, he delivered the speech, and it might have been possible for note takers to have jotted down and then circulated a "printed" version. Third, the orator edited and circulated the speech to friends or to a wider audience, and this process gave rise to the text that we read today. These editorial changes could conceivably add to, rather than subtract from, the historical information contained in the speech. Points that the orator had prepared but was forced to omit in his delivery for reasons of time could be restored. Perhaps a defense orator would include rebuttal arguments that occurred to him too late to use in the trial; these arguments would reflect what the prosecutor had actually said, even though the defense speaker added the arguments only after the trial was over. Corrections could be made in the edited version of improvised sections, such as a list of people present at the trial. Thus, while changes were made in the published version of a speech, they were not of a sort that should compel us to view the published defense speech as an imaginary response to an imaginary prosecution speech.

Finally, we need consider, from the point of view of the potential reader as well as that of the orator, why anyone would want to read these speeches. For Quintilian, education may have loomed large, and certainly in the case of Cicero, neophyte orators and even accomplished *patroni* may have been interested in reading his finest efforts, even if they were never actually delivered. For Stroh, the purpose of publication was primarily pedagogical, rather than to be a vehicle for political propaganda.[74] But surely most potential readers would be curious to know what Cicero really said at a sensational trial, not to possess a literary exercise that showed just how clever Cicero could be when, with the trial behind him, he was able with the advantage of hindsight to compose the best possible speech. Readers would not expect a verbatim transcript, because that was almost impossible to produce, but they would have wanted something that gave them the feeling that they were there.[75] While publication did serve a pedagogical function and while some, though not all, of these published speeches were political pamphlets, an important—and perhaps the primary—motive for publication was *gloria*. Given that there was an audience of people who wanted to read the speeches of great orators, a speaker like Cicero would have wanted to satisfy that demand and thereby display his excellence as an orator in the narrow sense and also enhance his stature as a statesman as he defines that role in the *De oratore*. That glory provided a sufficient motive for him to undertake the task of reconstructing and publishing his speeches.

In summary, the published texts of Cicero's forensic speeches were close enough to what he actually said that there is no compelling reason to dismiss these texts as valid sources for the trials in which they were delivered. The discrepancies between the delivered and published speeches are not so great as to exclude the possibility of understanding the case for the prosecution from the published texts.

THE RELIABILITY OF THE SECOND *Verrines*

Cicero's speeches against Verres constitute a fundamental resource for the study of prosecution in the last decades of the Republic, for the obvious reason that they are the only extant prosecution speeches, for this or any period of Roman history. But the five speeches from the second *actio* are not an obviously reliable source, since the second *actio* of that trial never took place and since the speeches are published versions not of what Cicero did say but of what he might have said. Since I make use of evidence from these five speeches, I need to present some argument in favor of their connection to the historical trial. I wish to present a novel argument in support of the proposition that when the speeches of the second *actio* describe the first *actio*, which of course did take place, they reflect reality. It should be noted that this proposition is different from saying that a written version of a speech reflects what was actually said in the spoken version of the same speech. It is likewise different from the proposition that the five speeches of the second *Verrines* reflect what Cicero would have actually said in a second *actio* if the trial had proceeded to a second hearing, in which he could have delivered those speeches. This argument is based on the list in appendix 2 of witnesses and documents that are mentioned in the second *Verrines*, specifically on two sections of that list: the list of witnesses mentioned in these speeches as having testified in the first *actio* and the corresponding list of witnesses who, Cicero says in the course of these five speeches, will testify after he and the defense *patroni* have spoken.

These five speeches deal with (1) Verres' career before his governorship of Sicily (73–71 B.C.), (2) his administration of justice in Sicily, (3) his man-agement of the grain tithe and other agricultural matters, (4) his art-collecting activities, and (5) his military management of the province. It is remarkable that in the first two of these speeches, Cicero does not mention by name one single witness who will testify in the second *actio*. In other words, from the first two speeches of the second *actio*, it seems that Cicero has already presented in the first *actio* virtually all testimony relevant to these two topics. Furthermore, to judge by all five speeches, while Cicero had, in the first *actio*, called witnesses relating to all five topics, by far the highest proportion of these witnesses had testified to matters relating to the first two topics. If there were an even distribution of witnesses, about 20 percent of the witnesses (i.e., eleven or twelve) would testify to each of the five topics. But out of fifty-six individual witnesses specified by Cicero in the first *actio* as having been called to testify, Cicero mentions fifteen (27 percent) in the first speech of the second *actio*, nineteen (34 percent) in the second speech, five (9 percent) in the third speech, eight (14 percent) in the fourth speech, and nine (16 percent) in the fifth speech. The distinction between the first two topics and the last three is so clear that it cannot be accidental.

Admittedly, this calculation is somewhat biased toward assigning wit-nesses to the first two speeches, because I have assigned witnesses who are cited in more than one speech to the earliest speech in which Cicero men-tions them. (The reason for this procedure will shortly become clear.) For example, I have counted in the second speech Cn. Cornelius Lentulus Mar-cellinus, who had testified in the first *actio* that Verres had allowed a trial to be conducted in the absence of the defendant (2 *Verr.* 2.103) and also about Verres' depredations of art works (2 *Verr.* 4.53). But the seven witnesses from the first hearing who are mentioned as such both somewhere in the first two orations of the second *Verrines* and also in the last three speeches are not numerous enough to explain the pattern.

The logical explanation of this pattern is that it reflects Cicero's method in presenting witnesses in the first *actio*, given the constraints of time under which he was operating, as he so clearly explains in his short speech in the first *actio*: the trial had to be finished that year (70 B.C.), because in the next year, Verres' allies would be so firmly in power that he could never be con-demned. The data are consistent with the suppositions that Cicero had a long list of witnesses to present to the court and that he started with those witnesses who could testify about Verres' pre-Sicilian career. He then

methodically moved on to those witnesses who testified about his administration of justice in Sicily, and since this subject was more recent, he naturally had more witnesses to present. When he saw that he had used up a
considerable amount of time on his first two topics, he called only a few
witnesses on his final three topics, enough to make his most persuasively
damning points, such as Verres' involvement in the crucifixion of the
Roman citizen P. Gavius (2 *Verr.* 5.158). Of course, Cicero knew that he
would have a second *actio* in which to bring forward the rest of his witnesses. A few witnesses had something to say about more than one topic,
and if they had something to say about one of the first two topics, he called
them and also let them present their testimony then and there on the later
topics, since it would have been foolish to ask them to testify in the first
actio and then make them wait several months before testifying again in the
second *actio*. It is reasonable to suppose that Cicero or a secretary of his
kept a record of which witnesses had been called and which witnesses
remained and that he consulted that list when he wrote the five speeches of
the second *Verrines*. Cicero must have consulted that record and used it to
distinguish between those witnesses whom he had called in the first *actio*
and those whom he would have called in the second *actio* had it taken place.

The preceding analysis does not absolutely prove that Cicero operated
in this way. As with any such claim that a fictitious speech has verisimilitude, one can always argue that Cicero artfully and artificially arranged the
Verrines to make it appear that he acted in the manner I have described and
that he thereby made the speeches of the second *actio* more realistic. This is
logically possible, but it is implausible for two reasons. First, such a process
would have been enormously arduous and time-consuming. Second, by
artificially creating the distinction between the first two and the final three
speeches, Cicero would have been detracting from the overall artistry of the
speeches, since he would have been introducing an element of asymmetry
and imbalance—making himself look like the lecturer who has not timed
the talk well and has to rush at the end.[76]

METHOD

But even if the published texts accurately reflect what happened at a trial,
other serious problems of method remain. It is obviously difficult to understand one side of an adversarial procedure from the partial and often dis-

torting presentation of the opposing side. To understand a case for the prosecution, it would be best to possess a complete transcript of the trial from beginning to end, and failing that, we would certainly at least like to read the prosecution's speech(es) and evidence. Relying on what the defense says about the prosecution is a third choice at best. The Roman forensic speaker did not have as his primary aim the transmission of facts; Gotoff is right to say as a rule, "In his judicial speeches the only thing Cicero needs to create in his listeners is a disposition to acquit."[77] Moreover, in many cases, we have a speech by only one of several speakers for the defense, Cicero, and his speech may not be the most informative about the prosecution (see chap. 3).

Despite these difficulties, it is normal to extract information about the prosecution from a defense speech; commentaries on defense speeches typically contain a section on charges. Those who study classical antiquity are often required to reconstruct the missing pieces of a puzzle from the extant pieces. I do not claim to possess a new method that makes this process easy or even easier. But in assessing the credibility about various statements made by the defense about the prosecution, there are some helpful guidelines.

Harris has identified six guidelines, which I quote verbatim, for evaluating the evidence found in Greek forensic speeches:[78]

1. Statements that are supported by relevant evidence can be regarded as reliable.
2. It is important to determine whether the evidence cited by the speaker could actually have proven the truth of his statement.
3. While we can trust a statement of fact that is corroborated by relevant evidence, nothing compels us to accept the speaker's interpretation of that fact.
4. All statements not supported by evidence should be regarded with suspicion.
5. The only kinds of unsubstantiated assertions that can be trusted are those made about public events in the recent past and charges made by the prosecutor that are mentioned by the defendant without being refuted.
6. The failure of the defendant to respond to a charge made by his accuser is not strong grounds for considering the charge to be true.

Harris arrives at these guidelines on the basis of his examination of opposing speeches of Aeschines and Demosthenes, and unfortunately, the equivalent Latin corpus never provides us with such pairs. Thus, as far as the sixth guideline is concerned, if the defense totally failed to mention or allude to a charge, it is very doubtful that we would know about it, unless a *testimonium* with that information existed in another source, such as Cicero's *Letters* or the commentary of a scholiast. The consideration that leads Harris to frame the sixth guideline is that the defendant might well not have time to respond to every attack made by the prosecutor, whether a formal charge or just personal abuse. Since the time constraints on the Roman orator were normally more lenient than those on his Athenian counterpart, a failure by the Roman *patronus* to deal with a formal charge (in other words, his alluding to it without mounting any challenge to it) suggests that he has no way to counter it. That failure is then a consideration in favor of the prosecution on that point, though fairness to the defense dictates recognition of the difficulty of proving a negative. The fifth guideline can be modified to the extent that even evidence from the distant past should be credited if it could effectively be challenged if it were false (as could, e.g., a quotation from the Twelve Tables). The first four guidelines can be accepted, as long as one realizes that they provide points in favor of or against the credibility of evidence, without any claim to being probative.

To Harris's first four guidelines, I would add the following, more general guidelines about the credibility of charges, guidelines that have no claim to originality but reflect the skeptical practice common to classicists:

1. When the defense alludes to a charge very briefly without refuting it, we should entertain the suspicion that the charge has merit.
2. When the defense dwells on a charge to what seems an excessive length, we should entertain the suspicion that it may not have been as central to the prosecution as the defense makes it out to be.
3. A charge should receive additional credence when the defense's refutation of it involves obfuscation.
4. When the *patronus* contrasts himself with the prosecutor in some way, we should be wary of accepting the judicial relevance of such statements.

Cicero's brevity in dealing with the allegation that Caelius attempted to bribe the slaves of Lucceius to murder the philosopher Dio is an example of my first guideline (see chap. 12). Cicero's expatiation on the *iudicium Iunianum* in the trial of Cluentius is the most obvious example of the second (see chap. 9). An example of the third is the confusion created by Cicero between homicide plots in July and November 63 (see chap. 10). Finally, the fourth stricture is appropriate since the defense in these trials was presented by an advocate, rather than the defendant himself, as was the case at Athens. Cicero's contrast of himself with Cato in the prosecution of Murena provides an example of material that should be viewed with skepticism (see chap. 6). These guidelines provide useful standards for weighing the credibility of a statement found in one of Cicero's forensic speeches. But they cannot be used in a mechanical fashion, and they do not provide a totally reliable calculation of its credibility.

THE ROLE OF LAW IN ROMAN TRIALS

It may seem obvious that law plays a role in trials, regardless of the legal system. But a lay reader who dipped into the scholarly literature on the trials of Ciceronian Rome might be pardoned for coming away with the conclusion that Roman forensic speakers and Roman jurors paid little heed to the law as it applied to the case in hand and perhaps could not even comprehend the difference between what was legally relevant and legally extraneous. Selections from one major book that expresses the point of view of this school give a flavor of how the legal history of this period was written in the sixties and seventies.

> Legal sophistries abounded on both sides; the slippery character of *maiestas* encouraged them. But it would be a mistake to dwell on the legal arguments. Politics was the central issue in this case.
>
> The technical charge against C. Antonius, it seems, was *res repetundae*, in connection with alleged behavior in Macedon. But the technical charge was a minor issue. The prosecutors, as in all Republican trials, had a free hand to raise any matter that might bring discredit upon the defendant. . . . C. Antonius was duly convicted, and

departed into exile. The verdict was difficult to avoid in view of the varied interests lined up against him.

Once again, analysis of criminal indictments serves to illuminate the whole complex political fabric.[79]

To take another example, Gotoff, having described the ways in which Cicero created personae for himself, his client, and the prosecutor, writes, "The implication of the above thesis, that fact and law mean less in a judicial speech than imagination, psychology, and showmanship, would not have surprised Cicero's contemporaries or earlier generations of Roman orators."[80] Zetzel dismisses any attempt to determine which party in a trial had right on its side.

> Truth is not an issue in a Ciceronian forensic oration: winning is.
> . . . unless we have some "objective" external evidence, we might as
> well dispense with trying to figure out what the "truth" of a case is,
> and how Cicero manipulates it. We will never know, nor should it
> matter. Where the real problem arises is in trying to decide whether
> the truth of the case made any difference to the judge or jury
> either.[81]

Yet at the same time, Zetzel makes the judgment that Cluentius, Archias, Sestius, Murena, Flaccus, and Milo were all guilty as charged and that possibly all of Cicero's clients were guilty in strict law. So it may be worthwhile to establish that law and legally relevant facts were indeed part of the business of the Roman juror and therefore of the Roman forensic orator. While Gotoff is certainly right that factors other than fact and law played an important role in a Ciceronian speech and, furthermore, that modern British and American trial lawyers would not be as shocked by such elements as some Ciceronian scholars are,[82] I wish to stress that fact and law did make an important difference in a case. This point of view deserves some amplification and explication, since it informs my analysis of the individual trials in a significant way.[83]

It would be a mistake to think that the ancient Greeks and Romans could not distinguish between a legally relevant fact or argument and a legally extraneous fact or argument. Aristotle contrasts the relevant matter (τὸ πρᾶγμα) with what is extraneous (ἔξω τοῦ πράγματος).[84] However, the ancient standard of relevance may have been different from prevailing standards today and may strike us as unreasonable. On the subject of laws, Aristotle expands that category to include "unwritten laws" of a very general, moral nature.[85] Several centuries intervened between Aristotle, on the one hand, and, on the other, Cicero and the rhetorical writers. But some continuity existed in the ancient intellectual tradition on rhetoric.[86]

Quintilian makes the same distinction between artificial and inartificial proofs, citing Aristotle as the source of this distinction, which, Quintilian writes, finds almost universal acceptance. Quintilian refers to a view that he rejects: while some rhetorical writers do not consider inartificial proofs to be worth writing about, because they require no art, he takes the opposite view, because he believes that great oratorical skill is required to neutralize and refute these proofs. Quintilian identifies the inartificial proofs as *praeiudicia* (prior judgments), rumors, torture, documents, oaths, and witnesses (*Inst.* 5.1.1–2). According to Quintilian, the category of *praeiudicia* is closest to Aristotle's law but not the same (5.2), and documents (5.5) are similar to contracts; torture (5.5), oaths (5.6), and witnesses (5.7.1–32) are the same for both writers. Quintilian divides *praeiudicia* into three categories: precedents (similar cases), judgments related to the case itself, and a rehearing of a previously decided case. Quintilian provides many details about oaths, running through the arguments that can be made by someone who challenges his adversary to take an oath or does not and someone who does take an oath or does not. He divides the category of *testimonia* into written and oral subcategories (5.7.1). He divides witnesses between those who are subpoenaed by the prosecutors and those who appear of their own volition (5.7.9); of the subpoenaed, some are hostile to the accused, and some are not (5.7.15). Like a modern lawyer, the ancient orator, according to Quintilian, had to exploit these witnesses without letting them sabotage his case by saying something unexpected (5.7.10–31). Quintilian includes many valuable pieces of advice, starting with knowing your witness (5.7.26), and he contrasts his approach to that of the rhetorical schools, who do not deign to treat this as a matter appropriate for instruction (5.7.28).

The kinds of evidence that can be cited in a forensic case today are quite different from what we can expect to find in an ancient case. Obviously, forensic evidence (fingerprints, blood type, DNA, and many other modern tools) was not employable, and evidence that we would consider irrelevant or useless was available and exploited. Witness testimony was important but impeachable. The arguments against evidence obtained through tor-

ture—especially the argument that people will tell lies to end their suffering—were present in the teachings of rhetorical writers, although those
writers also presented arguments in favor of evidence taken through torture. As Cicero has Antonius say (*De or.* 2.100), the orator needed to master the facts and documents in relation to a case and the characters of those
involved, before he made his speech, although not every orator did prepare
himself adequately.

The emphasis on character as an argument for guilt or innocence is one
aspect of Roman forensic rhetoric that contributes to a suspicion that
Roman trials had little or nothing to do with Roman law.[87] The prosecution's frequent use, explicit or implicit, of the argument that this was just
the sort of crime that one would expect the defendant to commit or the
corresponding use of the converse argument by the defense, that no one
could imagine this defendant committing such a crime, can easily mislead
us into thinking that the whole trial was just a test of personalities. But if
one accepts the idea that character is a constant, arguments from character
can be seen in a different light.[88] The character of the defendant can render
the charges plausible or implausible. In those kinds of case where overwhelming evidence is difficult to collect and present, these arguments from
character will necessarily play a greater role. Moreover, it would be a mistake to conclude that Cicero's personal attacks on the prosecutors represent
mere slanderous obfuscation, because his strategy is often to defend his
client by charging that the prosecutors themselves or people associated
with them have committed the crimes in question.

The rhetorical writers confirm that this use of character is normal. The
author of the *Rhetorica ad Herennium* (2.5), under the heading "vita
hominis" [the man's life], advises the prosecutor to bring in previous
crimes of the same nature that the defendant is charged with or, failing that,
any sort of vice he can uncover. Cicero makes it clear in his *De inventione
rhetorica* (2.28–37) that it is only as a last resort, when nothing discreditable
is known about the defendant, that the prosecutor would omit discussion
of the character of the defendant, and pari passu, that it is only as a last
resort, when the defendant is notorious, that the defense speaker would
argue that the court should examine nothing other than the actual charge,
not the defendant's past life. Quintilian likewise, in his description of the
arguments that can be made on the basis of character, suggests that only an
advocate with no character arguments to make will urge the court just to
ignore the defendant's character and past record. He adds the characteris-

tically sensible advice to the prosecutor that it is better to say nothing about the defendant's past life than to rely on frivolous and false slurs (7.2.33–34).

Plausibility was, after all, the issue, for the prosecution as well as the defense. Perhaps one of the reasons why students of Roman republican history come away from Cicero's speeches with a feeling that legal issues are not really at issue is that it seems obvious to them that the prosecution has not proven its case "beyond a reasonable doubt," as modern criminal courts are supposed to require today. Partly, this feeling is due to Cicero's skill as a defense lawyer, but it also has to be kept in mind that Roman prosecutors did not have to prove the defendant guilty beyond a reasonable doubt, as the Roman terminology for a verdict shows. *Fecisse videtur* means "to be convicted," and *non fecisse videtur* means "to be acquitted." In a discussion of epistemology, Cicero (*Luc.* 146) cites with approval the use of the word *videri* in the formula. In his *Letters,* he announces, "Drusus, Scaurus non fecisse videntur" [Drusus and Scaurus are found not guilty] (*Att.* 4.17.5). Although we may think that this standard is too easy on the prosecution and too hard on the defendant, it was the standard, and as long as juries followed it, we have no reason to view them as players in a legal sham.

Equally disconcerting to the modern reader as the personal material on the defendant is the space in some of Cicero's defense speeches that is devoted to his own character. This can indeed be an integral part of a defense, as Thierfelder has described in a masterfully compact survey of Cicero's forensic oratory. Thierfelder demonstrates that, possibly as a remainder from the time when a *patronus* in the nonjudicial sense served as an advocate for his *cliens,* the Roman advocate vouched for his client with his own reputation, to a greater or lesser extent, as the case demanded.[89] Correspondingly, as we shall see, the prosecution might make an issue of a particular advocate's involvement in the case, and for that reason, the defense counsel might have to justify his own participation.

It may seem like a truism, needing no argument, to say that the jury was the main audience of the advocate in a jury trial, since the jurors decided the outcome of the case. But two passages in Cicero's *Brutus* might seem to support the view that the *corona* (circle of onlookers) standing around the edges of the trial was as much the orator's target as was the jury.[90] This view rests, in my opinion, on a misinterpretation of these passages. In both, Cicero is arguing that the reaction of the rhetorically unsophisticated listener provides a good indicator of rhetorical effectiveness, not that these listeners are necessarily the main focus of the orator's efforts, though it happens that the jurors do constitute that focus. Cicero argues at *Brutus* 290 that one can gauge the effectiveness of an orator by his ability to hold the attention of an audience of ordinary onlookers (including jurors), untrained in rhetoric. In a similar passage, *Brutus* 200, he describes how an effective orator holds the attention of the jurors whom he is addressing. In these passages, he explains that if the audience laughs at an orator's jokes and weeps at his purple passages, an onlooker will know that the orator is doing his job well, but if the jurors yawn, gossip with each other, or check the time, the onlooker will realize that the orator is in trouble. These people could not analyze and describe why an orator is holding their attention, but they recognize a good orator when they hear one.[91] The reaction of the *corona* was not devoid of importance, but it was important only as it might influence the primary audience, that is, the jurors. An orator might try to influence the jury indirectly by eliciting a favorable response from the *corona,* and he certainly had to be concerned if lack of enthusiasm among the onlookers in the *corona* spread by contagion to the jurors. But these possibilities in no way contradict the primacy of the jurors as his audience.

The legal question before Roman juries was whether the defendants did or did not seem to have violated the law. Arguments from character were entirely valid and relevant to show the plausibility or implausibility that they had done so or possibly that someone other than the defendant had done so. Other attacks, whether they were related to some criminal statute or were personal abuse, were irrelevant. Thus, Cicero can say that only two things matter in the trial of Caelius, *aurum* and *venenum.* "Omnia sunt alia non crimina sed maledicta" [All the other things are not charges but insults], Cicero argued, "iurgi petulantis magis quam publicae quaestionis" (in Austin's words [*Pro Caelio*[3], 87, ad loc.], "more suited to some loutish brawl than to a court of justice"). Cicero concluded, "'Adulter, impudicus, sequester' convicium est, non accusatio" ["Adulterer, profligate, bribery agent" is abuse, not accusation] (*Cael.* 30).

How conscientiously did Roman jurors fulfill their responsibility to come to a legally rational judgment on the defendant? Obviously, we cannot know the answer to this question two millennia later, and the answer must be different for different trials and different jurors. Frier's analysis of the role of law in the trial involving Caecina (*TLRR* no. 189), which probably occurred in 69 B.C., provides a way to view the problem. In his analysis of the "problem of litigiousness," Frier argues that before the trial was on the horizon, the parties to the case operated with social and economic purposes in the "front region" of their interactions, with law in the "back region," but that when it became likely that a will (that of Caesennia) was going to lead to legal wrangling, the positions were reversed, and law moved into the "front region."

> Now the frame of reference for their interactions was inverted: private law became not only the means to an end, but also a large part of the end itself, in the sense that both parties consciously and overtly prepared their positions in lawsuits, without necessarily committing themselves thereby to carrying one out; while their normal, more purely social ambitions were ostensibly retired into the "back region" of their interactions. Each party began to think, both of himself and of his opponent, no longer as "ordinary" Romans, but rather as potential adversaries in a court of law. In essence, they began behaving less as "ordinary" Romans, and more as incumbents of a special social role or position.[92]

Frier's analysis of the role of law for the litigants can be extended to the jurors. When they took their solemn oath (*lex repetundarum*, lines 36–38) and were empaneled, they may have ceased to be "ordinary" Romans. They were now *iudices*, and law may have moved to the front region of their minds. Of course, one cannot prove that this change normally occurred, but Frier's analysis provides a basis for comprehending the process whereby normal upper-class Romans could have suddenly transformed themselves into instruments of the law, and the burden of proof is just as much on those who would argue that they did not move law to the "front region" as on those who argue that they did.

We cannot know to what extent the jurors came to a trial with an open mind or whether they entered it with a strong inclination to condemn or acquit. But even if they were initially inclined to vote a certain way, they had to be given, during the course of the trial, a good reason to do so. Rigsby writes:

> Obviously not all arguments are equally effective, and the difference lies in the local context. We cannot meaningfully ask what jurors find persuasive without asking more specifically what they find persuasive under these particular circumstances, i.e., sitting as jurors. . . . Truth, that is to say the production of a truth, a plausible

account of reality, is a trope or strategy. . . . for forensic oratory truth
was not just any trope, but a distinctive and obligatory one. The orator's case must appear true.[93]

The speakers had to provide the jury with good reasons for the vote they
were trying to get from it, the defense *patronus* for acquittal and the prosecutor for condemnation. Which was the easier task?

ADVANTAGES FOR THE PROSECUTION

Cicero's record of success as a defense speaker is all the more remarkable in
view of the inherent advantage that the Roman procedure for criminal trials
afforded the prosecution. In this section, I will advance reasons why, all
things considered, conducting a prosecution demanded less in the way of
improvisational rhetorical skills than conducting a defense. I concede that
neither task was easy in absolute terms and that the task of the prosecution
required more preparation (as I will show in the next section of this chapter).

At several points in his *Institutio oratoria*, Quintilian assesses the advantages and disadvantages of the two sides of a legal case. It must be conceded
that he finds advantages for the defense as well as for the prosecutor. He
points out that in the defense lawyer's exordium, the defense has only to
remind the jurors about what the prosecutor had to explain to them for the
first time. Quintilian maintains that in the examination of witnesses, the
defense has the advantage that it knows what a witness has said already in
the direct examination by the prosecution, but the defense has to deal with
the difficulty that the defense lawyer generally does not know what a witness will say (5.7.22).[94] Quintilian argues that prosecutors have to be careful
about trying to anticipate defense arguments and then trying to refute them
before the defense makes them. He admits that there may be good reasons
for doing so (4.1.49), but he warns that by raising an expected defense argument, the prosecutor is in danger of lending credence to it (5.13.45–50).
Quintilian maintains that while this practice may be desirable—even necessary—in the schools of declamation, where there is no real opponent, the
prosecutor using this practice in real trials can expose himself to ridicule.
Quintilian gives two examples: Cicero scoffs at the idea that the prosecution in the case of Cluentius had any real access to a defense plan to bring
up a legal technicality, and thus he is really admitting that the law itself is so

clear on this point that it can, so to say, speak for itself; Vibius Crispus, in Quintilian's own time, responds with the witticism that the prosecutor's statement of an argument obviates the need for him to make it himself (5.13.48). Doubtless, too, the general prejudice against prosecutors that Quintilian describes (12.7.1–4) constituted an obstacle for the prosecution, as necessary as prosecutors may (unfortunately) have been for the efficacy of the laws.[95]

Overall, however, Quintilian puts forward the view that defense is more difficult than prosecution. The most relevant passage (5.13.2–3) is worth quoting in full.

> Non sine causa tamen difficilius semper est creditum, quod Cicero saepe testatur, defendere quam accusare. Primum quod est res illa simplicior: proponitur enim uno modo, dissolvitur varie, cum accusatori satis sit plerumque verum esse id quod obiecerit, patronus neget defendat transferat excuset deprecetur molliat minuat avertat despiciat derideat. Quare inde recta fere atque, ut sic dixerim, clamosa est actio: hinc mille flexus et artes desiderantur. Tum accusator praemeditata pleraque domo adfert, patronus etiam inopinatis frequenter occurrit. Accusator dat testem, patronus ex re ipsa refellit. Accusator <a> criminum invidia, etsi falsa sit, materiam dicendi trahit, de parricidio sacrilegio maiestate: quae patrono tantum neganda sunt. Ideoque accusationibus etiam mediocres in dicendo suffecerunt, bonus defensor nemo nisi qui eloquentissimus fuit. Nam ut quod sentio semel finiam, tanto est accusare quam defendere quanto facere quam sanare vulnera facilius.

[Not without reason, however, has it always been believed, as Cicero often gives evidence of,[96] that it is harder to defend than to accuse. First of all, the latter is simpler; for the prosecutor states the case in one way, whereas the defense refutes it in many ways, since it is largely enough for the prosecutor that what he charges is true, whereas the defense speaker denies, justifies, changes the legal basis of the case, excuses, seeks pardon, mitigates, minimizes, diverts, scoffs, and pokes fun. Therefore, the speech from the prosecution is almost always straightforward and something that can be, so to speak, shouted, whereas the speech for the defense requires a thousand twists and ploys. Moreover, the prosecutor brings along from home very many things that have been previously thought out, whereas the defense speaker counters a host of unforeseen things. The prosecutor provides the witness, the defense speaker rebuts from the matter at hand. The prosecutor draws matter to speak about from the hatred against the charges, even if they are false, such as charges of parricide, sacrilege, or treason, but the defense speaker can only say that the charges are false. Therefore, even middling orators have been adequate for prosecutions, but no one has been a good defender unless he has been very eloquent indeed. For, to finish my thought with one stroke, it is as much easier to prosecute than to defend as it is to make wounds rather than to cure them.]

Quintilian here presents four reasons why it is easier to prosecute than to defend:

1. It is simpler. The prosecutor chooses one tactic, while the defender must use many; for example, the latter must argue both "non fecit" [He did not do it] and "si fecit, iure fecit" [If he did it, he did it rightfully].
2. The defender must improvise (see my discussion of the time allowed for the defense to prepare a response, later in this section), whereas the prosecutor can prepare his case in advance.
3. The defender can avail himself only of artificial proofs, without inartificial proofs, such as documents and witnesses.
4. The crime itself provides an emotional advantage to the prosecutor.

In view of these considerations, it is not surprising that some orators were better at prosecution than at defense.[97]

The second point requires some elaboration, because it is not obvious that it is valid. In a modern trial, the prosecution is required to reveal to its opponents both the charges, in the form of an indictment, and the evidence, according to the process of discovery.[98] The governing principle is that it is only fair that the defendant and his or her lawyers know exactly what the charges are and what evidence the prosecution has in its possession and plans to present in court. The fact that prosecutors are officers of the state, rather than private citizens, and have at their disposal the resources of a police force serves as at least part of the justification for this policy, since in its absence, the private citizen (the defendant) would have almost no hope of warding off an attack launched by the government. In Rome, perhaps because the prosecutor was a private citizen like the defendant, albeit granted a limited power to subpoena witnesses, and because no investigatory staff existed to collect evidence for the prosecution, the need to weight the scales to put the defendant on a level with the prosecutor was not as great as it is today.

In particular, I have argued that the prosecutor in a Roman criminal trial did not specify exactly what charges he would make, although I certainly admit that the evidence is not conclusive and that the point is far from proven. Elsewhere, I began with an interpretation of line 56 of the *lex repetundarum,* its restriction on double jeopardy, which is defined in a fundamentally different way from the modern idea of double jeopardy, and then I connected that view with the argument that Roman criminal trials were not initiated by an *inscriptio* with specific charges.[99] Having already expressed my view of this knotty problem, I will limit my discussion here to two points. First, a general *inscriptio* (i.e., one that did not list specific charges) could have existed even if my interpretation of double jeopardy is incorrect. The *inscriptio* might not have expressed the exact charges, but they would have come out in the trial itself, and they could have formed the basis for excluding a new trial involving precisely the same charges. Second, the evidence for specific charges presented in advance of the trial is very scanty. In the following paragraphs, I summarize it briefly.[100]

Paul (*Dig.* 48.2.3) provides a clause from an *inscriptio* initiating an adultery prosecution under the Augustan *lex Iulia de adulteriis.* Some specifics of the charge are provided: the name of the "co-respondent"; the location of the offense, defined by city and house; and the time of the offense, defined by year and month. But the wording of this *inscriptio* may relate to the specific provisions of the adultery law; the specific connection with that law may have been clear when Paul wrote, in a work on adultery ("de adulteriis"), "libellorum inscriptionis conceptio talis est . . ." [The layout of forms of indictment is as follows: . . .] (*Dig.* 48.2.3 pr.; trans. Robinson, ed. Watson), and the generic appearance of the formula that he provides may be a result of its later appearance in a collection, such as the *Digest.* The rationale for providing these details about where and when the trial occurred may relate to requirements of the adultery law with regard to the admissibility of the case, since the month of the offense in relation to the time of bringing the case was a condition that could bear on the right to sue

(Ulp. *Dig.* 48.5.4.1) and since the place where the crime occurred could also be relevant; for example, if a third party makes his house available for the rendezvous, he can be punished as an adulterer (Papinianus *Dig.* 48.5.9).[101] Because the adultery law involves these special features, it is not typical enough to provide a reliable model for reconstructing other laws. In addition, it may be of a kind that occurred only after the *lex Iulia publicorum iudiciorum* (17 B.C.?), so it would not provide a good guide for republican legislation.[102]

Seneca the Younger presents a parody in the *Apocolocyntosis* (14.1; cf. Suet. *Claud.* 29) in which he posthumously indicts the emperor Claudius under the *lex Cornelia de sicariis.* The indictment lists thirty-five senators, 221 knights, and, without any attempt at precision, a number of other people whom Claudius is accused of having murdered. If this *subscriptio* or *inscriptio* provides the pattern, we would have to conclude that many details are omitted, such as the names of the individuals. Of course, this passage contains a strong element of comic exaggeration, so it is possible that a real indictment would have provided many more specifics.

Cicero (*Inv. rhet.* 2.58–59) provides an example of a trial under a *lex de sicariis* that was specifically for parricide. Failure to demonstrate parricide caused the whole case to fail. This particular charge was specified in advance because it afforded the prosecutor an advantage (an earlier hearing than ordinary murder trials) and carried a more gruesome punishment in the event of a guilty verdict.[103]

A prosecution under the *lex Plautia de vi* specified an act of violence involving a strategic location and the use of a weapon (Asc. 55C). As with parricide and homicide, this charge may have constituted an aggravated form of violence, with special provisions.[104]

Tabulae publicae provided documentation about what a trial that had ended was about (Cic. *Clu.* 62). But these are not, as Giuffrè argues,[105] a record of the *inscriptio* but rather a record of the testimony of the trial, which can be used to establish what the charges in the trial were.[106]

After the *postulatio* (application to prosecute) but before the formal *nominis receptio* (admission of the charge), the would-be defendant was asked whether he wished to contest the charge. This procedure is called *legibus interrogari,*[107] for which we have three pieces of evidence. First, Cicero (*Dom.* 77) writes: ". . . at fuit iudici. Cuius? quis me umquam ulla lege interrogavit? quis postulavit? quis diem dixit?" [. . . but there was [a penalty] of a trial. Of what trial? Who ever lay charges against me? Who prosecuted me? Who summoned me?]. Cicero's point is that he has never been a defendant in a trial, and he lists the stages in a trial, one of which is the *legibus interrogari*. Second, Pseudo-Asconius (207St, on 2 *Verr.* 1.5) writes: "Quid est reum fieri nisi apud praetorem legibus interrogari? Cum enim in ius ventum esset, dicebat accusator apud praetorem reo: aio te Siculos spoliasse" [What is it to be brought to trial except to be arraigned before the praetor? For when it had come to court, the prosecutor said before the praetor to the defendant: "I say that you have robbed the Sicilians"]. Even if we interpret this passage to mean that Cicero's prosecution of Verres was limited to his alleged extortion in Sicily, the statement "aio te Siculos spoliasse" does not provide Verres and his *patronus* Hortensius with any new information about the upcoming trial. Given that Verres had just returned from three years of governing Sicily, they must have known that the extortion trial would have to do at least partly with his administration of that province. Santalucia suggests as a typical formula for this stage in the trial the statement "aio te veneno Titium necasse" [I say you have killed Titius with poison], made before the presiding officer of the *quaestio de sicariis et veneficiis*.[108] If Santalucia is right, the procedure of *legibus interrogari* conveyed some new information to the defendant and his or her advocate, that is, which individuals the defendant is charged with having poisoned. But it remains an open question whether the prosecutor was limited in the main trial to the charges he had mentioned in the *legibus interrogari* stage. We know of no instance where the defense attorney objected that the prosecutor had no right to introduce a new charge in the main trial. The only possible exception, the aforementioned parricide case discussed by Cicero at *De inventione rhetorica* 2.58–59, suggests that if the prosecution was compelled to be somewhat more specific in the preliminaries to the trial (alleging that the defendant had committed parricide, though not necessarily a specific act of parricide), the defense could raise an objection if the prosecution failed to substantiate that allegation.[109] Moreover, one has to wonder whether the Romans would have wanted to prevent a prosecutor from bringing charges based on new material that he had uncovered in the course of his officially sanctioned investigation. Third, *Scholia Bobiensia* 170St ("de aere alieno Milonis") reads: "legibus etenim sic interrogabantur: inquirente accusatore an omnia secundum legum praescripta gesserit is cui crimen intendebatur" [for he was arraigned in this way: with the prosecutor posing the question whether he against whom the charge was being directed has done all things according to the rules of the laws]. A reply to the question whether the defendant had done everything according to the rules of the laws would obviously not give any clue to the defendant as to the precise nature of the charges faced.

The prosecution could subpoena a number of witnesses up to a specified maximum (forty-eight), in addition to any "voluntary witnesses," that is, those who testified without the compulsion of a subpoena.[110] The prosecution told the praetor who these witnesses were, as well as bringing before the praetor written evidence that would be submitted, such as accounts, books, and public and private letters (*lex repetundarum*, line 34). Although there is no evidence that the prosecution had to provide the defense with the witnesses' names in advance, it is very possible that this information was available to the defense.[111] Of course, any evidence about who had been compelled to testify that the defense could glean from its intelligence in advance of the trial would help the defense better understand the case. However, there would still remain the problem of "voluntary witnesses," whose identity the defense might have no way of knowing.

None of this evidence demonstrates that the prosecution in ancient legal cases presented a specific and authoritative statement of the charges it intended to bring. That lack of evidence does not demonstrate the opposite, but we can say that, as far as we know, the defendant was informed of the basis of the accusation in very general terms through *legibus interrogari* and in specific terms only during the prosecutor's speech.[112] To this lack of evidence, we can add the argument from silence that we never hear Cicero, when speaking for the defense in a criminal case, claiming that the prosecution has introduced a charge improperly because it was not present in the *inscriptio*, although when speaking in a civil case, he does try to have charges dismissed from consideration because they were not included in the *formula* (the judge's statement of the issue).[113] Given the corpus of Ciceronian defense speeches that we possess, this argument from silence is as strong as such an argument can ever be.

Having heard the prosecutor's first speech in a case, the defense had little time to adjust, probably just overnight after the end of the presentation of the case by the prosecution. But it is possible that the prosecution's presentation took more than one day, depending on how one calculates the maximum times for making speeches. Cicero (*Flac.* 82) mentions a six-hour time limit for Decianus, a *subscriptor* for the prosecution. If this refers to the number of hours Decianus had, rather than the number of hours that had to be divided up among all the prosecution speakers, then clearly it could take several days to present the case, during which the defense lawyers could start to plan their response while still listening to their opponents.[114] Clark (1927, 76) argues, on the basis of a two-hour limit for a *subscriptor* in the *lex Ursonensis,* that the reading *VI horas* at this point in Cicero's speech is a corruption for *II horas,* since he does not believe that a trial would have taken so much longer at Rome than at Urso. If the rule at Urso follows republican practice, then with Clark's emendation, the prosecution speeches might take something like eight hours (four for the main speaker and two for each of two *subscriptores*). So even if we accept this view, the defense would have had at least the night to think about its response. Pompey's judicial legislation in 52 B.C., whereby the prosecution had two hours and the defense three, with other restrictions designed to speed up the trial so that the trial could have been completed in one day, must have been exceptional. It appears that the presiding magistrate could create an interval between prosecution and defense, though the evidence comes from the imperial period (Tac. *Ann.* 3.13, 67).[115] If there was a *comperendinatio* (adjournment prescribed by law) or *ampliatio* (renewed hearing) in the trial, then during the second hearing, the defense would have had more time to think about the prosecution case. Nevertheless, if it is correct that the defense speakers were not supplied with a precise list of charges in advance of the trial, then certainly by any standard they had to react to the prosecution speeches in a very short period of time and with extraordinary agility.[116]

It is not surprising, then, that Cicero (*De or.* 2.102) has Antonius say that he carefully interviews his client before the trial and tries to argue his opponent's case to the client, to try to extract the basis of his defense from the client. In a typical civil case, where the *formula* established the legal issue, the defense would have had more guidance, but in a criminal case, the defense speaker must have benefited greatly from a client's willingness to forecast frankly (in private, of course) the points that would be made against him, so that his advocate was not taken by surprise in open court.

THE DIFFICULTIES OF THE PROSECUTOR

In terms of rhetorical ability and mental agility, the defense speaker's role may well have required more than the prosecutor's. But in terms of preparation, planning, and labor, the prosecutor's task was probably considerably more difficult. In this section, I will use Cicero's prosecution of Verres as an example to show just how much effort was involved in preparing for a prosecution. Readers who think that a Roman trial involved empty rhetoric devoid of a factual basis will come to realize, I hope, just how much evidence Cicero collected, both in the form of testimony and in the form of documents, to vanquish his opponents, Verres and his *patronus* Hortensius.

Cicero himself testifies to the difficulty of the prosecutor's task. He does this explicitly when he presents his credentials in the *divinatio,* as he competes with a rival for the right to prosecute Verres. This relatively unknown senator, Q. Caecilius Niger, had served as quaestor at Lilybaeum under Verres in 73.[117] Cicero's main argument is that he himself is the prosecutor whom the alleged victims most want and the defendant least wants (*Div. Caec.* 10). To diminish his opponent's attractiveness, Cicero stresses the skill and conscientious effort that will be required, "aliqua facultas agendi, aliqua dicendi consuetudo, aliqua in foro, iudiciis, legibus aut ratio aut exercitatio" [a certain command of pleading, a certain familiarity with speaking, a certain way and practice in the forum, the courts, and the law] (35). He maintains: "Dicenda, demonstranda, explicanda sunt omnia, causa non solum exponenda, sed etiam graviter copioseque agenda est" [You must say, show, and explain all things. You must not only set out the case, but also plead it in an authoritative and ample way] (39). He asks Caecilius if he is ready to take up all of Verres' crimes, those committed as quaestor, legate, and praetor before he was governor of Sicily, as well as in Sicily itself, and present them in an appropriate manner to the court (38). Cicero ridicules the idea that T. Alienus as a *subscriptor* will be able to make up for Caecilius's deficiencies, since he will be constrained to understate his case so as not to upstage the lead actor, Caecilius (48). For at least two reasons, there is no doubt that Cicero is being somewhat unfair to his opponent. First, Caecilius has an incentive that Cicero lacks: he has been injured by Verres (see 58, 60). Second, it was common for a prosecutor lacking experience and/or of junior standing, as prosecutors often were, to seek the support of more experienced speakers to help them present their case.[118]

As much as Cicero is portraying the role of the prosecutor for the concrete purpose of obtaining the assignment, some truth emerges from his presentation. First, the cooperation of the alleged victims in supplying evidence is vital. Cicero claims that the Sicilians will not appear at the trial if Caecilius is chosen as prosecutor and will not supply documents, for fear

that Caecilius is more interested in hiding those documents that incriminate himself and his activities as quaestor than in revealing those that
incriminate Verres and his activities as governor (28). Second, Cicero
speaks of a shortage of capable prosecutors. As he describes the situation,
supporters of continuing the senatorial hold on the juries in criminal trials
are worried by the fact that the courts are failing to convict the guilty, and
for that reason, qualified prosecutors are reluctant to come forward and
devote themselves to the task (8). The implication is that few people want
to make the necessary exertions only to find out that they have wasted their
time and that the outcome, an acquittal, is a foregone conclusion. Cicero
argues that for this case, more than *pueri nobiles* eager to launch their
careers and *quadruplatores* (prosecutors) eager for financial rewards but
devoid of real rhetorical skill are needed, especially against so accomplished
an advocate as Hortensius (24).

To describe the situation more dispassionately, Cicero implies that a
reform accomplished by one of the Servilian laws on extortion in the late
second century—allowing as prosecutors Roman citizens, rather than
provincial victims aided by a Roman *patronus* as the *lex repetundarum* stipulated (lines 9–12)—had failed to provide a sufficient incentive to take on
this massive task.[119] Cicero claims that he will do an excellent job in prosecuting Verres. He will be the most "paratus" [ready], "vigilans" [watchful],
and "compositus" [well-prepared] of prosecutors (1 *Verr.* 32). He argues
(31–32) that he is facing a conspiracy to delay the trial into the next year, 69
B.C., when Verres' friends the Metelli[120] and their ally Hortensius can be
sure to secure an acquittal, because Hortensius will be consul, along with Q.
Metellus, and because M. Metellus will serve as praetor for the extortion
court. Cicero notes also that several excellent jurors, as well as M. Metellus,
will have to be replaced if the trial is delayed (29–31). Of course, the last
point is a way of flattering some of the jurors before whom Cicero is speaking. Although Cicero began proceedings in January 70, it appeared that the
trial might well not be completed within the calendar year, because of the
divinatio, another extortion trial that for procedural reasons took precedence over Cicero's, and four sets of games in the latter part of the year.[121]
Cicero announces that he will foil the defense strategy by eschewing a *perpetua oratio* (continuous speech) in the first hearing; rather, after a short
speech—really just an explanation and justification of his strategy—the
defense will be able to speak, and then the witnesses will be heard. Cicero
says that during that section of the trial, he will describe a charge and pre-

sent the witnesses relevant to this charge (33, 55). In this way, Cicero hopes to enable to court to finish its work before the end of the year.[122]

Cicero says that *tabulae* (records) and *testes* (witnesses) constitute the basis of such a case as that against Verres (2 *Verr.* 1.27). In part, this is a tendentious defense of his not having delivered a *perpetua oratio* in the first *actio,* but Cicero has a point: in the kind of case "ubi aliquid ereptum aut ablatum a quopiam dicitur" [where something is said to have been stolen or carried off by anyone] (1.27), evidence was available and accessible, even in the ancient world. So in extortion, peculation, and electoral bribery cases, documentary evidence could play a decisive role.[123] (By contrast, no such evidence would be likely to exist to help judge a crime of violence.) Cicero claims to have performed the task of gathering evidence in an exemplary way (3.175).

The work of gathering documentary evidence and collecting witnesses throughout the island of Sicily in such a short space of time must have been enormous.[124] The importance of witnesses is confirmed by the fact that jurors in trials under the *lex repetundarum* swore specifically to listen to their words (line 37).[125] Managing the witnesses was an enormous task, described by Quintilian (*Inst.* 5.7.3–32); this task fell on both prosecutors and defense speakers, but more on the former, since their power of compelling witnesses to testify was a key advantage that they possessed over their adversaries. The witnesses had not only to be located and interviewed but then to be persuaded to come to Rome, which required a great sacrifice of time and resources on their part, even apart from gubernatorial obstruction (see the discussion of Metellus's interference in the next paragraph). At Rome, they had to be coached to prepare themselves for cross-examination, so that they did not contradict themselves. This preparation was standard practice at Rome, although when on the defense, Cicero (*Rosc. Am.* 101; *Flac.* 10, 22) and possibly also Hortensius (2 *Verr.* 2.156) complain that the prosecution witnesses are parroting what they have been told to say by the prosecutors.[126] Moreover, Quintilian (*Inst.* 5.7.11) warns that apparently friendly witnesses sometimes prove turncoats.[127] Therefore, the advocate must try to find out as much as possible about witnesses' current attitude toward the other side in the case. Cicero argues that in Verres' trial, the witnesses had to be dissuaded from listening to the insinuations spread by Verres that Cicero had been bribed to commit *praevaricatio* (2 *Verr.* 1.17). Cicero had to deal with confederates of Verres who were trying to secure immunity for themselves by informing on him; he eschewed this convenient source of assistance (1.97–98). Travel in the ancient world, even in the relatively secure countryside of Italy and Sicily, was still dangerous; indeed, though Cicero scoffs (in the fifth book of the second *actio*) at Verres' claims that as governor he faced a troubled military situation, Cicero himself says (2.99) that his return trip to Rome (from Vibo to Velia, about a year before Verres became governor) was dangerous because of *fugitivi* (runaway slaves) and *praedones* (brigands), as well as threats from Verres.

Even under ideal conditions, the task of prosecuting an extortion case was enormous, but conditions for Cicero were far from ideal, if we can believe what he tells his audience. The enormous effort of collecting and presenting documentary evidence and testimony was made more difficult, according to Cicero, by the alliance that was arrayed against him, particularly by L. Metellus, the current governor of Sicily (1 *Verr.* 28). Cicero asked for and received 110 days for the collection of evidence. In this period, he had to travel to Sicily, assisted by his younger cousin L. Tullius,[128] collect the evidence there, bring it back to Rome, and, in addition, collect enough information, primarily at Rome, to deal with the charges (whether they were formal charges or just *reprehensio vitae ante actae* [censure of previous conduct])[129] about Verres' life prior to his governorship, charges to which Cicero devotes the first book of the second *Verrines*. As far as documentary evidence was concerned, the prosecutor had to follow certain procedures to prevent tampering. Cicero reports that he put a codex containing business records of Verres under seal and that Verres used that fact to absolve himself of responsibility for producing it to the court (2 *Verr.* 1.149). Verres had made the same excuse in 78 B.C., when Scaurus was using evidence obtained from him to prosecute Dolabella (*TLRR* no. 135); Cicero mocks this excuse by pointing out that it was permissible to make copies (2 *Verr.* 1.98). Although we need not accept at face value the way Cicero recalls his work as prosecutor, he does bring to light some ways in which the governor could try to hinder the *inquisitio*. The prosecutor had to deal with the current governor: to him, he gave the names ("nomina edere") of witnesses whom he was officially summoning ("denuntiare") (2.12, 65). In this case, the governor, Metellus, detained at least two of these witnesses, Epicrates of Badis and Heraclius of Syracuse, even though they were eager to cooperate with Cicero and tell him what they knew (2.65, 139; 5.129). In addition, Metellus pressured Sicilians to provide evidence favorable to Verres (2.139, 4.141).[130] To demonstrate improper alteration of records by Carpinatius, a friend of Verres, Cicero took him to court before Metellus. It is not clear from Cicero's account what Metellus did, if anything, but Cicero, with the help of the leading men of the area, made an exact copy of the document, including erasures and alterations, to bring back to Rome as evidence (2.187–90; for erasure, see 3.41). Metellus also refused to allow a suit against Afranius, a *decumanus,* or tithe collector, associated with Verres. Cicero says that the reason for his decision was to protect his friend Verres, although Metellus's reasoning was that such a trial would constitute an improper *praeiudicium* (prejudgment) on the extortion trial of Verres (3.152).[131] Cicero was able to obtain from the Syracusans public records that they had kept hidden, so that he could bring them to Rome as evidence (4.140). Cicero successfully maintained his rights as prosecutor under the law when the governor tried to prevent him from making a copy of a Syracusan senatorial resolution rescinding their eulogy of Verres (4.145–49). The difficulties imposed by the current governor will have been added to those created by his predecessor (the defendant), who had prevented information from being put on the public record and removed information that had been recorded (1.88). Cicero had to appeal to the presiding magistrate of the extortion court to compel Verres to hand over captured pirates (5.76).

Another difficulty faced by Cicero and almost any ancient prosecutor was that those cities and individuals who could provide information, in the form of either testimony or documents or both, were not necessarily happy to do so, even if the prosecutor had the right to compel them to do so. As Dilke has shown, although Cicero may have imagined that *Sicilia tota* spoke with one voice (*Div. Caec.* 30), Verres enjoyed some support in Sicily, particularly in the eastern part of the island. Messana was on Verres' side, Syracuse had some sympathy for him (2 *Verr.* 4.136–38), and other city-states had a lukewarm attitude. Dilke points out that (1) Leontini did not help Cicero in an official, corporate way (*publice*); (2) at Syracuse, some people, possibly the poor and even some of the wealthy, may well have supported Verres (2 *Verr.* 2.35–38, 45, 154; 4.136–38); (3) we hear of no agricultural complaints from Agrigentum; and (4) the senate and people of Centuripa decided not to send any official delegation (2 *Verr.* 3.108).[132] Along the same lines, Classen enumerates the many individuals who stood on the defendant's side.[133]

It may be objected that this analysis of the task of the prosecutor should be discounted because it is based on a collection of speeches of which most were never delivered. Why should we place any credence in the words that

Cicero claims he would have uttered, when his strategy in the first *actio* had been so successful that he never needed to deliver the last five speeches? The answer lies in Cicero's motivation for publicizing the second *Verrines*. Surely one motive was to get credit among the reading public for all the effort he had expended and facts he had uncovered. Cicero was proud of his accomplishment, too proud to leave it to molder among his private papers. That the five orations are much larger than he could ever have actually delivered suggests that most Ciceronian speeches tend to lead us to underestimate the amount of evidence that a prosecutor could have on hand, especially in the kinds of trial, such as extortion trials, where records and witnesses played a crucial role. The orator faced two kinds of limit. The first was the patience and retentive powers of the jurors. The second was the legal time limits. These apparently did not apply to the examination of witnesses, but they do seem to include the reading from documentary evidence by the clerk, since that occurred inside the *perpetua oratio* (unless there was a way literally to "stop the clock" when the clerk was reading from a document). So while it is true that in a real trial, the prosecutor would excise and compress his material to render it manageable, presentable, and comprehensible, this piece of abbreviation did not make the task of the prosecutor easier, at least if he was conscientious. He had to collect all the relevant evidence and then separate what was crucial from what could be omitted. (Of course, Hortensius might have been able to undercut and discredit much of the documentation and testimony presented by Cicero, just as Cicero so often did when he was the *patronus* for the defense, but that threat only made the prosecutor's task harder.) More specifically, he had to travel throughout an entire province to collect evidence and talk to potential witnesses over an extended period of time (Cicero's 110 days are about three and a half months), and then he had to winnow and edit what he collected. When we consider that even the second *Verrines* do not reflect all the failed leads and dead ends that Cicero must have pursued, the task seems all the more daunting.

CONCLUSION

The extant ancient sources provide a substantial, though not always satisfactory, basis on which to re-create the contents of missing prosecutions. The defense speeches themselves bear a meaningful resemblance to what the defense speaker, Cicero, said by way of rebuttal. Even though most of the speeches in Cicero's *Verrines* were never delivered, they allow us to envisage what happened in the trial of Verres and thus provide a usable example of a Roman prosecution. Roman law, about which we are exceptionally well informed, provides meaningful ground rules for what happened during the trial and the way the outcome was determined. The rhetorical handbooks confirm what the legal situation suggests and the forensic speeches exemplify.

The prosecutor in these criminal trials was much more in control than the defense speaker. He decided what charges to include, which to stress, and which to downplay. He re-created for the jury the character of the defendant. When he walked into the physical area in which the trial was to be held, he knew what he was going to say. The defense speaker had to rely largely on guesswork to forecast the nature of the case to which he would have to react. He might write out the introduction and conclusion for his speech, but he would have to improvise during the trial the central rebuttal to the charges. The prosecutor had vastly more work to do in preparation, gathering documents and interviewing potential witnesses. The defense speaker, precisely because he could do much less in the way of preparation, must have done much less preparation. Both sides needed some rhetorical skill, but whereas the prosecutor could rely on diligent research and assembly of information, the defense speaker needed to employ shrewd guesswork and quick wits.

As I stated earlier in this chapter, this book covers the eleven prosecutions that took place in the standing criminal courts and were countered by Cicero with an extant speech. The trials are divided by subject into three categories (official extortion, electoral malpractice, and crimes of physical violence) and arranged chronologically within parts dealing with those categories. In each part, the chapters dealing with the trials are prefaced by a summary of the legal background pertaining to their subject.[34] In each of the chapters within the book's three parts, I discuss the date and circumstances of a trial, the participants in it (defendant, prosecutor, and defense speakers), the legal charges and any other allegations made by the prosecution, the ways in which the prosecution might have tried to counter Cicero's rebuttal to its case, and the outcome.

Presenting the case for the prosecution inevitably involves a discussion of the defense, because the process of recognizing the merits of the prosecution case requires consideration of the defense rebuttal and its strong points and weaknesses. This requirement is inherent in understanding an adversarial proceeding and is not just a rationalization formed in view of the fact that for each of these eleven trials, we have one defense speech but no prosecution speech. I have tried to avoid summarizing Cicero's speeches, partly because that has often been accomplished, but mainly because the speeches themselves can be read. Rather, I try to show how the prosecution could have responded to counter the defense rebuttal. It might be objected that this constitutes an academic exercise, since the prosecution was not given the opportunity to deliver a speech of counterrebuttal. But the Roman trial did provide the prosecution with some opportunities to reply. First, in those trials where there was a second *actio*, the prosecutors could respond to the speech made by the defense in the first *actio*. Second, after the two sides had delivered their speeches, there was the examination and cross-examination of witnesses, in which the prosecution could attempt to counteract the rebuttal given by the defense, and the *altercatio*, in which the two sides engaged in questions and answers. Part of the case for the prosecution was the refutation or undermining of the defense arguments, so those arguments need to be considered here.

With this book, I do not claim to have uncovered a novel method to extract the prosecution's case from a speech for the defense. Nor can I claim to have found a new source of information. Some of the trials that form the subject matter of this book will be familiar to most of its readers, and all of them will be familiar to some readers. But cases do not speak for themselves, so speakers are needed, as Cicero says (*Clu.* 139). In the eleven trials that form the subject of this book, the defense has an indisputably eloquent spokesperson, and his words have been scrutinized, elaborated, and interpreted by generations of scholars. The case for the prosecution also deserves a coherent presentation, which I will try to provide, within the limits of the evidence that we possess. By examining these trials in a systematic and synoptic fashion from the point of view of the prosecution, rather than the defense, I hope to put them in an unfamiliar and interesting light.

Part One

Extortion

T he extortion[1] court dates back to 149 B.C., when a permanent investigatory committee of senators was established by a *lex Calpurnia de repetundis* to handle accusations that Roman officials abused their powers to deprive complainants of something material, usually money. Such complaints, since they generally originated with those living under the power of Roman governors, were naturally brought to the Senate. The *lex Calpurnia* established a permanent committee of the Senate to adjudicate these complaints. The law of 149 provided for the return of simple damages to aggrieved parties who won their cases. It was logical for the jurors in these courts to be senators, but later, the staffing of juries for these courts became very controversial, and later laws admitted to the juries members of other orders: knights or knights and another group called *tribuni aerarii,* sometimes along with senators.

Extortion laws had an ambiguous character; they were in part criminal laws, but in a much more obvious way, they defined a civil wrong, in that people could claim that they had been wronged by the defendant and demand pecuniary compensation for their losses.[2] This double nature seems less surprising when we consider that the Roman delict of theft (*furtum*) also provided for pecuniary restitution. In a sense, extortion was a special kind of theft committed by a Roman official, and it is doubtless no

accident that Mommsen, in his *Strafrecht,* puts his chapter on theft immediately after his chapter on extortion.[3]

Several tralatician statutes (that is, statutes that borrowed substantial
sections from previous laws relating to the same subject) were passed in later
decades, and one of them, probably from the Gracchan era and usually
identified with the *lex Acilia,*[4] has survived, albeit with major lacunae; it provided for double damages. In the approximately forty years between the *lex
Acilia* and Sulla's reform of the courts, the composition of the juries became
a major issue, and the basic structure of an extortion trial was changed, in
that the principle of only one mandatory rehearing of the whole case (*comperendinatio*) was specified. Most importantly for our purposes, the prosecutor was changed from the aggrieved party or parties represented by a
Roman *patronus* to a Roman citizen representing the aggrieved.

In the period of Cicero's judicial activity, two extortion laws were in
force: first, a *lex Cornelia,* passed by Sulla, and then, replacing it, a *lex Iulia*
of 59 B.C. The prosecution of Fonteius and probably also the prosecution of
Flaccus[5] took place under the *lex Cornelia,* and the prosecution of Scaurus
and the legal action (not really a prosecution) against Rabirius Postumus
were held under the *lex Iulia.* Aside from what we know about extortion
laws in general from the epigraphically preserved law and what we can presume to have formed part of the *lex Cornelia* in a tralatician way, we know
very little specifically about Sulla's law. It did include a provision (applying
only to senators) against accepting bribes in a judicial case.[6] We know
much more about the *lex Iulia.* Since it was still in force during the classical
age of Roman law, its content was discussed by imperial jurists. Compared
to the epigraphic law, the *lex Iulia* seems to have been aimed more directly
at restraining the rapacity of officials by telling them what they could or
could not do than at just providing monetary restitution and (in the case of
multiple damages) monetary profit to aggrieved individuals. But since we
know so little about the *lex Cornelia,* it is difficult to know whether this
innovation should be credited to the *lex Iulia* or whether some or all of
these features were included in the *lex Cornelia.* Nevertheless, it seems
likely, on the basis of the *Verrines,* that the *lex Iulia* was indeed the innova-
tor, since Cicero, prosecuting Verres under the *lex Cornelia,* states his case
in a way that suggests that the recovery of pecuniary damages is the main
goal of the prosecution, even though gubernatorial lust, cruelty, and
wickedness are cited as part of the reason for convicting the defendant (1
Verr. 56). Another novelty in the *lex Iulia* may have been its distinction

between simple extortion and aggravated extortion, where the exaction of money was accompanied by particularly heinous acts, although the primary evidence for that distinction dates from imperial times.[7]

I would not go as far as Riggsby does when he writes that the character of the *lex Iulia* was radically different from that of the *lex Acilia*.[8] He sees a shift from a "recovery function" to a "regulatory function," that is, toward control over Roman officials by the Roman government. But recovery is still very much at issue; in every provision cited in the *Digest,* the receipt of money is an essential attribute.[9] The *lex Iulia* as reported to us in the *Digest* is much more specific than the epigraphic *lex repetundarum* about which official actions are improper if money is received. Undoubtedly, this greater precision was directed toward plugging legal loopholes devised by ingenious Roman officials in the past. For example, the law forbade receiving money in advance for the performance of various public functions (Macer *Dig.* 48.11.7.2). The Julian law must have had teeth. It is clear from Cicero's letters when he is serving as governor of Cilicia (51/50 B.C.) that he felt that the provisions of the law were sufficiently strict that he and his staff needed to follow them, if only to make sure that he did not give his enemies, of whom he thought he had many, an opportunity to prosecute him for extortion (Cic. *Att.* 5.9.1, 5.16.3; *Fam.* 2.17.2, 4).

The element of restitution, which was always at least part of the extortion law, leads to an important distinction between the extortion law (and probably also the *peculatus* [embezzlement] law) and most of the other criminal laws of the *quaestiones perpetuae.* Where the punishment was the loss of *caput* (civil status), which for upper-class Romans (and the defendants in this book were all upper-class) meant de facto exile, there could be no sliding scale of punishment. If the jury convicted, the loss of *caput* followed as the only possible outcome. This is clearly true of trials relating to violence and murder, though not, as we shall see, of trials relating to electoral malpractice. In the extortion court, however, the *litis aestimatio* determined the actual damages, which could range from nugatory to bankrupting. The distinction is blurred somewhat if one believes that the sums that governors typically extorted, combined with multiple damages, meant that no defendant could actually pay off his penalty and thus that bankruptcy and accompanying *infamia* were the almost inevitable result of conviction.[10] Moreover, the practice of funding an election campaign with money borrowed against expected revenues from a governorship made it likely that someone convicted of extortion would not be able to pay the damages assessed against him, since much of his profits might have already gone to repay the loan.[11]

The compensatory side of the extortion law must have rendered an extortion prosecution different from those falling in the other two main categories that are within the scope of prosecution in this book (electoral malpractice and violence), in two ways. First, in those other trials, the prosecution was aiming at one goal alone, conviction, with its necessarily concomitant penalties. It did not really matter how many charges the jury accepted, as long as they were moved to convict. In the extortion trials, however, the prosecutor wanted to convince the jurors, in the trial stage, of the validity of as many charges as possible, so that those same jurors would vote, in the *litis aestimatio,* for as high a level of damages as possible. The second difference relates to the benefits emanating from a successful prosecution. In most trials, the prosecutors and those who aided the prosecution must have received considerable psychological gratification from the ruin of the person whom they had labored so hard to vanquish, but they got no concrete benefit (other than legal *praemia* awarded by some laws)[12] from the punishment of the convicted defendant (again electoral malpractice is a partial exception: if, as was often the case, the defendant had defeated the prosecutor in the election, the prosecutor stood to gain from his removal). In extortion cases, the complainants represented by the prosecutor received cash (or at least a legal claim for cash) on the basis of each grievance that the prosecutor was able to substantiate to the satisfaction of the jurors. Although we need not share Cicero's assumed horror, in his defense of Rabirius Postumus, at the prospect that someone who was not mentioned in a main extortion trial would find himself a target of a related subsidiary hearing (see chap. 5), there is probably validity to his point that it was normal for the jury to reckon damages only on the basis of what had been presented and proven to their satisfaction in the main trial. By the time of the *lex Cornelia,* the prosecutor himself no longer was a victim who could receive damages, but he was representing the interests of injured parties whom he could call to testify, and they had a financial interest in securing a conviction and obtaining an award of damages.

Extortion cases therefore required an enormous organizational effort, as we have seen of Cicero in his prosecution of Verres. The task of convicting a Roman ex-governor of praetorian or consular status was formidable, especially if the prosecutor was relatively young and inexperienced, as he often was.

CHAPTER TWO

In M. Fonteium

I n 69 B.C., on the heels of his successful prosecution of Verres for extortion, Cicero defended Fonteius, charged with the same crime. A later rhetorical writer reveals that Cicero tried to distinguish between the two cases: ". . . ut pro Fonteio Marcus Tullius exsequitur, quod eius causa non sit eadem quae Verris" [. . . as in his speech for Fonteius Cicero develops the argument that his case is not the same as that of Verres].[1] Since Cicero had just prosecuted Verres and was now defending Fonteius, it is quite natural that he would want his audience to think that the two cases were entirely different. The initial reaction of the modern reader may be to agree with Cicero, since Cicero's *Verrines,* which occupy a thick Oxford Classical Texts volume, dwarf what remains of his *Pro Fonteio,* only twenty-one pages in length in an Oxford Classical Texts edition. Moreover, the outlooks of the two speeches are so different—not surprisingly, given the two opposing roles of the same orator. Yet an analysis of the *Pro Fonteio* reveals hints, noted by commentators, that the charges made by the prosecution against Fonteius and the methods used to support them were similar to those that Cicero had used against Verres.

Therefore, we can use the extensive material on the prosecution of Verres as a model by which to understand better the prosecution of Fonteius.

Moreover, the result of such an analysis will, I hope, help us not only to better understand the role of Fonteius but also to see the trial of Verres in a
more realistic light, as Gruen has urged us to do—as a commonplace and
typical example of an extortion trial.[2] If the trial of Verres was, as Gruen
says, a minor event, rather than the scandal of the century, it provides us
with a typical example of an extortion trial that is useful for understanding
how extortion trials worked in general. By showing Cicero trying to refute
in his *Pro Fonteio* the prosecutor's lines of argument that he himself had
employed the year before with such apparent conviction in the *Verrines,* I
hope to convey the message that in both trials, the case for the prosecution
was presented, not the views of the individual prosecutor. Similar kinds of
trials gave rise to similar accusations, regardless of who the prosecutor was.

This chapter on the prosecution of Fonteius has a different structure
from the following ten analyses of other prosecutions. Here, the material
on the participants, the charges, and the procedural and substantive arguments (specifically, chronology, defendant, *patroni,* prosecutors, the
provinces involved, allegations not constituting extortion [involving the
defendant's actions prior to the governorship and his military performance
while governor], charges of extortion, witnesses, documents, and the outcome) will be presented in explicit comparison with the trial of Verres. The
result will be to magnify somewhat the importance of the trial of Fonteius
and to bring the trial of Verres down to the level of a typical extortion case.

Verres and Fonteius held governorships during roughly the same
period. Verres served as urban praetor in 74, governed Sicily in 73–71, and
was prosecuted immediately on his return. Fonteius served as governor in
Transalpine Gaul for three years in the mid-seventies (Cic. *Font.* 32); he
may have served as praetor in the first of these years and as propraetor in
the next two or as propraetor in all three years.[3]

For those trying to understand the 69 B.C. trial of Fonteius based on his
activities as governor, either possible chronology presents a problem,
although the latter possibility presents a lesser one. We (perhaps rashly)
expect an extortion trial to occur immediately after the termination of the
office in which the extortion is said to have occurred. Was there a gap of at
least two and possibly three years in which the case was not pursued, even
as the evidence grew cold? We can only speculate on the answer. It may be
a mistake, in the absence of sufficient evidence, to date extortion trials to
the year immediately following a governorship. It may have taken a long
time to gather the necessary evidence and locate appropriate witnesses in

an area where the spread of civilization was uneven. Also, the passage in 70 B.C. of the *lex Aurelia,* which turned two-thirds of the seats on the jury over to nonsenators (*equites* and *tribuni aerarii*), may have made a prosecution of Fonteius much more attractive than before, for some reason unknown to us. But this reason is hard to discern if one accepts the conventional view that the *equites* had strong ties to the business world, since Fonteius seems to have enjoyed cordial relations with Roman businessmen in his province. To judge by Cicero's portrait of the defendant, his record as a friend of the Roman businessman would have made a mixed jury, two-thirds of whom were not senators and might have had important commercial connections, more favorable to him, not more hostile to him, than the all-senatorial juries that prevailed before the *lex Aurelia* was passed.

The backgrounds of Verres and Fonteius were somewhat different; Fonteius possessed a much more established family background than did Verres. Fonteius came from a long line of senators who had reached praetorian rank ("continuae praeturae" [an uninterrupted series of praetorships], Cic. *Font.* 41); we can trace this line back as far as M. Fonteius, praetor in 166.[4] Fonteius's sister was a Vestal virgin and had been at least since 91.[5] In terms of social standing, then, Fonteius was superior to Verres and, all other things being equal, was probably in a better position to gain an acquittal, although, as we shall see, Verres was able to mobilize a powerful network on his behalf. Verres' father was a senator (Cic. 2 *Verr.* 2.95) and had worked as a *divisor* (distributor [of bribes]) in political campaigns (1 *Verr.* 23; 2 *Verr.* 3.161); he was, as far as we know, the first member of that family to enter the Roman Senate.[6] The only description that we possess of his actions in the Senate could be interpreted as proof of either his influence or his insignificance. On the one hand, he had enough power to organize a successful filibuster against a motion condemning his son; on the other hand, if we interpret Cicero's words very literally, he had to use surrogates to conduct his fight, perhaps because, as a lowly *pedarius* (backbencher), he could not speak for himself. Cicero describes his son, the defendant, Verres with obvious sarcasm as deserting Carbo, proconsul in Gaul in 83 B.C. because he preferred his own class, the *nobiles,* to *novi homines.* Cicero means that Verres was in reality closer to a *novus homo* than to a *nobilis,* though he was definitely not a *novus homo,* since his father was a senator.[7]

Both defendants were able to acquire first-rate advocates to speak for them. Fonteius had Cicero, who, because of his success against Verres and

his *patronus* Hortensius the previous year, was starting to take over from
Hortensius the leading position among Roman orators (Cic. *Brut.* 320).
Cicero portrays the advocacy of Hortensius for Verres as an example of the
former's attempt to be *dominus* of the law courts (1 *Verr.* 35; 2 *Verr.* 2.77), as
if he is flaunting a claim to be able to secure an acquittal for anyone, no
matter how wicked. Yet a simpler explanation of Hortensius's role is simply that Verres had the connections to obtain the best advocate in Rome.
This network of connections is suggested by the other advocates working
for Verres. As *subscriptores,* he had the services of Sisenna, praetor in 78 and
distinguished historian (Cic. 2 *Verr.* 2.110, 4.43), and Q. Caecilius Metellus
Pius Scipio Nasica, consul in 52 (4.79).[8] Although Cicero remarks that
Hortensius was neither a *necessarius* (friend) nor a *cognatus* (kinsman) of
Verres (5.176: his point is that Hortensius has no excuse for defending such
a scoundrel),[9] he reports that Verres was not only a friend but even a relation to his supporter L. Metellus (2.64, 138).[10] According to Cicero (3.7–8),
Hortensius and other nobles supported Verres in a way that was inconsistent with their general hatred of upstarts, and Cicero chides them for preferring people who are totally dependent on their favor and protection.
Thus, he manages to mock both Verres, for his common ways, and the
nobles, for their superciliousness. As far as we know (and, of course, our
knowledge of the trial of Fonteius is based on a fragmentary speech),
Fonteius did not enjoy even a minor combination of established powers
working on his behalf. In summary, then, if we compare the social sources
of protection for the two defendants, Fonteius was of somewhat better
birth than Verres, but Verres had working for him a coalition of very well-
born people, whereas Fonteius did not.[11]

   In the case of Fonteius, the prosecution was led by someone who was
not particularly distinguished at the time, although he did go on to have a
successful political career, M. Plaetorius Cestianus. He came from a fairly
obscure family. His father had been a senator until his execution in 82 B.C.
at Sulla's orders. By the time of Fonteius's trial, Plaetorius had already held
the quaestorship, and he went on to become aedile (possibly in 67), praetor
(possibly in 64), and thereupon governor in Macedonia.[12] Perhaps his conduct of the prosecution gives us an idea of what the prosecution of Verres
would have been like if Caecilius, rather than Cicero, had been successful in
the *divinatio,* the hearing to select the prosecutor from among those competing to conduct the prosecution. Yet Plaetorius may have had some help
from a distinguished quarter. His *subscriptor* was M. Fabius (*Font.* 36).

Cicero makes it clear that this Fabius shared the luster of the loyalty that the Gauls felt for the family of their conqueror, Q. Fabius Maximus Allobrogicus (consul in 121). It is debated whether Q. Fabius bore his name as a client of that eminent individual or as his actual descendant.[13]

The *Verrines* and the *Pro Fonteio* may seem at first to present totally different pictures of the mood inside the province involved in each case. Broadly speaking, Cicero paints a picture of a Sicily united in hatred of Verres, not only hatred from the Sicilians themselves, but also hatred from the Roman citizens of all ranks doing business there. He describes Transalpine Gaul as split between natives who are implacably hostile to Fonteius and Roman citizens who value his accomplishments. A closer analysis, however, of the mood in the two provinces that had allegedly suffered depredations reveals, on the one hand, greater complexity in both of them than the broad picture suggests and, on the other hand, greater similarity between the two provinces than appears at first glance in terms of the support and opposition to the respective defendants.

With remarkable frankness, Cicero declares that opposed to Fonteius is a "Gallorum consensio" [consensus of the Gauls] (*Font.* 16). This bluntness is not to be attributed to an uncontrolled impulse of honesty on the part of the advocate. Rather, it forms a logical part of a consistent strategy. The jurors have heard at least some of the hostile witnesses, since the extant speech was delivered at the second *actio* (37, 40).[14] Rather than trying to discredit their testimony by picking it apart and discrediting it, Cicero attempts to discredit these witnesses en bloc as untrustworthy, prejudiced against the defendant, and hostile to Rome. Cicero dignifies by the mention of his name only one Gallic witness, Indutiomarus, and that witness is mocked as ignorant of what it means to bear witness in a Roman court (29), *minax,* and *adrogans,* "threatening" or "insolent" (36).[15] Cicero implies that he forbore for the most part to cross-examine these witnesses, so as not to give an additional platform to the expression of their ire (22).[16]

One city in Transalpine Gaul, not inhabited by Gauls, supported Fonteius. This city was Massilia, the modern Marseilles, a Phocaean colony founded around 600 B.C., which represented the focus of Roman involvement in southern France. An old ally of Rome (*Font.* 13), having lent Rome military assistance in the Second Punic War, it had appealed to Rome for help against the Ligurians in 154 and again in 125. From then to 120, Rome campaigned vigorously, accomplishing the conquest of the entire area between the Alps and the Pyrenees. This expansion led to the building of the Via Domitia, the strategic link between Italy and the Spanish provinces, and to the foundation of Narbo in 118 or somewhat later.[17] Badian stresses the role of Massilia in Rome's Gallic policy. He maintains that until Rome organized the province of Gallia Transalpina, later called Gallia Narbonensis, with Massilia as an independent allied state within it, the thrust of Rome's measures there was to help Massilia. The coastal part of the Via Domitia was put under the protection of that city (Strabo 4.1.5 [C 180]).[18] The famous prohibition against the planting of grapes and olives by "transalpinae gentes" [peoples on the other side of the Alps] (Cic. *Rep.* 3.16) can be explained as a concession, probably dating back to 154 B.C., to the Massiliotes, who, as citizens of a merchant city, would benefit from the increased importation of Italian products and, if the prohibition did not apply to them, from an agricultural monopoly in those products.[19] Moreover, Marius gave to Massilia the canal that his troops dug from the Rhone to the Mediterranean, bypassing the estuary of the river, which tended to silt up (Strabo 4.1.8 [C 183]). In view of this long-term historical link between Rome and Massilia, it is not surprising that Massilia supported the Roman governor. Cicero implies that the Massiliotes are reliable witnesses like the colonists from Narbo and all other Roman citizens (*Font.* 34). Along with Roman businessmen in Gaul and the colony of Narbo, the entire community of Massilia ("Massiliensium cuncta civitas," 45) comes to the defense of Fonteius, since, according to Cicero, it is grateful to the defendant for preserving the city and, more generally, regards itself as Rome's bulwark against the Gauls.

The trial of Verres provides a parallel. Verres had one base of support in Sicily, the city of Messana, which was, like Massilia, a Greek colony in origin. Only this city sent a legation to the trial to praise the defendant (2 *Verr.* 2.13).[20] Cicero has an explanation for the support afforded by Messana to Verres: he both allowed them to share in the profits from his depredations ("socia furtorum ac flagitiorum tuorum" [partner in your thefts and outrages], 2.114) and also freed them from the many obligations that other cities had toward Rome (4.23), such as ships, sailors, and soldiers (5.43).

The charges against Fonteius are on the whole quite similar to the charges against Verres.[21] Both trials were conducted under the *lex Cornelia de repetundis,* although the intervening passage of the *lex Aurelia,* which established juries composed of equal parts of senators, *equites,* and *tribuni aerarii* instead of wholly senatorial juries, significantly changed the juries and therefore the audience whom the prosecutors and the *patroni* had to address.[22] Each defendant was on trial primarily—and perhaps entirely—for what he had done as governor of a province.[23] Sicily was a much older and more settled province than Transalpine Gaul[24] and was a more much important economic force within the Roman Empire, whereas Gaul possessed a much more obvious strategic importance as the link to Spain, especially because Spain was at that time the site of Sertorius's revolt. Nevertheless, Cicero's fifth *Verrine* shows that Sicily, too, faced military dangers, from pirates and from slave revolts. For both defendants, charges relating to money acquired in an improper manner by the defendant in his capacity as magistrate constituted the core of the case. In addition, the *vita ante acta* and the military record of each governor were under examination.

In an extortion case, one promagistracy typically provided the basis of the prosecution, as did Verres' governorship in Sicily and Fonteius's in Gaul (see chap. 1, "Advantages for the Prosecution"). Substantial practical difficulties in gathering stale evidence in the form of records and testimony presented themselves to a prosecutor who would have attempted to search further back in the case, although records at Rome from five or ten years previous would not be so difficult for him to obtain. But it was standard practice to include an account of the defendant's conduct in his previous offices, which formed part of the *vita ante acta*. Thus, Cicero contrasts the plain facts of the case ("res manifestae") with inference ("coniectura"), suspicion ("suspicio"), the character testimony of individuals ("virorum bonorum testimonia"), resolutions of polities within the Roman Empire ("civitatum auctoritates ac litteras"), and the reputation of the defendant's past life ("ante actae vitae existimatio") (2 *Verr.* 3.146). Unclear is the extent to which discussion of past conduct is meant merely to be indicative of the character of the defendant and therefore to render it more or less plausible that he did commit the acts with which he is charged, or whether this discussion relates to charges that constitute part of the formal matter of the case.[25] In the *Verrines*, Cicero devotes an entire oration (the first speech of the second *actio*) to Verres' life prior to becoming governor of Sicily in 73. Some passages seem to imply that incidents from this period constitute charges in the case, and others imply the contrary.

Just as Cicero raises, in the first book of the second *Verrines*, matters relating to Verres' official activities before his governorship in Sicily, Plaetorius raised objections to at least one aspect of Fonteius's official life before his governorship, as urban quaestor in 83.[26] Whether this should be viewed as mere slander concerning the defendant's *vita ante acta* or as a real charge, it certainly was intended to sway the jury to vote for condemnation. More-over, it involved financial dealings, and a real monetary amount was named,[27] suggesting real damages. Unfortunately, since the discussion of this charge comes in a fragmentary passage (*Font.* 1–5), we lack a context in which to understand it.

Plaetorius complained of the way that Fonteius, as quaestor in 83, han-dled debt reduction as provided for by the *lex Valeria* of 86 (*Font.* 1–3). As far as we can tell, a 75 percent portion of some debts was annulled by law, and the quaestor had to keep records of these transactions, possibly because they involved public debts.[28] The passage in Cicero that discusses Plaeto-rius's complaint has been explicated in a way that reveals what the nature of Plaetorius's accusation might have been: Fonteius possibly took 50 percent of the debt for himself from state funds and returned 25 percent to the cred-itor. This would explain why no witnesses complained and why the records seemed to be in order. In this scenario, the creditor would have received as much as he or she could under the *lex Valeria,* and the records might have shown legitimately—or almost legitimately—payment in full.[29] That this offense seems to be more *peculatus* (embezzlement) than *repetundae* (extortion), since these are state funds, counts somewhat against this inter-pretation, if one tries to see it as germane to the business of the extortion court. If Fonteius was in some way raking off an extra commission from the creditor who was being repaid (in exchange for the 75 percent forgiveness mandated by the *lex Valeria*), the charge would fall squarely in the purview of the extortion court.

Here, the prosecutor was not on particularly strong ground, for there was a case to be made for the way that Fonteius had dealt with this debt problem. Cicero retorts that he had only followed the procedures estab-lished by the first quaestor who had to attend to this debt reduction, Hir-tuleius (quaestor in 86), for whom Plaetorius had expressed approval. It is possible that the measure seemed excessively *popularis* (aimed at mass appeal) by the year 69 and that the resulting distaste for it worked against Fonteius, whereas at the time the measure was taken, before Sulla's return exacerbated political friction, a consensus existed in its favor. Scholars have made the case that the *lex Valeria* made economic sense, by balancing debts and land prices.[30]

The other seemingly extraneous matter that, it appears, must be dis-cussed in an extortion prosecution is the military record of the governor. In his speech defending Fonteius, Cicero connects this theme to the main matter of the speech by lamenting the fact that such supposed enemies of Rome as Indutiomarus are attacking and threatening with their testimony such a defender of Rome as Fonteius. In a similar fashion, Cicero had tried to use against Verres his allegedly poor military record. In his introduction to the fifth oration in the second hearing, in which Verres' exploits as commander against pirates and rebellious slaves are discussed, Cicero imagines that his opponent Hortensius will expatiate on this theme, as if Hortensius was going to follow Cicero with a speech for the defense in the second hearing. Cicero responds prospectively, even though he could insist on legal strictness and avoid the issue altogether as irrelevant.

> Non agam summo iure tecum, non dicam id quod debeam forsitan obtinere, cum iudicium certa lege sit, non quid in re militari fortiter feceris, sed quem ad modum manus ab alienis pecuniis abstinueris abs te doceri oportere; non, inquam, sic agam, sed ita quaeram, quem ad modum te velle intellego, quae tua opera et quanta fuerit in bello. (2 *Verr.* 5.4)

> [I will not deal, totally justifiably, with you in the following way. I shall not make the point that I perhaps ought to carry, since this trial is being held under a specific law—that we should be told by you not what you bravely accomplished in military affairs, but how you kept your hands from other people's money. I will not, I say, so deal with you, but I will ask in the way I understand that you wish, what your activity in war was, and how great it was.]

In defending Fonteius, Cicero alludes to Fonteius's military record, both as governor in Gaul and in previous positions: the travel through Gaul to Spain under Fonteius's tenure and the wintering of Pompey's army in Gaul (*Font.* 16, 20), the war against the Vocontii (20), Fonteius's defense of Macedonia against Thrace while legate there in 77 and possibly 76 (44),[31] and his defense of Hispania Ulterior while legate there in 81 (6, 45).[32]

The first charge against Fonteius from his governorship is that he made money off road construction, by accepting bribes either (a) to grant an exemption from the task or (b) to certify work already done as acceptable:

> Obiectum est etiam quaestum M. Fonteium ex viarum munitione
> fecisse, ut aut ne cogeret munire, aut id quod munitum esset ne
> improbaret. (*Font.* 17)

> [It has been further charged that Marcus Fonteius made a profit
> from the construction of roads, either for not compelling their con-
> struction or for not rejecting that which had been constructed.]

Cicero attempts to refute this charge with two counterarguments, the first
of which has two parts: (1a) no exemptions were granted, (1b) some people
were told that their work was unsatisfactory, and (2) Fonteius had delegated the work to two *legati* (17–19). The *Verrines* give us a good idea as to
how the prosecutors would have presented the two charges and would have
responded to the defense counsel's attempt to refute them.

We have no way to judge whether Cicero's claim that no exemptions
were actually granted is true. His dismissal of the accusation with four
words—"cum immunis nemo fuerit" [because no one was exempt] (*Font.*
17)—is suspiciously brief, though it is only fair to point out that it is
difficult to prove a negative. His rebuttal of the charge that Fonteius took
bribes to grant approvals of work done is more transparently unconvincing. If Fonteius was extorting money from some people to grant approval
or, more precisely, not to reject ("ne improbaret," 17), there could still be
some other people, perhaps those unwilling to pay, whose work would be
declared unsatisfactory. In fact, the fate of such people would presumably
make it easier to extort money from future prospects, who would have
before their eyes the fate of the uncooperative. In the second *Verrines*
(3.172–80), Cicero discusses a similar problem. As governor, Verres bought
grain for Rome, in addition to what he collected as tithe. Cicero says that
Verres rejected what the Sicilians tried to sell him: "improbas frumentum
Siculorum" [You reject the Sicilians' grain] (3.172). Verres' response is
imagined by Cicero to be that he did approve of the grain from some Sicilian cities, Centuripa and Agrigentum being mentioned by name. One
might expect that Cicero would maintain that they must have bribed Verres to accept their grain, but instead, he merely says that even these cities
never actually received payment for what they had shipped. The reason
why he does not make this claim could be that he does not want to discredit
two cities that testified against Verres[33] and that provided private witnesses
who testified on their own behalf. The vagaries of obtaining certification

that a public works project has been completed in a satisfactory manner are illustrated by the toils created by Verres for the young Iunius and his guardian, L. Habonius, by insisting that the columns on the temple of Castor be exactly plumb ("ad perpendiculum," 2 *Verr.* 1.133).

Cicero's attempt to defend Fonteius by putting the responsibility for road repair on the shoulders of his two legates, C. Annius Bellienus and C. Fonteius,[34] is questionable, especially in light of Cicero's attacks on Verres on similar grounds. In his defense of Fonteius, he makes two points: (1) M. Fonteius had written letters in which he assigned the task to his legates, letters that were entered as evidence in the trial; and (2) these legates are above reproach ("quos nemo possit reprehendere" [whom no one can rebuke], *Font.* 19). In the *Verrines,* Cicero alludes to this sort of argument—that the governor can shift responsibility from himself to his legates—but he does not claim that Verres or his defenders made it. Cicero implies that Verres did not use this defense (". . . nihil ad se istam rationem pertinere, per quaestores rem frumentariam esse administratam" [. . . that the affair does not have anything to do with himself, that the business with the grain had been conducted through quaestors], 2 *Verr.* 3.225) because Verres had written letters that showed his involvement in these matters.

The question whether a superior can be held responsible for the acts of his subordinates is particularly crucial in extortion cases. As prosecutor, Cicero makes the valid point that if juries accept the argument that the defendant himself must have received the extorted funds directly, the extortion law will be a dead letter.

> Tu mihi ita defendas, "Non est ista Verri numerata pecunia"? . . . Quicquid ab horum quopiam captum est, id non modo tibi datum, sed tua manu numeratum iudicari necesse est. Nam si hanc defensionem probabitis, "Non accepit ipse," licet omnia de pecuniis repetundis iudicia tollatis. Nemo umquam reus tam nocens adducetur qui ista defensione non possit uti . . . . Neque nunc tam isti mihi Verrem defendere videntur quam in Verre defensionis temptare rationem. (2 *Verr.* 2.26–27)

> [Would you offer this sort of defense to me, "That money was not disbursed to Verres"? . . . Whatever was taken by anyone of them, it is necessary that it be judged not only to be given to you, but disbursed by your own hand. For if you give your approval to this

defense, "He himself did not receive it," you might as well do away with all the extortion courts. No defendant will ever be brought to court so guilty that he cannot use that defense. . . . Those people do not now seem to me to defend Verres as to try out a line of defense on Verres.]

Cicero implies here that all unscrupulous governors can take care to cover their tracks enough so that they never actually take money illegally directly into their own hands.

Even if the argument that superiors cannot be held responsible for the actions of their subordinates threatens to undermine the extortion statute, it is one that the defense can be expected to present. Clearly, it was attractive enough for Cicero to use just a year later when defending Fonteius. It is an argument that Cicero, for all his indignation, imagines the defense presenting to the court in the trial of Verres; he does not say that they actually did make this argument,[35] although when Cicero has sufficiently ridiculed it, he does speak of it as if the defense had put it forward (2 *Verr.* 2.27). One suspects that it was the sort of argument he expected to encounter as prosecutor and, therefore, that he saw fit to include his refutation of it when he published the speeches of the second *actio*.

It may have been in connection with this charge that Cicero made the comment, "Si nulla pecunia numerata est, cuius pecuniae quinquagesima est?" [If no money was disbursed, of what money is that 2 percent?] (*Font.* 7). Clearly, the prosecutor had charged that Fonteius extorted 2 percent of some payment or 2 percent in addition to some payment, and Cicero's defense was to deny that any such payment was made to Fonteius in the first place. This could apply to fees in connection with road building, but it could refer as well to any of the other financial accusations, since the comment occurs in a fragment, cited by Iulius Victor (Halm, *Rhet. Lat. Min.* 397.18).

The most important and most damaging accusation made by the prosecution ("quod illi invidiosissimum et maximum esse voluerunt" [[a charge] that they want to be the most odious and the greatest], *Font.* 19) relates to *portoria* (duties) charged on wine, the *crimen vinarium*.[36] Cicero's refutation of it is as illogical as it may have been rhetorically effective, so the charge may well have been valid: the duties do not hurt the Romans, only the Gauls. Cicero resorts to the argument that the Gauls ought to dilute their wine with water rather than drink it neat: "Gallos post haec dilutius esse poturos, quod illi venenum esse arbitrabuntur" [after this the Gauls will drink it mixed with more water because they will think that it is poison] (9).[37] This mockery relies on a commonplace about the Gauls,[38] comparable to what Herodotus says about the Scythians.[39] Even if residents of a province consume more of a product than they ought, that fact does not justify a governor in extorting money on the trade in that commodity.

As well as summarizing some of the discussion of this charge with the rubric "DE CRIMINE VINARIO" [CONCERNING THE CHARGE RELATING TO WINE],[40] Cicero supplies (just before in our text) a few tantalizing details about it (*Font.* 19). He provides a list of various sums (from two and one-half denarii to six denarii) connected to geographical points that are on the road from Narbo to Toulouse or thereabouts.[41] It has been argued that these numbers represent cumulative amounts to be added on at various points, rather than total amounts. Clemente, however, shows persuasively that the fees were calculated on the basis of distance and possibly trade routes.[42] Hermon suggests that Fonteius instituted a policy that favored Toulouse by charging more for wine transported without going through that city, either to other *oppida* (towns) or to enemy territory.[43] Cicero explains that Plaetorius made the claim that Fonteius first conceived of his new wine duties in Rome before he left for the province, rather than in the province. Interestingly enough, Cicero never refutes this point. Why is it a charge at all? Clemente is right to conclude that Plaetorius is implying that Fonteius had formed a pact with some group at Rome to the disadvantage of the Gauls.[44] One can speculate that Fonteius claimed that the duties on wine were an emergency measure that he was forced to impose by financial exigency while he was in Gaul, while Plaetorius is making the contrary point that Fonteius had in fact decided on this scheme before departing for his province.

Following the rubric "DE CRIMINE VINARIO" are two more rubrics, "DE BELLO VOCONTIORUM" [CONCERNING THE WAR WITH THE VOCONTII] and "DE DISPOSITIONE HIBERNORUM" [CONCERNING THE LAYOUT OF WINTER ENCAMPMENTS] (*Font.* 20). Clemente suggests that these two items do not constitute charges against Fonteius and are therefore not essential enough to be included in the published version.[45] Weighing against this point of view is the fact that the first rubric, "DE CRIMINE VINARIO," clearly is a charge, as well as the fact that Cicero's first words on resuming his text are "At hoc Galli negant" [But the Gauls deny this]. These words are put in quotation marks in the Oxford

Classical Texts edition to indicate that Cicero is going to deal with a statement made by the prosecution. Whatever was said in the passages summarized by these two rubrics, the Gauls took issue with it; therefore, it could have represented an attempt to refute their charges. However, it is also possible that Cicero expatiated on his client's valorous campaigns against the Vocontii and his good service in providing winter quarters for troops of other commanders to promote sympathy for his client, rather than in response to specific charges. In any case, all the two rubrics tell us is that Cicero described in some detail the military campaign of Fonteius against the Vocontii and the winter camps that he provided Pompeius (*Font.* 16) and possibly also Q. Caecilius Metellus Pius.[46]

After this description of the parallels between the trials of Verres and Fonteius, it is necessary to turn to the major difference between the two cases. We have seen that in his prosecution of Verres, Cicero gathered an enormous amount of evidence, both in the form of testimony and in the form of records, and that even though this collection must have required a lot of work on his part, it was there for him to find. Plaetorius had a much more restricted pool of evidence from which to draw.

Plaetorius was in a less favorable position as prosecutor of Fonteius than Cicero had been in as prosecutor of Verres the year before. In terms of testimony, Plaetorius clearly had an ample supply of hostile Gallic witnesses but a paucity of Roman witnesses. In terms of records, he suffered from a lack of Gallic records that incriminated Fonteius (the Gauls probably did not maintain written records as much as the Sicilians) and from a shortage of Roman records to support his case.[47]

Plaetorius's use of a large number of hostile Gallic witnesses can be inferred from Cicero's attack on the reliability of the Gauls. Cicero says that they are hostile to Rome and to Fonteius and inherently untrustworthy. He claims that they are traditional enemies of Rome, who have waged war against Rome not only in ancient times but in recent memory (*Font.* 12). He reports that some of them have fought against Fonteius himself and that some have seen their lands taken away by order of the Roman Senate (ibid.). In his view, they are prejudiced witnesses. One wonders if Hortensius had the nerve to claim that the Sicilians' complaints about the exactions they suffered at the hands of Verres should be disregarded precisely because those exactions biased them against their oppressor. Obviously, witnesses who are victims of the defendant will always be hostile to him or her, but their testimony should not be dismissed out of hand for that reason. Cicero's response to this objection might have been that the Gauls were protesting actions decided by the Senate, which Fonteius was merely implementing, rather than actions that Fonteius chose on his own authority and for which he was responsible. Three other reasons that Cicero gives for the Gauls' hostility are the requisitions of cavalry, money, and grain for the war against Sertorius in Spain (13); it is less clear that this was done at the behest of the Senate. Cicero claims that such witnesses are obviously unreliable (14) and, moreover, since they are sacrilegious, that they cannot be trusted to honor an oath (30–31). Cicero mentions only one Gallic witness by name, Indutiomarus, and asks whether he feels the respect and awe that any Roman would feel for the role of witness. He mocks this leader of the Allobroges for prefacing his statements with *scio* rather than *arbitror* (29), as if that choice of verb ("I know" rather than "I think") demonstrates impudence (see also 36, 45). Cicero's decision to cross-examine these witnesses only briefly or not at all can probably be attributed to his inability to refute their testimony, although he claims to have adopted this course to avoid giving them greater exposure than they have already enjoyed (22).[48] It is reasonable to conclude that Plaetorius presented an impressive body of testimony from native Gauls against their former governor.

Plaetorius's use of Gallic witnesses contrasts with the "all-Roman" cast that Cicero brings before the jury as advocate for Fonteius: *publicani,* farmers, herders, and merchants from Gaul, as well as colonists from Narbo (*Font.* 46). Cicero declares that the lowest Roman should be preferred to the most eminent Gaul (27). But this principle does not prevent Cicero from calling to the witness stand or making use of the resolutions of many non-Romans: people from Hispania Citerior and Macedonia, where Fontieus had served as legate, and, closer to the subject matter of the case, the people of Massilia (44–45).[49] Clearly, Cicero had no fundamental objection to non-Roman witnesses, and his apparent failure to call a single Gaul as a witness suggests the unanimous detestation in which Fonteius must have been held by the Gauls, similar to the hatred felt by Sicilians toward Verres.

It seems reasonable to conclude that in terms of testimony, Plaetorius had the upper hand over Fonteius's advocate, Cicero, because the latter urges the jurors to feel free to trust their own judgment over the evidence of witnesses (especially these witnesses) (*Font.* 21, 23–27, 36–39). Here, Cicero uses historical exempla from past trials with the following logic: these are instances where Roman jurors have rejected the testimony of eminent Roman leaders; therefore, if their testimony can be rejected, surely the testimony of Gauls can likewise be rejected.

On the matter of records (*tabulae*), Cicero has less to say, at least in the extant text of his speech. He asserts that Fonteius has nothing to fear from the records, both private and public, of his service as *triumvir monetalis* (member of the board of three in charge of the mint) and quaestor (*Font.* 5). But records of Roman citizens preserved at Rome were obviously much more accessible than were records from Gaul, especially since most Gauls presumably failed to keep financial records in the Roman style. To overcome this objection, Cicero resorts to an interesting argument from silence (11). It is alleged that under Fonteius, Gaul was overcome with debt. From whom would the Gauls have borrowed money? Cicero asserts that they would have borrowed from Roman *negotiatores* (traders) in Gaul. He then makes the claim, often cited by economic historians, that no financial transaction occurs in Gaul without involvement by Roman businessmen. Cicero argues that since the businessmen's records have produced no trace of money given to Fonteius (presumably representing a loan from a businessman to a Gaul), clearly no such transaction has ever occurred. But since Fonteius had the Roman business community on his side, it is quite likely that they refused to produce records that would incriminate their friend, as did Verres' supporters in Sicily.

In the *Verrines,* Cicero is wont to emphasize the importance of evidence and witnesses—not surprisingly, since he has a more than adequate supply of both. In the first *actio* (1 *Verr.* 33), he claims that he is eschewing the normal *perpetua oratio* (continuous speech) in favor of evidence: financial records, witnesses, and the written statements and resolutions of both private individuals and public bodies. In the second *actio* (2 *Verr.* 1.128), he recalls both documents and testimony that the jurors heard in the first hearing and alludes to those that they will hear after his speech and the speech for the defense in the second hearing. Sometimes Cicero uses an argument from silence, as when he refutes Hortensius's contention that Verres simply bought the art objects that he acquired in Sicily; Cicero says that no entry appears in the books of the supposed seller (4.28). In some situations, he makes his attack without the benefit of evidence that Verres failed to pay *portoria,* on the grounds that it has been destroyed by the supporters of Verres (2.176–77). Similarly, in the case of dealings in grain, Cicero claims that the *decumani* (tax farmers) have voted to take joint action to destroy records incriminating to Verres and will not testify against him (2.175–76). Cicero argues that in other cases, records have been altered, so that they name a "Verrucius" instead of Verres (2.186–89). Although *publicani* were exempted from the prosecutor's power of subpoena, Cicero arranged a kind of volunteer "bucket brigade" to copy their documents, and he took these copies back to Rome. According to Cicero, there were also cases in which payments that ended up in the hands of Verres were registered as paid to his friend, freedmen, or subordinate (3.170–71; see also 2.27).

Drumann believes that Fonteius deserved to be punished as much as Verres.[50] Heinze takes exception to this judgment, placing some faith in Cicero's positive characterization of his client (*Font.* 37, 40) and pointing out that we no longer have the more substantive parts of Cicero's two speeches, in which he might have rebutted the prosecution charges.[51] Obviously, because the extant evidence is so scanty and partial, it is very difficult for us to render a verdict now. The purpose of highlighting the similarities between the prosecutions of Verres and Fonteius, as far as we can extrapolate the latter from Cicero's defense, has been not to compare the two defendants to the advantage of one or the other but to compare their trials, particularly the attacks made on them by their prosecutors. Whether Verres was more guilty of extortion than Fonteius or not, their prosecutors used similar lines of attack, and their defenders used similar lines of defense. To the extent that readers of the *Verrines* are inclined to conclude that Verres was guilty of extortion, they should be open to the possibility that they would feel much the same way about Fonteius if they were able to read the speeches of Plaetorius and Fabius.

Seen in comparison with the trial of Verres, the trial of Fonteius illustrates a fundamental dilemma for the prosecutor in an extortion case. In defending Fonteius, Cicero blames the prosecutor for, in crude terms, preferring foreigners to Romans. One may well retort that this is intrinsic to an extortion case, since the aggrieved parties are almost certainly foreigners[52] and since the defendant is quite certainly a Roman. But the prosecutor in Fonteius's case perhaps helped impale himself on this dilemma by arguing that an acquittal of Fonteius might incite rebellion in Gaul (*Font.* 33). This rationale for condemnation allowed Cicero to respond that this would be a good reason to acquit the defendant, even if he were guilty, so that the Gauls would not start to think that they could frighten the Romans into submission (34).

In contrast, when prosecuting Verres, Cicero skillfully avoids this dilemma. He takes pains to try to escape the consequences of the dilemma in three ways. First, he emphasizes the good qualities of the Sicilians and their loyalty to Rome: far from being aggressive, they are timid and reluctant to come forward (1 *Verr.* 28), happy just to be left alone to live in peace (2 *Verr.* 3.67); Sicily is an "inlustris provincia" (2 *Verr.* 1.10, 21; 4.90), full of goodwill toward Rome (for whom success in the province of Sicily paved the way for future overseas conquests) and therefore deserving of Rome's charity. As he begins to describe the injustices wreaked on Sicily by Verres, he launches into an encomium of the island as a loyal ally of Rome who provided an encouraging opening to Rome's pursuit of overseas conquests (2 *Verr.* 2.2). He argues that the people of Segesta and Centuripa are not only loyal to the Romans but related to them (5.83). (Plaetorius obviously has a much more difficult task when he tries to engender sympathy for the oppressed peoples of the still turbulent Transalpine Gaul.) Second, Cicero highlights injustices done by Verres against Roman citizens as well as against Sicilians: most outrageous is Verres' crucifixion of Gavius of Consa (5.160–65). Third, Cicero steers his audience, the jurors, away from the aforementioned dilemma by underscoring what Verres is doing not only to individual Roman citizens but to the Roman people as a whole: the summary execution of a Roman citizen endangers the confidence that all Romans feel against attack anywhere in the world, even in the remotest parts (5.166). Cicero closes the *Verrines* (5.183) with a characterization of what he (Cicero) has accomplished not only in fulfilling his obligation to the Sicilians but also in doing his duty for the Roman people. Moreover, he goes on to warn that if the court has been corrupted (in other words, if Verres is acquitted), he will fight against the perpetrators on behalf of the Roman people.

> . . . existiment in iis hominibus quorum ego inimicitias populi Romani salutis causa suscepero multo graviorem atque acriorem futurum.
>
> [. . . let them think that I will be a far sterner and keener opponent of those men whose hostility I will have undertaken for the sake of the safety of the Roman people.]

From the point of view of Fonteius as defendant, the ultimate and most crucial point of comparison between himself and Verres must have been the outcome of the trial. Would he suffer the same fate? In point of fact, we do not know the answer to this question. His lack of progress past the praetorship in the *cursus honorum* cannot prove anything, because many praetorians never obtained the consulate for one reason or another. Cicero (*Att.* 1.6.1) reports that an M. Fonteius bought a house in Naples in 68. If the purchaser is our defendant, that might possibly indicate an acquittal, in that he still had sufficient funds to buy the house, but it might be rash to assume that someone convicted of extortion could not protect some of his money in some way.[53] It would be wiser to conclude that we do not know the outcome of this trial.[54]

CHAPTER THREE

In L. Valerium Flaccum

Valerius Flaccus was prosecuted in 59 B.C. for his activities as governor in Asia in 62. In the year before his governorship, as praetor in 63, he had aided Cicero in the suppression of the Catilinarian conspiracy, and Cicero now defended him. He was one of Cicero's most distinguished clients; not only was he a patrician, but with the exception of his grandfather, C. Valerius Flaccus, he came from a direct, six-generation line of consulars going back to his namesake, the consul of 261.[1] Yet Cicero's brief was a difficult one, and while he was able to secure an acquittal for Flaccus (according to Macrobius [*Sat.* 2.1.13], despite the defendant's obvious guilt and by means of a joke no longer extant in the text of the speech in Macrobius's day),[2] his client's career came to a virtual close. Except for a legateship under L. Calpurnius Piso Caesoninus in Macedonia in 56–55, Flaccus never held public office again, at least as far as we know, and most significantly, he never held the consulate, although he should have been a candidate for that office, as Cicero implies at the very beginning of his speech: "sperabam, iudices, honoris potius L. Flacci me adiutorem futurum quam miseriarum deprecatorem" [I hoped, jurors, that I would be supporting Lucius Flaccus rather than making entreaties to ward off his afflictions] (*Flac.* 1).[3]

The strategy followed by the prosecution in this case is one that modern readers often scorn Roman advocates for not following: concentrating only on what is strictly germane to the charges of the case, vigorously collecting all available evidence, and disregarding the character and past life of the accused.[4] Since Flaccus was acquitted, this was apparently not a successful strategy, and the reason is likely to lie, at least in part, in Cicero's overall response to that strategy: Cicero argues that even if Flaccus has committed some misdeeds as governor, it is wrong of the prosecutors to pass over the defendant's public service to Rome before his praetorship (*Flac.* 6) and the probity of his private life (7). Cicero maintains that any offenses Flaccus committed in the brief period when he was praetor should not outweigh his accomplishments over his entire lifetime: "annui temporis criminationem omnis aetas L. Flacci et perpetua vita defendet" [The whole lifetime of Lucius Flaccus and his entire life will fend off an indictment relating to a one-year period] (100).[5] Cicero expresses the view that the prosecution's strategy in the trial of Flaccus stood as a test to the Roman judicial system. Would it allow a Roman of distinguished family and background to be convicted on the basis of overwhelming evidence submitted primarily by foreigners?

The trial of Flaccus took place in 59 B.C. and was probably ongoing in September of that year.[6] It was probably held under the *lex Cornelia de repetundis,* rather than the *lex Iulia de repetundis,* which was passed during that year, but this is the subject of controversy. In his speech, Cicero refers to a new law ("lege hac recenti ac nova" [this freshly passed and new law] *Flac.* 13), but not necessarily as the law under which the trial of Flaccus was being held.[7] The main effect that the identity of the statute could have on our understanding of the prosecution involves the number of witnesses. We know that the *lex Iulia* allowed the prosecution to summon up to 120 witnesses (as compared to forty-eight under the epigraphic extortion law [line 34]), and it is possible that the *lex Iulia* first provided for this increase.[8] If the trial was held under the earlier law, the prosecutors in the trial of Flaccus did not have the advantage of being able to call as many witnesses as they could have if the trial took place under the new law.[9] It is possible, although not necessarily the case, that the two extortion laws may have provided for different time limits for the speakers.[10] The controversy about the law under which the trial was held depends in part on whether a prosecution authorized under one law, the *lex Cornelia de repetundis,* could have led to a trial under a new law on the same subject, the *lex Iulia de repetundis.*[11]

The prosecutor and his *subscriptores* could not match the defense team (described later in this chapter) in either prestige or rhetorical experience.

With one possible exception, none of them appear elsewhere in the Roman courts, as far as we know. In number, they may have been as many as five or as few as three.

Since the chief prosecutor, D. Laelius, served as tribune of the plebs in 54 B.C., he was probably born in the late nineties and would have been in his early thirties at the time of this trial. He later went on to serve under Pompey as envoy and a prefect of the fleet in 49 and 48 B.C. His father had died serving under Pompey in Spain in 77(?).[12] Cicero describes him as "optimi viri filium, optima ipsum spe praeditum summae dignitatis" [the son of an excellent man, himself [the son] endowed with excellent prospects of the highest political success] (*Flac.* 2) and as "adulescens bonus, honesto loco natus, disertus" [a fine young man, honorably born, and eloquent] (18). He had probably been present in Asia when Flaccus was governor there in 62 (see *Flac.* 14).

The *subscriptor*[13] most frequently mentioned in the speech is C. Appuleius Decianus, probably the biological son of P. Decius Subulo (praetor in 115) and adopted into the family to which belonged L. Appuleius Saturninus, the seditious tribune at the end of the second century B.C.[14] His father had prosecuted the father of Flaccus at the beginning of the century (*TLRR* no. 78)—probably unsuccessfully, if the father went on to become the suffect consul of 86[15]—and, shortly after the trial, was himself successfully prosecuted and went into exile in the realm of Mithridates (*TLRR* no. 81). Cicero mentions this past history for two reasons: (1) it establishes an *inimicitia* between Decianus and Flaccus, which, while providing a good reason for Decianus's joining the prosecution, undermines his objectivity;[16] and (2) it serves to allow Cicero to contrast the illustrious ancestors of Decianus with his own life as an obscure *eques Romanus* living and conducting business in Asia Minor.[17] The role of Decianus in the trial is clouded by the fact that Laelius claimed that Decianus had been bribed by Flaccus to betray the prosecution, and Cicero's very unconvincing rebuttal—that Flaccus had no motive to do so because Decianus contributed so little to the prosecution (*Flac.* 81–82)—makes it seem more, rather than less, plausible that the charge was justified.[18]

The Bobbian scholiast (93St) names an "L. Balbus" as another *subscriptor* in this case. Three nomina have been suggested to complement the praenomen and cognomen and complete this *subscriptor*'s name: *Laelius, Cornelius,* and *Herennius.* The first, *Laelius,* suggested by Drumann-Groebe (D.-G. 5:614) has little to recommend it. Schöll suggests *Herennius:*[19] in the

Pro Caelio (25), Cicero mentions L. Herennius, "meus familiaris," who was a *subscriptor* against Caelius.[20] But that the scholiast's L. Balbus was L. Cornelius Balbus, suffect consul in 40, is an even more intriguing possibility. As Münzer points out,[21] we have specific testimony from Valerius Maximus (7.8.7) that a Cornelius Balbus arranged many private suits against an L. Valerius Heptachordus and finally prosecuted him on a capital charge. If this anecdote refers to L. Valerius Flaccus, it would provide one piece of evidence (although hardly enough to prove the connection) to view Pompey as an instigator of the accusation (see discussion later in this chapter), because L. Cornelius Balbus had received his Roman citizenship through Pompey's efforts (see Cic. *Balb.* 6, 19, 38; Plin. *HN* 5.36, 7.136) and was a follower of Pompey.[22]

The final two *subscriptores* are much more shadowy figures, and if Webster (*Pro Flacco,* 56) is right, they did not exist at all. Cicero admits that Laelius has charged that Flaccus attempted to bribe not only Decianus but also a "Lucceius" for two million sesterces (*Flac.* 83). Cicero attempts to refute that charge by ridiculing the idea that it would have been worth that much money to remove this Lucceius from the case. Webster maintains that since several manuscripts have the name *Lucius* in the text of the speech and since the Bobbian manuscript has *Laelius,* this could be a corruption of the name *L. Balbus.* The other figure mentioned is "Caetra," whose name is preserved by the Bobbian scholiast (95St) in a lemma from the speech, but whose name Schöll[23] removes by suggesting that the reading be changed from "Quid sibi meus necessarius Caetra voluit?" [What did my friend Caetra want for himself?] to "Quod sibi meus necessarius cetera voluit" followed by a verb like *mandari,* to be translated "because my relative [or "my friend"] wanted everything else to be handed over to him."[24] Webster's approach has the advantage of preserving the sense of the very opening of the extant Bobbian commentary, "<subscri>bentibus L. Balbo et Apuleio Deciano" (93St), implying two *subscriptores,* though caution ought to be exercised before Occam's razor is applied too vigorously to resolve dubious manuscript readings. Moreover, as Classen notes, the plural *ceteros* in the scholiast's comment "Subscribserat hic inter ceteros Decimo Laelio accusatori" [He had served as an assistant prosecutor among the others to the main prosecutor Decimus Laelius] (*Schol. Bob.* 95St) suggests the presence of at least three *subscriptores.*[25]

The prominence of the defendant in this case was matched by the eminence of his two *patroni,* Hortensius and Cicero. We know of seven instances where these two advocates worked together, sometimes with others as well (in defense of Rabirius, Murena, Sulla, Flaccus, Sestius, Plancius, and Scaurus [respectively, *TLRR* nos. 221, 224, 234, 247, 271, 293, 295]). One fact stands out about their forensic partnership: when working together, they never lost a case, at least as far as we know. This record may testify not only to their rhetorical prowess and to jurors' respect for them but also to the prominence of the clients whom they agreed to defend. It would be unfair to claim that they took only easy cases, as their defense of Flaccus shows. At the time of this case, Cicero was at the height of his influence, though already under attack from his political enemies. Hortensius's position had been somewhat eclipsed by Cicero's success, starting with Cicero's victory over him in the case of Verres in 70 B.C., but he was still the second most prominent orator in Rome (see Cic. *Brut.* 320, 325–28; Quint. *Inst.* 11.3.8). He usually handled the refutation of the prosecution's factual arguments, leaving the more emotional peroration to Cicero (see Cic. *Brut.* 190; *Orat.* 130).[26] Therefore, for the purpose of reconstructing the prosecution's case against Flaccus or any other defendant in whose defense Hortensius and Cicero were cooperating, Hortensius's speech, if we had it, would probably be more useful than Cicero's, which in this case summarizes arguments with which Hortensius has already dealt more fully (see *Flac.* 41, 54).

The picture that has emerged from this discussion is that two illustrious advocates defended someone of the most distinguished lineage against a prosecution team that lacked personal prestige: an *adulescens*, a Roman knight from the fringes of the empire who was seeking revenge for his father's disgrace, and a (possibly) foreign-born man from the other end of the empire. But the picture changes when we take into account the role of Pompey, the most powerful man in Rome:

> sermo est tota Asia dissipatus Cn. Pompeium, quod L. Flacco esset vehementer inimicus, contendisse a Laelio, paterno amico ac pernecessario, ut hunc hoc iudicio arcesseret, omnemque ei suam auctoritatem, gratiam, copias, opes ad hoc negotium conficiendum detulisse. (*Flac.* 14)

> [a rumor was circulated throughout all of Asia that Gnaeus Pompeius, being a fierce enemy of Lucius Flaccus, had demanded from Laelius, a friend and close connection through his father, that he summon the defendant to this court, and that Pompey had turned

over to him all his prestige, goodwill, resources, and wealth to accomplish this business.]

It was obviously not in Cicero's interests to bring up the possibility that Pompey may have been the motivating force behind the prosecution, so we must assume that such a belief was current, whether or not it was true. It is quite clear that the defense did not aim to use the trial as a platform to attack Pompey, who enjoyed prestige at least as high in Asia as in Rome, as the Roman general who had defeated Mithridates with a command that lasted six years (66–61 B.C.) and who had organized all of Asia Minor and Syria. In fact, Cicero deferentially uses Pompey as a standard of sound administration, citing Pompey's naval policy (*Flac.* 29, 32), his policy toward the Jews (68), and his distrust of Greeks (20). In any case, in the year 59, as attacks on Cicero mounted, the orator had no wish to alienate the most powerful politician in Rome. His failure to mount a convincing rebuttal to the widespread belief that Pompey was behind the prosecution suggests that there was some truth to this belief.

There are two scholarly views on Pompey's motive here, both of which may have some merit, though I offer a third possibility. The first is that Flaccus was the object of an attack by the so-called triumvirate of Pompey, Crassus, and Caesar against the nobility to which he belonged.[27] The testimony of P. Servilius Vatia Isauricus (consul in 79) and Q. Caecilius Metellus Creticus (consul in 69) in favor of the defendant is adduced as evidence. Epstein[28] argues vigorously against this point of view, attributing the motivation of Pompey and others to *inimicitiae* rather than factional politics. He posits a deep enmity between Flaccus and Pompey, on the basis of Cicero's words (just quoted) that "sermo est tota Asia dissipatus Cn. Pompeium, quod L. Flacco esset vehementer inimicus, contendisse a Laelio, paterno amico ac pernecessario, ut hunc hoc iudicio arcesseret" (*Flac.* 14).[29] According to Cicero, the testimony of Servilius and Metellus may be attributed simply to their debt to the defendant as his former commanders.[30] Moreover, as Epstein points out, after the trial, Flaccus went on to serve in 57–56 under L. Calpurnius Piso Caesoninus (consul in 58), who was Caesar's son-in-law. Gruen (1968a, 166) argues that Piso was no friend of Pompey, although Piso was linked to Caesar. But to the extent that Gruen undercuts the idea of a united triumvirate by suggesting that Piso's ties to Caesar were much closer than his ties to Pompey, he also weakens the likelihood of a "triumviral" role on the trial of Flaccus. The most straightforward explanation of Pompey's role in the trial is probably the best: he was a patron of the people of the province of Asia,[31] much as the Marcelli defended Sicilian interests and encouraged Cicero to prosecute Verres (Cic. *Div. Caec.* 13–14 and 2 *Verr.* 3.45; cf. 2 *Verr.* 4.86).[32]

The chief prosecutor, Decimus Laelius, mounted a well-substantiated case. To translate Cicero's opprobrium into neutral language, Laelius devoted himself to the case with great energy, assisted by many others. He made use of the power to summon witnesses that was granted to him by the statute under which he was trying the case, and he used not only public money but even his own private resources to provide a travel allowance to witnesses whose means did not allow them to travel to Rome. Not only did he conduct his investigations among all social strata in Asia, but he sought out his evidence in the remotest corners of that province. He had to repel attempts by the defense not only to suborn these witnesses but also to co-opt even one of his own *subscriptores*. Finally, he may have devoted a remarkable length of time to his prosecution, if he began it soon after Flaccus's governorship in 62, because the case did not come to court until 59.[33] In short, the case featured a model prosecutor and a model prosecution,[34] against which it is hard to imagine what could be said.

Yet, of course, Cicero could imagine what could be said against Laelius and said it. His attacks on the prosecutors provide information about their presentation of the case, as long as we translate Cicero's vocabulary into more temperate language. Cicero says that Laelius was "vehemens" (*Flac.* 13), a term that could be flattering (translated as "forceful") or pejorative (translated as "violent"). What one might call Laelius's determination, Cicero terms an unreasonable passion ("inflammatus incredibili cupiditate"). Cicero calls the large staff that Laelius gathers an *exercitus* (army) and says that the Asian witnesses have been not just legally summoned but "compulsi" [rounded up] and "concitati" [incited] (3).[35] The prosecutor's solicitude for those witnesses who needed help not only to travel to Rome but to stay there—in other words, all witnesses but the independently wealthy, who did not need to work to support themselves—is used by Cicero to show that they cannot be trusted as witnesses, since they are not independent of the prosecutor. Cicero maintains that Flaccus was handed over not to the witnesses of Asia but tent mates of the prosecutor.[36] Cicero portrays the prosecutor's use of his legal power of subpoena as designed to strike fear into potential witnesses, and he portrays those who need travel funds as too poor to stay at home, that is, bankrupt ("qui domi stare non poterant" [who cannot stay at home/who cannot stand on their own resources] (14).[37] Cicero argues that the witnesses are too closely associated with the prosecutor to be considered witnesses at all (21), that they not only rise up from the prosecutor's benches but stay at his home, where the prosecutor has taught them what to say (22). In case the jurors miss the point, Cicero claims that the witnesses will be out on the street if they slip up in their testimony: "si verbo titubaverint, quo revertantur non habebunt. An quisquam esse testis potest quem accusator sine cura interroget nec metuat ne sibi aliquid quod ipse nolit respondeat?" [if they stumble in speech, they will have no place to return to. Can anyone be a witness whom the prosecutor questions without concern and who does not fear that he might respond to him with something that he does not want?] (22).[38] In short, the more conscientiously Laelius performed his duties as prosecutor, the more Cicero mocked him as a young man goaded by an irrational passion to cause the ruin of a model Roman noble. The more carefully the prosecutors managed the case down to the last detail, the more Cicero implied that the need for such management showed that it was an inherently bad case.

The prosecutors presented to the court powerful testimony to support their case. It was only natural that most of the witnesses in a prosecution of a Roman governor who had served in Asia would be Asian Greeks. The ridicule that Cicero aims at Laelius's efforts to compile an overwhelming case against Flaccus speaks to the persuasiveness of the evidence presented by the prosecution. The witnesses are predominately not only Greeks, says Cicero, but Asian Greeks, whose national failings Cicero stresses, taking flight on the wings of ethnic abuse,[39] as one would expect the defense orator to do when his case is weak. Cicero argues (*Flac.* 24) that contemporary Asian Greeks combine the worst characteristic of Greeks, *levitas* (fickleness), with the worst characteristic of barbarians, *crudelitas* (cruelty), and can be relied on to produce nothing of value in their *contiones*. Therefore, he argues, the resolutions of support for Laelius and against Flaccus should have no value. To illustrate further the worthlessness of the Asian Greeks, as compared to the Greeks who have come to testify for Flaccus from other parts of the Hellenic world (Athens, all Achaea, Boeotia, Thessaly, and Marseilles [see *Flac.* 62–63]), Cicero cites for each of the four parts of Asia (Phrygia, Mysia, Caria, and Lydia) a folk proverb or comic stereotype that shows the low regard in which they were held (65). Cicero's more factual—though undoubtedly overgeneralized—reason for discounting the testimony of the Greeks is that they supported Mithridates in the eighties (see *Flac.* 60–61).

Not only are Greeks in general unreliable witnesses according to Cicero (*Flac.* 23), but these particular witnesses called by the prosecution come from such obscure origins that Cicero has, he complains, no basis for a character attack: "Quid dicam in ignotum?" [What should I say against an unknown person?] (23). He argues that the *psephismata* (resolutions) from Greek cities are the product of an unruly rabble (23). Laelius's complaint that the public testimonial given for Flaccus by the city of Acmonia is forged allows Cicero to claim that all such statements, for or against the defendant, are unreliable and should be discarded (36). Cicero maintains that in their attacks on Flaccus, Greek witnesses did not exercise the restraint shown by Roman witnesses (10–11). To establish that Greek records are always unreliable, Cicero cites correspondence between Pompey and Hypsaeus, who served under Pompey in Asia as quaestor and probably proquaestor in the mid-sixties—letters that obviously complained about some financial records (20). The defense lawyer's criticism of the opposing witnesses is not always consistent; while he implies, on the one hand, that they are reckless blabbermouths ("impudentissimus loquacissimusque deligitur" [the most brazen and talkative person is chosen], 11) who begin to answer the question before it has even been posed to them and at greater length than even the prosecutor intended (23), he complains, on the other hand, that he cannot effectively cross-examine witnesses who answer questions with a curt "dedimus" [we gave] (23).[40]

Cicero's complaint about the brevity of witness responses suggests that Laelius was trying to establish his case on a factual basis. The witness or witnesses who answered so curtly may have quite simply been supplying the essential fact for an extortion case, namely, that he or they had given money. Laelius's coaching of the prosecution witnesses may indicate the careful planning in which he engaged to build his case piece by piece. Keeping them in his own house may have been his response to the possibility that the witnesses would be suborned or would suffer some worse fate. Laelius attributed the death of a witness from Dorylaum to Flaccus (see *Flac.* 41),[41] and the witness Mithridates of Pergamum, after giving two days of testimony, walked around wearing a *lorica* (breastplate) to show his fear of assassination at the hands of Flaccus or his followers.[42] The prosecution's efforts to collect compelling evidence, as we see those efforts reflected in Cicero's ridicule of them, remind us of the conscientious diligence that we are ready to credit to Cicero himself as prosecutor of Verres. The more Cicero rails against the ethnic origin of the prosecution witnesses, the more we should suspect that their hostile testimony was compelling.

Laelius complained that Flaccus had tried to corrupt the prosecution effort, and the weakness of Cicero's rebuttal suggests that the charge had merit. Laelius charged that Flaccus had bribed Decianus and that Decianus had deserted the case as a result (*Flac.* 81).[43] Cicero responds that it makes no sense both to charge someone with *avaritia* (greed; e.g., to lay an extortion charge against him) and also to charge him with bribery (83). Such a rejoinder is unconvincing, since even a rapacious person might be willing to invest some of his ill-gotten money to secure the rest of it.[44] Cicero also argues that Flaccus had nothing to gain from suborning the two *subscriptores*, though he sarcastically raises the possibility that Laelius might have been jealous of the skill of Decianus in conducting his part of the case and that Balbus's weak performance might suggest that he had been bribed (83). Kurke (1989, 75) shrewdly suggests that Cicero's description of Decianus's performance ("Invidisti ingenio subscriptoris tui; quod ornabat facile locum quem prehenderat, et acute testis interrogabat [You envied the talent of your assistant prosecutor because he adorned the topic that he had grasped and pointedly questioned the witnesses], *Flac.* 82) indicates that Laelius believed that his *subscriptor* was taking up too much time with excessive elaboration. All in all, Cicero's feeble rebuttal suggests that Flaccus had tried to buy off his attackers and, therefore, that Laelius would have been quite justified in offering accommodation to his witnesses in his own house to keep a watchful eye on them.

Cicero's speech for the defense yields some overview of the charges made by the prosecution, although the possibility has to be kept in mind that Cicero fails to mention charges with which Hortensius had already dealt. Cicero divides his rebuttal into four parts, dealing first with the charges made by Asia as a whole (*Flac.* 27–33), second with the charges from individual cities (34–66), third with the complaint of the Jews (66–69), and fourth with the complaints of Decianus and other Roman citizens (70–93). Since he is responding to speeches made by at least three prosecution speakers, as well as their witnesses, he was probably reorganizing the prosecution material to some extent, but this four-part division provides the best framework for reconstructing the prosecution arguments.

The one charge against Flaccus that all the cities of Asia Minor make ("de communi totius Asiae crimine" [concerning the common charge of all

Asia], *Flac.* 34) is that they were improperly required by Flaccus as governor to pay for a fleet: "classis nomine pecuniam civitatibus imperatam queruntur" [They complain that money was levied on the cities under the heading of a fleet] (27).[45] Cicero makes a tripartite defense on this charge, arguing that the prosecution must show that the fleet was (a) unauthorized, (b) unnecessary, or (c) unused and was therefore just a way to exact money. On the first point, Cicero argues that the Senate had authorized a fleet in 63, when he himself had been consul, just as it had in previous years. On the second, he counteracts the prosecution argument that Asia did not need a fleet because Pompey had pacified the waters around Asia[46] and that, in fact, Flaccus took no prisoners (31). Laelius had supported this point by noting that Quintus Cicero, both the brother of the orator and Flaccus's successor as governor of Asia, did not demand money for rowers, preferring to call up a fleet as the need arose (33).[47] Cicero maintains that the provision of a fleet can be valid even in the absence of any specific naval threat and that he has eminent witnesses who will testify that people were being captured by pirates (31).[48] Laelius's final point—and probably his primary one, as was appropriate in an extortion case[49]—is that Flaccus failed to account for the money exacted for this purpose (33). Cicero can only weakly respond that he did not profit by his omission, but of course, in the absence of accounts, it is impossible to trace the use to which the money was put. While it is relevant to argue, as Cicero does, that a bipartite fleet was launched, that Flaccus used only half as many ships as Pompey had used, and that Flaccus divided the cost among the cities according to a formula devised by Sulla, it must have been impossible to tell whether Flaccus used all the money that he had exacted for the fleet for its ostensible purpose. Cicero also claims that Flaccus cannot be criticized for failing to account for the money when he would be providing grist for his prosecutors by admitting that he did demand the payment from the cities.

Cicero's defense appears all the more questionable when one compares it to the attack he made on Verres in his final oration against him, in which he employed the same fundamental argument regarding military security as did Laelius. Just as Cicero would later argue that Asia had suffered no military reverses while Flaccus was governor, so Hortensius argues (or at least Cicero pictures him as arguing [2 *Verr.* 5.1]) that Sicily was safe during the three years that Verres governed it. Sallust confirms the military value of Verres' activities for the defense of Italy: "C. Verres litora Italia propinqua firmavit" [Verres fortified the neighboring shores of Italy] (*Hist.* 4 frag.

32 Reynolds). In their role as prosecutors, both Laelius and Cicero ridicule the idea that the defendants can claim any credit for this relative peace. Both mention dubious record-keeping practices, since the charge was extortion and since the expenditure of money, not the results achieved, was primarily at issue. However, Cicero at least does not place primary stress on this question of relevance, though he does refer to it. He ostentatiously eschews this line of argument, preferring to stress Verres' inadequacy as a commander (2 *Verr.* 5.4, quoted in chap. 2). Yet his charges that the navy under Verres was inadequately manned (5.86, 87, 110, 131) and ill fed (5.87, 99, 101, 131) and that this logistical failure led to the navy's humiliating defeat at the hands of pirates (5.87–91) implicitly raise the financial issue. Cicero argues that because Verres issued exemptions from duty to rowers and soldiers (5.133, 136)—for a fee, of course—the fleet was ill manned. Cicero notes that Verres had compelled cities to pay for a fleet (5.136) and that inadequate preparation suggests that the money had not been spent for the purpose for which it was allocated. According to Cicero (5.95–100), the fact that the pirates were satisfied, after burning the Roman fleet, simply to sail around the harbor of Syracuse and then to sail away was lucky for Verres, for Syracuse, and maybe for all of Sicily but did not really alter the legal issue. The major difference between Verres' situation and Flaccus's is that at least Verres had apparently kept some records of the naval tax, since Cicero nowhere claims that he did not,[50] whereas Flaccus did not even keep records of his naval taxation.

I turn now to charges laid by individuals and individual cities.[51] Mithridates of Pergamum presented a charge of unknown nature ("Mithridaticum crimen") that was evidently supported by an assembly of the people of Pergamum (*Flac.* 17). This charge was evidently fairly weighty, because Mithridates, the supposed son of Mithridates VI and a concubine,[52] had testified about it for two days; Cicero claims that after cross-examination and extensive treatment of Mithridates' testimony by Quintus Hortensius in his speech, Mithridates was a broken man (41). The first charge to which Cicero presents a detailed response comes from Asclepiades of Acmonia, who claims that he paid a large sum (206,000 drachmas) to Flaccus on behalf of the city of Acmonia. Since he himself did not have that much cash, he borrowed it from A. Sestullius and his brothers (34–36).[53] Cicero's response is to challenge the factual basis of the claim; neither Asclepiades nor A. Sestullius can produce records to substantiate the claim, and Asclepiades cannot produce any of the Sestullii in court to corroborate his testimony.[54] A similar complaint comes from Dorylaum. Someone from that city testified that he had provided funds to Flaccus, presumably again on behalf of the city. Again, Cicero argues that there are no records to substantiate the claim, though the prosecution claims that relevant records made it as far as Speluncae, in southern Italy (39–41). Here, Cicero somewhat contradicts his general claim that the Greeks have no respect for the need for accuracy in testimony and documentation. He suggests that the reason why these claimants from Dorylaum say that they have lost the records is that the laws of that city are particularly harsh with regard to forgery, so the claimants do not dare produce forged records.[55] A similar contradiction becomes apparent in a complaint from Temnos. Witnesses from there claim that they had given fifteen thousand drachmas to Flaccus and his staff (43). Cicero argues that though this city keeps very careful records, with a total of twelve elected officials whose job it is to monitor the municipal finances, none of these has been produced in court to substantiate the charge. Cicero also contests the plausibility of the charges by pointing out that the witnesses claim they gave this money to Flaccus personally yet also say that they gave a larger sum of money ostensibly for temple repairs.[56] Using a false dilemma (false because while it may be true that the Temnians should have acted consistently, it is not necessarily true that they did so), Cicero argues that they must claim one or the other: "nam aut omnia occulte referenda fuerunt, aut aperte omnia" [for either all things should have been secretly recorded, or all things should have been openly recorded] (44). Cicero claims he cannot even deal with this charge unless he is given all the particulars, yet if one thinks of the *Verrines,* it is easy to see that it would be almost impossible to do that in extortion cases, where a multiplicity of charges can only be briefly described in the *actiones,* leaving the detailed documentation to the *litis aestimatio.* A prosecutor who wished to mount an overwhelming case, as did Laelius, finds himself criticized for not expatiating on every aspect of the case. Yet if Laelius had chosen to highlight just a few of these charges, presumably the ones for which he could produce reams of evidence and hordes of witnesses, one can well imagine that Cicero would have ridiculed him for wasting the time of a Roman jury with such massive support for just a few charges.

The level of complexity that can be reached when an orator goes into detail is illustrated by the next allegation that Cicero handles, involving Heraclides of Temnos (*Flac.* 45–50). To strip the episode down to its essentials, Flaccus as governor had appointed arbiters (*recuperatores*) to decide a private case between two local inhabitants, one of whom was Heraclides. They ruled against Heraclides, who charged that Flaccus had used force and fear to compel them to do so. Cicero goes to unusual lengths to persuade the jury of the worthlessness of Heraclides' claim.[57] Yet it is not even clear that Flaccus's actions in this case were the basis for a formal charge. Cicero begins by complaining that though the resolution of Temnos alleges that their most eminent citizens who had held the highest offices were unjustly condemned by Flaccus, none of them is present or specifically named. Then, he ridicules the idea that Heraclides, who is present, could be referred to in this resolution. It turns out that Heraclides held the office of *sitophulax* (grain inspector),[58] probably in 66 and 65, but disappeared in disgrace when it was discovered that in this capacity, he had billed both the Roman governor and the city for the grain. He was not appointed as a member of the delegation to Rome by the city but had attached himself to it apparently while it was already en route. It is not even apparent whether the legal narrative that Cicero goes on to relate in detail represents any kind of charge against Flaccus, for he introduces it merely as the reason why Heraclides was so hostile to Flaccus. If Cicero is right that Heraclides was not one of the city's leading men whom Flaccus had wronged in a way that formed part of the grounds for his prosecution, Cicero is introducing the case of Heraclides as a red herring.[59]

The narrative of the case goes as follows. From Rome, Heraclides bought an estate at Cyme with money borrowed from Sextus Stloga (who happened to be a juror in 59), with a guarantee from P. Fulvius Neratus. To pay Stloga, Heraclides borrowed money from C. and M. Fufius, with a guarantee from Hermippus. When Heraclides was not able to obtain money from his rhetoric students, he secretly returned to Asia. Eventually, Hermippus found out that the debt had not been paid, made good on his guarantee to the Fufii, and sued Heraclides before assessors appointed by Flaccus. They ruled for the plaintiff, and the defendant was forced to sell a few slaves to him to satisfy the obligation. In the next year, Heraclides went before the new praetor, Cicero's brother, Quintus, to ask for a rehearing, on the ground that Flaccus had interfered in the trial against him. Quintus agreed to this request, with the proviso that the liability would be doubled if the defendant was found guilty. Heraclides declined this opportunity, and when Quintus's legate refused to alter Quintus's decision, Heraclides returned to Rome. There, he sued another former legate in Asia, C. Plotius, for some slaves whom he said he had been forced to sell when the previous

judgment had gone against him. He agreed to the arbitration of Q. Voconius Naso, an ex-praetor, but abandoned the case when he realized that
Naso would rule against him.[60]

That Cicero goes on at such length about the foibles of Heraclides does
not imply that Laelius lay equal stress on this one witness. Evidently, Cicero
had opportunities to gather information on this one case, certainly from his
brother and probably from other senators as well, and uses this one example to imply that he could similarly demolish the character of the other witnesses against Flaccus, even though he does not do this. Thus, he ends the
narrative with a reminder to the jurors that they should be grateful that he
does not generally go into such detail about each witness but instead deals
with them in general terms.

> Satisne vobis, iudices, videor ad singulos testis accedere neque, ut
> primo constitueram, tantum modo cum universo genere confligere?
> (*Flac.* 50)

> [Do I seem to you, jurors, sufficiently to come to grips with the wit-
> nesses one by one, and not, as I had first decided, to do battle only
> with the whole group?]

But all Cicero has shown of relevance here is that in one minor private case,
Flaccus appointed *recuperatores* who rendered what seems to have been a
fair verdict.

Another case from Temnos receives only a short description in Cicero's
speech. The witness involved has not yet spoken, and Cicero does not want
to respond until he has heard the testimony. According to Cicero (*Flac.* 51),
a young man, Lysanias, borrowed money from Decianus, putting up his
family estate as security, and was forced to forfeit that estate, presumably
because he could not pay the debt. Cicero claims that Decianus forced
Lysanias to testify because he was still hoping to get his estate back.[61]

Next, Flaccus was accused of having taken money from a fund that had
been deposited at Tralles by various cities to pay for games in honor of his
father, L. Valerius Flaccus, suffect consul in 86 (*Flac.* 52–61).[62] This charge
is all the more remarkable because the defendant and his ancestors acted as
the patrons of this city (52). Laelius also claimed that Mithridates had
seized the money.[63] This must have occurred between the elder Flaccus's
proconsulate in 95 and/or 94[64] and the younger Flaccus's governorship in

62, probably in the early eighties. This money is in some way related to the town's bitter quarrel with a Castricius, to whom it had unwillingly paid a debt; unfortunately for us, Cicero refers to the "Castricium nomen" [entry for Castricius] only fleetingly, since Hortensius has already discussed it in his speech (54).[65] Even Cicero admits that he always believed that there was some merit to the complaints of Tralles on this score: "itaque civitatis pudentis, ut ego semper existimavi, et gravis, ut ipsi existimari volunt, iustum dolorem querelasque cognoscite" [And so hear the just distress and complaints of a decent city, as I have always thought of it, and of a responsible city, as they themselves wish to be thought of] (55).

Cicero's counterarguments against this accusation are so weak as to give credence to the prosecution's case. First, Cicero notes that the respectable people of Tralles want to have nothing to do with this complaint and that the city has delegated the matter to a poor and positionless man, Maeandrius. Second, Cicero argues that it is ridiculous for the city to complain about the loss of something that did not belong to it.

Queritur gravis, locuples, ornata civitas, quod non retinet alienum; spoliatam se dicit, quod id non habet quod eius non fuit. (*Flac.* 56)

[A responsible, wealthy, and magnificent city complains because it does not keep something that belongs to someone else; it says it has been robbed, because it does not have that which it did not own.]

Yet it is a principle of the Roman law of theft that someone who holds someone else's property can under certain circumstances be held liable for its safe return and that if it is stolen, the holder of the property has suffered a loss by its disappearance and may sue the thief.[66] Since extortion is a kind of theft, it is quite possible that the city of Tralles was liable for the safekeeping of the funds and therefore had legal standing to seek restitution for it. Third, Cicero defends Flaccus by means of a dilemma that is so opaque that editors have suspected corruption of the text (59).[67] He argues that if the elder Flaccus could legitimately use the money for games in his own honor, the son could legitimately take the money (for the same purpose?), whereas if the elder Flaccus was not allowed to take the money, the son or any other heir could take it at his death. Fourth, Cicero maintains that the Trallians were angry because they had for years lent out this money at high interest. Fifth, Cicero argues that the Trallians have no right to complain about the fact that Mithridates took the money, because they had shown themselves sympathetic to him and disloyal to Rome. None of these arguments undermines the apparent legitimacy of the Trallians' claim that money that had been deposited with them by neighboring cities to honor the senior Flaccus should only be used for that purpose and that his son could not tap into those funds for his personal enrichment any more than the father could have in his own lifetime. That Cicero does not dispute that the son did appropriate these funds for his own use strongly suggests that he had in fact done so.

Decianus also brought complaints against Flaccus, presumably during the first *actio,* when Decianus was still working for the prosecution. Cicero claims that Flaccus, during his governorship, had ruled against Decianus in some matter (*Flac.* 77) and that this action caused the *inimicitia* that caused Decianus to report Flaccus to Laelius (81).[68] The main charge Decianus brings relates to the inheritance of Valeria, which Flaccus adjudicated as belonging to himself. Decianus's main contention is that Flaccus should not have rendered judgment in a case where he had a personal stake.

> Relinquitur illud quod vociferari non destitit, non debuisse, cum praetor esset, suum negotium agere aut mentionem facere hereditatis. (85)

> [One matter remains that he has not ceased to declare loudly, that, since he was praetor, he should not have looked after his own interests or made mention of the inheritance.]

This complaint accords with modern ideas of conflict of interest, and M. Aufidius Lurco had made the same point ("negavit a privato pecuniam in provincia praetorem petere oportere" [he said that a praetor should not seek money in his province from a private person], 86), so it certainly was one that the ancient mind could comprehend. But Cicero argues that it is quite acceptable for governors to render judgments from which they themselves profit (85). Decianus has a good point here, regardless of the merits of the case itself, but Cicero distracts his listeners from the procedural point by arguing at some length for those merits.

The case involved the inheritance of one Valeria, the wife of Sestullius Andro (*Flac.* 84–89). She was a freeborn woman but was related to Flaccus probably as the descendant, possibly the daughter, of a *libertus* (freedman) of the Valerii.[69] She died intestate, in which case her inheritance would go to her husband if she was in his *manus* (under his control) or, failing that, to the descendants of the original manumittor, including Flaccus himself. Cicero argues that she could not have made a *manus* marriage without the consent of her *tutores* (guardians), among whom was Flaccus himself, and the implication is that he did not issue his approval.[70] The same argument counters the claim of Decianus that she had settled her estate on her husband as a dowry; for that arrangement, she would have also needed the approval of Flaccus. Cicero rejects the idea that Flaccus might have given his consent to any of these arrangements.[71] But the possibility that Flaccus acted dishonorably has to be considered; he might have given his consent to the marriage and property arrangements and then, when it became clear that he stood to lose by what he had approved, did an about-face and, as praetor, refused to recognize the validity of what he had done as a private citizen. Against the conflict-of-interest claim, Cicero argues that Flaccus gave up his part of the inheritance to an *adulescentulus,* L. Valerius Flaccus, the joint heir, and so did not directly benefit from the decision (89). Finally, Cicero notes that Andro himself is not present to give evidence.

Interwoven with the Andro matter is the complaint of M. Aufidius[72] Lurco (tribune of the plebs in 61), who apparently took part in presenting the complaint of Andro, perhaps as the representative of the patronal family, the Sestullii (he was C. Sestullius's maternal uncle). He was angry because his freedman had been condemned by a decision of Flaccus (*Flac.* 87–88), just as P. Septimius saw his *vilicus* condemned for murder (11, 88).

Decianus also complained about Flaccus's decision not to support his claim that land at Apollonis should be registered in his name and about another decision of Flaccus regarding a claim to the slaves of Amyntas, the leading citizen of that city, whose wife and daughter still resided in the house of Decianus (*Flac.* 71–80). Both Apollonis and Pergamum refused to register the land in Decianus's name,[73] although the land was registered in his name under the Roman census of 64 B.C.[74] The matter was brought before three Roman governors: P. Orbius in 64, P. Servilius Globulus in 63, and Flaccus in 62. In 63, the Senate passed a senatus consultum on which Flaccus probably based his decision.[75]

The final Roman complaint comes from Falcidius, who says he gave fifty talents to Flaccus (*Flac.* 90–93). Falcidius gave this money to secure for himself the tax-farming rights for Asia, which he had bought under the previous praetor, Globulus.[76] Webster (*Pro Flacco,* 104) is probably right that

Flaccus demanded in the year of his governorship that Falcidius repurchase the rights at a higher price.[77] Cicero ridicules the evidentiary basis of this claim, letters from Falcidius's mother and sister, rather than oral testimony from Falcidius himself. Cicero also claims that there is no reason that Falcidius would have been forced by this transaction to sell his Alban estate.

Besides the complaints of the Greeks and Romans residing in Asia, there is the complaint of the Jews against Flaccus (*Flac.* 66–69). Flaccus took it on himself to prevent the traditional Jewish tax (half a shekel, or two denarii) from each adult male Jew from being sent to its destination at Jerusalem. This is a matter of several hundred pounds of gold.[78] The prosecution argues that Flaccus, unlike Pompey, who spared the Temple at Jerusalem after he took that city in 63 B.C., has trampled on the traditional rights of the Jews. On this matter, the response of modern readers is likely to be hostile toward Cicero's arguments, especially his contention that the military defeat of the Jews shows that the gods are hostile toward them (69).[79] But to be fair to Cicero, we need to take into consideration some points raised by Marshall (1975b), who provides salutary support for some of Cicero's arguments.[80] In legal terms, Cicero's response is that because Flaccus paid into the Roman treasury the gold that he seized, no theft has occurred. The behavior of the Jews may have constituted a contumacious defiance of an existing ban issued by Flaccus, either as an ad hoc ruling or as part of the governor's annual edict for his province. Marshall argues (1975b, 145) that the exception to the Senate's decision on precious metals made by previous Roman officials on behalf of the Jews was a matter of customary tolerance or indifference, not of firm privilege. In political terms, Cicero's response is that the Jews are a rebellious people and that Laelius is appealing to the Jews in Rome to create *invidia* against Flaccus: "a iudicibus oratio avertitur, vox in coronam turbamque effunditur" [the speech is turned away from the jurors, and his voice is poured out on the gallery and the crowd] (*Flac.* 69). Moreover, Flaccus's edict may have been an attempt to implement the latest in a series of senatus consulta[81] that were designed to reduce the flow of gold and silver from Asia.[82] It is only fair to point out, however, as Marshall admits (1975b, 143 n. 17), that however rational this policy may have been, Quintus Cicero almost certainly did not renew it in his edict, since his brother would have mentioned such a reaffirmation.

Did Flaccus deserve an acquittal? Marshall criticizes the readiness of earlier scholars to accept the guilt of Flaccus as proven on the basis of Macrobius's testimony.[83] He rightly points out that the statement of guilt is put into the mouth of one of the characters in Macrobius's dialogue and that this dialogue could have been based merely on a reading of the speech, rather than on independent evidence. Yet it is hard not to obtain an overall impression of Flaccus's guilt from Cicero's speech. As we have seen, his arguments do little to refute the contention of the prosecution that Flaccus had violated the extortion law while governor in Asia.

The outcome of this case testifies to the difficulty in convicting even a defendant who was technically guilty of certain criminal acts, in the absence of evidence from other periods of his life that rendered such accusations plausible and in the presence of a distinguished family tradition. A strong case that the defendant's *vita ante acta* showed serious faults may have been a necessary condition for conviction, even if it was not a sufficient condition. Nevertheless, the acquittal of Flaccus was in some sense a Pyrrhic victory, because the Roman people never entrusted Flaccus with the consulate, which his record and family almost guaranteed him. Whereas legal guilt was not always enough for conviction, legal acquittal did not always bring total absolution.

CHAPTER FOUR

In M. Aemilium Scaurum

caurus was prosecuted in mid-54 for his activities as propraetor in Sardinia in 55. Our understanding of the case
against him is exiguous, because we do not have a full
record of the defense that was made on his behalf. There
are two reasons for the gaps in our knowledge: first, we have only part of
Cicero's speech, contained in two large fragments from palimpsests and in
fragments from Asconius and a few other authors; second, Cicero defended
only "part" of Scaurus's case (". . . cum ego partem eius ornatissime
defendissem" [. . . part of him being defended by me in my best style], *Att.*
4.17.4; trans. Shackleton Bailey).[1] In contrast, our understanding of the
trial's background is unusually full, because of Asconius's *argumentum*
and commentary on the *Pro Scauro*. It is therefore easier to understand this
trial in political terms than in legal or rhetorical terms, but it should be kept
in mind that this situation results partly from the nature of the sources.

Cicero provides an outline of his speech.

> Dicam enim primum de ipso genere accusationis, postea de Sardis,
> tum etiam pauca de Scauro; quibus rebus explicatis tum denique ad
> hoc horribile et formidolosum frumentarium crimen accedam.
> (*Scaur.* 22)

[For I will speak first about the particular type of accusation, there-after about the Sardinians, then also a few things about Scaurus; when I have explained these things, then finally I will approach this dreadful and alarming charge relating to grain.]

According to Cicero (23–37), the case is characterized by insufficient inves-tigation and excessive *inimicitia*. The Sardinians are portrayed as totally untrustworthy (38–45), and Scaurus is defended from the criticism of avarice. But in the extant part of the text, the "frumentarium crimen" is hardly mentioned (21). Perhaps it was merely summarized with a rubric (cf. "DE CRIMINE VINARIO" at *Pro Fonteio* 20), and the region of the speech where it would naturally fall is full of lacunae. But even before his summary of the structure of his speech, Cicero has already dealt with a scandalous incident: the suicide of the wife of Aris because of Scaurus's harassment of her, explained by Cicero either as a suicide or as a murder commissioned by Aris so that he might remarry and disguised as a suicide (*Scaur.* 2–14).

The cast of characters involved in this trial seems vast compared to the number of people who took part in the other trials on record.[2] The fact that we possess Asconius's commentary partly accounts for the plethora of names, but that commentary in turn reflects the reality that an unusually large number of individuals took part in this trial. Even more striking than the number of participants is their standing and political heterogeneity.

The prosecution side, while not small, lacked distinction. The *nominis delator* was P. Valerius Triarius.[3] His participation was probably due to the connection with Sardinia that his father had established as propraetor there in 77, fighting against Lepidus.[4] The only personal advantage the prosecu-tion had derived from that fact was that Triarius and his mother, Flaminia, were close friends of Servilia (Asc. 19C), the half sister[5] of M. Porcius Cato, the presiding magistrate. The *subscriptores* were two brothers, M. and Q. Pacuvius Caldus (or Claudus or, some think, Claudius),[6] and L. Marius,[7] all of them obscure. Rather than attempt to specify a reason related to faction or patronage for their supporting roles, it may be wiser to opt for a simpler explanation: they were perhaps injured parties, as was Decianus in the trial of Flaccus.

The only source of prestige for the prosecution came from the backing of Ap. Claudius Pulcher, consul in the year of the trial. Cicero downplays the *inimicitia* between Ap. Claudius and Scaurus with the argument that Claudius was trying to prevent Scaurus's election to the consulate to allow the election of C. Claudius Pulcher (praetor in 56), his brother, since both candidates were patricians (*Scaur.* 31–37).[8] But Cicero gives another clue to the role of Ap. Claudius when he says that it is natural for a predecessor (*decessor*) to be envious of his successor (*successor*) and for them to become enemies (33).[9] It seems likely that the Sardinians, after suffering for a year under Scaurus, had sought aid from their previous governor Claudius, whom they may have even respected and who was now consul at Rome, much as the Sicilians, in their case against Verres, sought the aid of Cicero, who had served as quaestor in Sicily (Cic. *Div. Caec.* 2). Though Ap. Claudius did not take part in the trial himself, he did help arrange for the prosecution.

The group that Triarius and his *subscriptores* confronted was by any account a varied lot.[10] There were six *patroni*. As Asconius remarks (20C), this was an exceptionally high number, four being the usual maximum. The *patroni* were (in the order in which Asconius names them, with their magistracies held by the time of the trial):

P. Clodius Pulcher (curule aedile in 56)
M. Claudius Marcellus (praetor by 54)
M. Calidius (praetor in 57)[11]
M. Tullius Cicero (consul in 63)
M. Valerius Messala Niger (consul in 61, censor in 55)
Q. Hortensius Hortalus (consul in 69)

All of these men, with the exception of Cicero and Clodius, are described in the *Brutus* as significant orators, and it is easy to see why Cicero leaves himself out of his own work[12] and also omits Clodius, his mortal enemy.[13] All in all, Scaurus had the best team available speaking on his behalf.[14] Their rhetorical qualifications provide a sufficient explanation for their selection. Any attempt to explain this coalition in political terms runs into difficulties, not only because of the bizarre coalitions of Cicero[15] and Clodius or of Clodius and Milo, archenemies, but also because of Hortensius's connections with Cato and Servilia, both of whom were thought to be supportive of the prosecution.[16]

The *laudatores* constitute an equally impressive group, here in terms of prestige rather than ability. Nine of the ten were consulars, and the exception was Sulla's son.[17] The group included (again in the order given by Asconius [28C], with their magistracies held by the time of the trial):

L. Calpurnius Piso Caesoninus (consul in 58)

L. Volcacius Tullus (consul in 66)

Q. Caecilius Metellus Nepos (consul in 57)

M. Perperna (consul in 92, censor in 86)

L. Marcius Philippus (consul in 56)

M. Tullius Cicero (consul in 63)

Q. Hortensius Hortalus (consul in 69)

P. Servilius Vatia Isauricus (consul in 79, censor in 55)

Cn. Pompeius Magnus (consul in 70 and again in 55)

Faustus Cornelius Sulla (quaestor in 54)

It is hard to imagine a more stellar cast. The eleven *supplicatores,* who threw themselves at the knees of the jurors, divided themselves into two groups (listed here with their magistracies, if any, held by time of trial):

M. Aemilius Scaurus	Faustus Cornelius Sulla
(praetor in 56)	(quaestor in 54)
M'. Acilius Glabrio	T. Annius Milo (praetor in 55)
L. Aemilius (Lepidus?)[18]	C. Peducaeus
Paullus (curule aedile in 56)	
L. or P. Cornelius Lentulus	C. Porcius Cato (praetor in 55)
(Cruscellio?)	
L. Aemilius Buca	M. (Popillius?) Laenas Curtianus
C. Memmius[19]	

As these lists show, the *supplicatores* were much more junior than the *patroni,* containing no consulars and several individuals who had held no major office.

Not surprisingly, those with a prosopographical inclination have tried to discern a political explanation of this constellation, but without success. Courtney (1961) argues that the prosecution represents the Marian tradition; the defense, the Sullan. Gruen counters with the observation that whereas the son of Lepidus (consul in 78) supported Scaurus in this trial, the father had led a revolt against the Sullan system,[20] and Marshall points out that the father of the chief prosecutor had opposed Lepidus in Sardinia.[21] Ciaceri (1926–30, 2:125) argues that the triumvirs were backing the prosecution; the anti-triumviral party, the defense. But the support provided to the defense by Pompey and individuals with ties to him, as well as by Clodius, speaks against this point of view.

The quest for a prosopographical explanation runs into both general and specific difficulties. The general problem with it involves the fact that the Roman aristocracy was composed of a small number of families, interlocked by adoption and marriage (serial marriage at that, with frequent death and divorce). Most Roman aristocrats were connected to each other by some link, so a link between two individuals may explain nothing about of their political alliances, in terms of either *amicitia* or *inimicitia*.[22] The specific problem here for the prosopographer is the ambiguous role of Pompey. The marriage link between Pompey and Scaurus (Scaurus married Tertia after Pompey had divorced her for *impudicitia,* "unchastity") created a cause of both connection and enmity. Scaurus placed faith in the fact that his son was half brother to Pompey's children, but as Asconius explains (19–20C), Pompey felt that Scaurus had shown too little respect for the judgment he had made on Tertia's character, and therefore Pompey provided Scaurus only lukewarm support. Cicero confirms that Pompey's attitude was ambiguous: "Pompeius fremit, queritur, Scauro studet: sed utrum fronte an mente dubitatur" [Pompey is fuming and growling. Ostensibly, Scaurus is his man, but does he mean it? We have our doubts] (*Att.* 4.15.7; trans. Shackleton Bailey). Since Pompey was governor of both Spains, although he in fact remained in Italy, he could not enter Rome and sent his *laudatio* into the city in writing (Asc. 28C). Besides illustrating the ambiguity of prosopographical facts (does marriage to the same woman cause friendship or hostility?), the role of Pompey is too murky to allow us to analyze either the defense or the prosecution as a Pompeian effort.

There are two different ways to explain the motives of the two sides in this trial and the relationship between those motives: either as an attempt to shore up the existing constitution or as a sign of a constitution in collapse. Gruen (1974, 336–37) stresses the aristocracy's attempt to preserve normality by defending the freedom to hold elections without interference from the judicial process. He argues that the aristocracy rightly saw the trial as an attempt through judicial means to prevent the election of Scaurus to the consulate and that the aristocrats were determined to prevent this interference, whereas they were quite ready to allow Scaurus to go down to electoral defeat after the trial. The alternative explanation for the large opposing coalitions stresses the highly unusual situation that existed in 54, which was an annus mirabilis in terms of electoral wheeling and dealing. Gruen describes the situation.

The two men [C. Memmius and Domitius Calvinus] concluded a private agreement with the consuls of 54, Ap. Claudius Pulcher and Cn. Domitius Ahenobarbus, for the mutual benefit of all four. The consuls would exert their influence to obtain the election of Calvinus and Memmius; in return, the latter two, if elected, would secure proconsular *imperium* and desired provinces for the outgoing consuls by providing phony witnesses to a *lex curiata* and a senatorial decree which never existed. As a personal guarantee of their good faith, the candidates put up an enormous sum of money which would be forfeit should they fail to carry out their obligations. The whole transaction was put in writing with several copies![23]

As a result of this public scandal, all four candidates were prosecuted for *ambitus,* and no consular elections were held that year.

Three pieces of evidence connect, in different ways, the outcome of the trial to the outcome of the election. The first explains how a trial would affect an election. Cicero claims that Ap. Claudius Pulcher, consul in that year, wished to assist the campaign of his brother, C. Claudius Pulcher, for the consulate of 53 by ruining Scaurus's chances; both were patrician, and two patricians could not hold the office together.

> Quam ob rem se consule neque repelli fratrem volebat neque, iste si patricius esset, parem Scauro fore videbat, nisi hunc aliquo aut metu aut infamia perculisset. (*Scaur.* 34)
>
> [Therefore he did not want his brother to be defeated when he himself was consul, and he saw that he would not be a match for Scaurus if he [Gaius] was a patrician, unless he had struck him down with either some threat or some disgrace.]

The preceding passage argues that if Scaurus either was expected to be condemned in an upcoming trial (*metu*) or had been condemned and was therefore *infamis* (*infamia*), his chances of election would be very seriously reduced. But Marshall shows that the fact that someone was a defendant in a trial did not legally disqualify him from running for office.[24] He cites the trial of Catiline *inter sicarios* in 64 (*TLRR* no. 217) while he was running for the consulate, the trial of Clodius in 57 (*TLRR* no. 262) while he was running for the aedileship,[25] and the trial of Scaurus in 54. It seems reasonable to add that the *infamia* that usually followed condemnation would prevent an elected magistrate-designate from assuming office, although perhaps *infamia* was not legally automatic.[26] Electoral offenses were a special case, since those who had gained election through illegal means ought not to secure immunity from prosecution for their crime by virtue of having successfully committed it. It is clear that condemnation under an *ambitus* law did disqualify the condemned from holding the office to which he had been improperly elected; that, after all, is the reason why Paetus and Sulla (*TLRR* nos. 200–201) could not take up the consulate of 65 to which they had been elected. Shackleton Bailey (1970) has shown that trials of magistrates-designate were predominantly held for electoral offenses. *Ambitus* laws must have contained special provisions that allowed prosecution of a magistrate-designate—after the election, of course, because that would have been the logical time to launch such a prosecution.

The second piece of evidence deals with the political effect that the election might have on the trial. It comes in a letter of Cicero to Atticus (*Att.* 4.15.9) and can therefore be viewed as a frank assessment of the chances of Scaurus, whom Cicero had by this time (27 July) taken on as a client for the extortion trial. Cicero, referring to the possibility that he himself may have to serve as *patronus* for the consuls-designate, presumably in trials for election offenses, writes:

> Fortasse accedent etiam consules designati. In quibus si Scaurus non fuerit, in hoc iudicio valde laborabit.

> [Perhaps the Consuls-Designate will come next. If Scaurus is not one of them, he'll have a difficult passage in this trial.] (trans. Shackleton Bailey)

Cicero's argument is that if Scaurus is not elected, he will have a hard time in the extortion trial. In other words, defeat at the polls will make it more likely that Scaurus will be condemned.

The third piece of evidence also deals with an effect that the election might have on the trial, but with the judicial, rather than the political, effect. Asconius says prosecutors feared that Scaurus, using extorted funds, would bribe his way to electoral victory and then extend the trial until he took office on 1 January 53, so that he could go on to hold another governorship (in 52) before ever justifying his conduct as governor in 55.

Qui [the prosecutors] inquisitionis in Sardiniam itemque in Corsi-
cam insulas dies tricenos acceperunt neque profecti sunt ad
inquirendum: cuius rei hanc causam reddebant, quod interea comitia consularia futura essent; timere ergo se ne Scaurus ea pecunia
quam a sociis abstulisset emeret consulatum et, sicut pater eius
fecisset, ante quam de eo iudicari posset, magistratum iniret ac rur-
sus ante alias provincias spoliaret quam rationis prioris administra-
tionis redderet. (Asc. 19C)

[These men were each granted 30 days for their investigations in Sardinia and Corsica [*that is, 30 days in each island*], but did not leave to
begin their inquiries; they explained that the consular elections were
imminent, and they were afraid that Scaurus might buy the consulship with the money he had extorted from the province, and then
enter office before the case could come to court (like his father); he
might then begin robbing other provinces before he could be made
to account for his earlier term of duty.] (trans. Squires, italics mine)

As Weinrib points out, this passage shows that the status of magistrate, not
the status of magistrate-designate, brings a trial to a halt.[27] In other words,
the prosecutors faced a problem similar to the one Cicero faced in prosecuting Verres, and they adopted a similar solution. Both Cicero and Scaurus's prosecutors wanted to make sure that their trials reached their conclusions within the calendar year (70 B.C. for Verres, 54 B.C for Scaurus),
though their reasons were somewhat different: Verres would then be protected by powerful magistrates (see chap. 1), whereas Scaurus would be a
magistrate himself. Cicero waxes eloquent about his thorough investigation in Sicily (*Scaur.* 24–26), visiting the farmer in his cottage and at the
plough. But in fact, he used only 50 of the 110 days granted to him for his
investigation (1 *Verr.* 6; 2 *Ver.* 1.30), and he abbreviated the first *actio* as
much as possible, just as Triarius tried to do by calling only one witness in
the first *actio* (*Scaur.* 29). Weinrib is right to note that the longer Scaurus
campaigned for office, the more money he would spend for electoral
bribery, and the less likely it would be that Scaurus would be able to pay
damages to the Sardinians, even if he were convicted.[28] Scaurus's prosecutors clearly wanted to finish their trial before the consular elections, in the
hope that they would be able to convict Scaurus by then and that, therefore,
he would not be able to stand for office as a matter of law, he would not be
a viable candidate as a matter of practical politics, or both.

These three pieces of evidence relating to this trial support the view that while a guilty verdict could adversely affect the success of a candidate and while the failure to secure election could adversely affect a defendant in a trial, there was no automatic legal effect of a trial (except a trial for electoral misconduct) in progress on an election or vice versa except that the actual assumption of office, as a result of electoral victory, would bring a trial to a halt.[29] Scaurus returned from Sardinia on 29 June to stand for the consulate and apparently did become a candidate. On 6 July, he was *postulatus* (indicted) for extortion by Triarius (Asc. 18–19C).[30] The bizarre coalition on behalf of Scaurus as an extortion defendant probably reveals more about the chaos that had already developed in Roman politics than about a principled attempt to protect a traditional balance of power between the courts and the electoral *comitia*. This chaos was leading to the formation of large coalitions, precisely because the republican aristocratic ethos of individual effort, albeit supported by familial and other connections, was no longer adequate to achieve success.

It is striking that this combination of a trial and an election campaign was unusual. One might expect that it would be common, since the situation of the younger Scaurus was typical under Roman *leges annales:* praetorship in 56, governorship in 55, trial for extortion and campaign for consulate (of 53) in 54. Yet the implication seems to be that this is a fairly rare occurrence; Asconius (19C, quoted earlier in this discussion) refers to a prosecution of the defendant's father, M. Aemilius Scaurus, consul in 115 (*TLRR* no. 37), who avoided prosecution by taking up a magistracy before the trial was over.[31] It would have been natural to prosecute a prospective rival for office in the year when he could be expected to run for office according to the rules of the *cursus honorum,* and that such a prosecution did not often happen, though there was no legal bar against it, suggests some social convention against the practice, as Gruen suggests.[32]

The extortion prosecution of Scaurus that took place during his campaign was certainly politically unwelcome to him, but it did not legally preclude him from running for the consulate. All we know is that a major criminal conviction would have ended his political career and that no prosecution of him could have begun during the period when he held the consulate, had he obtained that office. But as it turned out, he was not elected to the consulate of 53.

A fragment at the beginning of the text of the *Pro Scauro,* fragment g, characterizes the prosecution's case as an unorganized mass of disparate charges: "et quoniam congesta fuit accusatio magis acervo quodam criminum, non distinctione aliqua generum et varietate . . ." [And since the prosecution was heaped up with, one might rather say, a certain pile of charges, without any separation or variety of types . . .] (Halm, *Rhet. Lat. Min.* 357.11). The impression we get from the extant text of Cicero's defense, however, is that the case against Scaurus consisted of a very limited number of charges. This is misleading for three reasons. First, we possess only part of Cicero's speech. Second, that speech was only one of six given by the speakers for the defense. Third, Cicero refuses to refute individual charges made by the prosecution, preferring to speak at a more general level (*Scaur.* 19–20) and thereby allowing himself a much shorter speech. Whether or not the defense was justified in its claim that the *accusatio* lacked a coherent structure, it probably contained complexity on the order of Cicero's *Verrines*. For example, the prosecution in the case against Scaurus probably presented a section on Scaurus's *vita ante acta,* analogous to Cicero's first speech in the second *actio* of the trial against Verres.[33] There may well have been a tradition hostile to Scaurus, one that specifically related to avarice. Josephus (*AJ* 14.80–81 and *BJ* 1.159; see also App. *Syr.* 51) preserves the tradition that in 62 B.C., Scaurus, as Pompey's proquaestor in Syria, took a bribe to withdraw the army under his command from Nabataean Arabia. Asconius (27C) reports that Scaurus's house was lavishly decorated, containing four elegant marble columns.[34] Asconius (18C) also records that Scaurus gave unusually lavish games as aedile in 58 B.C.,[35] constructing a luxurious temporary theater that held eighty thousand spectators,[36] and that he went deeply into debt as a result. These sorts of allegation would have made a charge of extortion more plausible.

The prosecution did allege that Scaurus committed acts that met the formal criteria for extortion: "poposcit, imperavit, eripuit, coegit" [He demanded, requisitioned, seized, constrained] (*Scaur.* 18). Chief among these acts must have been those that constituted the "frumentarium crimen," which must have been analogous to the charges made by Cicero in the second *Verrines* (3). Cicero says that the prosecution lacked the financial accounts necessary to support such charges (*Scaur.* 18), but he admits that they have produced a mass of witnesses who all paint the same, consistent picture (18–20).[37] Sardinia was a major grain producer and supplier, and the governor's involvement in the grain business, which Cicero describes in all its complexity in the *Verrines,* must have presented Scaurus with the same opportunities in Sardinia as Verres had found in Sicily. But

since the text of the *Pro Scauro* ends while Cicero is dealing with the character of Scaurus, which precedes the section on the "frumentarium crimen"
(21), we can only guess at the nature of the detailed charges that Triarius
and others had brought against Scaurus.

The prosecution in the case against Scaurus argued that various acts of
violence and sexual transgression rendered Scaurus's extortionate activity
more *atrox* (heinous), much as Cicero caps his presentation of Verres'
extortion with a depiction, in the fifth speech of the second *actio*, of Verres'
penchant for cruelty and sexual excesses.[38] The two separate but related
incidents we hear about in the *Pro Scauro* relate to Bostar, a resident of
Nora, and to the wife of Aris. Although Bostar was planning to flee from
Sardinia before Scaurus arrived, he dined at the residence of Scaurus and
died immediately (*Scaur.* frags. h–i). It is possible that the prosecutor
claimed that Scaurus's motive for Bostar's death was financial and thus
strictly relevant to an extortion case. Scaurus intended, it was charged (as
far as we can judge from the relevant fragments), to supervise to his own
advantage the distribution of someone's (possibly Bostar's) estate (frags.
m–n). Whatever was involved, the prosecutor blamed Scaurus, whereas
Cicero reviled Bostar's mother. He relates that Aris fled Sardinia, leaving
his wife behind; she committed suicide (frags. o–p, *Scaur.* 5). The connection between the two incidents is the fact that the mother of Bostar is present in court (*Scaur.* 8), apparently as a witness. Cicero charges that she and
Aris planned to get married at Rome, once the wife of Aris was put out of
the way. Whereas the prosecution alleged that the wife of Aris had committed suicide to protect her chastity against the designs of Scaurus, Cicero
ridicules the idea that his client or any man would have desired her, who,
he says, was an ugly old woman; he argues that either she committed suicide when she discovered her husband's perfidy[39] or a freedman of Aris was
commissioned to murder her in a way that her death would appear to be
suicide. Cicero implies that the latter is the more likely scenario, and he
tries to strengthen this line of argument by pointing out that the freedman
immediately set out to Rome to report the news to Aris.[40] Cicero reports
that when Aris heard the news of his wife's death, he married Bostar's
mother (6–12).

Since Cicero does not deign to answer the prosecutor's charges one by
one, we cannot know what they were, but Cicero's unconvincing rebuttal
suggests that those charges had some claim to credibility. Cicero restricts
himself to the kind of argument recommended by Quintilian to dispose of

non-Roman witnesses: attack the credibility of them as a group.[41] Against the witnesses, Cicero makes three points—none very convincing, at least to a modern reader. First, Cicero argues that the fact that their testimony is consistent and unanimous shows that they are in a conspiracy against Scaurus (*Scaur.* 38). Second, he notes that this case is based on what one person has said and that this person is motivated by financial gain. If Cicero is not just referring here to the damages that would be awarded to the victims of Scaurus in the *litis aestimatio* should the jury vote to condemn him, perhaps he has in mind legal *praemia* offered to the person most responsible for the conviction of Scaurus.[42] Finally, Cicero argues that the Sardinians are untrustworthy (although Cicero admits that he himself is using the *laudationes* of Cn. Domitius Sincaicus and others who had received Roman citizenship from Pompey), alluding to their Punic and African ancestry and, to make matters worse, to the fact that many of them had been transported to Sardinia as a punishment for their crimes (39–44). The case against Scaurus was probably similar to the case against Verres, with one important difference, the lack of Roman citizen complainants. If Triarius was unable to find any Roman citizens who were willing to testify of wrongs done by Scaurus to them, that was a substantial weakness in his case. It might have been due simply to his haste in putting together the prosecution without traveling to Sardinia. Or perhaps Scaurus had been careful enough not to commit the same error as Verres and had limited his depredations to noncitizens.

Scaurus was acquitted, overwhelmingly. Asconius (28C) gives us the vote. Of twenty-two senators voting, only four voted to condemn; of twenty-three knights, only two; and of twenty-five *tribuni aerarii,* only two. Moreover, popular pressure forced Cato, the presiding magistrate, to poll the jury as to whether any of the prosecutors had committed *calumnia* (or, possibly, made it easier for him to do so, depending on how one reads the text of Asconius at this point). While Triarius escaped with no votes in the affirmative, Marius received two and each of the Pacuvii ten. Though not enough to convict them of *calumnia,* this process must have made it clear just how far short of victory the prosecution had fallen.[43]

CHAPTER FIVE

In C. Rabirium Postumum

he final case involving extortion for which we have an extant speech is the prosecution of Rabirius Postumus under the *lex Iulia de repetundis* (*TLRR* no. 305), probably at the end of 54 B.C. It is an atypical prosecution—in Cicero's phrase, "quasi quaedam appendicula causae iudicatae atque damnatae" [a sort of small addition to a case that has already been decided and in which a guilty verdict has been rendered] (*Rab. Post.* 8). This legal procedure took much less time than a regular trial; in fact, Ramsey argues that it was of a type that could conceivably be completed from start to finish within one day.[1] The *causa,* which had already been *iudicata* (adjudicated) by the time this case went to court, was a prosecution of Gabinius, the second of three he had to face that year. In the first (*TLRR* no. 296), he had already been acquitted on a charge of *maiestas* (roughly, "treason"), though by a fairly narrow vote (thirty-eight to thirty-two). In the second (*TLRR* no. 303), extortion was the charge, for his activities as governor of Syria between 57 and 54. He was at the same time being prosecuted for *ambitus* (*TLRR* no. 304).[2]

Cicero, in a letter to his brother, Quintus (*Q Fr.* 3.1.15), writes that C. Memmius (tribune of the plebs in 54) was one of a number of people who were interested in prosecuting Gabinius in 54. Clearly, Gabinius was seen as a likely target for prosecution after his return from the East, probably all the more so after his narrow acquittal in the *maiestas* trial. Memmius's position that year as tribune, a traditional platform for prosecution, made the task appropriate for him, but we do not know of any particular personal or political grounds for enmity. L. Ateius Capito (quaestor by 52), whom Cicero lists, in the same letter, as *subscriptor,* was a relative of the staunchly antitriumviral C. Ateius Capito (tribune of the plebs in 55), so it is possible that antitriumviral sentiment had something to do with his desire to participate. When Gabinius had been convicted by Memmius and Capito, Memmius went after Rabirius (*Rab. Post.* 7, 32). After this year of forensic activity, Memmius disappears from view.

Presumably, Cicero defended Rabirius because he had defended Gabinius in the main part of the trial. That act was, of course, bizarre by any account. Cicero had been a bitter enemy of Gabinius, who was one of the two consuls in 58 who supported Clodius, the tribune who drove Cicero into exile. Cicero had in fact been urged to prosecute Gabinius in the first trial (for *maiestas*) but had decided to adopt a neutral stance, at least in public, primarily to avoid offending Pompey, but also because he feared that a prosecution by him might backfire to Gabinius's advantage (*Q Fr.* 3.2.2).[3] Rabirius Postumus was the nephew and adoptive son of the man whom Cicero had defended before the people in 63 on a charge of *perduellio.*[4]

The legal basis for the prosecution of Rabirius Postumus was the *quo ea pecunia pervenerit* clause (translated "into whose hands the money had passed"), which was included in the *lex Iulia de repetundis,*[5] but which extended back to its predecessor, the *lex Cornelia* of Sulla, and to the *lex Servilia* (*Glauciae*) from the late second century B.C.[6] Cicero goes to some pains to emphasize that, although the *lex Iulia* is in general stricter than its predecessors, in this respect, it merely adopts the language of the earlier extortion laws. (His point is that his vast experience in dealing with extortion cases in different capacities, mostly under the *lex Cornelia,* is still relevant [*Rab. Post.* 9]). To understand the prosecution's case against Rabirius, we need to understand the legal implications of a case under the *quo ea pecunia pervenerit* clause of the *lex Iulia.*

Was Rabirius a *reus?* He probably was not,[7] although Cicero describes him as such, in very explicit terms.

Non igitur reus ex ea causa quae iudicata est redundat Postumus, sed est adreptus unus eques Romanus de pecuniis repetundis reus. . . . Quo de reo? De equite Romano. (*Rab. Post.* 11–12)

[Postumus is therefore not a defendant who is flowing over from a case that has already been decided but the one and only Roman knight who has been brought into court on a charge of extortion. . . . [A vote] about which defendant? About a Roman knight.]

Cicero's point is that it is outrageous that a Roman knight should be prosecuted for extortion. Cicero's language is clearly tendentious, since his failure to claim that the prosecution constituted a violation of the terms of the statute shows that the prosecution was in fact legal. Although, as I shall show later in this chapter, there are grounds for arguing that the prosecution did try to blacken the image of Rabirius, it may have made no legal difference how he had come into the money that Gabinius had been judged to have extorted.

It was enough for the prosecution to show that Gabinius's illegal proceeds had made their way into Rabirius's hands—possibly through perfectly legal transactions and even if Rabirius himself had done nothing illegal—and that this money should be used to complete the payment of damages owed by Gabinius, since insufficient funds had been collected from Gabinius himself. The rectitude of Rabirius's conduct was not a real issue. In fact, Cicero correctly points out that if funds sufficient to pay the assessed damages had been realized from guarantors (*praedes*) or from Gabinius's property, there would have been no question of seeking funds from Rabirius (*Rab. Post.* 37). Moreover, the fact that the *quo ea pecunia pervenerit* clause applied to anyone, whether senator or not, makes sense, because the point of this clause was not to punish someone who had committed extortion but to make sure that the victims received the damages awarded to them. As much as Cicero protests against the fact that a knight was the *reus* of an extortion case (10–12), he never complains that the prosecution is a violation of the statute.[8]

The *quo ea pecunia pervenerit* clause introduced by the *lex Servilia* (*Glauciae*) added an additional safeguard to protect the interests of victims in their claims to restitution, since it made it more likely that the full amount would eventually be collected and less likely that victims would have to settle for partial compensation. To the extent that extortion laws moved in the direction of multiple damages, it became less likely that the full legal amount would ever be collected.[9] The *lex repetundarum* (lines 56–57) had laid down that money to pay the damages assessed would be taken from guarantors (*praedes*) or from seizure of a requisite part of the condemned man's estate. In the *litis aestimatio,* the jury that had rendered the verdict would make an assignment to individuals (or to their representatives) of the sum appropriate for the level of damages they had suffered. The provision of double damages made it much less likely that funds sufficient for this purpose could be found. In other words, it was quite possible for a governor to extort more money in one year than he possessed in the rest of his estate. The *quo ea pecunia pervenerit* clause of the *lex Servilia* (*Glauciae*) may have been designed to solve this problem that the epigraphic extortion law had created.[10]

The trial of Gabinius provides a clear example of the need for the *quo ea pecunia pervenerit* provision. In it, we see in part a reflection of the procedures of the *lex repetundarum,* which were retained in the *lex Cornelia.* Damages were assessed against Gabinius, but insufficient funds were drawn from *praedes* and his estate. Then, the *quo ea pecunia pervenerit* provision of the *lex Iulia* took effect (see n. 5). It is not surprising that sufficient funds were not forthcoming, for the amount of money was enormous: Ptolemy was alleged to have promised to Gabinius the sum of ten thousand talents,[11] as a bribe to restore him to power.[12] Even if Gabinius had saved every sesterce that he took from Ptolemy, it is hardly likely that he would have had either another ten thousand talents available to pay double damages or more if the *lex Iulia* stipulated an even higher multiplier. The prosecution charged that this money had found its way into Rabirius's hands.

We need to try to reconstruct the order of financial events that led to the trial, although Cicero does not make any effort to provide a clear narrative in his speech. Shatzman provides the following summary of events in the fifties regarding Ptolemy Auletes and Rome.

> One group of Roman bankers and financiers, of whom we know only the name of Rabirius Postumus, made a large loan to Auletes in the year 59, intended to provide some of the money needed for the payment due to Caesar and Pompey, who seem to have had some responsibility towards the lenders. After his escape from Egypt, Auletes appeared in Rome and applied for further loans and the creditors consented, being assured that Pompey would restore the king. It appears that this did not satisfy the king's needs and, being short of money, he resorted to more borrowing, this time from a group of bankers associated with Lentulus. The first group succeeded when Gabinius, Pompey's associate, restored the king and

Rabirius got an office that enabled him to collect the money. The others did not expect Rabirius to take care of their interests, and some of them set out for Egypt, but, so far as we know, in vain.[13]

In 59, Caesar arranged for recognition of Ptolemy as king for six thousand talents, or thirty-six million denarii, and Ptolemy contracted a debt of six thousand talents to Pompey and Caesar (Sue. *Iul.* 54).[14] A few years later, Rabirius lent money (his own and his friends') to Ptolemy, when the latter was in exile at Rome, for his "travel expenses" [ad sumptum itineris] (*Rab. Post.* 6) and for maintaining a royal establishment. Once back in power (in 55),[15] Ptolemy paid a bribe of ten thousand talents to Gabinius;[16] this money could have come from Ptolemy's subjects or at least in part from Rabirius's loan, and in any case, the source for the repayment of the loan would have been Ptolemy's royal revenues.[17] When the bribe was paid,[18] Rabirius, who was functioning as Ptolemy's treasurer (*dioecetes; Rab. Post.* 22, 28),[19] took a 10 percent commission (or so the prosecution charged); Cicero professes doubt as to whether this was charged in addition to the ten thousand talents or deducted from that sum (*Rab. Post.* 30).[20] It is unclear how the actual transfer of the money took place; Rabirius may have registered a debit in his account for Ptolemy and a credit in his account for Gabinius, as well as a credit in his own account for the commission, with no physical money actually changing hands.[21] The prosecution charged that Rabirius had the money hidden away: "at habet et celat. Sunt enim qui ita loquantur. . . . 'occultat pecuniam Postumus, latent regiae divitiae'" [But he possesses the money and is hiding it. There are those who talk in this way. . . . "Postumus is hiding the money, royal riches lie concealed"] (38–45). It was commonly believed that Rabirius had made use of his activity in maritime commerce to launder the money, while at the same time realizing a profit on it. Though most of his cargo was comprised of cheap gimcracks, the cargo of one small ship remained unknown, and Cicero cannot deny the common belief, based on the crew's course and on their bragging, that this cargo was very valuable (40). On this basis, the prosecution can claim that Gabinius's money had reached Rabirius and that, therefore, Rabirius's property could be seized to pay off the unpaid damages.

If this reconstruction is correct, what Rabirius did before Gabinius received the ten thousand talents from Ptolemy is not legally relevant, nor is the rectitude of his conduct thereafter. In essence, he was holding Gabinius's money, which he had possibly invested in maritime commerce, and the state had the right to recover that property.[22] If the ten thousand talents were extorted funds—and the court had already ruled that they were—they could not come into the legitimate ownership of Rabirius by possession (*usucapio*). Paul records the relevant prohibition: "Quod contra legem repetundarum proconsuli vel praetori donatum est, non poterit usu capi" [Anything given to a proconsul or praetor in breach of the statute on extortion cannot be usucapted] (*Dig.* 48.11.8 pr.; trans. Robinson, ed. Watson).[23] This prohibition parallels the prohibition against acquiring ownership of *res furtivae* (stolen goods) through *usucapio* (Gai. *Inst.* 2.45, 49), a prohibition that goes back to the Twelve Tables.[24] If Yaron is right, this prohibition was confirmed by the *lex Atinia,* which he dates to the early or middle second century B.C.—in other words, in approximately the same period as the first extortion law (the *lex Calpurnia* of 149 B.C.).[25] Since extortion is a kind of *furtum,* it makes sense that the same principle regarding *usucapio* would apply to both extortion and theft.

Cicero attempts to cloud the matter with a misleading argument, one that is all the more confusing because the text seems to be corrupt. In Clark's Oxford Classical Texts edition (1909), it reads:

> Age, cedo, cum is qui pecuniam Postumo debuit non huic, sed Gabinio dederit, condemnato Gabinio utrum illi quo ea pecunia *pervenerit* an huic dicenda causa *est.* (*Rab. Post.* 38)

> [Come, tell me, since he [Ptolemy] who owed the money to Postumus has given it not to him [Postumus] but to Gabinius, who should stand trial now that Gabinius has been condemned, that person in whose possession the money has ended up, or the defendant [Postumus]?]

Cicero is highlighting the fact that Postumus is a victim in this whole matter, not a beneficiary, since he has not received repayment of the loan he made to Ptolemy. Olechowska, in her Teubner text (1981), adopts the reading "condemnato Gabinio utrum illo <capite> QUO EA PECUNIA sit an UNDE EA" [whether, after the condemnation of Gabinius, [the matter should be investigated] under the heading WHITHER THE MONEY or WHENCE THE MONEY]. According to this reading, the contrast is not between Ptolemy and Postumus but between a focus on the final destination of the money and a focus on the original source of the money. Both the destination and the source could be Rabirius Postumus, since Rabirius had lent money to Ptolemy, who had paid money as a bribe to Gabinius, some of which was deducted by Postumus on his own account. Klodt favors Clark's solution but tentatively modifies Clark's text to read, "utrum illi de ea pecunia an huic dicenda est" [whether the former [Ptolemy] or the latter [Postumus] should stand trial about this money], since, Klodt argues, the king could not be prosecuted under the *quo ea pecunia pervenerit* clause of the extortion law but could be tried for unpaid debts.[26] Cicero's overall point seems to be that since Rabirius Postumus did not benefit from this financial triangle (i.e., Ptolemy has failed to pay back his loan to him), it is not fair that he should be the one to suffer for Gabinius's misdeeds.

Cicero bases his interpretation of the extortion laws, or, rather, his understanding of how they have been administered in the past, on his experience as a prosecutor, juror, praetor in the extortion court, and *patronus* in many extortion cases. He says that to his knowledge, no one has ever been brought to trial under the *quo ea pecunia pervenerit* clause who had not already been summoned in the *litis aestimatio,* and no one was summoned to that proceeding who had not been named as involved in the case by witnesses or records. Since the name of *Postumus* had not come up in the *litis aestimatio* resulting from the condemnation of Gabinius or in the main trial of Gabinius that led to the *litis aestimatio,* it makes no sense, Cicero argues, to bring his name up at this point (*Rab. Post.* 9–10).

There is no logical reason why the receiver of extorted monies would necessarily be mentioned in an extortion case.[27] It is possible that such a person would not have been named in the *litis aestimatio* because he had suffered no damage at the hands of the condemned defendant and that he would not have been named at the trial itself because he had not played a significant role in the extortion. In the case of Postumus, specifically, there is a further reason not to mention him. It is important to remember that in an extortion trial, the normal role for the governor is villain, and the inhabitants of the province are usually the victims. In the trial of Gabinius, the defendant must have been cast by the prosecution as villain, with Ptolemy, the king of the long-suffering Egyptians, as his victim. In that trial, Rabirius, Ptolemy's *dioecetes,* was neither villain, since he was not working for Gabinius, nor victim, since he was an agent, not a principal. There was no reason for either the prosecutor or the *patronus* to bring up Rabirius's name in the trial of Gabinius.

In the quasi trial against Rabirius, the prosecution attacked the character and conduct of Rabirius, rather than just limiting itself to the legal argument. Evidently, the prosecutors believed that it was too risky to present a limited, purely legal argument and that it was advisable to rouse the jurors against the defendant. They had a store of ill will against Rabirius to draw on. He had lorded it over the people of Alexandria ("dominatus est enim . . . Alexandreae," *Rab. Post.* 39), and as a result, witnesses from Alexandria testified against him, although they had spoken for Gabinius (31). Rabirius had a reputation for display and boasting ("ostentatio" and "gloria," 38), which Cicero tries to use to his client's advantage by arguing that such a person would not hide his wealth, as the prosecutors allege that he has done (38, 45).[28] Rabirius had evidently incurred enmity by enriching himself, although Cicero claims that he had done so legitimately ("remque praeterea bonis et honestis rationibus auxisset" [he had moreover increased his wealth by good and honorable means], 38). Finally, Rabirius had even ostentatiously adopted Greek dress (25).

We can conclude that Rabirius had earned general and undeniable disfavor. This conclusion is based on the primary defense that Cicero offers: that Rabirius was acting under compulsion. Cicero argues that when in Egypt and Alexandria, Rabirius was *in custodia regia* (22), his lending of his own and his friends' money had put him in a position where he had to support Ptolemy to be able to recoup these funds (25), he had no choice but to become the *dioecetes* of the king (28), he was like someone who has fallen into the hands of enemies or brigands (29), and he had to obey the king (29). He acted foolishly, admits Cicero (22); some would say he had excessively high hopes, others that he had made a serious error, and he himself that had been crazy (25).[29] It is no wonder that the prosecutors believed that Rabirius's unpopularity could only clinch the case against him.

Not surprisingly, the prosecution in the case against Rabirius relied on the evidence of witnesses from the East, specifically Greeks from Alexandria. As one must expect, Cicero tries to discredit their testimony, on both general and specific grounds. The general ground is that in comedy (*mimi*), the Alexandrians are stereotypical tricksters and cheaters (*Rab. Post.* 35).[30] The specific ground is that in the trial of Gabinius, the Alexandrians had argued against the charge that Gabinius had received a bribe of ten thousand talents, yet now they affirmed the opposite (34). Cicero claims that this is an example of their clumsiness ("insulsitas," 36),[31] but the justification for the inconsistency put forward by the prosecution may have been closer to the truth. Memmius alleged that Pompey had twisted the Alexandrians' arms to support Gabinius, just as he had done to Cicero to obtain his services as *patronus* for Gabinius (32). Pompey's name clearly

exerted great influence in this pair of trials. At the trial of Gabinius, a deposition from Pompey that the defendant had taken money only for military
purposes was repeatedly read (34). A much more minor point, but at least
as telling, is Cicero's attempt to establish a connection between Rabirius
and Pompey and almost to imply that Pompey had encouraged the original
relationship between Rabirius and Ptolemy. Cicero mentions the legally
irrelevant point that the loan documents were written at Pompey's Alban
villa, albeit when Pompey was away (6). The most likely conclusion is that
Pompey was determined to save Gabinius and compelled both Cicero and
the Alexandrians to defend him, whereas he was willing to sacrifice such
small fry as Rabirius Postumus or might have been willing and able to help
make good the financial loss to Rabirius, huge as it would be. Therefore, in
the trial of Rabirius, the Alexandrians were free to say what they really
thought of the defendant. There is no doubt that they genuinely detested
him; they had imprisoned him and forced him to flee (39).

It is hard to tell whether the prosecution won its case against Rabirius,
for two reasons. First, we are not sure about the career of Rabirius Postumus after the trial. Second, since this was not a true extortion trial, there
was no question of a guilty verdict that would necessitate exile or *infamia*
and consequent exclusion from office holding; therefore, we cannot gauge
the outcome of the trial by Rabirius's subsequent career.[32] Moreover, it is
not clear that a verdict of "redigam" [I shall restore] would have resulted in
Rabirius's bankruptcy and ruin. On the first point, Rabirius served as proconsul in Cilicia, probably in 47,[33] but this might have been due to Caesar's
influence, rather than to normal eligibility. On the second point, the
pathetic picture Cicero paints of Rabirius in dire poverty ("umbram equi-
tis Romani et imaginem" [a mere shadow—a mere wraith—of a Roman
knight], *Rab. Post.* 41) should not be accepted without question. It is conceivable that Rabirius was required to pay the money but that Caesar (who
Cicero says was sustaining Rabirius), Pompey (who had worked hard to
secure the acquittal of Gabinius), and perhaps also their wealthy triumviral
colleague Crassus came up with the funds to pay the court for Rabirius and
leave his civil status intact.[34] In that case, since Rabirius would have been
saved from bankruptcy and would have avoided *infamia* (not having been
charged with, or found guilty of, any crime), he would not have been disqualified from future office holding. That Cicero published his *Pro Rabirio*
is an argument, though not an irrefutable one, for a judicial outcome in
Rabirius's favor.[35]

Part Two
Electoral Malpractice

T he post-Sullan period saw a growth of legislation against various kinds of electoral malpractice.[1] The Sullan increase in the number of quaestorships from eight to twenty (Tac. *Ann.* 11.22) must have considerably increased the number of candidates eligible for higher office,[2] and this competition must have been particularly intense for the consulate, which was still held by only two people each year. Cloud suggests that the breakdown of traditional *clientela* (clientship) relationships and an increased role for money may have created a need for this kind of legislation.[3] That view might seem to reflect unwarranted nostalgia for the past, but the introduction of the secret ballot may well have provided voters with more independence.[4] The law may have discouraged bribery by making it more difficult for the person supplying the bribe to know whether the recipient was living up to his end of the bargain.

The law on bribery became stricter over time. Before the *lex Calpurnia* of 67 B.C. was an *ambitus* law almost certainly passed by Sulla (*Schol. Bob.* 78St). All we know about this law is that those who were convicted under it were forbidden to hold office for the next ten years. The *lex Calpurnia* was passed as the result of intense political pressure to pass a tougher law, possibly due to pressure from former tribunes who could run for office now that the Sullan disabilities on them had been lifted.[5] Its punishments were permanent disqualification from office holding, expulsion from the Senate, and a fine. In 63, the consul Cicero successfully proposed a law that enjoined a ten-year period of exile.[6] The law was further strengthened by Pompey in 52, possibly by exile for life and a stiffer fine.[7] It appears that these laws dealt only with the giving of bribes and that the candidates themselves were the primary targets, although the trend in later legislation was to include the candidates' assistants,[8] as well as to define the crime of *ambitus* more specifically.[9] A provision of the *lex Tullia* made it harder for defendants to claim poor health to delay proceedings (Cic. *Mur.* 47).

A related law, probably handled by the *ambitus* court, was the *lex Licinia de sodaliciis,* passed by Crassus in 55. This law forbade electoral combinations, which the Roman system of multiple voting for multiple offices encouraged. It is debated whether this law was related to bribery; it seems that bribery was not an essential part of these illegal combinations but that where there was bribery, there would almost necessarily be illegal combinations, since organization was required to distribute money to enough people to make a difference. Under the *lex Licinia,* the selection of jurors was done in an unusual way that gave more power to the prosecutor, so it may have been easier to secure a conviction under this law than under an *ambitus* law.[10] Also, the punishment under the *lex Licinia* was capital, so the consequences of conviction were more severe.

Electoral bribery and illegal electoral combinations are inherently charges that involve many people, since organization is necessary for both of them. But the people involved have no incentive to come forward as prosecutors, and the victims—the defeated candidates—may well have been quite ignorant of the details of the hidden machinations that were happening behind the scenes, although they may have known of or at least suspected foul play and were ready to prosecute. For that reason, the *ambitus* laws made extensive use of *praemia* to encourage those with knowledge of electoral misconduct to come forward with what they knew, so as to encourage at least a few of the many people involved to inform on their confederates (see chap. 7, n. 47).

CHAPTER SIX

In L. Licinium Murenam

he prosecution of L. Licinius Murena in 63, when he was consul-elect, presents a straightforward case for electoral bribery, or *ambitus*. A disappointed candidate put together a coalition to prosecute one of the victors, who responded by collecting a team of highly competent and politically influential orators. They were able to fend off the attack, and Murena went on to serve as consul in 62.

That Ser. Sulpicius Rufus (praetor in 65) prosecuted calls for little comment, as it was probably quite usual for a defeated candidate to participate in the prosecution of a successful rival, as had P. Rutilius Rufus, L. Aurelius Cotta, and L. Manlius Torquatus (respectively, *TLRR* nos. 34, 200, 201). The goal of such an effort was what the defeated candidates for the consulate of 65 accomplished in 66: the disqualification of their successful rivals and the substitution of themselves. Münzer makes the case that the *adulescens* Ser. Sulpicius who joined Ser. Sulpicius Rufus in the prosecution was the son of the defeated candidate, although this is nowhere explicitly stated. Münzer points to the parallel of L. Manlius Torquatus supporting his father in the prosecution of P. Cornelius Sulla for bribery in 66. If the identification is correct, Cicero's wording is rather indirect: "Accusat Ser. Sulpicius, sodalis filius,[1] cuius ingenio paterni omnes necessarii munitiores esse debebant" [one of the prosecutors is Servius Sulpicius, the son of a fraternity brother [to Murena] and by whose talent all his father's friends ought to have been rendered safer] (*Mur.* 56). Rather than just saying that Sulpicius senior is a *sodalis* of Murena, Cicero implies this by saying that Sulpicius junior is a son of a *sodalis* of Murena and that he should therefore spend his time defending his father's *sodales*, rather than prosecuting them.[2] C. Postumius[3] is described by Cicero as a *paternus amicus* of Murena (56), but he was probably related to Sulpicius senior by marriage, possibly through his sister. The "star" of the prosecution team ("fundamentum ac robur totius accusationis" [a foundation and mainstay of the whole prosecution], 58) was M. Porcius Cato, *tribunus plebis designatus* in 63.[4] He had sworn to prosecute anyone who used bribery in connection with the consular elections for 62, with the exception of his brother-in-law, D. Iunius Silanus, who was married to his sister Servilia (Plut. *Cat. Min.* 21). Cato was a more than competent orator.[5]

The team for the defense was more distinguished, including Cicero, the best orator in Rome and incumbent consul; Hortensius (consul in 69), the second best orator in Rome; and Crassus (consul in 70), the second most powerful politician at Rome after Pompey, who was still in the East. Cicero (*Brut.* 233) ranked Crassus as one of the most powerful orators at Rome for a period of years, despite his rather pedestrian speaking.[6]

Unfortunately, relatively few facts about the prosecution case survive, because Hortensius and Crassus provided the detailed rebuttal of specific charges of bribery, leaving Cicero as the final speaker to concentrate on the political consequences of the case (*Mur.* 48, 54). Following the division established by the prosecution, Cicero divides his speech into three parts: (1) the defendant's private life, (2) merits of the candidates (*contentio dignitatis*), and (3) *crimina ambitus* (11). He deals with all these areas to some extent, and he even covers the most technical and already discussed area (the *crimina ambitus*) at the defendant's request, or so he says (54). But the extant text omits some of the technical rebuttal, summarizing it with the rubrics "DE POSTUMI CRIMINIBUS" and "DE SERVI ADULESCENTIS (CRIMINIBUS)" (57).[7] A little earlier in the text (54), Cicero refers to the fact that Postumius spoke about the revelations of the bribery agents ("de divisorum indiciis")[8] and the money that had been seized from them ("de deprehensis pecuniis"). These phrases suggest that the prosecution had found a "smoking gun": cash that bribery agents admitted was to be distributed in the consular elections. We do not know how the defense tried to deal with this concrete evidence, but we can surmise that it argued (1) that the *divisores* (distributors [of bribes]) were not reliable witnesses and (2) that the money was being spent to support another candidate. The prosecution would have surely argued that the money was likely to have been spent to benefit the candidates who actually won the election.[9] Sulpicius junior spoke about the centuries of knights, to which he belonged as a young man of senatorial standing who had not yet entered the Senate himself (54). While we do not know what the related charges were, it is reasonable to speculate that those committing the bribery had targeted the eighteen equestrian centuries, since they possessed considerable influence in the centuriate assembly.[10]

The accusations of Cato relating directly to *ambitus* were based on a senatus consultum passed in 63 to clarify certain points about the *lex Calpurnia* (*Mur.* 54, 67).[11] In 63, on the motion of the consul Cicero, the Senate made three clarifications of the provisions of the *lex Calpurnia* (*Mur.* 67), concluding that *ambitus* had occurred:

1. "si mercede obviam candidatis issent" [if the candidates paid to have people meet them],
2. "si conducti sectarentur" [if people were hired to accompany candidates about], and
3. "si gladiatoribus volgo locus tributim et item prandia si volgo essent data" [if places at gladiatorial games were given out indiscriminately by tribe and if dinners were given out indiscriminately by tribe].

Cato charged Murena under each of these points. First, a huge crowd had met Murena when he returned to Italy. (Cicero countered that they had turned out without any financial inducement and had included clients; neighbors; fellow tribesmen; soldiers of Lucullus, under whom Murena had served from 73 to 69 B.C.; and even Postumius himself [69].) Second, a retinue went out with Murena in his campaign—but not for pay, retorts Cicero (70). Third, games and meals were provided indiscriminately to tribes (72). Here, Cicero seizes on the meaning of *volgo* and on the distinction between the candidate and his supporters, who can perform favors for the voters that it would be illegal for the candidate himself to perform. For example, he argues that whereas L. Pinarius Natta,[12] the stepson of Murena, engaged in this sort of activity to win over his fellow knights for Murena,

Murena did not engage in the activity himself and therefore cannot be held responsible. Cicero also notes that a Vestal virgin[13] gave Murena her seat at the gladiatorial games. Cicero argues that Cato's interpretation of the provisions would prevent the leading men in the state from surrounding themselves with their *tribules* (fellow tribesmen), and he points to a mere *praefectus fabrum* (aide-de-camp)[14] who was apparently criticized for once providing seats to his *tribules* (73, after a lacuna). Just as Cicero defends Murena against charges based on his own *lex Tullia,* so he defends him on charges relating to the senatus consultum about the *lex Calpurnia,* a senatus consultum that Cicero had proposed.[15] If the prosecution anticipated Cicero's presentation of a lenient interpretation of the statute, it probably argued that a much stricter interpretation was necessary if the laws were not to be a mere sham, since presumably any viable candidate could find someone in whose name he could act. If the friends of a candidate could shield him from the charge of giving out favors indiscriminately, by doing so on his behalf to people to whom they had some preexisting connection, presumably any viable candidate could find enough supporters to do so and thereby circumvent the law.[16]

Beyond this legal argument, Cato made the general point that it was wrong to let appeals to the appetites influence decisions about the election of magistrates (*Mur.* 74). He even argued that to seek imperium by such appeals was more appropriate to "lenocinium" [pandering] to spoilt youth. This is part of Cato's Stoic outlook, which Cicero mocks (60–66).

The second part of the prosecutor's case relates to an argument from plausibility that was apparently specific to cases of electoral bribery. If a long shot as candidate was successful in the election, it was plausible—so the argument went—that this candidate had committed bribery.[17] Along these lines, Sulpicius senior argued that he came from a patrician family of a much more distinguished lineage than Murena's plebeian family, which had never held the consulate. He noted that Murena and he had competed at earlier stages of the *cursus honorum* and that he had been returned before Murena in the election for quaestor (*Mur.* 18) and again in the election for the praetorship (35); in other words, he had shown himself a better vote getter.[18] Moreover, Sulpicius argued, instead of spending his time abroad, fighting against Rome's enemies, he had devoted himself to the support of his fellow citizens, providing them with legal advice as a jurisconsult (21). Cicero (15–16) attacks the premises on which Sulpicius's argument was based. Murena's family, though plebeian, was by no means undistinguished, Cicero argues. His father had reached the praetorship (88 B.C.?),[19] whereas the family of Sulpicius, although of ancient distinction, had slipped into obscurity in the two generations previous to him. The prosecutor's father was *equestri loco,* though his grandfather probably had reached the Senate.[20] Cicero's most memorable criticism of the prosecution's argument from plausibility comes in his celebrated *Juristenkomik* (23–29), his disparagement of the jurisconsult and the technicalities in the law that are Sulpicius's specialty, as opposed to a military or oratorical career (29–30). Although Cato had dismissed the Third Mithridatic War as having been fought against "mulierculae" [little women] (31), Cicero maintains that it was crucial to Rome's security (31–34). Cicero also contrasts the opportunities for gaining political popularity in his role of urban praetor, by handing down fair decisions, as opposed to the ill will that Sulpicius must have incurred as praetor in the *peculatus* court, from which condemned scribes and disappointed Sullan veterans were sure to leave bearing a grudge, not to mention the jurors who were compelled to sit on this court (41–42).[21] Finally, Cicero argues that Sulpicius's announced intention to prosecute for bribery while still a candidate cast a pall over his campaign (43–45), on which he should have concentrated, and distracted him from it (45–47), leading him to desperate measures, such as giving more voting power to freedmen.[22] Cicero argues (43–49) that this conduct contrasts with the comportment of an effective candidate, as described in this speech and in the *Commentariolum Petitionis.*

The remaining part of the case against Murena related to his private life (*Mur.* 11). To judge by Cicero's refutation of it, this came under two headings: Asia and dancing. The prosecution raised his career in Asia: "obiecta est enim Asia" [Asia was laid as a charge against him] (11), and "habet Asia suspicionem luxuriae quandam" [Asia carries a certain suggestion of extravagance] (12). Murena's experience of Asia came from two military campaigns: first with his father in the early eighties, ending with a triumph of his father in 81, in which the son took part (11, 15); and second as legate to Lucullus (20; 73–69 B.C.). It is likely that the prosecution brought forward specific incidents that had taken place in Asia. The prosecution also called Murena a *saltator* (dancer), a term of abuse (13).[23] In his rebuttal, Cicero does not discount the seriousness of the charge but rather takes the opposite tack: since the charge is so heinous, for it to be credible it must be accompanied by concomitant actions—in this case, debauchery. Cicero argues that in the absence of such evidence, the charge must be false, but it is likely that the prosecution had referred to some specific incident or incidents, which Cicero ignores rather than trying to palliate their effect.

The other personal argument voiced by the prosecution in Murena's trial revolved around Cicero's own participation in the case, which both Sulpicius senior and Cato attacked. Sulpicius accused Cicero of inconsistency: Cicero had supported Sulpicius in the campaign but now defended his competitor, the man whom Sulpicius was prosecuting (*Mur.* 7–10). In a tripartite attack (3–6), Cato also attacked Cicero for an alleged reversal: (1) Cicero is a consul, (2) he carried a law against *ambitus,* and (3) his leniency toward Murena contrasts with the severity he has already shown (toward Catiline, who at the time of the trial had already fled Rome and taken to arms). Cicero replies (1) that it is entirely appropriate for a consul to defend a consul-designate, (2) that support for a law is not inconsistent with the defense of a man who has not violated that law, and (3) that he is by nature full of "lenitas" [leniency] and "misericordia" [mercy] but that duty forced him to defend the state with vigor. Cato's attack affords Cicero an opening to "conciliare" [win over] the jurors with a "captatio benevolentiae" [attempt to capture goodwill],[24] which may explain why he leads his speech with this section, after his exordium.

An apparent inconsistency in the tone of the *Pro Murena,* which ranges from serious to light, may seem puzzling.[25] In fact, however, a consistent strategy imbues the speech. Cato and Sulpicius senior—and probably the two lesser prosecutors as well—conveyed a sense of moral outrage against Murena: a candidate for the consulate had profited from election bribery. Cicero, by contrast, projects an image of liberal generosity: not only should one overlook the defendant's shortcomings, but one should allow the "homines tenues" [lowly people] their little pleasures in supporting the candidates to whom they feel allegiance (*Mur.* 70). In keeping with this tone, Sulpicius and Cato are treated as deserving respect—even if they have taken themselves too seriously. Cicero does not make use of the argument that Cato's threat of prosecution against electoral bribe givers excluded Cato's brother-in-law Silanus, who was also elected to the consulate of 62 (Plut. *Cat. Min.* 21). Such a criticism would have been inconsistent with the persona adopted by Cicero of someone who wants to "live and let live," in keeping with traditional Roman social ties and values. The mood of leniency prepares the audience to take seriously Cicero's stance that Murena's possible conviction at the end of 63 and the subsequent vacancy in the consulate for the next year posed a grave danger to the state. As Leeman (1982, 228) concludes, this anxiety may have been sincere. By adopting a mild-tempered and generous persona in most of the speech and implying that he, unlike his opponents, is not philosophically inclined to doom-and-gloom diatribes, Cicero makes his listeners take seriously the picture of a government threatened with crisis that he presents to the jurors.

Murena went on to lead an unremarkable life. Whether or not his disqualification from the consulate would have exacerbated the political crisis at Rome, his tenure of the consulate was undistinguished. Cicero mentions a Murena in 47 and 45 B.C. (*Att.* 11.13.1, 13.50.4), but Münzer ("Licinius," no. 118, *RE* 13 [1927]: 443–44) and Shackleton Bailey (*CLA*, 5:281; see also *CLF*, 1:371) argue that this cannot be the consul of 62 reemerging after all those years.[26] It is possible that despite the acquittal, Murena had been damaged by the trial and quickly became a political nonentity. His absence from the sources may indicate that he suffered obscurity in his later years or that he died soon after 62.

CHAPTER SEVEN

In Cn. Plancium

Iuventius Laterensis was, as far as we can tell, a more than usually upright person. As quaestor and proquaestor in Cyrene (Cic. *Planc.* 13, 63), he balanced his obligations to Roman subjects and the *publicani* ("Cyrenis liberalem in publicanos, iustum in socios fuisse" [At Cyrene he was generous to the tax farmers and fair to the provincials], 63). In 59, rather than put himself in a position where he would have to swear to uphold Caesar's two agrarian laws, he withdrew his candidacy for the tribunate of 58 and was thought to have acted honorably in so doing ("Laterensis existimatur laute fecisse quod tribunatum pl. petere destitit ne iuraret" [Laterensis . . . is thought to have made a gentlemanly gesture in giving up his candidacy for the Tribunate rather than swear it], Cic. *Att.* 2.18.2; trans. Shackleton Bailey]). In 51, he was the presiding magistrate whom we have seen struggling conscientiously, if not always correctly, to master the intricacies of the extortion law (Cic. *Fam.* 8.8.2; see, in the present book, chap. 5, n. 8). In the kaleidoscopic events of 43, he is described by L. Munatius Plancus (consul in 42) as a "vir sanctissimus" [very upright man], but despite his good qualities, he appears to be somewhat at sea (Cic. *Fam.* 10.21.3; cf. 10.23.4). When, against Laterensis's advice, Lepidus joined forces with Antony although Antony had been declared an enemy of the state, Laterensis committed suicide,

128

showing himself, in the judgment of Velleius Paterculus (2.63.2), "vir vita ac morte consentaneus" [a man consistent in life and death]. This exemplary citizen, moreover, had consular ancestors on both sides of his family; if his virtue had not sufficed, one would have expected that his ancestry would have prevailed over a weak field of *novi homines* in the election for curule aedile. That did not happen, however, nor was he able to unseat one of his rivals by an *ambitus* prosecution. Why did this candidate and prosecutor, "nec minore facundia quam generis nobilitate praedit(us)" [endowed with no less eloquence than nobility of origin] (*Schol. Bob.* 153St), fail in both endeavors, when he had a strong prima facie case that his opponent could not have won without foul play of some kind?

The trial of Cn. Plancius (*TLRR* no. 293) took place in 54, under the *lex Licinia de sodaliciis,* which had been passed by the consul Crassus the previous year.[1] The trial ended by September 54 (Cic. *Q Fr.* 3.1.11). We know that electoral *comitia* had been held in 55, in which Plancius had been victorious. But that result had been disqualified because of violence,[2] and the concern voiced about bribery at the time may also have been part of the rationale for overturning the results, though Cicero (*Planc.* 49) claims that the time between the declaration of this election and the voting was so short that no bribery could have taken place.

Cicero's portrayal of the two prosecutors, Laterensis and L. Cassius Longinus (tribune of the plebs in 44),[3] is distorted not by vituperation but by an almost ostentatious display of goodwill toward them. They appear to be beyond reproach, a defeated candidate of high caliber serving as *accusator* and a young talented orator supporting him as *subscriptor*.[4] Rather than denying his ties of *amicitia* with Laterensis and his gratitude toward him, Cicero gladly admits their relationship (*Planc.* 5). As Craig points out,[5] this description of their relationship is supported by the ten passages in other works where Cicero refers to him. Moreover, Cicero pointedly declines the invitation of Cassius Longinus to find *vitia* in the character of Laterensis (63). Laterensis came from a distinguished family, had shown loyalty and patriotism in Cicero's hour of need, and was clearly a strong candidate for the aedileship. L. Cassius Longinus receives similar praise from Cicero, who describes him as "ille omni et humanitate et virtute ornatus adulescens" [that young man equipped both with all culture and all virtue] (58). But by mentioning the study that Cassius has devoted to reading Cicero's published speeches (66) and by complimenting Cassius on his speech (58), Cicero deftly suggests to the jurors that they should be

on their guard against rhetorical cunning, while at the same time emphasizing his opponent's youthful inexperience and his own seniority. As Craig
suggests,[6] by emphasizing that Cassius is an orator, he implicitly highlights
Plancius's unfamiliarity with and indifference to rhetoric (62).[7]

The defense team is equally distinguished, although unoriginal, comprised of Cicero and Hortensius. It has been disputed whether Hortensius
in fact appeared for the defense. The key passage from Cicero's speech says
that Hortensius had spoken the day before about the method of jury selection and the correct interpretation of the relevant legal language and,
moreover, that he spoke with authority, since he had previously (in February 56) proposed this method in the form of a senatus consultum.

> Quid? huiusce rei tandem obscura causa est, an et agitata tum cum
> ista in senatu res agebatur, et disputata hesterno die copiosissime a
> Q. Hortensio, cui tum est senatus adsensus? (*Planc.* 37)

> [Well, I ask you, is the rationale of this decision obscure, or was it
> discussed both on that occasion when the matter was brought
> before the Senate, and argued very fully yesterday by Quintus Hort-
> ensius, with whom the Senate on that occasion agreed?]

Linderski (1961b) has shown that Cicero's phrase "cui tum est senatus
adsensus" refers to a speech of Hortensius on the subject, delivered in the
Senate in 56, while "disputata hesterno die" refers to a second speech, delivered the day before by Hortensius as the first advocate for the defendant.[8]
Cicero's support for Plancius might seem natural enough because Plancius,
as quaestor in Macedonia, had protected him in exile,[9] were it not for the
fact that Laterensis had also rendered him outstanding service in that
period (*Planc.* 2, 86). Although Laterensis can claim to be hurt by Cicero's
desertion of him (5) and can attempt to downplay Plancius's service to
Cicero (4), he cannot claim, as Sulpicius could in the trial of Murena, that
Cicero had deserted in the trial the candidate supported by him in the election, in favor of his victorious opponent.

The trial presents a chronological question: was Plancius aedile in 55
and then prosecuted in 54, or was he elected in 55 for office in 54 and prosecuted in 54? The former chronology leads to the view that the year 54 saw
a concerted attack on the magistrates of the previous year; the latter
chronology suggests that the prosecutor was trying to accomplish the con-

crete goal of disqualifying the magistrate-elect and then obtaining the office himself.

Taylor (1964) has forcefully made the case for the first scenario, according to which Plancius was prosecuted in 54 after he had already completed his term of office. Her argument runs as follows: We know that A. Plautius and the defendant Cn. Plancius were tribunes of the people in 56. They were able to run for office in the year 55 because elections were delayed until after they had ceased to hold that office. In 55, with Pompey presiding, elections were held, in which Plancius was *renuntiatus* (proclaimed as a successful candidate), but these elections were canceled by violence. Plancius and Plotius were victorious in the second election, and their opponents Q. Pedius and M. Iuventius Laterensis were defeated. They held office in 55,[10] and Plancius was prosecuted in 54 under the *lex Licinia de sodaliciis,* which had been passed the previous year.

Sumner refurbishes the case that Plancius was elected to office for 54, arguing that the law may have specified a waiting period in which magistrates-elect would be liable to prosecution for electoral malpractice.[11] This would explain how Plancius could have been prosecuted in the same year as (but not at the same time as) he held office. (Sumner cites the parallel of a senatus consultum proposed in 55 but suppressed by the consuls, stipulating that praetors-elect should remain *privati* for sixty days after their election so that they could be prosecuted [Cic. *Q Fr.* 2.8.3]; the rationale would have been that in view of the delayed elections, the candidates would otherwise assume their office immediately and therefore be immune from prosecution.) Sumner argues *ex silentio* that if Plancius had already served as aedile in 55, Cicero would have made mention of his splendid accomplishments.[12] But Broughton notes two considerations that are probably fatal to Sumner's reconstruction of events.[13] Plancius's colleague in the curule aedileship celebrated the Ludi Megalenses (in April), as is shown by a coin that he issued with the head of Cybele pictured on the obverse,[14] and the trial of Plancius occurred around the time of the Ludi Romani, that is, at the end of August or in early September, since Cicero says that Laterensis tried to prevent the trial from taking place around the time of these games, so that Cicero could not make use of religious themes in defense of his client as he had previously done for other aediles (83).[15] Sumner's reconstruction is based on the trial occurring before the aediles took office, so if he is right, these very short aedileships could have commenced only in September. Yet Plautius was performing his duties in April, so it seems better

to conclude that Taylor is right to put these aedileships in 55 and that Plancius stood trial after his year of office.[16]

This chronological crux is important for understanding the motivation
of the prosecution in this case. Taylor argues that a Catonian faction in 54
not only saw their candidates Domitius Ahenobarbus as consul and Cato
himself as praetor but also went after magistrates from the previous year
whom Pompey and Crassus had brought to victory through electoral corruption: P. Vatinius (praetor in 55, consul in 47; *TLRR* no. 292), Nonius
(praetor in 55; *TLRR* no. 285), and C. Messius ([curule?][17] aedile in 55; *TLRR*
no. 289), as well as Plancius.[18] If she is right, the prosecutors engaged in a
concerted attack for a broad political objective. The prosecutors used as
their tool the *lex Licinia de sodaliciis*, although the use of this statute might
have raised questions of retroactivity; perhaps it allowed retroactive application or had been sufficiently foreshadowed by the senatus consultum of
56 to allow prosecution in 54 for acts committed before the passage of the
law in 55,[19] or perhaps, because of the delay in the elections for 55, the law
was passed before the relevant campaigns.[20] If Sumner is right, however,
the prosecutor in this case, Laterensis, had the same objective as Sulpicius
Rufus in the trial of Murena: to obtain the office vacated by the convicted
magistrate-elect, Plancius. For Taylor and against Sumner, it should be said
that the argument from silence—that Cicero would have mentioned Plancius's accomplishments if he had already held the aedileship—is only as
strong as such an argument can be. It can be argued that Hortensius might
have mentioned Plancius's aedileship in his speech on behalf of Plancius.
Or the argument from silence can perhaps be countered by the speculation
that Plancius's record as aedile may have been notoriously bad and, therefore, that Cicero did not want to remind the jury of it. For example, if Plancius, as Sumner suggests, had given lavish games, this liberality might have
confirmed an image of an excessively wealthy son of a *publicanus* with vast
amounts of money to spend, not only on games, but also on electoral
bribery.[21] Taylor does establish a pattern of prosecution for electoral malpractice after the year of office; perhaps some aspect of the *lex Licinia de
sodaliciis* made this activity particularly easy or attractive.[22]

The legal basis for the trial was the *lex Licinia de sodaliciis,* passed the
year before by the consul Crassus. The legal difficulty that this trial raises
reflects a more general problem, the relationship between the crimes *de
sodaliciis* and *de ambitu.* Linderski, in his seminal discussion (1961a),[23]
argues that the law was based on a senatus consultum proposed by Horten-

sius in 56, the year before the *lex Licinia* was passed.[24] This law created a crime of "aggravated[25] electoral corruption" (*ambitus infinitus,* as opposed to *ambitus communis*) through the use of *sodalitates,* or organizations of influential people, who were sometimes organized into *decuriae* within the thirty-five tribes.[26] Since the compilers of the *Digest* had no interest in electoral matters (Mod. 48.14.1 pr.), we have no commentary on the statute, much less the text of the law itself. As a result, we do not possess a definition of the *crimen sodaliciorum.*[27] However, Cicero's speech does provide us with some idea of what the law's target was. He says that the "decuriatio tribulium" [division of the members of the tribes], "discriptio populi" [distribution of the people], and "suffragia largitione devincta" [voting restricted by bribery] caused the Senate to take action, and he challenges Laterensis to prove that "decuriasse Plancium, conscripsisse, sequestrem fuisse, pronuntiasse, divisisse" [Plancius divided, enrolled, served as depository of bribes, made promises, parceled out]; then, he will be in a position to use the tools with which the law supplies him (*Planc.* 45). The vocabulary used here is repeated shortly thereafter: "sic tu doce sequestrem fuisse, largitum esse, conscripsisse, tribulis decuriavisse" [so it lies with you to prove that he was a depository, that he engaged in bribery, that he enrolled and divided up the tribe members] (47).[28] The statute, whose terminology is probably reflected in the phrases repeated by Cicero, increased the penalty for certain kinds of electoral misconduct, possibly to lifelong exile,[29] and may have laid down a penalty, unknown to us, for the *divisores.*[30]

The prime question about this law is whether it specifically prohibited electoral *coitio* (collusion). It is clear that the use of this tactic could be a cause for opprobrium ("suspicionem coitionis" [suspicion of collusion], *Planc.* 53), but it is not clear that this statute prohibited electoral *coitio* as such, in the absence of bribery.[31] The issue is clouded by alternate readings of *Scholia Bobiensia* 152St, where the reading adopted by Stangl specifies the use of "sodales" as what the law prohibited, whereas Mommsen (1899, 872 n. 2) reads the vaguer "alios" [others].[32] Mommsen and Taylor (1949, 68) argue that *coitio,* in and of itself, was illegal, but Hall (1964, 302) maintains that while *coitio* itself was not illegal, the members of such alliances were liable for the bribery that would be necessary to make these alliances work.[33] Staveley agrees: "*Coitio* can hardly have served much purpose and have been particularly effective except when it found expression in some form of electoral bribery."[34] According to this view, allegations of *coitio* in the context of formal bribery charges corroborate the charges and cast opprobrium on the candidates who had formed the coalitions. There can be no doubt that in the fifties, electoral bribery was widespread.[35]

Staveley's certitude is unwarranted. On the second point, whether *coitio* could be effective in the absence of bribery, the answer hinges on the power of candidates to influence voters by nonmonetary means, such as persuasion and prestige. Some candidates may well have possessed that influence. On the first point, *coitio,* in and of itself, could certainly serve a purpose, for it enabled a candidate to magnify his electoral power. The Roman system of group voting, multiple candidates, and multiple positions (e.g., two curule aedileships) clearly made *coitio* a rational way to maximize one's resources, in terms of influence and money, by concentrating on some groups to the exclusion of others and, for that reason, "trading" voting units. It is therefore possible that vote swapping might have occurred in the absence of bribery, and the *lex Licinia* might have criminalized this activity, which had been frowned on but not prohibited before the senatus consultum of 56 and the *lex Licinia* of 55; perhaps the increased factionalization of politics in this period made such a formal prohibition more necessary than before.[36] In other words, the *lex Licinia de sodaliciis* may have prohibited the use of *sodales* in electoral combinations. The prohibited *sodalicia* need not have been bound together by money,[37] but they often were, at least in part. Depending on the evidence available, in some trials, it may have been relatively easy to substantiate the charge of *coitio* by showing that money had been distributed, whereas in others, it may have been easier to prove the *coitio* and to use that proof as a basis for suggesting bribery. In either situation, the key to a successful prosecution would be to persuade those who were involved in the illegal combination to come forward with their testimony, since electoral bribery clearly required considerable coordination among many people, all of whom had benefited in some way from the bribery and none of whom was in any obvious sense a victim of the crime.[38]

The first part of the prosecution case involved the actual conduct of the election campaign. The highly irregular circumstance of having to hold a second election for the curule aedileship had created a situation in which *coitio* was especially likely to occur. Cicero claims the opposite for his client (*Planc.* 49): what motive did he have to bribe anyone in the second election when he was the clear winner in the first election, which had been carried almost to conclusion, up to and including the *renuntiatio* (official return) of votes? But when one considers how Roman elections worked, it is clear

---

that after the first election showed each candidate where his voting strengths and weaknesses lay, the second election was likely to be the scene of exactly the kind of vote swapping that the *lex Licinia* tried to deter. Candidates would have gained a very good idea of their support in the various tribes. A winning candidate knew that he had more votes than he needed to carry one tribe or that he could dispense with the vote of a certain tribe altogether; correspondingly, the candidates who came up short in the first election would know in which tribes they lacked votes to reach a majority of voters or how many tribes they needed to achieve a majority of tribes. Moreover, as Yakobson observes, "[t]he votes received by a candidate in a voting unit carried by a rival were to him wasted votes."[39] So it would be in the interest of both winners and losers in the first election to reach an agreement with another candidate to agree to swap votes in the second election and to get the word out to their supporters. If Plancius really was certain that he would win in the second election, he clearly had votes to spare and could use them as bargaining chips to curry favor with a competitor and likely colleague-to-be or to influence the voters' choice for his future colleague. Moreover, he might have reckoned that his competitors who had not done so well in the first election could now, with the knowledge gained in the first round, work together to use in the most efficient manner the voting support that they knew they had. That consideration would explain why Plancius, as well as Plotius, was concerned about a close outcome the second time around (*Planc.* 54). The tactic that Laterensis says Plancius and Plotius used against himself and Pedius—creating a Plancius-Plotius slate and persuading the supporters of each of them to cast their two votes for both—makes perfect sense in that situation. Thus, Plancius and Plotius got almost the same number of votes in some of the tribes (53).

Cicero's speech does not provide clear guidance as to whether the gravamen of the case is an electoral coalition, the disbursement or receipt of bribes, or some combination of these. The closest he comes to defining the *crimen sodalicium* is when he ridicules the prosecution for not making the charges that one would expect to find in such a case.

> Decuriatio tribulium, discriptio populi, suffragia largitione devincta severitatem senatus et bonorum omnium vim ac dolorem excitarunt.[40] Haec doce, haec profer, huc incumbe, Laterensis, decuriasse Plancium, conscripsisse, sequestrem fuisse, pronuntiasse, divi-

sisse; tum mirabor te eis armis uti quae tibi lex dabat noluisse. . . . sic
tu doce sequestrem fuisse, largitum esse, conscripsisse, tribulis
decuriavisse. (*Planc.* 45–47)

[It is the division of the members of the tribes, the distribution of
the people, and the voting restricted by bribery that in the past have
awakened the severity of the Senate and the forceful indignation of
all good men. Demonstrate your contentions, support them, apply
yourself to them, Laterensis, that Plancius divided up the members
of the tribes, enrolled them, served as depository of bribes, made
promises, parceled out money; then I shall be surprised that you
refused to avail yourself of those weapons that the law gave you. . . .
so you must show that he was a depository, that he engaged in
bribery, that he enrolled and divided up the tribe members.]

It is quite possible that Laterensis was unable to adapt to the requirements
of prosecuting under the new law *de sodaliciis* and relied too heavily on
arguments that were more appropriate for an *ambitus* court (47). Cicero
wants the jurors to believe that whatever the focus of the statute, Laterensis
has chosen to prosecute under it to take advantage of the method of jury
selection it stipulates (36; see discussion later in this chapter and *Planc.* 47)
and that his charges really involve *ambitus*. This objection to what the prosecution has done can be interpreted in two ways: (1) an *ambitus* case can be
brought under the *lex Licinia de sodaliciis,* since that is allegedly what Laterensis is doing; or (2) an *ambitus* case is fundamentally different from a
case *de sodaliciis* and that is why Cicero is objecting to the procedure used.
The solution may be that the charge focused on the improper creation and
use of electoral collusion between two candidates and that because this
coalition used bribery as one of its tools, evidence of this bribery helped
Laterensis establish to the court the existence of this collusion.

The actual results of this voting also supported the prosecution case.
The prosecution charged that the outcome of the voting in the second election was very suspicious, in that Plancius and Plotius not only carried the
same tribes but carried them by almost the same number of votes within
each tribe (*Planc.* 53).[41] Craig refers this argument back to Cicero's complaint that Laterensis is conducting an *ambitus* case under the guise of a
"sodaliciorum tribuarium crimen" [tribe-related charge of illegal associa-
tions] (47).[42] But the outcome of the second election, as described by

Cicero, suggests the high level of coordination that may have been the target of Crassus's law. Also, Cicero's suggestion that the case amounted to *ambitus* rather than *sodalicia* (47) is separated from his account of the vote in the second election by two sections, one to demonstrate that Plancius was a strong candidate (48–50), the other to argue that the distinguished ancestry of Laterensis was no guarantee of victory for him (51–53). Therefore, the point of his account of the second election is not to show that Laterensis has really charged Plancius with bribery. Rather, Cicero needs to make some response to Laterensis's charges, which are very embarrassing for the defense, and the very unconvincing nature of his response (that the law made provision for casting lots when the candidates' votes were tied)[43] suggests that the prosecution has a valid and legally relevant point in the identity of the number of votes cast in some tribes for Plancius and Plotius.

Laterensis also made a charge with regard to the conduct of the first election, the results of which had been disqualified. He says that Plotius had agreed to deliver the vote of his own tribe (Aniensis) to Pedius and that Plancius had agreed to do the same (Teretina) for Laterensis but that after the results of that election, Plotius and Plancius had second thoughts about their generosity, fearing defeat in the second election, and took back their own tribes (*Planc.* 54).[44] Although it is hard to tell from Cicero's account what the quid pro quo was in this agreement, it clearly constituted *coitio*. Craig argues on the basis of this passage that *coitio* could not have been by itself grounds for accusation, since Laterensis was in effect admitting that he had been involved in a *coitio* in the first election and therefore would have been incriminating himself by bringing up this matter.[45] This argument is a strong one.[46] But I would argue, on the contrary, that the fact that Laterensis brought this matter up can be explained by the fact that it puts the character of Plancius in a bad light, since he not only entered into the deal but then failed to follow through on it. Since all four candidates were evidently involved in it, he may have been fairly confident that none of them would be brazen enough to launch a prosecution in which that candidate was clearly as guilty as the others.[47] There is no doubt that Romans would have considered such an agreement improper, even if, as Craig is arguing, it was not illegal. The fact that Cicero tries to show that this agreement never occurred, rather than that it reflects as badly on Laterensis as it does on Plancius, suggests that he had decided, for reasons he does not want to make clear, to deny the whole business, rather than to try to measure out the blame. While Craig is right that *coitio* would not be illegal if it was "simply a pledge of support between two candidates" (1990, 76 n. 6) it is quite possible that *coitio* was illegal, even when it involved not bribery but the subversion of basic principles of electioneering, such as deliberately "throwing away" some votes to another candidate.

Laterensis also alleged vote fraud, that is, that he had not been credited with all the votes that were in fact cast for him. He claims that he has more witnesses from the Voltinian tribe than votes cast for him (*Planc.* 54); presumably, these are witnesses who can testify that they voted for Laterensis. Cicero, in another confusing and unconvincing rebuttal, treats this charge as if it involved bribery, rather than a miscount of the vote. He attacks the credibility of these witnesses: either these witnesses were bribed by Plancius to desert Laterensis, in which case they could have been bribed by Laterensis to bear false witness (that they had voted for Laterensis), or they accepted bribes from Laterensis to vote for him.[48] If their votes were not bought by Plancius, Laterensis may have simply been unpopular in that tribe.

Cicero claims that Plancius prosecuted under the *lex Licinia de sodaliciis* rather than the *lex Tullia de ambitu* simply because he wanted to use, or rather abuse, its provisions for jury selection. Instead of the system of choosing decuries for a case, with a right of rejection of individual jurors, the *lex Licinia* created a system of *editicii iudices* (nominated jurors), for which the *Pro Plancio* provides our main evidence (36–44). The prosecutor chose four tribes, of which the defendant could reject one.[49] Cicero claims, citing Hortensius's speech the day before as his authority, that the legislative intent of this provision was to add the role of witness to the role of juror. Therefore, he claims, Laterensis was duty-bound to choose the tribes where he claimed bribery had taken place, primarily the Teretine and to a lesser extent the Voltinian. Instead, he chose three tribes that had nothing to do with the case and one that he knew Plancius would reject. But as Linderski and Gruen point out, the fact that Cicero does not claim that Laterensis's selection was illegal strongly suggests that nothing in the law compelled the prosecutor to follow the Hortensian logic.[50] Indeed, it might seem much more reasonable to avoid a tribe in which the defendant had practiced widespread bribery, so that it would be less likely that a bribed voter would find his way onto the jury. Moreover, even if legislative history were considered decisive or at least strongly persuasive, the rationale behind a senatus consultum passed by the Senate in 56 with regard to electoral combinations might not have been the same as the people's rationale for passing a similar measure in 55.

Whether bribery is intrinsic to a charge *de sodaliciis,* there is no doubt that Laterensis did claim in the trial to have evidence that bribery had occurred. Cicero positions his treatment of this evidence so as to downplay its importance. He mentions it briefly in his discussion of jury selection (*Planc.* 37). Later, he demands that the prosecution substantiate its charge of bribery by challenging it to make the case that Plancius had practiced bribery in any given tribe, listing the *sequestres* and *divisores* in it; he claims he will be able to demonstrate how Plancius won any given tribe without bribery (48). Only a little later in the speech do we learn that there was concrete evidence of bribery: coins seized in the Circus Flaminius and a *divisor* whom the consuls investigated. The *divisor* complained that he had been treated unfairly by the supporters of Laterensis, and Cicero wants the jurors to conclude that he has been working for Laterensis, not Plancius ("Atque is quidem eductus ad consules qui tum in crimen vocabatur se inique a tuis iactatum graviter querebatur" [Indeed, he who was brought before the consuls and then subjected to a prosecution made serious complaints that he had been unfairly shaken up by your people], 55). But the *divisor*'s complaint is ambiguous. Whichever side had employed this *divisor* had delivered the money, since it was there (unless the *divisor* had advanced the money on the promise of reimbursement from the candidate), so his complaint might have related to some other aspect of the agreement into which he had entered. For example, he might have believed that Plancius, who could have been the source of the money, was acting in concert with Laterensis. Given the level of *coitio* that had existed in the first election, this would hardly be surprising. He may then have felt and expressed outrage when the followers of Laterensis reported him to the authorities. Cicero tries to undermine the significance of the incident by arguing that a successful prosecution of Plancius's *divisor,* who was summoned before the consuls and accused (55),[51] might have provided a useful *praeiudicium* (previous legal judgment affecting the present trial) for this trial ("Qui si erat divisor, praesertim eius quem tu habebas reum, cur abs te reus non est factus? Cur non eius damnatione aliquid ad hoc iudicium praeiudici comparasti?" [But if this person was a distributor, especially someone working for a man whom you regarded as a defendant, why was he not prosecuted by you? Why did you not procure by his condemnation something of a favorable verdict for this trial?], 55). If Laterensis could have secured the conviction of this underling, he could have argued that this provided a precedent that would reinforce the case against Plancius. An example of this tactic is the two prosecutions and convictions (*TLRR* nos. 147–48) of minor figures in the case involving Oppianicus and Cluentius (*TLRR* no. 149), which, Cicero claims (*Clu.* 46–61), made the conviction of the principal, Oppianicus, inevitable. That Laterensis did not embark on this course showed, according to Cicero, that he had very little evidence against the candidate.

The analogy with the trial of Oppianicus in 74 points up a possible difference between the two situations. The two minor defendants were tried under the same law, and before the same jurors, as Oppianicus (Cic. *Clu.* 62). But although Plancius's *divisor* may well have been open to prosecution, we do not know that, as a *divisor*, he could be tried under the *lex Licinia de sodaliciis,* as opposed to the *lex Tullia de ambitu.* If he could have been tried under Crassus's law, Cicero had created a new difficulty for his client. For if the *divisor* could be tried *de sodaliciis* for distributing bribes, it stands to reason that the candidate could be tried under that law for providing the bribes. Therefore, Cicero's contention that the prosecution had brought the trial to the wrong court would have been invalidated. In fact, the prosecution might have been quite right to present the evidence about the *divisor* in a trial of Plancius *de sodaliciis,* as showing an elaborate and improper coordination of effort to secure his election, as evidenced by a large amount of money seized in a public place. Yet it might not have been permissible to prosecute the *divisor* under this law, and a preliminary prosecution under an *ambitus* law would have meant using a different court and different jurors and so would not have provided a clear *praeiudicium* that would have almost obligated the jurors to convict Plancius.

The second part of the prosecution case relates to the electoral prospects of the two candidates. As one would expect on the basis of the *Pro Murena,* Laterensis argues that he was the obvious favorite and that the contrary result can only be explained by an extraneous cause, that is, bribery: "Quaerit enim Laterensis atque hoc uno maxime urget qua se virtute, qua laude Plancius, qua dignitate superarit" [For Laterensis inquires and presses hard especially on this one point, with respect to what merit, virtue, or esteem did Plancius surpass him (*Planc.* 6). Laterensis had the clear edge in *dignitas;* he was of consular rank on both sides of his family, whereas Plancius and the other two candidates were the sons of knights, thus *novi homines* (17).[52] As quaestor, the prosecutor had given games at Praeneste and got on well with Roman businessmen in Cyrene (63). Moreover, Laterensis argued, the father of Plancius was not only an *eques* but a *publicanus,* and although Cicero calls him "princeps iam diu publicano-rum" [someone who has for a long time been a leader of the tax farmers] (24), Laterensis considers this a mark against him, especially since the father had offended people by unusually harsh language in one matter (33–34)—usually taken to be the appeal by the *publicani* to the Senate for the cancellation of their contract for the taxes of Asia, which had failed to provide them with enough revenue to meet their bid.[53] Against this undistinguished opposition, argues Laterensis, the *imagines* (masks of ancestors) of his household should have assured him of victory (51). Moreover, claims the *subscriptor,* L. Cassius Longinus, Plancius had done little to recommend himself, either in the military sphere or in the forum, as orator or jurisconsult (61–62). The prosecution also attacks Plancius's general character (see discussion later in this chapter).

In response to a challenge from the *subscriptor* to find faults in Laterensis, Cicero eschews a personal attack and, rather, brings out all the elements that contributed to the defeat of Laterensis. He develops a theme he had mentioned before, namely, that Laterensis had not shown enough willingness to court the Roman people. Cicero argues that Laterensis, like Sulpicius Rufus (see chap. 6), had been so confident of victory that he failed to mount a vigorous campaign (*Planc.* 12), and Cicero maintains that Laterensis's withdrawal from the campaign for tribune of the people in 59, even if from high-minded motives, left doubt as to his steadfastness in a crisis (13). When answering Cassius Longinus, Cicero points to the time Laterensis had spent in the provinces; his proquaestorship of Cyrene in the late sixties[54] took him away from Rome at a critical time (63; Cicero here recalls an argument he made at sec. 13).[55] Moreover, Laterensis's home region of Tusculum had seen so many of its native sons succeed in Rome that it failed to support them enthusiastically, whereas the people of the prefecture of the Atina and even of surrounding areas were keen to have one of their own reach the aedileship at Rome; furthermore, the area of Plancius's support possessed a much larger and denser population than Tusculum (19–24). Plancius's father campaigned assiduously for him (24), as did Cicero (24–26). Although the *subscriptor* had argued to the contrary (61), Cicero maintained that the public career of Plancius was at least respectable. He served under A. Manlius Torquatus in Africa in 69 and under Q. Caecilius Metellus Creticus in Crete in 68–67 with his relative Cn. Sentius Saturninus, quaestor or legate at the time (27).[56] He saw service in Macedonia, first in 62 as *tribunus militum* and later in 58 as quaestor. According to Cicero, not only was Plancius *gratiosus* (a popular person), but his supporters, whom Laterensis denigrated as *sodales,* were *amici* who themselves were *gratiosi* (46–47). Cicero argues that Plancius's lack of legal talent or training is irrelevant to obtaining the favor of the Roman people, who in these matters care nothing for the *cura* of the orator or the *scientia* of the jurisconsult (62).

While arguing that Plancius is a well-qualified candidate, Cicero also maintains that one should not expect the best-qualified candidate to win such an election as this one. First, Cicero says that even if Laterensis deserved to win, his defeat could be explained without resorting to the argument that bribery was used against him. Cicero argues that the Roman people often let themselves be moved by influence and campaigning ("gratia" and "preces," *Planc.* 9) rather than following a sober judgment of each candidate's qualifications, especially in the less important offices, where the people do not feel that their *salus* (safety) is at stake (7).[57] Cicero claims that *studium* (partisan spirit), not *iudicium* (judgment), is at work (10). Second, Cicero maintains that regardless of the merits of the candidates, the voters have a right to cast their ballot as they please. Cicero suggests that if it came to pass that any victorious candidate could be prosecuted on the grounds that a better candidate had been rejected by them, the courts would determine the elections, not the assemblies (10–16). Cicero even goes so far as to downgrade the role of family ancestry in determining elections. He develops this theme in response to a rhetorical question from Longinus: would Cicero not admit that he, as the son of a Roman knight, had a harder time in achieving office than would his son, coming from what was now a consular family (59)? Cicero counters that most Roman magistrates have never been the equals of the greatest Romans (60) and that all the Romans require from a magistrate is the qualities of a good slave steward (*vilicus*): frugality, industry, and vigilance ("frugalitas, labor, vigilantia," 62).

These two arguments—that Plancius was sufficiently respectable to be a viable candidate and that Laterensis's good character did not guarantee election in any case—are designed to undermine the prosecution's basic contention that the defeat of a better candidate constitutes a basis for suspecting bribery. Cicero's use of these two arguments suggests that he recognizes that his client's merits are somewhat weak. Since he cannot argue on substantive grounds that Plancius deserved to be elected, he argues on procedural grounds (1) that the people often choose to elect an inferior candidate and (2) that in any case, the voice of the electoral *comitia* should be final.

The prosecution's third area of attack in this case focused on the character of Plancius. Unless many of the prosecutors' arguments simply went unmentioned and unanswered by the defense, we can say that the prosecution did not lay great stress on this aspect of the case. Laterensis called Plancius a *bimaritus* (bigamist), alleging that he took a young male with him to a province as a sexual companion; he was also supposed to have raped a mime actress (*Planc.* 30). Cicero denies both charges, as well as claiming that local custom permitted the actions alleged in the second charge. Plancius also was supposed to have improperly allowed someone to be released from prison at the request of a powerful young man, but he apparently realized his error and reapprehended the prisoner (31). Otherwise, Laterensis used the reputation of the father to create odium against the son (31). Cicero not only objects that this is procedurally unfair but defends the father, as a powerful *publicanus* who deserves respect, even if, as we have seen earlier in this chapter, it could not be denied that he had expressed himself too harshly.

Laterensis and Longinus added one more line of attack, one that was not integral to bribery charges in general; they made an issue of Cicero's participation in the case. This aspect of Longinus's speech was probably a departure from the norm, at least in terms of the time he devoted to it. Longinus claimed that Cicero was under no special obligation to come to the aid of Plancius, because Cicero was in debt to many people for their support (*Planc.* 68). Laterensis complained that Cicero owed him his support because of the help Laternesis had provided Cicero in his time of crisis (73). Plancius's services to Cicero in protecting him when he sought refuge in Macedonia in 58 were not so great and should not be so considered, Laterensis claimed (4, 71–72). He argued that Cicero had not been in physical danger in 58; he had incurred more debt to L. Racilius, tribune of the plebs in 56 (95). Cicero maintains the opposite, while not denying the value of the services Laterensis had rendered him.[58] Laterensis also attacked Cicero for his tendency to characterize every prosecution of a client whom he was defending as an attack on himself (75): "'quo usque ista dicis? nihil in Cispio profecisti; obsoletae iam sunt preces tuae'" ["How long will you keep saying those things? You did not gain results with respect to Cispius; your entreaties are now worn out"] (75). Cicero had unsuccessfully defended Cispius (tribune of the plebs in 57; *TLRR* no. 279), possibly on a charge of *ambitus* and possibly in 56. Cispius, too, had helped Cicero, although relations between them had previously not been warm; Laterensis made fun of the "lacrimula" [little tear] that Cicero shed for his client (76). Cicero retorts that Laterensis himself had provided him with the evidence for his case on behalf of Cispius and had urged him to take it. Laterensis clearly took aim at Cicero's well-known and by now tiresome line that he was the real object of every prosecution, probably calculating that Cicero could not evoke sympathy for his suffering when his opponent was clearly free of any Catilinarian or Clodian taint. But whatever resonance Laterensis's attack on Cicero had, the jurors acquitted Plancius.[59]

Gelzer's overall description of the trial of Plancius is that it was a typical *ambitus* trial without general political interest.[60] Leaving aside the fact that it was a trial *de sodaliciis,* not *de ambitu,* he is right, as far as the trial itself is concerned, although Cicero's invocation of Pompey (*Planc.* 49) reflects the extraordinary power of certain individuals in these last years of the Republic. For the purposes of this book, the more typical the trial was, the more it tells us about trials involving electoral malpractice. Yet the circumstances that lay behind the trial reflect general phenomena of the greatest interest. The necessity of holding a second election to create aediles, after the first election had sent the presiding consul home to his wife splattered with blood, certainly reflected a severe problem, at least in the short term.

The circumstances of the trial reflect a fundamental change that was in progress, the Roman revolution that gave its name to the book on Roman history that is now the best known since Gibbon's. According to the standards of the Republic, even of the early first century B.C., Laterensis deserved to win the election. His record was clean, his lineage was consular, and all his opponents were weak candidates. Instead, he lost, and the son of an abrasive *publicanus,* of someone who had been dependent on the favor of Laterensis's ancestors in the Senate for his success, was victorious. Neither Laterensis nor Cicero told the real story of what was happening: a Roman revolution, in which obscure people from obscure places superseded the Roman nobility. Laterensis probably did not comprehend the change, and Cicero, although he himself was part of that process, did not comprehend or was unwilling to admit the subversive nature of the historical process that had brought him to the apex of the Republic.[61] The earnest expression of wounded pride evinced by Laterensis signaled the approaching end not only of an era but of a political system.

Part Three

Homicide and Violence

L ate republican criminal law had at least two statutes aimed at crimes against the physical safety of individuals, though the fact that these crimes were prosecuted in standing criminal courts may indicate that although individuals were directly harmed by these crimes, the threat to public law and order provided the rationale for these statutes.[1] Such crimes were different from extortion and electoral malpractice—as well as from the crimes of *maiestas* and *peculatus* (treason and embezzlement), neither of which gave rise to a trial that produced an extant speech of Cicero—in that they did not relate to a public office; therefore, people well below the level of senator had opportunities to violate them. To some extent, the trials in this section will take us somewhat down the Roman social scale, though no further than the *domi nobiles* (local nobility) of Italy after the Social War. The homicide and violence court saw the greatest use of *iudices quaestionis* as presiding magistrates, generally ex-aediles who performed the duties that a praetor performed in the more prestigious[2] and less busy courts, such as extortion and treason courts. In the year 66 B.C. we know there were three courts operating under the *lex Cornelia*, two *de sicariis* and one *de veneficiis*, though I will argue that this division between the two parts of the statute is informal and for the sake of convenience and that any of these courts could adjudicate all matters falling within the purview of the statute (see chap. 9).[3]

Sulla passed a law that, roughly speaking, covered what we would call homicide, the *lex Cornelia de sicariis et veneficiis*.[4] But both the origins of the statute and its field of application militate against thinking of this law as simply directed at what we call murder. As its double-barreled name suggests, it represents a union of two preexisting statutes, a union that may have occurred before Sulla or that he may have initiated. Luckily for us, Cicero quotes from various provisions of the law to make a point about the applicability of one of its provisions (*Clu.* 148, 157). The poisoning part (*de veneficiis*) included not only the use of poison to kill someone but a variety of activities connected with poison: manufacture, sale, purchase, possession, and dispensing (*Clu.* 148). The other part (*de sicariis*) seems to have originally been something similar to our gun laws; it takes its name from the dagger (*sica*) used by urban criminals.[5] It prohibited walking around with a weapon for a criminal purpose and only later evolved into a law also directed against the use of that weapon, that is, murder. Special provisions applied to parricide, which were later replaced by a separate *lex Pompeia de parricidiis,* probably passed by Pompey (*Dig.* 48.9).[6] It appears from the *Digest* (Marcianus *Dig.* 48.8.1 pr.) that the Cornelian law also covered arson. Finally, it contained a provision directed against "judicial murder," the use of the courts to bring about the condemnation of an innocent person on a capital charge—a provision that Cicero (*Clu.* 151, 154) identifies as originally contained in the *lex Sempronia ne quis iudicio circumveniretur,* dating from the Gracchan period.

Unlike the other provisions, that against judicial murder applied only to senators. This limitation created gaps in coverage that varied in extent according to the legal situation at various times. In terms of punishing jurors who accepted bribes to condemn an innocent person, this restriction presented no problem for the Sullan *quaestiones,* since all jurors were senators, but after the *lex Aurelia* (70 B.C.), two-thirds of the jurors were not. Moreover, to the extent that it applied to prosecutors—who would not necessarily be senators—who might provide bribes to jurors or even to witnesses giving false testimony against a defendant (*Clu.* 157), the limitation of liability under this clause to senators created an anomaly.

The first major addition to the *quaestiones* created or re-created by Sulla was a court to deal with violence (*vis*). It is generally thought that the insurrectionary activities of M. Aemilius Lepidus motivated the passage of the *lex Lutatia de vi* in 78 B.C., but another law, the *lex Plautia* (or *Plotia*) *de vi* was passed afterward, probably in 70 B.C. How the two laws were related is not known, but it is the *lex Plautia* of which we hear in the last decades of the late Republic. It was aimed at violence that in some way disrupted the public safety, and for the sake of a speedy trial, it allowed trials on *dies festi* (Cic. *Cael.* 1).[7] In 52, Pompey, as sole consul, passed a law establishing a special court to repress the violence that was tearing Rome apart, most notably the death of Clodius at the hands of Milo (Asc. 36, 38C).[8]

These two *vis* trials show that it is not possible to draw a clear line of demarcation between murder and *vis* trials. Clearly, Caelius and Milo were charged with offenses that could have formed the basis of murder charges, but the prosecutors chose the *vis* court instead. Despite this overlap, however, murder and *vis* had different core meanings, to judge by the different types of cases brought before the two kinds of courts. Prosecutions under the *lex Cornelia de sicariis et veneficiis* generally involved homicides that were in some sense private, although they threatened public order because of their heinous nature. *Vis* prosecutions were based on accusations of more general mayhem that constituted a direct attack on the state and that usually involved groups of people acting in concert, such as the Catilinarian conspiracy and the gang warfare of the fifties.

CHAPTER EIGHT

In Sex. Roscium Amerinum

icero's presentation of the case for Roscius conveys such a compelling picture—with the exception of one major structural problem—that it is hard not to be swept away by it: An unsophisticated young man of fine family, Roscius, finds himself accused of arranging the murder of his father. Two kinsmen, who had been engaged in an intrafamilial quarrel with the murder victim, ally themselves with an upstart freedman potentate in the camp of a victorious general, Sulla, and arrange to have all the family property stripped from Roscius and given to themselves. To guarantee their undisturbed possession of their newfound wealth, they hire a professional orator to deliver the case against Roscius. Erucius, the prosecutor, provides the "confictio criminis" [fabrication of the charge]; the two kinsmen, the "audacia" [effrontery] to arrange for the prosecution; and the freedman, the "potentia" [power] (Cic. *Rosc. Am.* 35). Given the Sullan connection of the freedman, they are all confident that no orator of any note will be willing to speak for the defendant. But young Cicero, in his first criminal speech, dares the impossible—and if his readers could vote, he doubtless would secure an acquittal, just as he was probably able to do.

Yet when we marshal the facts provided by Cicero and consider them as dispassionately as we can, the case becomes much less clear. The facts are too meager, the social setting is too confused, and the legal question is too much a matter of burden of proof, rather than a clear-cut abuse of power, to allow us to conclude that we are dealing with an innocent defendant hounded by insatiably greedy malefactors. In dealing with crimes of violence, such as homicide, the Roman courts were often forced to rely on evidence so incomplete and inconclusive as to leave the rational juror—or reader—in a state of indecision.

The defendant came from Ameria, about fifty Roman miles north of Rome. His father, Sex. Roscius senior, had been one of the *domi nobiles* and preferred to spend most of his time at Rome. Roscius senior owned thirteen rich farms in the Tiber valley, and he left some of them in the care of his son, also called Sex. Roscius, who is the defendant in this trial. Roscius senior had another son, about whom we know only that his father preferred to have him with him at Rome (*Rosc. Am.* 45), and a wife, about whom we learn nothing other than her existence (96).[1] At Rome, Roscius senior enjoyed friendly relations with some of the most prominent Roman families: Caecilii Metelli, Servilii, Scipiones, and Valerii Messallae (15, 149). Cicero describes him as a "nobilitatis fautor" [supporter of the nobility] (16), in a context that implies that he sided with Sulla, and Cicero says that he seemed to glory in the Sullan victory. Though this description fits Cicero's rhetorical purpose here, disassociating the murder of Roscius from the murder of those vanquished by the Sullan victory, there is no specific reason to doubt Cicero at this point.[2] Sometime after the end of the Sullan proscriptions ("aliquot post mensis" [after some months], 128), which took place on 1 June 81 (128), Roscius senior was slain at Rome. Roscius junior was in Ameria at the time of the slaying. At this point, two other Roscii enter the picture, relatives of the defendant and his father, T. Roscius Magnus and T. Roscius Capito.[3] The former was at Rome at the time of the killing, the latter at Ameria.[4] Magnus sent a freedman of his to Ameria with the news, and that emissary arrived overnight, in record time, and reported the death of Roscius senior to Capito (19). Four days later, the news was reported to L. Cornelius Chrysogonus, a freedman of Sulla, at Sulla's camp in Volaterrae (20). Then, the name of Roscius senior was retroactively added to the proscription list, and his property (thirteen farms) was confiscated by the state and sold; it was purchased by Chrysogonus.[5] Capito eventually received three farms, and Magnus took the other ten as procurator (or agent) in Chrysogonus's name (21). Cicero claims that Chrysogonus paid only two thousand sesterces for property worth six million.[6]

Roscius junior was driven off the ancestral property, on which he had been residing, though he had not owned it as long as his father was alive. The ten leading men of Ameria (including Capito) went to Sulla at Volaterrae to complain, and having received assurances from Chrysogonus that these injuries would be undone, they returned to Ameria. But nothing was done to correct the problem, and Roscius junior fled to Caecilia, the daughter of Q. Caecilius Metellus Baliaricus (consul in 123) and sister of Q. Caecilius Metellus Nepos (consul in 98) (*Rosc. Am.* 27, 147, 149). His enemies then accused him of parricide, the murder of his own father. Messalla, probably M. Valerius Messalla (consul in 53) (149; see discussion later in the present chapter), not being old enough himself to serve as *patronus,* found an advocate for Roscius, Cicero. The case was the first to take place under the *lex Cornelia de sicariis et de veneficiis,* probably in 80, although late 81 cannot be ruled out.[7]

C. Erucius delivered the speech for the prosecution. He may have gone on to become somewhat of a regular prosecutor, enough, at least, to project a characteristic rhetorical style.[8] The scholiast terms him "quodam ex novis accusatoribus" [someone from the new [i.e., post-Sullan] prosecutors] (*Schol. Gron.* D 301St). We know little or nothing about his past.[9] Cicero mocks him as someone who has no personal interest in the case and has taken part simply for mercenary reasons (*Rosc. Am.* 55). However, those who wished to prosecute for personal reasons often brought in a professional speaker to present their case (see chap. 1, "The Difficulties of the Prosecutor"), so the role Erucius played may have been quite normal and acceptable.

Cicero says that T. Roscius Capito and T. Roscius Magnus each participated in the trial. Cicero describes them as working together, the former as the experienced survivor of many battles, the latter as a young apprentice whom Capito is training. Cicero says that he understands that Capito will come forward as a witness, and he threatens him with a rough cross-examination ("De Capitone post viderimus, si, quem ad modum paratum esse audio, testis prodierit" [We'll see to Capito later, if he comes forward as a witness, as I hear he has been made ready to be], *Rosc. Am.* 84). Cicero somehow predicts that Capito will rely on written material ("volumen"), which Cicero says was clearly prepared by Erucius (101). As for Magnus, Cicero says that he sat with the prosecutor and, in fact, that he was the only one to do so ("istic sedes ac te palam adversarium esse profiteris" [you sit on that side [with the prosecutors] and openly declare yourself to be an opponent], 84; ". . . alterum sedere in accusatorum subselliis video" [. . . one of whom I see seated on the prosecutors' benches], 17; "potissimum tibi partis istas depoposcisse ut in iudicio versarere et sederes cum accusatore" [To think that you specifically demanded that side for yourself, to get involved in a trial and sit with the prosecutor!], 95; "solus tu inventus es qui cum accusatoribus sederes atque os tuum non modo ostenderes sed etiam offerres" [you are the only one who has been found to sit with the prosecutors and to not only show your face but even force it upon our attention], 87). Scholars disagree on whether Magnus appeared as a witness.[10] Cicero leaves open the possibility that Magnus might appear as witness, but he claims that Magnus would not be credible testifying against the defendant if he rose up from the prosecution bench. Although Magnus might have participated in the case as a *subscriptor,* he apparently contributed nothing in that capacity.[11] One does not have to assume that Magnus was expected to appear as a witness and that it was for that reason that Cicero was trying to discredit him in advance,[12] since it is central to Cicero's strategy to blacken the reputation of Magnus. Cicero wanted the jurors to believe that he committed the murder or at least masterminded it, since he was at Rome when it occurred (see discussion later in this chapter). Cicero implies that there may be other prosecution witnesses to come (*Rosc. Am.* 30, 82). Because the defense speech precedes the testimony, there was no way the *patronus* could know for sure whom the prosecution would call as witnesses, as Cicero's apparent reliance on hearsay implies ("audio," 84), unless the prosecution was required to disclose the names of the witnesses whom it was compelling to appear (see chap. 1). Therefore, to the extent that our text of this speech reflects his actual speech at the trial, one would not expect him to know this information. It is not surprising that he denigrates the prosecution testimony in advance, since, as Ayers shrewdly notes, it appears that there will be no witnesses for the defense.[13]

Cicero tells the jury that there was an old quarrel between Roscius senior and the other Roscii, Magnus and Capito (*Rosc. Am.* 17), and he refers later to a property dispute ("magnas rei familiaris controversias" [major disputes about family matters], 87). This dispute may provide an alternate explanation to Cicero's as to the reason for this disposition of the property, which would undercut the argument of cui bono that Cicero employs to suggest that since Magnus and Capito benefited from the chain of events started by the murder of Roscius senior, they must have had a hand in it. Cicero says they have profited handsomely in the final disposition of the thirteen farms of Roscius senior, Capito with an outright gift of three farms—indeed, the three best (99, 115)—and Magnus with the procuratorship of the remaining ten (21, 23), of which Chrysogonus is the owner. Chrysogonus's immediate profit came in the form of objects that he took to a new house he was building in the vicinity of Veii.[14]

As portrayed by Cicero, L. Cornelius Chrysogonus is the central character in the prosecution. The defense claims that until he has gotten rid of Roscius junior, this *adulescens,* a freedman of Sulla's, does not feel that he can be secure in his ownership of the confiscated property that he has purchased from the state. For that reason, says Cicero, Chrysogonus has caused this trial to take place (*Rosc. Am.* 6). According to Cicero, Chrysogonus is providing the *potentia* that he confidently believes will neutralize any opposition (35). Even Cicero admits—or feigns—a reluctance to talk about Chrysogonus for fear of offending other people, clearly Sulla and his supporters (124). Yet the freedman played no formal role in this trial, except in the negative sense of preventing his slaves from testifying in it; his informal role, such as it was, will be discussed later in this chapter, in connection with the political context of the trial.

To return to the two Roscii, Magnus and Capito, Kinsey (1985) presents a careful and penetrating critique of Cicero's account of their role. First, Kinsey treats the supposed *inimicitia* (enmity) between them and Roscius senior. Kinsey points out that Capito, at least, may not have been an enemy of Roscius senior, since the leading men of Ameria included him in their delegation of ten representatives to Sulla in Volaterrae (*Rosc. Am.* 26).[15] Certainly, the leading men of the town would have known of any such *inimicitia* and would have known enough not to make him part of their protest delegation and, moreover, not to depend on him in the way that Cicero says they did. By the same line of reasoning, Mallius Glaucia, the underling of Magnus who delivered the news of the murder to Capito, may have had no reason to believe that Capito was an enemy of the dead man. If so, that he brought the news from Rome to Capito first (19, 96)[16] could show simply that he wanted a family member to break the news to Roscius junior.[17] Cicero's detailed knowledge of what happened as the first dawn broke after the death of Roscius suggests, as Kinsey (1980, 176) correctly notes, that Mallius may have gone from the house of Capito to that of Roscius, perhaps accompanied by Capito. Cicero knows the kind of vehicle used, a *cisium.*[18] Also to be noted is Cicero's knowledge, presumably also gained from his client, that Mallius brought the weapon, still bloody with the dead man's gore, to Capito (*Rosc. Am.* 19). Cicero wants us to believe that this fact reflects gloating over the success of the plot, but Mallius—or he and Capito—may have thought that the weapon would be of interest to Roscius junior as crucial evidence of the crime. As Kinsey also argues (1980, 176), the speed with which Mallius traveled may reflect not careful planning but simply a determination by this lowly figure to please his superiors by providing good service to them.

Kinsey (1980, 180) also dissects the argument of cui bono that Cicero makes. Cicero's opening account (*Rosc. Am.* 13) implies that a group of (as yet unnamed) accusers have profited by the death of Roscius. Only as the narrative unfolds do we realize that even Cicero does not claim that there was a preconceived plot to exploit the murder of Roscius for personal enrichment. Only after Magnus had informed Capito of the murder and after Chrysogonus heard, four days later, about this event, did Chrysogonus realize the value of the Roscian property and the opportunity it afforded him (20).[19] Chrysogonus then had the property confiscated and bought it for a ridiculously low sum. Chrysogonus may have appointed Magnus as procurator of the property as a convenience to himself, since he needed a local man to administer it. Moreover, Capito's acquisition of the three farms could have come about as a settlement of a claim on the property that Capito had made previously, referred to by Cicero (when describing the enmity between Capito and Roscius senior) by the phrase "magnas rei familiaris controversias":[20] "Inimicitias tibi fuisse cum Sex. Roscio et magnas rei familiaris controversias concedas necesse est" [You must admit that ill will existed between you and Sextus Roscius and there were major disputes about family matters] (87). Cicero's account puts Capito's actions in the most treacherous light possible, but an alternate scenario can be envisioned.

Capito had been on good enough terms with Roscius senior that the notables of Ameria included him in the protest against the confiscation of his property. But there had been some property dispute within the family before the death of Roscius senior. In fact, if Capito had some claim on the property of the (now deceased) Roscius senior, that claim gave him an interest in disputing the confiscation, since the seizure by an outsider made it less likely that he would ever make good on his claim. Perhaps Chrysogonus, then, when he met with the delegation from Ameria at Volaterrae (*Rosc. Am.* 26), bought Capito off by a promise to honor that claim (which may or may not have been a good claim), presumably calculating that two thousand sesterces was a very good price to pay for ten farms and that the sacrifice of the three others was worthwhile to neutralize potential opposition. Perhaps Capito, in turn, persuaded his colleagues that the name of Roscius senior should be removed from the list of those proscribed. This scenario requires that we postdate Capito's possession of the three farms to a time after the delegation from Ameria has arrived at Volaterrae. Admittedly, this interpretation runs somewhat contrary to Cicero's account at this point, but as we have seen, that account is studiously ambiguous here. Moreover, as Kinsey points out (1980, 178), Cicero says at a later point that Capito came to terms with regard to his share in the booty at the same time as he was keeping the Amerian delegation from Sulla (110, 115).[21] All in all, it is hard to believe that the Amerians would have included Capito in the delegation if he was already blatantly profiting by the confiscation. Alternatively, it is possible that his possession of the three farms—if it had indeed already occurred—was seen in Ameria as a way of keeping the farms within local control, against the encroachments of Chrysogonus and his agent Magnus, who, though belonging to the Roscian family, lived at Rome. But even if Cicero's first version of events is correct (21), that is, even if this *societas* was formed when the news of Roscius's death first reached Volaterrae, this *societas* clearly did not exist before the murder and in no way could have motivated it. Indeed, even Cicero admits that Chrysogonus had nothing to do with the murder itself (122).

Kinsey, in a later article, points out another complicating factor, the presence of the wife of Roscius senior and many other kinsmen in Ameria.[22] Cicero asks,

Cum Ameriae Sex. Rosci domus uxor liberique essent, cum tot propinqui cognatique optime convenientes, qua ratione factum est ut iste tuus cliens, sceleris tui nuntius, T. Roscius Capitoni potissimum nuntiaret? (*Rosc. Am.* 96)

[When Sextus Roscius had at Ameria a home, wife, and children, when he had so many relatives and kinsmen who were on excellent terms with him, for what reason did it come about that that client of yours, the messenger of your crime, announced it above all to Titus Roscius Capito?]

Cicero asks this question to suggest impropriety in the fact that the messenger of Magnus went to Capito rather than to the wife or other kinsmen to announce the murder of Roscius, yet, as Kinsey points out, his remark raises the question of why these relatives are not present at the trial. One would have expected the wife of Roscius senior, especially if she is the mother of the defendant and not just his stepmother, to appear in court in mourning and, if this had been the case, that Cicero would have exploited her grief at some point in his speech.[23] The absence of the wife and other kinsmen at the trial raises the possibility that they did not support Roscius junior.[24] We can only speculate about why they did not support their kinsman. One reason might have been that they were fearful of appearing for the defense for the same reasons that prominent *patroni* did not want to speak for Roscius; even if we know with hindsight that Sulla was willing to let the courts function in a legal manner, this would not have been a foregone conclusion at the time. A second possibility is that they knew that he was guilty. A third possibility is that they suspected that he was guilty. The murder of Roscius senior had brought about their downfall too (at least the downfall of the wife and other children); even if, for the sake of argument, we assume that they might not have hoped to acquire ownership of the thirteen farms, they certainly had been enjoying the profits from them. Now they were destitute, and it would be only natural, especially in the psychological context of civil war and an authoritarian government, for them to fall to blaming the individual who was the apparent cause of all their grief, namely, Roscius junior. It would be naive to assume that people in such a position rally around the oppressed; they are at least as likely to look for a scapegoat.

To summarize the defendant's situation, he has been accused of the murder of his father. Two relatives have aligned themselves with the prosecution, and have profited from the defendant's apparent downfall. The other relatives are failing to support him. The picture is somewhat brighter when we look at what the powerful friends of the deceased are doing for his son.

The main player in the defense of Roscius was Cicero, who managed to convert the liability of his inexperience—this was his first criminal case[25]—into an asset. Cicero says that there were others present at the trial who could have spoken but that they did not because they were of such eminence that anything they said would have been taken too seriously—a reference to the dangers of this time, just after Sulla's victory.[26] Cicero says that he can speak freely, because he will be either ignored or pardoned (*Rosc. Am.* 3). He also suggests to the jurors that he is not a skilled orator, thus disarming them and lowering their resistance to the rhetorical tactics that he employs throughout the speech (5). Cicero claims that Erucius was happy to discover, after he had delivered his own speech and as Cicero rose to speak, who the *patronus* for the defendant was, since he felt he had nothing to fear from such a tyro (60). It is interesting to note that Erucius, when he delivered his speech to the court, did not know for sure who would be speaking on the other side of the case. Cicero suggests that he probably looked around to see who was sitting on the defendant's benches and, seeing no eminent orator, felt excessively confident of his own success. Presumably, then, if he had seen a well-known orator with ample experience in criminal cases, he would have been likely to guess that he was a *patronus,* but a prosecutor apparently received no official notification as to who was speaking for the defense, at least not in this *quaestio.*

Cicero also says that people whom he deeply respects have urged him to take the case (*Rosc. Am.* 4). The implication is that Roscius junior had some powerful backers, as indeed he did. Cicero maintains that a certain Messalla would have spoken for Roscius if age had allowed (149). Landgraf (270, ad loc.) makes the reasonable suggestion that this Messalla served as *advocatus* in this trial. Scholars have debated whether this was M. Valerius Messalla Niger (consul in 61) or his cousin M. Valerius Messalla Rufus (consul in 53). Drumann and Groebe (D.-G. 5:252 n. 3) and Landgraf (270) argue for the latter on the grounds of his young age, which they calculate as sixteen, and Landgraf cites a passage from Ulpian (*Dig.* 3.1.1.3) that says that no one under 17 can be allowed to prosecute. However, Münzer ("Valerius," no. 266, *RE* 2.8 [1955]: 163) defends the identification provided by the scholiast (*Schol. Gron.* D 303St) that this is the well-known orator (Cic. *Brut.* 246; *ORF* no. 124), Niger (praetor in 64,[27] consul in 61). He shows that Rufus was only two years younger than Niger, since Rufus was a candidate for the praetorship in 63 (Cic. *Sul.* 42). Therefore, Niger must have been born in 105 or 104[28] and Rufus in 103 or 102, and in 80, they would have at least reached the ages of 24 and 22, respectively. Thus, Cicero's use of his youth as an explanation why he did not play a more active role in the trial needs to be taken with a grain of salt; political allegiances and fears probably played more of a role. Roscius was also supported by Caecilia Metella, who was sheltering him at Rome in his homeless condition, and by mentioning her support three times (*Rosc. Am.* 27, 147, 149), Cicero clearly wants to suggest to the jurors that the defendant could count at least one member of Rome's most powerful family as his friend. As Kinsey (1980, 183–84) suggests, Cicero wants to have things both ways: he criticizes the prosecution for relying on the *potentia* of Chrysogonus, but he makes it clear that Roscius, too, has *potentia* on his side. The difference is that Messallae and Metelli may legitimately exercise *potentia;* freedmen may not.

The prosecutor, Erucius, had a relatively straightforward case to present. Roscius senior was definitely the victim of homicide. No one knew who had committed the actual deed, or, to be more precise, Cicero does not imply that Erucius has claimed to have that information, and Cicero only suggests, in a rather weak manner, that the assassin could have been Magnus (*Rosc. Am.* 92). Erucius takes the position that there were any number of potential *sicarii* (assassins) at Rome in the aftermath of the Sullan victory, of whom Roscius junior could have easily availed himself. Cicero quotes him as follows:

> Eius modi tempus erat . . . ut homines volgo impune occiderentur; qua re hoc tu propter multitudinem sicariorum nullo negotio facere potuisti. (80)

> [The times were such . . . that men were regularly killed without punishment; therefore, you [Roscius] could have done this without trouble on account of the plentiful supply of assassins.]

According to the impression conveyed by Cicero, Erucius conceded Roscius junior's alibi that he had not been at Rome at the time of the murder (74, 76), and Erucius charged that the defendant had accomplished the deed through an intermediary, such as a slave or a hired assassin (74).[29] He may have well used the same argument of cui bono that Cicero used: the son had clearly benefited from the death of the father and would have inherited at least part of the estate at his death. Since we do not hear from Cicero of anyone else who failed to inherit property that he or she expected on the death of Roscius senior, Roscius junior was possibly the sole heir; the brother mentioned by Cicero (45) was probably dead.

The argument of cui bono could apply in almost any murder case, at least any in which the murdered person had property to bequeath, yet no one would claim that all heirs try to murder the testators from whom they expect to benefit. Erucius argued that the father and son had not been on good terms ("'Patri non placebat'" ["His father disliked him"], *Rosc. Am.* 40), that the father had sent the son to the country as a punishment (42), and that the father had decided to disinherit him ("'istum exheredare in

animo habebat'" ["he intended to disinherit him"], 52). Erucius claimed
not that Roscius junior exhibited the hallmarks of a wild youth, marked by
lust and debt (he was in fact over forty years old [39]), but that he was a rus-
tic boor ("ut ipse accusator obiecit, ruri semper habitarit et in agro colendo
vixerit" [as the prosecutor himself said by way of accusation, he had always
lived in the country and supported himself by farming], 39), who not only
had been absent from Rome for several years and had never stayed there for
more than three days (74, 79) but rarely even left his estates (79).[30] He had
ample means to obtain someone else to do the actual deed: a hired assassin,
either at Rome or at Ameria, or a slave of the family (74, 76–77). Roscius
senior, at the time of his death, had attended a *cena* (banquet, 18), as he
often did (52), and so was walking about in the dark, quite possibly under
the influence of drink, and Erucius may have argued that the son would
have known of this. In 81, life at Rome was in an unsettled condition, murders were common (80), and the courts were not yet functioning. Although
modern readers may find that the dearth of physical evidence (fingerprints,
blood types, hair samples, etc.) weakens the case, the Roman jurors of the
time would not have expected such evidence. Testimony from eyewitnesses
would have been desirable, but that would have been presented after
Cicero's speech, and Erucius may not have revealed it in his (see Kinsey
1985, 190). Eyewitness testimony may have been forthcoming. Cicero
wanted his audience to believe that the prosecution was trying to hide such
evidence, because T. Roscius (probably Magnus, acting as procurator for
Chrysogonus)[31] did not allow two slaves to testify, slaves now in his possession but previously belonging to Roscius senior, who might have been able
to provide useful information (77, 119). But the link between Erucius and
Chrysogonus cannot be taken as a given,[32] and one motive of Chrysogonus
may have been to prevent the physical damage that the torture that always
accompanied the judicial examination of slaves could cause.[33] Erucius also
charged him with *peculatus,* the theft of state property (82). Cicero ridicules
this charge as totally irrelevant, as if Erucius had been quoting from a different speech on a different charge. But as Landgraf (168–69) rightly points
out, such a charge was related to the affair if Roscius junior had failed to
turn over to the state all the property that was to be confiscated as a result
of his father's posthumous proscription. Despite his dismissal of the
charge, Cicero refers to it again, addressing Chrysogonus, who had purchased this estate from the government (". . . si nihil de patris fortunis
amplissimis in suam rem convertit, si nulla in re te fraudavit, . . . si ex

omnibus rebus se ipsum nudum neque praeterea quicquam excepit . . ."
[. . . if he has diverted nothing from his father's very vast fortunes to his
own advantage, if he has in no way swindled you, . . . if from the whole
estate he has left himself not even the shirt on his back nor anything else
. . .], 144). Finally, Roscius was antisocial, and no one who knew him was
willing to testify to his good character, at least as far as Cicero lets us know.

Erucius presents a plausible account of how Roscius junior killed his
father, even if we today may find that it does not meet our standard of dis-
pelling all reasonable doubt. Cicero's attempt to discredit that account is
unconvincing, even though it is rhetorically clever. Cicero uses a device that
might be termed "antidilemma"; that is, instead of presenting his opponent
with several choices and showing that each one is impossible, he presents a
number of options, each of which is quite possible, and then attacks the
prosecution for its inability to specify which option it has selected. The
assassins could have been slaves or a free people. If free, they could have
been from Ameria or from Rome (*Rosc. Am.* 74). If they were at Rome,
Roscius could have arranged the assassination at a distance, by some messenger, although we do not know who or when.[34] He could have hired these
people by money, influence, expectation, or promises ("pretio, gratia, spe,
promissis," 76). Cicero never really deals with the possibility that slaves
(either Roscius senior's or someone else's) committed the crime; as Craig
(1993, 35) notes, he "slid[es] adroitly from slaves as murderers to slaves as
witnesses" (*Rosc. Am.* 79). This is not a dilemma, because Cicero does not
present a host of possibilities and then show that each is unacceptable;
rather, he lists many possibilities that are perfectly acceptable and then
merely criticizes the prosecution for not being able to specify which one it
wishes to claim as the true explanation of what happened.[35]

The trial of Roscius presents one major problem for scholars: why does
Cicero not just argue that Roscius junior, like anyone else, could have
legally killed Roscius senior since the latter had been proscribed and, therefore, that there can be no question of murder? This question relates to the
prosecutors' strategy, because one of the answers suggests that they never
intended to gain a conviction. The subtle answers that have been given to
this question justify the sort of criticism that Douglas (1980) gently directs
at Stroh's *Taxis* in his review of the book: "one begins to wonder if S. is not
a great deal subtler than the orator he is studying." It is easy for scholars in
their studies or libraries, analyzing a written text over a period of months or
years, to lose sight of what sorts of statement and implication the orator's

audience could reasonably be expected to grasp in a speech delivered orally within one day. The solution that has gained widespread acceptance is that Chrysogonus actually wanted an acquittal to come from the trial, on the grounds that Roscius junior had the right to kill his proscribed father. If the defense made this argument, it would then be accepting the validity of the proscription—which was in fact illegal because it occurred after the end of proscriptions on 1 June 81—and would thereby secure Chrysogonus's "purchase" of the Roscian estate and his title to that property. This point of view and its subsequent modification deserve careful study, even though they are ultimately unconvincing. Heinze provides the standard exposition of it.

> For even if only one possibility was available to represent the acquittal of the defendant as justified not by his proven innocence, but by his right to kill his proscribed father, then, on the one hand, the hatred of parricide remained attached to Roscius and all further steps on behalf of his restitution were hindered to the utmost; and on the other hand, the validity of the proscription had thus basically been admitted by the opposition, and also from this point of view, the hands of Roscius's friends were tied, Chrysogonus remained unchallenged in the possession of his loot: this, and nothing other, was exactly the goal of his prosecution.[36]

Stroh (1975, 61–63) modifies this reconstruction in one detail. He argues that Chrysogonus and his supporters relied on an acquittal to come from the trial not because Roscius senior had been proscribed but because he had been killed behind enemy lines (". . . ut eum apud adversarios occisum esse diceret" [. . . that he said that he had been slain among the opponents [of Sulla]], *Rosc. Am.* 127). He points out that it would be easier for Roscius junior to say that his father had been killed "in adversariorum praesidiis" [in the opponents' strongholds] than that he had killed his own father, albeit with legal impunity. Kinsey (1966a) argues that it was possible to speak of both the truly proscribed and those "qui in adversariorum praesidiis occisi sunt" [who were killed in the opponents' strongholds] as *proscripti*, even if this usage was not strictly correct, and thus that Cicero, in his speech, is able to disregard this technical distinction. In his conclusion, Kinsey accepts the basic contention of Heinze that Chrysogonus instigated the prosecution to enjoy his booty in peace, and in another article, Kinsey (1980, 179–80) suggests that Chrysogonus believed that Roscius junior was planning to try to regain his father's property. However, Kinsey (1988) also argues that Cicero glosses over the distinction between proscriptions, which were supposed to end by 1 July 81, and sales of confiscated property, for which no deadline may have been set by law. According to this reasoning, the only illegality about the sale was the proscription itself, in which Chrysogonus had played no role.

An analysis of the context in which the idea that Roscius senior was killed behind enemy lines occurs rules it out as a solution to the problem. Cicero deals with the issue in his description of the role of Chrysogonus (*Rosc. Am.* 125–28), who played no formal role in the trial. He says that Chrysogonus bought the property of Roscius senior. He quotes two clauses under which the property could have been sold: as that of a proscribed person (UT AUT EORUM BONA VENEANT QUI PROSCRIPTI SUNT) or as that of someone killed within the enemy's lines (AUT EORUM QUI IN ADVERSARIORUM PRAESIDIIS OCCISI SUNT" [. . . that the goods either of those who have been proscribed or of those who were killed in the opponents' strongholds be sold]). He then argues that the second clause cannot apply in this case, because as long as there were lines of battle, Roscius senior was within Sulla's, and because he was killed at Rome when the fighting had stopped.[37] Cicero then claims that Chrysogonus prevented Sulla from knowing the truth of these matters (". . . ut his de rebus a legatis Amerinorum doceri L. Sullam passus non sit" [. . . that he did not allow Lucius Sulla to be informed about these matters by the envoys of the Amerians], 127), by falsely claiming ("ut ementiretur") that Roscius senior's death took place among the enemy ("ut eum apud adversarios occisum esse diceret"). He then shows that Roscius's property could not have been legally sold as that of a proscribed person, since the proscription had ended on 1 June 81, before the death of Roscius. Cicero is not saying that the *in adversariorum praesidiis* argument was used by the prosecutor in the trial; rather, he is saying that it had been used earlier by Chrysogonus as an expedient to quash any investigation by Sulla into the Amerian delegates' claims, since presumably Sulla would have no sympathy for those who had fought against him. There is no reason why this argument should be consistent with the claims that the prosecutor made later at the trial, even if, as Kinsey claims (1966a), it was possible in common parlance to disregard the distinction between the proscribed and those killed within enemy lines.

Kinsey (1981) attempts a new approach to the problem by arguing that the date of 1 June 81 marks the point after which the killing of the proscribed could no longer take place legally, not just the date after which the proscription itself could no longer occur. However, Craig (1993, 45 n. 1) is right to object that the two passages Kinsey cites need not be read as Kinsey would want. The first says that by the time of the proscription of Roscius senior, those who feared the new regime believed that they were out of danger (" . . . cum etiam qui antea metuerant redirent ac iam defunctos sese periculis arbitrarentur [. . . when even those who had previously been afraid returned and thought that they were now rid of their dangers], *Rosc. Am.* 21). Cicero's words need not be taken as referring to people who had actually been proscribed but, rather, may refer to people who had previously thought that they would be proscribed or that they would suffer some other persecution from the Sullan government but who now (after 1 June 81) believed that they had outlived that danger and could live in peace. The second passage says that proscriptions and sales (of confiscated property) were, according to a statute (probably the *lex Cornelia de proscriptione;* see *Rosc. Am* 125), supposed to cease on 1 June ("Opinor enim esse in lege quam ad diem proscriptiones venditionesque fiant, nimirum Kalendas Iunias" [For I think that the law contains a deadline for proscriptions and sales to take place—namely, the first of June], 128). Although Cicero does not say categorically that those who had been proscribed before this date but had evaded death could still be killed with impunity, the text allows for that interpretation. If Kinsey were right, anyone proscribed at the end of May would be safe if he could only survive for a day or two at the end of the month, though admittedly his property would have already been confiscated by that point. We cannot accept with certainty (though we cannot disprove) Kinsey's claim that had Cicero relied on the argument that Roscius junior could legally kill his father, Erucius would have refuted the argument simply by showing that the homicide had occurred after 1 June.

The solution to the problem of why Cicero does not claim that Roscius junior killed his father legally if he did so is more likely to lie in the extreme delicacy with which a legalistic defense had to be made. Quintilian cautions that a denial of the facts is always stronger than the defense "Etiam si feci, recte feci" [Even if I did it, I did it according to the rules] (*Inst.* 3.6.10), but he argues that it is quite right to join a denial that the defendant committed the deed with the claim that even if the defendant did commit the deed, he would have acted legally (4.5.13).[38] That the charge is parricide makes the legalistic defense doubly dangerous. Even if we take Cicero's expression of pious horror at the very thought of parricide (*Rosc. Am.* 37–38) with a grain of salt, as dictated by rhetorical needs, everyone considered that crime as heinous in the extreme. If Cicero conveyed to the jurors the impression that his client thought that it was proper for him to kill his father, they would be more than likely to vote in disgust to condemn. Therefore, he couches the legalistic defense in two ways: first, by making it clear that it is his decision, not his client's, to raise this defense; and second, by raising it only with regard to the legality of the confiscation of property as a result of the proscription, not with regard to the legality of killing Roscius senior.

Cicero here takes full responsibility for raising the legal technicality, just as he later does in his speech in defense of Cluentius (see chap. 9). In that speech, before attempting to gain an acquittal on a legal technicality (that as an *eques,* his client was not liable under the "judicial murder" clause of the *lex Cornelia de sicariis et de veneficiis*), Cicero stresses that he is doing so on his own account and, in fact, against the express wishes of Cluentius (*Clu.* 144). In his speech in defense of Roscius (*Rosc. Am.* 129), Cicero draws a distinction between what he says on his own account ("pro me ipso") and what he says on his client's ("pro Sex. Roscio"). Cicero claims that issues of the first type, which relate to the sale of the property, its acquisition by the luxurious Chrysogonus, and praise of Sulla (130–42), do not interest his client, who, we are to believe, cares nothing about money. Cicero claims to raise these issues on his own, fired by a sense of indignation.

> Quae enim mihi ipsi indigna et intolerabilia videntur quaeque ad omnis, nisi providemus, arbitror pertinere, ea pro me ipso ex animi mei sensu ac dolore pronuntio. (129)

> [For those things that seem to me myself shameful and unbearable and that I think apply to everyone unless we take precautions, I state them on my own behalf from my mind's perception and outrage.]

As for appeals for Roscius to be left alone to live out his life in penury, Cicero makes these in the remainder of the speech (143–54), on his client's behalf.

> . . . quae ad huius vitae casum causamque pertinent et quid hic pro se dici velit et qua condicione contentus sit iam in extrema oratione nostra, iudices, audietis. (129)

> [. . . those things that pertain to the defendant's mortal risk and legal case, what he wants to be said on his behalf, and with what terms he is content, you will hear, jurors, at the end of our speech.]

In this way, Cicero attempts to insulate his client from the risk involved in attempting to avoid conviction on the basis of a technicality, since such an appeal could easily backfire.[39]

Since the Roman system of criminal justice contained no mechanism for appeal to or review by a higher level, this trial provides the only forum to raise this issue, and Cicero wants to do so. Therefore, he questions the legality of the proscription, but only in the context of the confiscation of property, not in the context of the homicide itself. He makes three claims:

1. Chrysogonus has instigated this trial as a way to get rid of Roscius junior, who constitutes the only bar to his peaceful enjoyment of the property of Roscius senior (*Rosc. Am.* 6, 8, 110, 132, 146, 150).
2. Roscius junior, however, has no hope of retrieving this property (7, 143–47).
3. In fact, the property still belongs to Roscius junior, since the confiscation of it by the state and, therefore, the sale to Chrysogonus were illegal (125–30).

Concentrating on the legal issue relating to property and omitting the legal issue relating to homicide have three advantages for Cicero and his client. First, doing so enables them to discredit their accusers (including Chrysogonus) by showing that they ultimately benefited from the crime and thereby to suggest that they should be the suspects (*Rosc. Am.* 13, 21, 23, 84, 99–100, 107–108, 110). Moreover, Cicero uses the silence of Erucius on the property issue to confirm the deviousness of the prosecution side (28). Second, Cicero's strategy allows this trial, should it lead to acquittal, to function as a persuasive precedent in a future action in which Roscius junior might try to acquire title to his father's property, though it would not dictate a successful result to such an action.[40] Establishing that the confiscation was illegal opens the way to possible material benefits for Roscius junior, despite his advocate's protestations that he has no interest in any such aim. Finally, the attack on the legality of the confiscation might lead some jurors to take the reasoning one step further and to raise the question that has occurred to modern scholars: if the prosecutors think that the proscription and resulting confiscation were legal, do they not have to admit that the murder of Roscius senior was legal? If some jurors themselves raised this question in their own minds, this was so much the better for the defendant, and no blame could attach to him.

Cicero, then, uses the distinction between the advocate's speech and the defendant's wishes to raise, without endangering his client, the issues that he thinks need to be raised. The Roman distinction between the advocate and the client suggests a major weakness of the theory of Heinze and Stroh mentioned earlier, namely, that Chrysogonus started a prosecution to force the defendant to argue for the legality of the proscription and, therefore, that he would be quite happy with an acquittal, since that would guarantee the legality of his title to the property confiscated as a result of the proscription. As Kinsey (1981, 150) and Craig (1993, 45) have pointed out, an acquittal would not have signified the jurors' formal validation of any particular line of argument made by the defense *patronus*. Roscius would have been free to disown it later, and even Cicero could have tried to do so, though such an effort might have proved embarrassing (cf. Cic. *Clu.* 138–42). The criminal trial of Roscius *inter sicarios* did not offer a formal *praeiudicium*, which would have dictated the outcome of a later civil action for the recovery of property; in other words, a verdict of innocent in this trial would not guarantee that Chrysogonus's title to the property could never have been challenged in the future. However, if Cicero had made the audacious claim that Roscius felt he had the right to kill his own father since the father had been properly proscribed, that claim would certainly have been thrown back at Roscius if he ever tried to reclaim his father's property on the grounds that the proscription had been improper. Cicero is exercising proper prudence to emphasize the defense that his client had not committed the crime and to question the proscription only on his own authority and only with regard to the property issues.

The Heinze/Stroh thesis relates not only to what argument Cicero made or did not make but also to the whole strategy of the prosecution. If we accepted this thesis as correct, we would have to accept that the prosecution strategy was dictated by Chrysogonus and, moreover, was aimed at an acquittal. Now that this thesis has been disposed of, it is time to examine the role of Chrysogonus. Was he the dominant, behind-the-scenes force for the prosecution? Does his importance in the case, if he has any, link it to the Sullan regime and its reconstitution of the Roman state?

As portrayed by Cicero, L. Cornelius Chrysogonus is the central, controlling character in the prosecution, and his aim is to secure the conviction of Roscius junior. According to the defense, this *adulescens*, a freedman of Sulla, cannot feel secure in his possession of the property that was confiscated from Roscius, property worth six million sesterces, which he bought from the state for the risible sum of two thousand sesterces (*Rosc. Am.* 6), until Roscius junior has been removed from the Roman scene. For this reason, argues Cicero, Chrysogonus has caused this trial to take place. According to Cicero, Chrysogonus provides the *potentia* that he believes will neutralize all opposition (35). Even Cicero admits—or feigns—a reluctance to talk about Chrysogonus for fear of offending other people, clearly Sulla and his supporters (124). His speech probably provided a vivid portrait of the luxurious lifestyle that this freedman enjoyed; although there is a lacuna within this section of the extant text (132–35), the scholiast (*Schol. Gron.* D 314–15St) gives us a good idea of what this section contained. In his *peroratio,* Cicero makes clear the prejudices that he hopes his speech will have aroused in the minds of the jurors: Roman nobles should cease to pay homage to this upstart. Cicero makes a clear attempt (*Rosc. Am.* 135–42) to exploit the uneasiness that the jurors, who under the new Sullan laws were senators (admittedly, some very new senators who owed their senatorial status to Sulla), must have felt about the *potentia* that the Sullan victory gave to Sulla's followers, including those of low birth.

Yet what evidence is there of Chrysogonus's involvement in the trial? The only evidence is that Chrysogonus's procurator had refused to let the slaves he had acquired from the Roscian estate testify at the trial (*Rosc. Am.* 77–78)—a move that constitutes, in a sense, a rejection of a move by someone else to involve Chrysogonus in the trial, rather than Chrysogonus's attempt to involve himself in it. Two facts weigh against the importance ascribed by Cicero to Chrysogonus for the case. First, Erucius never mentioned Chrysogonus, and Cicero provides a memorable description of the effect Cicero made on Erucius by bringing up his name several times (59–60).[41] Second, Cicero admits that Chrysogonus had nothing to do with the murder of Roscius senior and only found out about it and the victim's wealth after the fact, when he first heard about them at Volaterrae (105). Cicero (105–107) turns this prior ignorance of the man whom he portrays as his primary opponent to his own advantage by condemning (with an elaborate *praeteritio*) Capito and Magnus for betraying their own family, turning to the patronage of this upstart, and providing him with information, in preference to their connections with their "veteres patroni hospitesque" [people linked by traditional ties of patronage and hospitality] (105–7).

The obvious fact that Chrysogonus did profit by the chain of events that started with the murder of Roscius senior does not prove that he caused that chain of events or even played a key role in it. Rather, he exploited it for his own gain, as one would expect the successful belligerents in a civil war to do when they have secured peace. The greater one imagines the power of the Sullan party to be at the time of the trial, the less plausible is Cicero's contention that Chrysogonus could not rest until Roscius junior was removed from the state or that Chrysogonus needed Roscius junior to acknowledge the legality of his acquisition of the Roscian property for him to be able to ignore its illegality. According to Cicero, Magnus and Capito murdered or arranged the murder of a relative, Roscius senior, and then gained the support of one particularly unpleasant follower of a newly victorious coup leader to hide their crime, allowing that follower to share in their spoils. But it might be more accurate to say that when their kinsman, with whom they had some kind of a dispute, was killed in the unsettled climate that prevailed at Rome, Magnus and Capito, belonging to a distinguished family in a not very distinguished town, decided to exploit the situation as best they could, by cutting a deal with one of the less distinguished followers of the victorious coup leader and sharing the family property with him, thereby securing the coup's support for their claims. That they were willing in 81 or 80 B.C. to work with a member of the Sullan party tells us little about their moral character. That they were willing to cooperate with the prosecution of their kinsman Roscius junior, the son of the murdered man, or even to instigate it tells us equally little about their character, since they may have honestly believed that he had committed the crime. If he had done so, they may have reasoned that it was better that they share the family property with an outsider (who was in fact willing to use one of them as procurator over his share of that property) and thereby secure a claim that they had long made on it than that a member of their family should profit by his most heinous act of parricide—the murder of someone who was not only his father but their relative as well—and inherit all of it.

The question of the role of Chrysogonus leads naturally to the overall political situation and its role in the case. How should this case be viewed in its political context? How much of a role did politics play in this case, and how important was this case in Rome's political development? To what extent do the two sides in the case have different views on the relationship between politics and this trial?

This may have been a landmark trial in Roman political history, even though one would not expect the *quaestio de sicariis et veneficiis* to constitute the field for an important political struggle. As Jones points out, the presiding magistrate for this court and other less prestigious courts, such as those of *vis* and *falsum,* was usually a *iudex quaestionis,* of aedilician rank, rather than a praetor, and while the purpose of creating aedilician *iudices quaestionis* must have been simply to provide enough presiding magistrates to staff all the courts, the distinction must have reflected the glamor of the various courts.[42] Cloud explains this distinction, noting that these less desirable courts did not necessarily deal in less severe penalties (e.g., the penalty for *ambitus* was less severe than that for poisoning) and that the overall prestige of these courts was not necessarily lower than the prestige of the others.[43] Cloud correctly sees the status of the defendants in the various points as the key variable in the status of the courts. But despite the relatively low status of the court *de sicariis et veneficiis,* the time of this trial, probably 80 B.C., was a special case, in that this court was just beginning to function in a normal way, despite the abundance of murders to provide work for it (*Rosc. Am.* 11), and in that its president was a praetor, M. Fannius.[44] As people at Rome waited to see if Sulla would put aside his tyrannical ways and bring back the rule of law, it is plausible that murder trials could have attained symbolic political importance.

Badian (1984, 250) maintains that the trial constituted a turning point in Roman history.

> The point at issue was nothing less than whether the *nobiles* could maintain their influence in the Italian countryside, or whether the Italians—the new voters and legionaries—should be encouraged to follow any upstart—even a freedman—who acquired sufficient *potentia.* On the answer the future of the *res publica* depended, and Cicero was briefed to put the issue clearly and take a firm stand: it was thought that, if it were done with sufficient care, he, the unknown youth, could do it with impunity.

Cicero, Badian writes, was briefed by nobles and understood the importance of the trial for the whole nobility. As a result of the acquittal, Badian continues (251), the *nobiles,* in a striking example, had vindicated their *fides* and their power to protect their clients. Sulla, according to this view, needed to be shown that his policies might lead to the encouragement of upstarts like Chrysogonus and the collapse of the power of the nobility— the opposite of his stated, conservative aims. Gabba (1964, 10–14 = 1976, 137–40) attacks this view as exaggerating the importance of the case. The nobles were not united; many were absent, others were present but did not speak for the defense (*Rosc. Am.* 1–3), and others still allied themselves with the *libertus* Chrysogonus even though they had opposed the power of the *equites,* who possessed a much higher social standing than *liberti,* especially in the courts (140). Afzelius (1942) and Kinsey (1982) minimize the political significance of Cicero's speech, and Kinsey (1980, 185) argues that the *nobiles* would not have been afraid to speak out, as Cicero claims (*Rosc. Am.* 3–4), "since Sulla's acts of violence were confined to the earlier part of his dictatorship."

Badian's interpretation is correct so far as it explicates Cicero's strategy in using political arguments to bring the jurors over to his side, showing how Cicero exploits the contradiction that such conservative revolutionaries as Sulla have to face: in restoring the old order through novel means, new sorts of people will gain power. But the strategy constitutes a means to an end, the acquittal of Roscius, and Cicero made an issue of Chrysogonus for that purpose. It is a mistake to argue, as Kinsey (1980) does, that because we know with hindsight that Sulla acted quickly to lay down his dictatorship and restore constitutional government,[45] it must have been clear at the time of the trial that no reprisals needed to be feared or that some other form of tyranny would never reappear.[46] To maintain, as I have, that Cicero's strategy was motivated by the goal of an acquittal, rather than by the goal of making a political statement, is not to deny that it may have taken a good deal of courage on his part and perhaps also on his client's part to base this case on arousing prejudice against Sulla's henchman. Indeed, Cicero's willingness to do so, perhaps with the agreement of his client, may signal the desperation of Roscius's situation. Cicero went for broke and, as it turned out, probably won.

In what way and to what extent did Erucius make use of the political situation? He made no mention of Chrysogonus in his speech (see n. 32) and, according to Cicero, was shocked when the defense did. Although we need not fully credit Cicero's depiction of Erucius's casual attitude toward the case (*Rosc. Am.* 59), his overall description of how his opponent argued his case is believable, especially since Cicero would not have published a version that varied widely from what spectators perceived at the time. Erucius's primary argument must have been that Roscius had committed a crime—and a particularly heinous one at that—and therefore should be punished. To the extent that he may have alluded to the political situation, it would probably have been to urge a return to "normalcy," to regular constitutional government, including a judicial system functioning to repress crime. This was the first trial *inter sicarios* to take place after a period of much bloodshed, and the eyes of Rome were on the magistrate and the jurors to see if they were up to the challenge. Cicero attributes to the supporters of the prosecution the thought that the first defendant ought to be condemned to show that law and order had returned (28), and Erucius probably made an argument somewhat along those lines, just as Cicero also does (12), speaking, as he says, in a somewhat accusatorial vein (11–13). The difference, of course, is that Erucius claimed that Roscius junior had committed the crime; Cicero, that Magnus did so, abetted by his cronies. Erucius said that murder must not be allowed to go unpunished; Cicero urges the court to show that murder will be punished by, in this case, acquitting the defendant and thus leaving the way open to convict the real culprits. Both orators could use this argument without fear of offending Sulla, because he claimed to have reestablished the constitution and to have allowed traditional Roman institutions, reformed—or rather renewed—in accordance with *mos maiorum* (inherited custom), to function again. Other than to praise Sulla for his restoration of the Republic, there was no need for Erucius to bring up Sulla's name. We know that Erucius did not mention the name of Chrysogonus, and there was no need for him to mention Sulla's name, although Cicero tries to link Erucius to implicit criticism of Sulla because Erucius used the argument that Roscius junior could well have committed the crime in times when *sicarii* were committing crimes with impunity (80). (The pun on *sectores* as cutters of throats and cutters of purses [94] establishes a link to the Sullan proscriptions and the auctions that they caused.)

The prosecution of Roscius can be linked directly to the Sullan regime only if one accepts the involvement of Chrysogonus. Erucius had reason to be surprised that Cicero would make that connection. Chrysogonus was clearly not involved in the planning and commission of the crime, and Cicero's argument that Chrysogonus had instigated the prosecution to secure his ill-gotten gains by getting rid of Roscius junior, not a very convincing argument in any case, would not have been worth refuting in advance, even if it had even occurred to Erucius as something the defense would claim. If there was any truth to this argument, Erucius would have hardly drawn attention to the fact that he was speaking on behalf of a freedman, rather than for relatives of the murder victim, as he appeared to be doing. If Chrysogonus really did have any hand at all in the prosecution, any advantage in implying that Sulla and/or his party indirectly supported the prosecution would have been outweighed by the risk of angering Sulla by implicating him in a sordid seizure of property—property that, while it might have been a fortune to the people involved in this case, would have seemed a trifle to the conqueror of the East and Italy. Erucius must have presented the case as one of straightforward murder, committed by a wicked son whose avarice overcame his patience; Cicero turned it into a political drama involving one man in a high place.

It is reasonable to surmise that Roscius was acquitted. Cicero's speech enjoyed such acclaim that thereafter, Cicero writes, there was no case "quae non digna nostro patrocinio videretur" [that seemed unsuitable for our legal representation] (*Brut.* 312), and it makes more sense that a victory, rather than a defeat, made Cicero such a desirable *patronus*. Nevertheless, the only direct evidence for acquittal comes from Plutarch (*Cic.* 3) and the scholiast (*Schol. Gron.* D 301St), so some caution should be exercised, since these two authors may have jumped to a conclusion on the basis of the rhetorical success of Cicero's speech.

CHAPTER NINE

In A. Cluentium Habitum

icero's speech in defense of A. Cluentius Habitus is by far his longest forensic speech.[1] He delivered it at a trial (*TLRR* no. 198) in 66 B.C., launched in reaction to a trial eight years earlier (*TLRR* no. 149)—itself connected directly to two other cases (*TLRR* nos. 147–48)—that was so celebrated it even gained its own name (*iudicium Iunianum*), one which reverberated through at least seven other cases in the next few years (*TLRR* nos. 153–54, 159–61, 170, 172, possibly 162). Yet the individuals involved came from the lower end of the social strata visible to us today, the *domi nobiles* from *municipia* across the Apennines from Rome, who as individuals were politically dominant only in their own regions and were secondary actors within the city of Rome, though as a group they could be a significant force, and who therefore appear less in our extant literary sources than their real importance probably warranted. Cicero's *Pro Cluentio* provides us with more information about them, their families, and their environments than does any other source from the period, unlike most of the other extant criminal speeches, which involve people from the upper classes of the city of Rome.[2] Sex. Roscius senior and junior are partial exceptions, but as we have seen (in chapter 8), the father was well integrated into the Roman scene, and the son, despite Cicero's protestations of innocence and impotence, had strong ties to members of Rome's most powerful families.

In 66 B.C., Abbius Oppianicus, son of the defendant in 74 B.C., brought a prosecution against Cluentius, a member of the equestrian order (Cic. *Clu.* 156), under the *lex Cornelia de sicariis et de veneficiis*. In part, he claimed to be upholding his own interests, since he claimed that the defendant had tried to murder him (as is discussed later in this chapter), but the prosecution was an act of filial piety, as even Cicero admits (". . . qui pietate ad accusandum excitatus es" [. . . who were motivated by family feeling to prosecute], 172), for the defendant of 66 had in 74 successfully prosecuted the prosecutor's father. Oppianicus junior remained silent throughout the trial, with "tacita pietate" [silent family feeling] (65), and left the actual presentation of the case to the advocate, T. Attius[3] of Pisaurum, also a Roman knight. Cicero avoids attacking Oppianicus, since no one could blame him for attempting to gain revenge on the man who, without a doubt, had ruined his father. But Cicero portrays him as being in the grip of his stepmother Sassia, not only because she had been married to his father, but also because, three years before the trial, she had gotten him engaged to marry her own daughter by a previous marriage (179). With this tie and her own control over the will of his father, she planned to induce him to undertake the prosecution of Cluentius.[4]

Cicero provides a brief overview of Attius's speech.

. . . T. Attium Pisaurensem, cuius accusationi respondi pro A. Cluentio, qui et accurate dicebat et satis copiose, eratque praeterea doctus Hermagorae praeceptis, quibus etsi ornamenta non satis opima dicendi, tamen, ut hastae velitibus amentatae, sic apta quaedam et parata singulis causarum generibus argumenta traduntur. (*Brutus* 271)

[. . . Titus Attius of Pisaurum, whose accusation I answered in defense of Aulus Cluentius, who [Attius] spoke both with careful preparation and eloquently enough, and was moreover learned in the teachings of Hermagoras, by which certain rhetorical points are delivered, points that are appropriate and prepared for each kind of case, *like javelins fitted with thongs for the light-armed troops,* although insufficiently ample rhetorical ornaments are provided.] (The italicized words are from the Douglas commentary.)

The reference to Hermagoras carries two implications.[5] First, along with Cicero's previous representation of the teaching of Hermagoras, it suggests that Cicero judged that Attius possessed more technical competence in preparing material to be used in the speech than persuasive force: "ex hac inopi ad ornandum, sed ad inveniendum expedita Hermagorae disciplina" [[He was] from the school of Hermagoras, which is meager in adornment, though useful for invention] (263).[6] Second and more specifically, Cicero's evaluation of Attius's speech tells us something about its content. Hermagoras developed the (στάσις or in Latin, *status*) theory, which divided questions into four categories:

1. στοχασμός, or *coniectura,* or question of fact;
2. ὅρος, or *definitiva* or *proprietas,* or definition;
3. κατὰ συμβεβηκός or ποιότης, or *generalis* or *qualitatis,* or contingent or quality; and
4. μετάληψις, *translativa* or *translatio.*[7]

The final category deals with issues of procedure, such as whether the court had the right to hear the case or the prosecutor to prosecute, and was invented by Hermagoras (Cic. *Inv. rhet.* 1.16; Quint. *Inst.* 3.6.60). The author of the *Rhetorica ad Herennium* objects to making the fourth category separate from the second and subsumes it into the second as a legal question, *legitima constitutio,* of which *translatio* forms a part (1.18). He downplays the practical importance of such a question in the Roman trials, as opposed to preliminary hearings (1.22). Cicero, in the *De inventione rhetorica* (1.16), criticizes those who disagree with the four-part classification of *status,* as being motivated by *invidia* (envy) and *obtrectatio* (malicious attack). Cicero's description in the *Brutus* of Attius as a follower of the teachings of Hermagoras suggests first that he paid particular attention to the κρινόμενον in the case and that an issue of *translatio,* a specifically Hermagorean category, may have played an important part in the prosecution. As we will see later in this chapter, this issue was whether Cluentius, as a nonsenator, could be tried under the "judicial murder" clause of the *lex Cornelia de sicariis et de veneficiis.* Thus, Cicero's general depiction of the prosecutor's speech in the *Brutus,* in a passage in which he refers to the trial of Cluentius, corroborates the view that Attius made an argument about the suitability of such a charge before this court. Of course, as prosecutor, Attius argued that such a charge was indeed suitable.

Geography may help us understand Oppianicus's choice of advocate. Larinum was, from the Roman point of view, a backwater, difficult to get to; although, as the crow flies, it lies almost directly east of Rome, travel from Larinum to Rome must have been arduous and circuitous, necessitating a dip to the south to connect with the Via Latina, unless one went down to the Adriatic, traveled north along the coast, and then took the Via Claudia across the mountains. Larinum was therefore probably more part of an eastern Italian, northwest-southeast axis along the Adriatic than connected to western Italy.[8] Attius came from Pisaurum, which is far away from both Rome and Larinum but easy to access along the Adriatic coast, and it is clear that the family of Oppianicus had connections in the Ager Gallicus, a region in the northern part of the Adriatic coast (*Clu.* 22). Moreover, at one point, we hear about a traveling medicine man from Ancona who provided Oppianicus senior with the means to murder his mother-in-law (40), and his wife Sassia may have come from Histonium, a town on the Adriatic.[9] By contrast, Cluentius used the services of Cicero, who came from Arpinum, a town on the route from Larinum to Rome. Thus, Oppianicus's choice reflects the axis along the eastern Italian coast; Cluentius's choice reflects the axis across the Apennines to the western side of Italy and Rome.

Cluentius's only *patronus* was Cicero, serving that year as the praetor in the extortion court. His appearance in the case involved some personal inconsistency, which he tried to explain away (as is discussed later in this chapter).

The action of the case begins in the town of Larinum. Its soil is sandy and not as rich as the land lying below it, closer to the Adriatic. So pastoral farming was there mixed with agriculture, and ranchers were among those who sent testimonials to Rome on behalf of Cluentius (*Clu.* 198). Larinum was an important crossroads of the drovers' trails that traversed much of Italy, and a bailiff or bailiffs of Cluentius had gotten into a brawl with some shepherds who were taking their flocks on these trails (161). Cicero claims that the brawl was just a legitimate defense of the master's property rights; the prosecution had evidently claimed that this incident showed the violent and arrogant character of Cluentius. The town was big enough to have its own amphitheater, but because it joined the losing side in the Social War at the beginning of the first century B.C., it went into a decline, and cultivation there possibly yielded to pasturage.[10]

Larinum contained several intertwined notable families. The first is the Cluentii. The defendant's father, who died in 88, is described by Cicero

(*Clu.* 11) as being the leading man (*princeps*)·of not only the *municipium* itself but the whole *regio* (locality) and *vicinitas* (vicinity); his son was fifteen years old at the time. It is noteworthy that when his son Cluentius was in dire distress at the trial in 66, his testimonials came from a wide region around Larinum, from the Marrucini and Frentani along the coast and from people from Teanum, Luceria, and Bovianum (197). Cluentius senior and his wife Sassia had a daughter and a son. After his death, his daughter (the defendant's sister) married a member of the Aurii Melini. According to Cicero, a rift developed between Cluentius junior and his mother when she became infatuated with her son-in-law, and as soon as Cluentia, sobbing away her youth in her brother's arms, had divorced him, Sassia married him. Another local notable, Statius Abbius Oppianicus,[11] a Roman knight "in municipio suo nobilis" [distinguished in his community] (109) and the father of the prosecutor in 66 B.C., was busy securing the property of his current wife as his brothers-in-law died off; one of them, who had been captured in the Social War and was imprisoned in the area near Pisaurum, was murdered with a nudge from Oppianicus. When word of this crime got back to Larinum, Oppianicus was forced to flee to the pro-Sullan general Q. Caecilius Metellus Pius (consul in 80), but on Sulla's victory, he came back in triumph, became a local magistrate, liquidated the man who was accusing him of murder, and married Sassia (21–28). An inscription found at Larinum dedicated to Sulla as dictator and patron testifies to Sulla's following there.[12] So now Cluentius was the stepson of Oppianicus.

Thereupon, suspicious deaths occurred in this family (*Clu.* 30–42). Stepfather and stepson came into open conflict when Oppianicus tried to establish that the Martiales, priests of Mars at Larinum who had been considered to be the property of Mars, were free Roman citizens (43–44).[13] Cluentius's fellow townsmen persuaded him to defend their traditional rights at Rome, so they went to Rome to argue the case.[14] As Dyson (1992, 72) points out, the local notables were regrouping in the aftermath of Sulla's coup d'état, reasserting their traditional power, and counterattacking. According to Cicero, at this point (75 or 74 B.C.), Oppianicus plotted the murder of Cluentius, who was intestate and known to be such, so that upon his death, his property would go to Sassia, and he could then murder Sassia and thus obtain the wealth of Larinum's first family (*Clu.* 45). This led to the prosecution of Oppianicus by Cluentius in 74. From this point on, Cluentius spared no effort to ruin his enemy. He obtained as his advocate P.

Cannutius, "homo in primis ingeniosus et in dicendo exercitatus" [an out-standingly gifted man and trained in oratory] (50), and when he was him-self prosecuted in 66, this *domi nobilis* secured the services of Rome's best orator, Cicero, already busy enough as the presiding magistrate of the extortion court. It is curious that Cicero never presents any special reason why he took up this case—no ancestral bond of loyalty to the defendant, no friendship or joint service to the state. Cicero may have taken the case with an eye to strengthening his political support for an upcoming campaign for the consulate, just as he may have taken up the case of Tullius five years ear-lier to strengthen his political hand.[15] An alternative or coexisting possibil-ity is that Cluentius promised Cicero a handsome reward. Even if such a reward was illegal—in the sense that the *lex Cincia*, as a *lex imperfecta*, made any promise of reward legally unenforceable—Cicero may have believed that it was worth the risk.

Cicero describes the murder plot that caused Cluentius to prosecute Oppianicus in 74 as follows (*Clu.* 47): Oppianicus contacted a con man from Aletrium called C. Fabricius to arrange the murder. The latter tried to bribe a slave (Diogenes) belonging to Cleophantus, Cluentius's doctor, to poison Cluentius. The slave told his master of the plot, and a sting opera-tion was arranged. The freedman of Fabricius, Scamander, was witnessed in a lonely spot with a sealed purse of money that he had brought as payment for the poison, and the slave gave him the poison (50, 53). Scamander was put on trial on a charge of murder and convicted, Fabricius was tried and convicted, and then Oppianicus was put on trial—all under the *lex Cornelia de sicariis et de veneficiis* (homicide law). Cicero argues that it logically fol-lowed from the conviction of the two confederates that the principal in the plot, Oppianicus, ought to have been prosecuted and convicted. Since a guilty verdict was a foregone conclusion, Cicero argues, if any bribery occurred at this trial, it must have been done by the desperate defendant, Oppianicus, not the confident prosecutor, Cluentius. Yet although Cicero makes this out to be a straightforward chain of events, capable of being interpreted in only one way, it is in fact puzzling in two ways.

First, why was a slave with access to Cluentius handing the poison over to someone else? At this meeting, the slave Diogenes (whom Cluentius had now purchased so that, we are told, he could be in a position to get infor-mation from him) brought the poison, and Scamander brought the money. Yet why would Diogenes bring the poison? If he or the doctor was to administer it to Cluentius, it would make no sense to hand it over to Sca-

mander; he ought to keep it for further use. It seems unlikely that Diogenes
brought the poison just to prove that he had it, because Scamander would
not be able to tell that it was poison merely by looking at it. So the ostensible purpose of the rendezvous must have been for the slave to provide the
drug to Scamander, not to administer it himself; in other words, he was
functioning (in modern terms) as a pharmacist, not as a doctor or nurse.
That role would have been quite plausible. Indeed, Cicero, in defending
Scamander, had claimed that Diogenes was handing over medicine, not
poison (*Clu.* 53). Scamander was caught with both the poison and the
money on his person (53), so apparently Diogenes had already handed the
poison over to him, although Scamander had not yet paid the slave.[16] But if
Diogenes was just selling a drug, what was the importance of the fact that
he was the slave of Cluentius's doctor (or actually, though Scamander did
not know this, the former slave of the doctor)? As far as we know, Scamander could have administered the poison to anyone, and there is no particular reason to think that Cluentius was the destined victim. In fact, the existing doctor-patient relationship between Cleophantus and Cluentius, if it
has any relevance at all, would suggest that Cluentius was not a likely victim, because then there would have been no point in Diogenes transferring
the poison out of the doctor's storeroom; it would have been easier to have
the slave or the doctor administer it to Cluentius, since they were in a position to administer drugs to him.[17] Rather, a logical explanation for the
involvement of Cleophantus and his slave Diogenes (though not provable
as the only one, from the evidence at our disposal) is that Cluentius wanted
to poison someone, possibly Oppianicus, and went to a logical source to
obtain the poison, namely, his doctor. By purchasing Diogenes, Cluentius
could keep the slave from testifying against him. It has to be conceded that
to establish that scenario, one would have to show that it was Cluentius
who was using Scamander as a middleman.

Second, is it really credible that Cluentius tried to protect himself from
a poison plot managed by Oppianicus, when he could easily remove Oppianicus's motive by simply writing a will from which his mother did not
stand to benefit? Cicero wants us to believe that Cluentius feared that Oppianicus was about to have him poisoned so that Cluentius's estate would be
inherited by his mother, Sassia, who could then be dispatched so that Oppianicus could inherit her estate (*Clu.* 20, 45). Even if we grant that Oppianicus and/or Sassia had systematically plotted to kill about a dozen people,
including an unborn child, so as to inherit from their victims, why did Clu-

entius not protect himself by writing a will and leaving his money to someone other than his mother, especially if, as Cicero claims (47), he was in
poor health? Cicero tries to answer this question by arguing that Cluentius
was loathe to disgrace his mother by excluding her from his will and so
chose to remain intestate (45). But it is implausible that he could not bring
himself to disinherit his mother but was willing to prosecute her husband
on a capital charge that could and did send him into exile, wandering
around Italy, homeless and poverty-stricken (170).

It might be objected at this point that Cicero's speech cannot contain
these two flaws or any other evident flaws, because he would know that the
jurors would spot them and because such flaws would only hurt his case.
But jurors listened to Cicero's speech and reacted to it immediately; unlike
us, they did not have an opportunity to ponder his words over a period of
time, comparing and contrasting passages from different parts of this
unusually lengthy speech. For example, whereas Cicero says that it was
obvious that Oppianicus would be condemned, even before his trial began,
given that the same jury had just convicted Scamander and Fabricius (*Clu.*
59; Cicero thus argues that Cluentius had no motive to bribe the jurors to
vote for condemnation), he can praise those jurors who voted, after the
speeches had been given and the evidence had been presented, that they did
not yet have enough information to cast a vote (76). He even claims that at
least some of the five votes for acquittal could have been well motivated
(76).[18] Cicero could well have thought that the flaws in his argument would
not occur to his audience while he made his speech or even before they cast
their votes and that the superficial plausibility of his arguments would do
its work. He would be all the more likely to get away with his prevarications
because it is unlikely that the prosecutor had presented his own account of
the events leading up to the trial of 74; all the prosecutor had to do (or so he
thought) was to remind the jurors of the bribery and resulting scandal that
had cast a shadow over Cluentius ever since.

Cicero does have to confront directly an inconsistency in his own conduct, for he had served as the advocate for Scamander. He confronts this
matter directly and with amusing self-deprecation. The people of Aletrium,
whom Cicero elsewhere describes as being totally different in character
from Fabricius, asked Cicero, as a native of neighboring Arpinum, to take
on the defense of Scamander, which he did in total ignorance, he claims, of
the facts of the case. Cicero makes the best of the situation; he commends
himself to his audience by demonstrating his ability not to take himself too

seriously. Interestingly enough, only later in the speech, in quite another context, he argues for the license of an advocate to speak as best he can for the case, rather than expressing his own opinion (*Clu.* 138–39; cf. 1 *Verr.* 39).

None of the alleged perpetrators or victims in this case was in any way well known at Rome. But events at Rome were remembered, even after a period of many years, if they were as scandalous as Cluentius's prosecution of Oppianicus senior in 74 B.C. To judge by Cicero's misleading speech in defense of Cluentius, the trial at which he spoke in 66 B.C. revolved almost entirely around the trial that took place eight years earlier, although, as we shall see, Cicero may have exaggerated the connection between the trials.

Cluentius was fifteen in 88 B.C. (*Clu.* 11). Thus, he was born in 104 or 103, about twenty-nine or thirty years of age at the time he prosecuted Oppianicus, and eight years older when he himself was prosecuted by the son of Oppianicus. Cluentius and Oppianicus senior not only came from the same social stratum at Larinum but were closely related by interwoven matrimonial ties. Not only had Cluentius's mother, Sassia, married Oppianicus senior after the death of Cluentius's father, but both families were linked to the Aurii.[19] Politically, however, the Cluentii and the Abbii had been on different sides of the civil war of the eighties: the Abbii were pro-Sullan, and the Cluentii were Marian. But as Moreau points out,[20] political differences did not necessarily rule out marriage alliances. Cluentius not only had influence at Larinum, as is attested by his defense of the town's interests against the lawsuit to declare the local Martiales to be free Roman citizens (43–45),[21] but was also established enough at Rome to obtain the services of P. Cannutius (whom Cicero identifies as "homo extra nostrum ordinem meo iudicio disertissimus" [in my judgment, the most eloquent man outside our [senatorial] order], *Brut.* 205) as pleader for the prosecution. Cluentius was successful in his effort to ruin his enemy Oppianicus senior through this attack (*Clu.* 175), as Cicero willingly admits to make the argument that after the trial, Cluentius had no motive to bring about the death of Oppianicus (170). Clearly, Cluentius was a dangerous antagonist and could be expected to defend himself vigorously. We know he did, because he secured the services of Cicero, then praetor of the extortion court (147), as his *patronus.*

The legal basis of the prosecution has been much debated by scholars. Cicero's response falls into two parts, a very large section on a charge of "judicial murder" and a shorter section on a charge of poisoning. Cicero states that the former charge is a matter of *invidia,* not *crimen,* whereas the charge of poisoning is the proper business of the court (". . . qua de re lege est haec quaestio constituta" [. . . to deal with which this court has been established by law], *Clu.* 1). He says that answering the poisoning charges requires far less effort than countering the *invidia* that has been engendered by the *iudicium Iunianum.* He goes on to defend the emphasis he intended to give to the *invidia,* by presenting a legal argument of some profundity (3). He argues that the jury ought to view the defense discussion of the *crimina* in a purely adversarial role, considering only those arguments made by the defense in its presentation of its case and not supplying any additional arguments of its own, but that when it comes to *invidia,* the jurors should be prepared to discuss the matter among themselves and should enter into their decision-making process any arguments that they deem relevant. The reason that he gives for this distinction is that the *crimina* involve the interests of the defendant alone ("proprium periculum" [the defendant's liability]), whereas the *invidia* involves everyone ("causa communis" [the public interest], 3). We might respond to Cicero that, logically, this distinction might be understood to show that the defense lawyer could afford to devote less time, not more, to *invidia,* since the jurors' imagination and wisdom would constitute an auxiliary source, so to speak, of *argumenta* on that score. But Cicero wants the jurors to view his loquacity on the subject as a favor to them and to all Romans, making their job easier.[22] Only in section 164 (in a speech of 202 sections) does Cicero begin to deal with what he claims is the real basis of the case.

> Cognoscite nunc id quod ad vestrum ius iurandum pertinet, quod vestri iudici est, quod vobis oneris imposuit ea lex qua coacti huc convenistis, de criminibus veneni.

> [Investigate now that which pertains to your oath, what belongs to your court, what that law under whose compulsion you have come together has placed as a burden on your shoulders—investigate charges of poisoning.]

There follows an avowedly brief ("paucis verbis," 164) summary of the poisoning charges:

1. that Cluentius poisoned C. Vibius Cappadox (165);
2. that Cluentius attempted to poison Oppianicus junior (166–68) and that the victim was by accident Balbutius; and

3. that Cluentius instigated M. Asellius to poison Oppianicus senior (169–91).

In one short section (160–64), Cicero deals with several complaints that the prosecution had made against his client to bring *invidia* against him by showing that he was prone to violence and lawlessness:

1. that his slaves insulted Cn. Decidius the Samnite;
2. this his bailiffs (*vilici*) brought violence against the shepherds of Ancharius and Pacenus;
3. that he wormed his way into the will of P. Aelius to the disadvantage of a kinsman;
4. that he refused to pay a legacy owed to Florus;
5. that he treated a free woman, the wife of Ceius the Samnite, as his slave;
6. that he was improperly holding the property of Ennius; and
7. that he and his slaves assaulted Ambivius, an innkeeper, on Ambivius's premises.[23]

Cicero would have us believe that this collection of supposed misdeeds is laughably weak, but clearly the prosecutor thought he could make a case that Cluentius terrorized the local population with a band of followers and dependents.

The prosecution brought some testimony to bear on the third real charge, that Oppianicus senior had been poisoned, although Cicero attacked its credibility. Sassia interrogated three slaves about his death shortly after it occurred, but even under extreme torture, none of them could be compelled to admit any knowledge of a plot. She had purchased one of them, a doctor by the name of Strato, so that she could compel his testimony. When this interrogation produced nothing, she bought him his own shop so that he could set up a practice. (Even Cicero admits that it seems curious that Sassia, obsessed with extracting useful testimony from the doctor, would reward him in this way after he refused to provide it; he implies that this inconsistency is just more evidence of her deranged character.) Three years later, after Strato committed an unrelated theft, in the course of which he murdered two slaves, he was tortured again. The prosecution brought the records of this second investigation before the court that was trying Cluentius, and according to these records, Strato revealed the plot to commit homicide by poison. Cicero tries to undermine the importance of this investigation by the procedural argument that while the investigation was supposed to be only about the theft, nothing in the records contained anything about theft, and Cicero claims that Sassia had forged these records (176–87).

Was the "judicial murder" allegation—that Cluentius, by prosecuting an innocent Oppianicus senior in 74, had brought about his ruin by an improper use of the judiciary—a "real" charge in the trial? Scholars have found this question difficult to answer. On the one hand, Cicero clearly says that the poisoning is what is related to the jurors' oath and is their business to judge and that the poisoning is what the statute establishing the court, the *lex Cornelia de sicariis et de veneficiis,* has defined as a crime. He implies that this should be their exclusive concern, though, interestingly enough, he does not actually say so (*Clu.* 164). Moreover, Cicero makes a case that is persuasive—at least to many scholars—that Cluentius, as an *eques,* was not liable under the judicial murder section of the statute (148), since it pertained only to senators. It might seem impossible to believe that with the letter of the law so clearly against him, Attius would have dared expect to make judicial murder a formal part of the indictment against Cluentius. Yet, on the other hand, Attius clearly argued that it would be unfair not to apply the judicial murder clause—and, in fact, all laws—equally to everyone (150).

I maintain that the question is so difficult to answer because it is the wrong question. I would like to believe that Riggsby (1999, 54) is right to say that an article of mine (Alexander 1982) "allows us to cut the Gordian knot." In that article, I argued that it is wrong, at least for this period, to think in terms of a formal bill of indictment that detailed the particular charges that the prosecutor was bound to prove, to the exclusion of all other charges. Rather, I believe, the prosecutor had to persuade the praetor that he had a genuine case that deserved to go on the court docket, and if the prosecutor did obtain approval, he had every reason to adduce every possible violation of the statute that he could.[24] That is how the epigraphically preserved extortion law seems to have worked, judging by lines 55 and 56,[25] and many features of the criminal trials of the first century B.C. are consistent with—and none are obviously inconsistent with—the proposition that later republican laws also acted in this fashion. Since the penalty under this and many other criminal statutes—loss of *caput*—applied for any number of offenses, there was every reason for the prosecution to launch as broadly based an attack as possible against the defendant.[26] In the absence of a judicial procedure whereby the judge ruled on the admissibility of charges, statements, and evidence, the only restraint was imposed by the jury; presumably, if it found some of the charges wholly unconvincing, far-fetched, and/or irrelevant, it would be less likely to accept the more reasonable charges. The role of the defense lawyer was not only to refute as many of these points as possible but to make at least a nominal objection to all of them, since any one of them was enough to trigger the one (and only) penalty that the law applied.

The procedure of the *lex Cornelia de sicariis et de veneficiis* probably, if my approach is correct, did not call for Attius to present a bill of particulars to the praetor, and thus we cannot assume that the praetor had approved the judicial murder charge before the trial began. In the trial, the prosecutor clearly did present it to the jurors as a reason why they should vote to convict Cluentius. He must have known full well that according to the letter of the law, this defendant was not liable under that section of the statute. Why, then, did he think that the charge was worth making? He knew that a defendant who relies on a legal technicality to avoid conviction looks bad. Therefore, he predicted to the jurors that Cicero would make such a defense, thus trying to put him into the worst possible light (143). Moreover, he argued that there should be equal justice for all, specifically that a law that applied to senators should also apply to knights (145, 150). In view of Cicero's excuses for devoting so much of his speech to the judicial murder charge, it is very likely that the prosecutor had not devoted such a high percentage of his time to that charge; it was a subordinate charge, worth making as a way to discredit the defendant, but not the gravamen of the case.

Cicero responds to the predicted wiliness of the defense by using a technique recommended by Quintilian (*Inst.* 4.5.19–21), to claim that his client has begged him not to resort to a legal technicality and that therefore, honoring this request, he is doing so in his own name.[27] As for the claim that one law should apply to all, Cicero booms forth on the importance of the letter of the law, as opposed to its spirit (a stance that, along with its opposite, his earliest rhetorical education would have taught him to adopt, when it suited the case at hand), specifically to make the case that the judicial murder law is properly applicable only to senators who gain certain advantages from their office and therefore deserve to have special liabilities placed on them (*Clu.* 150–54).

Attius tried to persuade the jury that the defendant was liable to a judicial murder charge (and that he had committed that crime); Cicero, that he was not liable (and that he had not committed it). Giuffrè argues that Cicero had foreseen this type of situation in discussing a poisoning charge with a supplementary charge in the *De inventione rhetorica* (2.58).[28] As I have previously argued (Alexander 1982, 159), the parricide case there discussed is somewhat different from the case of Cluentius, because parricide brought with it certain procedural consequences (the case was heard *extraordinarius,* and the penalty was especially humiliating). In a parricide case, such a charge would have to be specified in the *nominis delatio,* and the defense would be in a stronger position than Cicero was to argue that the prosecutor was obligated to prove the charge. In any case, it is clear that Attius did far more than just mention the charge of judicial murder; he tried to substantiate it by presenting to the jurors the evidence for the opprobrium in which the *iudicium Iunianum* came to be held. All the convictions and other expressions of disapproval whose importance and relevance in this regard Cicero tries to minimize had been already mentioned by Attius (referred to by Cicero as "tu qui iudicia facta commemoras" [you who recall judgments that have been made], *Clu.* 112), or at least most of them had been, since it is unlikely that Cicero would have initiated the recollection of them in the jurors' minds. They include

1. a conviction of C. Iunius (*TLRR* no. 153; *Clu.* 89–96),
2. a conviction of M. Atilius Bulbus (*TLRR* no. 160; *Clu.* 97),[29]
3. a conviction of Ti. Gutta (*TLRR* no. 161; *Clu.* 98),[30]
4. a conviction of P.[31] Popillius (*TLRR* no. 185; *Clu.* 98),
5. a conviction of C. Aelius Paetus Staienus (*TLRR* no. 159; *Clu.* 99–102),
6. a conviction of P. Septimius Scaevola (*TLRR* no. 172; *Clu.* 115),
7. a censorial *nota* against M. Aquilius and Ti. Gutta (*Clu.* 127),
8. a vote by one censor against P. Popillius (*Clu.* 132),
9. a censorial *nota* against A. Cluentius Habitus (*Clu.* 133),
10. a disinheritance of Cn. Egnatius by his father (*Clu.* 135), and
11. a senatus consultum on corruption in *iudicium Iunianum* (*Clu.* 136).

That the prosecutor mentioned the two acquittals of C. Fidiculanius Falcula[32] is much less likely, not only because acquittals served the interests of his case less well, but because of the way Cicero introduces his discussion of these two cases: "Videamus ecquod aliud iudicium quod pro Cluentio sit proferre possimus" [Let us see whether we can produce any other trial that benefits Cluentius] (*Clu.* 103). The easy acceptance that Attius must have thought any charge associated with the *iudicium Iunianum* would have met is supported by Cicero's own damning references to it in the *Verrines* (1 *Verr.* 29, 39; 2 *Verr.* 1.157), which Cicero tries to explain away as a manifestation of an advocate's technique rather than his own opinion (*Clu.* 138–42).

It is worth considering, if only to dismiss it, a further reason why Cicero might have argued that only the poisoning charge was legally relevant. It was common, apparently because of the frequency of homicide cases, to have several quaestors for this law sitting simultaneously. Cicero describes the two other *iudices quaestionum* (besides Q. Voconius Naso, the presiding magistrate in this case), as if they were presiding over a different court, along with the *peculatus, repetundae, ambitus,* and other courts ("reliquae quaestiones"): "quid M. Plaetori et C. Flamini inter sicarios" [What about the murder court of Marcus Plaetorius and Gaius Flaminius?] (*Clu.* 147). This suggests some distinction between the *de veneficiis* and the *de sicariis* courts. How strict and formal is this distinction?[33] If this court were restricted to dealing with poisoning and if any other kind of homicide was there ipso facto irrelevant, Cicero would have made that argument. Instead, he argues only against the judicial murder charge, and he argues against that particular charge only because the defendant, as a senator, is not liable to a charge of that sort, not because this *quaestio* cannot hear such a charge.[34] Kunkel (1963, 741) is probably right that the *lex Cornelia* had united these two kinds of homicide under one statute and that there was no longer any legal distinction between them. Therefore, whether Sulla was the first to add the judicial murder clause to a homicide law or whether one of the two previous such laws (*de sicariis* and *de veneficiis*) had already absorbed that provision, it is clear that it would have made no sense to argue that the clause fell in one part of the law or the other. The distinction Cicero makes probably refers to a practice of dividing up the two kinds of homicide when the number of cases made it impossible for one magistrate to handle all of them. It is likely that the two branches of this law dealt with two different "clienteles"—the *de sicariis* with the more public homicides, the *de veneficiis* with the more domestic. Since most cases would naturally fall on one side or the other, this was a convenient way to distribute them.

Although there is no legal wall dividing the *lex Cornelia de sicariis* into

two parts, the assignment of the case to Q. Voconius rather than to M. Plaetorius or C. Flaminius supports the interpretation that from the prosecutor's point of view, poisoning was the main charge made against Cluentius,
whereas judicial murder was a subordinate issue. Cicero "threw dust in the
jurors' eyes" by reversing this order of importance. This reversal served two
purposes for the defense. First, that Cicero belabored the judicial murder
charge, with detailed discussion of the careers of individual jurors after the
trial, must have left the jurors exhausted and numb when he finally reached
the poisoning charges. They would be less likely to question why Cicero's
refutation of these charges is so perfunctory, and they might have wel-
comed the end of his speech at that point and felt well disposed toward him
for ending the speech quickly. Second, judicial murder was a charge that
Cicero could easily discredit on the basis of a legal technicality, even if the
prosecutor had never intended for it to be the focus of the case. Cluentius
probably had poisoned someone or some people, possibly including his
inveterate enemy Oppianicius senior, and probably deserved to be convicted for that offense.

CHAPTER TEN

In P. Cornelium Sullam

I n 62 B.C., someone who had been elected in 66 to be consul in 65—but who never held the consulate—appeared as a defendant in a *vis* trial. P. Cornelius Sulla, the nephew[1] of the dictator who had created or re-created most of the criminal courts of the period, lost his opportunity to hold Rome's highest annual office because of a successful *ambitus* prosecution in 66, as did his fellow consul-designate P. Autronius Paetus. As a result, under the provisions of the *lex Calpurnia de ambitu,* besides losing the consulate, he was expelled from the Roman Senate, could never again hold public office, and had to pay a fine, but he was not in exile.[2] He chose to spend most of his time in Naples (Cic. *Sull.* 17, 53), even though he could return to Rome if he wished, as he may well have done (see discussion later in this chapter). But this fall from near the pinnacle of Roman politics did not free him from the Roman *quaestiones.* He was accused primarily of participation in the Catilinarian conspiracy of 63, under the *lex Plautia de vi.*

The situation must have looked bleak to the defendant. All those who had been charged and tried under this law as Catilinarians had been convicted (Cic. *Sull.* 6, 71; Berry, 142, 279, ad locc.; Dio Cass. 37.41.4; *TLRR* nos. 226, 228–33). Acquittal by virtue of rhetoric seemed unlikely; Rome's leading orator, Cicero, could hardly be expected to take the case of an alleged

Catilinarian. Moreover, there must have been lingering resentment in some quarters against a defendant who had enriched himself through the proscriptions.[3] But Cicero, a man who had the previous year defended, against a charge of electoral bribery, a consular candidate against whom he had campaigned, Murena, had another surprise in store for the Roman people, as they experienced the relief of a coup d'état denied and the anxiety of finding out what Rome's greatest general, Pompey, would do on his return to Italy. Cicero and Hortensius took the case and won it for their client. Did Cicero takes this case because of politics or, as he would have us believe, a sense of justice and fairness (*Sull.* 14); was this an instance, as the prosecution claimed, of an arbitrary, capricious tyranny of one man who thought he could control the Roman courts; or was the reason the simplest of all, money?

The lead prosecutor, although young,[4] was experienced. L. Manlius Torquatus was the son of the consul, also L. Manlius Torquatus, who was elected in the place of P. Cornelius Sulla.[5] Like his father, the son had played a role in 66 B.C. in the successful *ambitus* conviction of his father's rival.[6] After this trial, he was a moneyer in 65 (Crawford 1974, 1:439, no. 411), and his coinage suggests that he served as a member of the priestly college of the *quindecimviri sacris faciundis*. At the time of the *vis* trial in 62, he was standing for some office (*Sull.* 24), possibly the military tribunate.[7] Torquatus may well have been confident that if he could have contributed, even in only a supporting role, to the conviction of a praetorian and consul-designate, he could lead a successful effort four years later to convict the same person—whose political career was now in a state of ruin—in a judicial environment that seemed solidly pro-prosecution.

At Torquatus's side stood a knight called Cornelius,[8] whose father, C. Cornelius, also a knight, had been involved in the Catilinarian conspiracy and had in fact been assigned to kill Cicero (*Sull.* 18). The father had been tried for *vis* as a result (*TLRR* no. 228), and Cicero's taunt that he lost whatever reward normally exists for informing ("quod praemi solet esse in indicio, reliquerit" [[he] has abandoned what is customary by way of reward for informing], *Sull.* 51) suggests conviction,[9] especially since no one thought him worthy of a defense (6). At the same time, Cicero goes on to mock the father for the fact that his son's defense virtually constitutes an admission of his father's guilt ("quod turpitudinis in confessione, id per accusationem fili susceperit" [[he] has taken on through his son's prosecution what is customary by way of disgrace in a confession], 51). This statement suggests that the younger Cornelius vouched for the fact that Sulla did participate in the Catilinarian conspiracy, and he could have given this assurance only if he possessed inside knowledge of the conspiracy, which he would have received from his father.[10] It is quite possible that the collapse of the conspiracy created a falling-out among its adherents and that Cornelius was acting simply out of spite against those participants who had not suffered as his father had.

Sulla received a much warmer welcome from the Roman establishment than did the other alleged Catilinarians, such as Vargunteius, Ser. Sulla and his brother P. Sulla (not the person defended by Cicero in the *Pro Sulla*), M. Porcius Laeca, and Cornelius, the father of the *subscriptor* (*Sull.* 6). Not only were Cicero and Hortensius there for the defense, but the consulars, the "ornamenta ac lumina rei publicae" [ornaments and leading lights of the state] (5), supported Sulla without making a speech, by their presence at the trial (4–5; see also 81). It is obvious why the prosecutors would not have expected Cicero to defend Sulla. The participation of Hortensius might also have been a surprise. He had already turned down Vargunteius (*TLRR* no. 232; *Sull.* 6), although he had spoken for him before (*TLRR* no. 202).

Hortensius handled the accusations against the defendant that pertained to the so-called First Catilinarian Conspiracy, which scholars since the mid-1960s have dismissed as a fiction. Cicero claimed to know nothing about it, since he had not participated in the *consilia* of Torquatus senior when the latter was consul in 65, and for that reason, Cicero claims, he dealt only with the one aspect of those charges with which he was associated, namely, a letter he had written to Pompey (discussed later in this chapter).[11] We possess only one fragment of Hortensius's speech (Gell. *NA* 1.5.2–3). Gellius writes that Hortensius was ridiculed for an excessively histrionic style of rhetoric because of his liberal use of gestures. In this trial, L. Manlius Torquatus taunted him for that reason with the appellation "Dionysia," after the name of a notorious dancing girl, and Hortensius responded that he would rather be a Dionysia than, like Torquatus, a stranger to the Muses, Aphrodite, and Dionysos. This gibe was a reference to the reputation of Epicureans as being uncultured.[12]

The prosecution obviously tried to make the best of the fact that it faced Rome's best lawyer, Cicero. It tried to persuade the jury that he was an arrogant upstart who was trying to run Rome in a tyrannical fashion. If he could attack some alleged Catilinarians but defend others, the prosecution argued, obviously he believed he could arbitrarily decide whom to condemn and whom to pardon: he was "inconstans" [inconsistent] and "levis" [fickle] (*Sull.* 10). For example, the prosecution argued that it was inconsistent of Cicero to attack Autronius with his testimony (*Sull.* 10, 14; *TLRR* no. 229) and defend Sulla. Cicero responds not only by asserting, as one might expect, that Autronius was guilty, whereas Sulla is innocent, but also by comparing Sulla's model behavior as a defendant to Autronius's attempt to raise a mob of gladiators and fugitive slaves to disrupt the trial with violence (*Sull.* 15). The prosecution asserted that Cicero's arrogation of power was no less than "regnum" [tyranny] (21–22) and, even worse, rule by a foreigner ("peregrinus," 22). Cicero defends his use of power (21) and points out that if he is a foreigner, so are many other Romans whose votes Torquatus will need in elections (24); he notes that even the patrician Torquatus has a mother whose family comes from Asculum (25). If it were not for Cicero, the prosecution says, the defendant would not have even ventured to come to trial but would have forfeited his *caput* and gone into exile (22). Cicero justifies his conduct not only by the example of the "summi viri et clarissimi cives" [leading men and most famous citizens] who are in various ways coming to the support of the defendant (4–5) but also by the example of Hortensius. Why, he asks, was it appropriate for Hortensius to defend Sulla but not appropriate for Cicero to do so (4)? The prosecution argued that Cicero had investigated and exposed the conspiracy of 63 B.C. (3). Cicero's response, not terribly convincing, is that Hortensius was just as familiar with the conspiracy as Cicero himself, because Cicero had publicized it so much (4). Later on, Cicero may be implicitly defending his participation in the trial with another comparison between himself and Hortensius: in this trial, just as Cicero dealt with charges relating to the second conspiracy, Hortensius dealt with charges relating to the first conspiracy three years before ("ergo istius coniurationis crimen defensum ab eo est qui interfuit, qui cognovit, qui particeps et consili vestri fuit et timoris" [Therefore, the charge relating to that conspiracy has been refuted by a man who was concerned with it, who investigated it, and who had a share both in your policy and your fear], 12). If, before the trial, the prosecution thought that it could make Cicero the issue, after Cicero's first *digressio* (2–10) and *partitio* (11–14), it must have wondered whether it had merely handed him an opening to sing his own praises.

The first substantive charge that Cicero attempts to refute is the charge that the Allobroges had implicated Sulla in the conspiracy of 63 B.C. (*Sull.* 36–39). According to Cicero, C. Cassius Longinus told the Allobroges about the plot and mentioned C. Autronius as a participant. They then asked whether P. Sulla was involved. According to Cicero, it was natural for them to think that Sulla might be acting in concert with Autronius, his fellow convict from 65. In order not to diminish the apparent power of the conspiracy in the eyes of these foreigners, yet not wishing to tell an outright lie, Cassius said that he did not know for sure. The prosecutor claimed that Cassius's response failed to exculpate the defendant. Cicero argues that Cassius knew who was involved in the conspiracy and readily revealed the identity of conspirators other than Sulla; when Cassius had been directly asked by the Gauls whether Sulla was involved, he had not been willing to state the outright falsehood that he was involved but avoided saying that he was not, to make the conspiracy seem stronger. Therefore, Cicero claims, Cassius's failure to say positively that Sulla was involved is tantamount to a denial that he was a conspirator.[13] But as Berry points out,[14] Cassius's response "se nescire certum" [that he did not know for certain] (*Sull.* 38) could mean that he really did not know, because Sulla had as yet not responded to an invitation to join the conspiracy. With regard to this charge, as with others, it is possible that Sulla was simply cautious, not committing himself to the conspiracy but interested enough in it not to say no. If that was the case, then from a legal point of view, he would not be guilty of illegal actions, yet he was not as morally innocent as Cicero would have us believe.

Related to this charge is the accusation that Cicero falsified the public records ("tabulae publicae," 40) that were made of the interrogation of Volturcius and the Allobroges in the presence of the Senate on 3 December 63 (Cic. *Cat.* 3.8–10; Sall. *Cat.* 47). This accusation is clearly related to the first charge and is not so much a separate charge against the defendant, who was not accused (at least not explicitly) of complicity in this falsification of the record, as it was a way to undercut some of the evidence that tended to exculpate him. Since the defense did not dispute the fact that Sulla was named by the Allobroges (*Sull.* 36), it would appear that the prosecution claimed that Cicero had altered the passages in which Sulla's name appeared, rather than excising them completely.[15] Cicero protests that he could not have succeeded in such deception, given that many other senators were present, and that he would have been a fool to try. He explains that he took extraordinary measures to ensure that a reliable record was kept of the interrogation, appointing four upright senators with particularly quick penmanship, as well as outstanding memory and knowledge, to keep a record (42).[16] Cicero then collated the four accounts and distributed the edited version as widely as possible throughout Italy. Gabba argues that Cicero could have introduced some distortion either in the process of collating the senators' notes or in the process of having the collated version ("*commentarius meus*," 45) recopied and distributed, and he argues that Torquatus, as Cicero's *familiaris* and *contubernalis*, would have been in a position to know of the deception.[17] Cicero asks rhetorically why Torquatus did not object to the written record that Cicero produced at the time (44). To this question, two possible answers come to mind: first, Torquatus was not permitted to attend a meeting of the Senate, since he was not a senator (unless the right of attending senate meetings had been granted him as a *praemium*, but Cicero does not say that he was present); second, in that time of crisis, Torquatus may not have wanted to hamper the suppression of the conspiracy by textual nitpicking. Certainly, Cicero is right that the account that he produced could not have been totally unlike the actual testimony (45), but there could have been nuances of phrasing that would work later to Sulla's advantage. If any intentional distortion took place on Sulla's behalf in December 63—a possibility that Cicero rejects out of hand as totally inconsistent with the course of action that he was following— Cicero could have been trying to protect Sulla well before the prosecution. That the consuls passed a law during the next year (62 B.C.) against secret placement of supposititious legislation in the official *aerarium* archive (*Schol. Bob.* 140St) suggests that "falsification was a live issue in 62."[18]

The next charge was brought by Cornelius junior. Cicero declines to deal with matters relating to the so-called First Catilinarian Conspiracy, which, he says, Hortensius has already discussed (*Sull.* 51; cf. 11–14); evidently, Cornelius had something to say about these events. Cicero turns to the plot of July 63 to kill Cicero and possibly others, either Antonius (the other consul) and/or the consuls-designate; the existence of such a plot is not a matter of dispute.[19] Cicero says that he saw Autronius in the Campus Martius on that occasion and asserts that Sulla would not have dared show his face there. Then, in a stratagem well explicated by Berry,[20] Cicero changes the subject to a second homicide attempt against him, plotted on the night of 6–7 November, when Cornelius senior was assigned the task of murdering Cicero at his house when he held his morning *salutatio* (18, 52; on Cornelius's involvement in the plot, see also Cic. *Cat.* 1.9 and Sall. *Cat.* 28.1–3). By changing the subject to a homicide attempt four months later, Cicero is able to produce an alibi for his client: he was at Naples at the time

(*Sull.* 53). As Berry argues, when Cicero has said that he saw Autronius in the Campus Martius and then speaks of Sulla's presence in Naples some time later, it is easy for the audience to make the assumption that Sulla was also at Naples during the consular elections, although Cicero never says that this was the case. In Berry's words, "Cicero's deviousness on this point strongly suggests that Sulla did indeed visit Rome for the elections of 63."[21]

Cicero attempts to discredit the testimony of Cornelius junior by mocking his father for the poor judgment shown by him in protecting his own interests: he gave up whatever reward he could have received by informing (*Sull.* 51), which, according to Sallust (*Cat.* 30.6), was immunity and two hundred sesterces for people of free status. It is quite possible that Cicero had negotiated unsuccessfully with Cornelius senior, who had been too stubborn to save his own skin by informing on his confederates. Now, finally ("tandem aliquando," 52), still hesitating somewhat,[22] he admitted, through his son, his involvement in the attempt to murder Cicero in November 63 ("quod turpitudinis in confessione, id per accusationem fili susceperit" [[he] has taken on through his son's prosecution what is customary by way of disgrace in a confession], 51). In other words, Cornelius junior has claimed direct knowledge of the conspiracy through his father, thereby admitting his father's participation.[23] Cicero mocks the father for letting his son stand in for him: "informat ad hoc adumbratum indicium filium" [he molds his son to this sketched-out informing] (52; translation based on Berry). As Berry says,[24] these words were designed to reduce the credibility of what Cornelius junior says. For the same reason, Cicero scoffs at "vos qui haec ab illo mandata defertis" [you who make these [accusations] as assigned by him] (54), referring to Cornelius junior as well as Torquatus. Yet Cornelius's charge, viewed objectively, ought to carry considerable weight, precisely for the reason that Cicero mocks his father. After all, the son has information directly from a participant, one who, at this stage, derives absolutely no benefit from his turncoat activity. If the son said that Sulla had participated in the conspiracy, what advantage did he now derive from making up this information?[25]

The alibi that the defendant was in Naples allows Cicero to pass on easily to the next charge, that Sulla was involved in the procurement of gladiators in support of Catiline (*Sull.* 54–55), since Campania was the center for the training of gladiators. This area of the prosecution was also handled by Cornelius junior, and Cicero scoffs at Cornelius for running errands on his father's behalf (54). But if Cornelius senior was in fact associated with Sulla in some insurrectionary activity, it stands to reason that his son would exploit this source of information. Cicero needs to undermine the charge that Cornelius the father was deeply involved in this wrongdoing. Through the *oratio recta* that Cicero puts in the mouth of his opponent, as part of an *altercatio* between the two of them, we learn that the defendant was accused of being responsible for hiring gladiators in a great haste—haste that probably was unnecessary in view of the fact that the games were not to be held for some time, ostensibly for his cousin Faustus Cornelius Sulla, the son of the dictator,[26] although without the approval of Faustus. Cicero's response is that he has a letter to Sulla from Faustus, who was campaigning in the East at this time,[27] in which Faustus requests the employment of this very company of gladiators, to fill an obligation placed on him by his father's will, and that the games in which they were to perform, in honor of the dictator Sulla, were not far off.[28] Copies of this letter were also sent to L. Julius Caesar (consul in 64), to Q. Pompeius Rufus (tribune of the plebs in 52), Faustus's nephew, and to C. Memmius (praetor in 58), the husband of Faustus's twin sister (55).

The prosecution claimed that (depending on the interpretation of the text) Sulla himself, a freedman of Sulla called (as one would expect) Cornelius, or, as I shall argue, possibly Cornelius senior was in charge of the gladiatorial troupe. Cicero says:

> "At praefuit familiae Cornelius." Iam si in paranda familia nulla suspicio est, quis praefuerit nihil ad rem pertinet. Sed tamen munere servili obtulit se ad ferramenta prospicienda: praefuit vero numquam, eaque res omni tempore per Balbum Fausti libertum administrata est. (*Sull.* 55)

> ["But Cornelius was in charge of the company of slaves." Now if there is no suspicion connected with procuring a company of slaves, it is irrelevant to the matter at hand who was in charge. But, however, while he volunteered to look out for weapons—a slave's job— he was in fact never in charge, and the whole time that matter was managed by Balbus, a freedman of Faustus.]

Berry maintains that it would have been apparent to the jury, which had already heard the statement from the prosecution, that the Cornelius mentioned by the prosecution was a freedman of Sulla.[29] I agree that this Sulla cannot be the defendant himself, for he is elsewhere called P. Sulla. But since the prosecutors assigned this charge to Cornelius junior, would it not make more sense to suppose that the Cornelius mentioned by the prosecution is the father of the *subscriptor?* Cicero's train of thought goes as follows: (1) there was no wrongdoing involved in recruiting the gladiators, so it does not matter who was in charge of the recruitment; (2) in any case, Cornelius volunteered to collect arms, that is, to act in a subordinate capacity, one more appropriate for a slave than a free man; and (3) a freedman of Faustus was in charge of recruiting the gladiators.[30] By this interpretation, there is no need to posit the existence of an additional freedman called Cornelius. Cicero tries to make Cornelius senior look somewhat ridiculous, while undermining his status as a leading figure in an insurrectionary plot involving gladiators and thereby undermining his credibility as a witness against Sulla on this charge.

Next, the prosecution charged that Sulla had sent P. Sittius of Nuceria in Campania to Further Spain to cause trouble in that province (*Sull.* 56–58). Sittius had been a wealthy Roman, probably a Roman knight, from the town of Nuceria in Campania, with business interests not only in Spain but also across the Mediterranean from Spain, in Mauretania. Cicero, writing to Sittius at some point after Cicero's return from exile in September 57 (*Fam.* 5.17.2), provides us with a synopsis of Sittius's life up to that point, at least from the point of view of the three services rendered to him by Cicero up until then. First (and this is before the *vis* trial of Sulla), when Sittius was absent from Rome, Cicero defended him as his name was brought into unpopularity and a charge ("in invidia absens et in crimen vocabare").[31] Second, Cicero defended Sittius's reputation when he was brought into the *vis* trial of Sulla: " . . . cum in tui familiarissimi iudicio ac periculo tuum crimen coniungeretur, ut potui accuratissime te tuamque causam tutatus sum" [. . . and when your closest friend was brought to trial and his ordeal was conjoined with the charge against yourself, I championed you and your cause as diligently as I was able] (trans. Shackleton Bailey). Cicero identifies Sulla as Sittius's "familiarissimus" who served as Sittius's procurator (or agent) while Sittius was conducting business with the king of Mauretania (*Sull.* 56); because of debts contracted in unsuccessful business dealings, Sulla, as Sittius's procurator, was assigned to sell off all his possessions. Sulla was then accused in this trial of having sent Sittius to Further Spain to stir up trouble on behalf of the Catilinarians.[32] Third, when Cicero returned from exile in 57, he found his friend Sittius embroiled in a trial of some sort (a trial that in some way was very unjust and in which a crisis relating to grain gave rise to prejudice against the defendant), and Sittius was condemned,[33] after which Cicero did his best to mitigate the effects of this verdict on Sittius's son (Cic. *Fam.* 5.17.2).

Berry argues that Cicero's refutation of the prosecution's charge involving Sittius is the most convincing of all.[34] Berry shows persuasively that Sittius's military activity must have started after 57, not as early as 64, where Shackleton Bailey places its beginning,[35] or as late as the forties, as argued by Syme.[36] He highlights the following points made by Cicero in his client's favor:

a. Sittius did not go to Spain and Mauretania just in 64 but frequently (*Sull.* 56) and, most importantly, well before the hatching of the conspiracy.[37]

b. Although he did have a debt problem, like many who were indeed Catilinarians, Sittius arranged for some[38] of his Italic holdings to be sold to pay off these debts.

c. If Sulla had wanted to use Sittius for a conspiracy in Rome, he would not have sent him far away.

d. In terms of character, Sittius was a *bonus* (loyal citizen). His father had sided with Rome during the Social War, and his debts were due not to extravagance but simply to bad business decisions.

I find none of these arguments decisive and therefore do not believe that we know whether Sittius was involved in the Catilinarian conspiracy. As to point *a,* the fact that Sittius had established business contacts in the West does not make it less likely that he could be employed for a political and/or military conspiracy by conspirators. Rather, it makes him a good choice for that role. It is possible that Catiline was laying the groundwork already in 64 for a coup d'état the following year, or Catiline might have first contacted Sittius in 63 when Sittius was already in Spain. In that case, while Cicero might be right that Sittius was not sent ("missus," 56) to Further Spain by Catiline, he was located in a good place to cause trouble. Or he might have traveled from Mauretania to Spain at the behest of Catiline. As to point *c,* if Sulla was involved in the conspiracy, Sittius would have been a natural person for him to draw into it, since they were such close friends (57). Moreover, Sertorius had shown that Spain provided an excellent base of operations against Rome, and some Romans were ready to believe—whether rightly or, more probably, wrongly—that the proquaestorship of Cn. Calpurnius Piso (65–64 B.C.) had something to do with seditious activity.[39] Hannibal had left Rome with an indelible fear of Spain as a threat to Rome, and the long campaign to conquer Spain throughout most of the second century must have reinforced that fear. As to points *b* and *d*, if Sittius had desperate problems with debt, as he evidently did if he had to instruct Sulla to sell "plurima et pulcherrima praedia" [a large number of his finest properties] (56), he might well have been led to desperate measures. As Berry points out,[40] Catiline himself claimed to be able to settle his own debts from his holdings (Sall. *Cat.* 35). All in all, Cicero's refutation of this charge seems no more or less convincing than his refutations of the others. Sittius's later career as a condottiere in Africa in the forties shows that he had the temperament for such activity, and certainly in 63 and possibly a year earlier, Catiline could have been lining up potential condottieri to fight on his side. Spain and Africa would be logical places to find such condottieri. Finally, Sittius had already lost most of his possessions and may have been attracted to desperate measures. None of these arguments constitutes evidence that Sittius supported the Catilinarians, but they do suggest that the idea is not implausible.

About fifteen kilometers west from Nuceria was Pompeii, whose inhabitants were not always friendly to their neighbors, at least not in later times (Tac. *Ann.* 14.17). Sulla was accused of having incited the citizens of Pompeii to join Catiline (*Sull.* 60–62). Specifically, the prosecutor claims that he capitalized on discord between the Pompeiani (the original inhabitants of the town) and the *coloni*, colonists settled by the defendant's uncle, another Sulla, to punish Pompeii for its participation in the Social War. The defendant Sulla was one of the founders and, thereby, one of the patrons of the town, and evidently he had played a part (along with other *patroni* of Pompeii) in settling a dispute between the two groups, in a way that was more to the favor of the original inhabitants.[41] Cicero's main defense is to say that neither group took part in the Catilinarian conspiracy and that they have both sent delegations to show support for the defendant.

Cicero's response to this charge is so brief that the modern reader must conclude either that the prosecution had a weak case with few specifics and thus there was little Cicero could say in response or that the prosecution had a strong case and Cicero preferred to pass over the subject hurriedly. He does tell us that the matter or matters that Sulla settled had something

to do with *ambulatio*, "strolling" or "a promenade," and *suffragia*, "voting."
Although attempts have been made to interpret these two words as referring to one charge relating to voting, campaigning, or freedom of move-
ment within the walls, Wiseman[42] has shown that these are probably two
separate matters: (1) some restriction on the voting power of the precolo-
nial population (as opposed to the Sullan colonists) and (2) exclusion from
a particular place for walking, or portico, that is, the *quadriporticus* just
behind the main theater, which is near the *theatrum tectum*. The evidence
for the latter issue consists of two inscriptions (*CIL* 10.844, 852 = *ILS* 5636,
5627) that show that two *duoviri quinquennales*, C. Quinctius Valgus[43] and
M. Porcius, played a part in the construction of both the amphitheater at
Pompeii and the *theatrum tectum*. Wiseman suggests that just as part of the
amphitheater was reserved for the *coloni*, the *quadriporticus* may have also
been restricted for their use. Vitruvius (5.9.1) mentions that this kind of
facility was useful for a crowd seeking to avoid the rain, so the Pompeiani
may have seriously resented any limitation on their right to make use of it,
especially since it covered a substantial area, about two thousand square
meters.

   The prosecution claimed that the purpose of mobilizing gladiators and
other resources was to apply force for the passage of a bill to reduce the disabilities suffered by Sulla and Autronius as a result of their conviction of 66
B.C. (*Sull.* 62–66). This measure would have turned back the clock as far as
the *ambitus* penalties that they had suffered, so that instead of being
expelled from the Senate in perpetuity and forbidden to run for office
again, as well as being assessed a fine, as the *lex Calpurnia* (under which
they had been tried) stipulated, they would only be prevented from holding
office for ten years, as the previous law, the *lex Cornelia*, had stipulated.[44]
The result of this message would have been to allow the two convicted consuls-elect to serve in the Senate and run for the consulate again in 56 B.C.
This *derogatio* (partial abrogation) of the *lex Calpurnia de ambitu* went
against the spirit of the times. Although another such *derogatio* was proposed for this very statute (Asc. 69C),[45] there was political pressure to
strengthen the law on electoral bribery, not weaken it (Cic. *Mur.* 47), and
Cicero himself as consul, the year before this trial, had passed a tougher law
containing a provision of ten years of exile for the convicted (Cic. *Mur.* 3,
45, 89; Cic. *Planc.* 83; Cic. *Sest.* 133; Dio Cass. 37.29.1; *Schol. Bob.* 79St).[46]

   The impetus for this proposal clearly came from Sulla's family. It was
proposed by Sulla's younger uterine half brother, L. Caecilius Rufus (prae-

tor in 57), who became tribune of the people on 10 December 64.[47] Stone argues that Sulla bankrolled the campaign of C. Antonius and Catiline for the consulate of 63 and furnished his house as a meeting place for these two candidates and their campaign staff (Cic. *Tog. cand. apud* Asc. 83C), to facilitate passage of this proposal.[48] When Sulla decided to give up on it, he delegated Q. Metellus Celer (praetor in 63, consul in 60) to speak on his behalf (*Sull.* 65); Celer was the half brother of Mucia, the wife of Pompey, who was Sulla's brother-in-law.[49] Apparently, Caecilius immediately abandoned the proposal and went on to support the cause of the *boni*.

Cicero tries to minimize the seriousness of this attempt in three ways. First, he minimizes its legal significance. Although, as consul later in the year, after the failure of this bill, he would denounce "iudiciorum perturbationes, rerum iudicatarum infirmationes, restitutio damnatorum" [disruption of the courts, annulment of previous decisions, [and] reinstatement of the condemned] (*Leg. agr.* 2.10), he is here at pains to distinguish between the overturning of a verdict, which he admits would constitute an unwarranted attack on *res iudicatae,* and the reduction of a penalty. Second, he makes the point that Sulla, speaking through the praetor Q. Caecilius Metellus Celer, urged that the bill be dropped. Third, he changes the subject as quickly as possible to the fear raised by Sulla's co-convict, Autronius, who obviously would have also benefited by the proposal, despite the fact that the political impetus came from Sulla and his family. Even Cicero cannot deny that the whole idea was a mistake ("errato L. Caecili" [the mistake of Lucius Caecilius], *Sull.* 64), which he ascribes to "amor fraternus" [love for a brother] (62). Although his opening sentence in dealing with this matter establishes the link between *vis* and the proposal, he never directly refutes the notion that Sulla had at least considered the use of *vis* to get the *rogatio Caecilia* passed. The prosecution must have vigorously argued three points: first, that the proposal was clearly linked to Sulla; second, that Sulla was ready to use force to overturn most of the effects of his prior conviction and thus that the Roman people might face a second consular candidacy of P. Cornelius Sulla in 56 B.C., as well as his immediate return to the Senate; and third, that Sulla was attacking the sanctity of *res iudicatae,* thereby threatening the stability of the state by undermining its judicial decisions.

Finally, Cicero dealt with the prosecutor's charge that Sulla had participated in the so-called First Catilinarian Conspiracy (*Sull.* 67–68), although, for the most part, the refutation of that charge had been assigned to Hortensius. Cicero responded to the part of that charge that rested on a letter written by Cicero to Pompey in late 63, in which he bragged of his exploits and in this way irritated the great general (*Schol. Bob.* 167St). In this letter, he spoke of a "furorem incredibilem biennio ante conceptum" [unbelievable madness conceived two years earlier] (67), which ought to refer either to December 65 (if by "biennium" Cicero meant literally twenty-four months) or to sometime in 65 (if he was thinking in terms of two calendar years).[50] Cicero had no motive to expatiate on the discrepancy between 66, the year when the so-called First Catilinarian Conspiracy was planned, and 65, specifically 5 February of that year, when a "caedes optimatium" (slaughter of the optimates) mentioned in his letter to Pompey was planned, for he could associate these events with people other than his client (Piso, Catiline, Vargunteius, and Autronius), people whom Cicero is happy to paint in the blackest terms.[51]

As Ramsey has shown,[52] Cicero here distorts the prosecution's allegation. The prosecutor charged that Sulla had used violence in attempting to seize the consulate for himself. Cicero wants his audience to believe that the prosecutor has contradicted himself: how could Sulla both campaign for the consulate for Catiline and try to seize it for himself? Both men could not hold that office at the same time, since both were patricians; no more than one patrician could be consul in any given year. Ramsey has shown that Cicero misleadingly telescopes two different stages in the events of 66. In autumn of that year, Sulla, who, along with Autronius, had already been stripped of his consulate, supported Catiline in a supplementary election. The implication is that if Sulla could not be consul in 65, he would not sit idly by while the man who had convicted him, L. Manlius Torquatus, obtained that office. The election of the patrician Catiline would preclude the election of the patrician Torquatus. But Catiline's candidacy was disallowed, possibly on the grounds that only the candidates in the original election (in July 66 for the consulate of 65) could be candidates in the supplementary election; Catiline had not originally been a candidate.[53] The victors in this election were thus Torquatus and Cotta. According to the prosecution, Sulla then ("patre tuo consule designato" [when your [Torquatus junior's] father was consul-designate], 11) adopted a new plan—to assassinate Torquatus on 1 January 65 and take his place. The prosecution evidently argued that Cicero's own letter to Pompey in 63 substantiated this charge, frequently citing it in the trial ("saepe recitas," 67). We know no more about the specifics of the charge or the evidence that substantiated it, because Cicero dismisses it rather hurriedly as inconsistent with Sulla's character and ends by proclaiming that he has dealt with "virtually all" the charges ("criminibus omnibus fere dissolutis" [now that I have refuted virtually all the charges], 69). One would like to know what charges, however trivial they may have been, Cicero declined to discuss and refute.[54]

Berry presents an ingenious argument to the effect that the order in which Cicero presented his refutation of the charges in this case reflects the order in which the prosecutors had made those charges. He points out that Cicero recommends in two of his rhetorical works (*Orat.* 50; *De Or.* 2.314) the practice of inserting weak points in the argument between the stronger points. Berry sees no such policy in the second *reprehensio,* where the third through eighth charges are discussed. Berry thinks that Cicero's refutation of the charge of conspiracy between Sulla and Sittius is ironclad, yet Cicero places that refutation neither first in the *reprehensio* (i.e., third overall) nor last, but rather third in the *reprehensio* (i.e. fifth overall). Therefore, according to Berry, no strategic reason lies behind the order in which the charges are refuted, and Cicero probably simply followed the prosecutors' ordering of the charges, which he sees as one of decreasing importance, an ordering that suited both sides.[55] But if the Sittius charge is viewed as possessing at least as much plausibility as the others, as I have argued earlier in this chapter, then this line of reasoning seems much less compelling.[56]

The division of the charges also weighs against this approach. Working from the proposition that Cicero followed the prosecutors' order, Berry assigns to Cornelius not just the third and fourth charges (massacre in the consular elections in 63 for 62 and gladiators) but also the fifth, sixth, and seventh (Sittius, Pompeii, and *rogatio Caecilia*). We know that Torquatus presented the second and eighth charges (falsification of *tabulae publicae* and participation in the First Catilinarian Conspiracy) (*Sull.* 40, 67 [cf. 68, "patre tuo"]), and Berry is working on the premise that Cornelius was in the better position to comment on the charges relating to the conspiracy of 63, whereas Torquatus focused on denigrating Sulla's defenders. Yet there is no particular reason to think that Cornelius dealt with the fifth, sixth, and seventh points, and it seems more likely that his participation was limited to the two points where he possessed special knowledge.[57] Whether Cornelius handled two or five charges, Berry's point of view that Cicero follows the order of charges as presented by the prosecution cannot account for the order in which all the charges are handled by Cicero in his speech (though it could possibly account for the order of charges just in the second *repre-*

hensio, the third through eighth charges), because Cicero there first deals with charges made by Torquatus, then deals with charges made by Cornelius, and then goes back to at least one other charge made by Torquatus. Obviously, Torquatus did not deliver two speeches, with a speech by Cornelius inserted between them. Moreover, given that the defense speeches dealt with Sulla's alleged participation in an earlier conspiracy both at the beginning (in Hortensius's speech) and at the end (in the latter part of Cicero's speech), whereas the prosecution presumably made that charge in one segment, it is fair to infer that at least in this one instance, the defense did not follow the lead of the prosecution. I conclude that we cannot use the order in which Cicero attempts to refute the charges to draw any conclusions about the order of charges as presented by the prosecutors. As Berry suggests (232), the relative importance of the charges may have been a factor for both prosecution and defense, leading them both to deal with the more important charges earlier in the speech, while the jury was still relatively fresh and attentive. But it is also plausible that Cicero was particularly anxious to refute the second charge (falsification of the evidence of the Allobroges by Cicero), since it was directed at himself, and that before he could refute this charge, he needed to deal with the first charge, the evidence of the Allobroges against his client. Since, as a defense speaker, his *auctoritas* was an asset for the defendant, Cicero was exculpating himself not just on his own behalf but for his client's sake as well.

Sulla was acquitted; although no source tells us this explicitly, the fact that he was in Rome in 54 makes it clear that he was not in exile, and therefore he cannot have been condemned (Cic. *Att.* 4.18.3; *Q Fr.* 3.3.2).[58] Did he deserve this verdict? As Berry rightly points out, Sulla was on trial for *vis,* not for Catilinarianism, and even if Sulla was waiting in 63 to see if Catiline was successful, keeping the option open of joining him if he was, that intention does not constitute violence.[59] Berry is right to find unconvincing Cicero's refutation of the third, sixth, and seventh charges (massacre in 63, Pompeii, and *rogatio Caecilia*),[60] and I do not believe that, with the evidence at our disposal, we are in a position to dismiss any of the charges outright. But that is not to say that we know that Sulla had committed *vis* or, even less, that the prosecution had presented convincing evidence that he had.

Berry is right to ask whether it is credible that Cicero would have defended anyone whom he genuinely believed to be a Catilinarian.[61] Cicero was accused of having received a loan of two million sesterces from Sulla when he was a defendant in 62 and of using that money later that year, after the trial, to buy a house on the Palatine.[62] Whether or not Cicero over-stepped the *lex Cincia de donis et muneribus* by accepting this loan,[63] it is not plausible that such a loan would have caused him to defend someone whom he believed to have joined himself to Catiline, though Sulla could have committed *vis* without being a Catilinarian. Whatever Cicero's feeling toward Sulla in 62, by the time of Sulla's death in 45, Cicero did not greatly regret his passing (*Fam.* 15.17.2, 9.10.3), and in 44, Cicero recalled how his career was marked from start to finish by profiteering from civil war, under both Sulla and Caesar (*Off.* 2.29).[64]

CHAPTER ELEVEN

In P. Sestium

icero's *Pro Sestio* presents at least two paradoxes. First, more than any other speech of his, it responds to the prosecutors' speeches; yet it provides fewer details about what the prosecutors had actually said than does any other speech. Second, given that one of the main voids we face is the lack of extant "inartificial proofs," such as testimony and documents, we might expect that we would gain a particularly close view of that aspect of this case from a speech by Cicero, the *In Vatinium*, that is supposed to be a response to the testimony of one of the witnesses, Vatinius; yet Cicero's attack on Vatinius reveals almost nothing about what he had said, and the little it does tell us seems to have little to do with Sestius or what crimes he was supposed to have committed. Indeed, the main piece of evidence that we gain from the *In Vatinium* about the *vis* case against Sestius is that—in the view of this prosecution witness, at least—it ought not to have been a *vis* case at all. If even a supporter of the prosecution had strong reservations about whether the defendant's actions fell under the definition of *vis*, it is difficult to feel confident that we can apply to this particular crime what we know about the crime of *vis* or the statute that established it as a crime.

Sestius aided Cicero in his period of banishment (March 58–August 57) and staunchly promoted his return in his capacity as tribune of the people in 57 B.C. (Cic. *Att.* 3.19.2; *Q Fr.* 1.4.2; *Red. sen.* 20; *Red. pop.* 15; *Sest.* passim), even suffering serious wounds (despite his sacrosanct status) in the effort (Cic. *Q Fr.* 2.3.6; *Sest.* 85; *Red. sen.* 30). In the violence of November 57 between Milo's and Clodius's supporters, Sestius was pro-Milonian to the point of irrationality ("Sestius furere" [Sestius was beside himself], Cic. *Att.* 4.3.3; trans. Shackleton Bailey). When Sestius faced prosecution, not only for *vis* but also for *ambitus* (*TLRR* nos. 271, 270), Cicero immediately offered his services as *patronus* (Cic. *Q Fr.* 2.3.5). Yet Cicero was not an unabashed admirer of Sestius. While in exile, he complained that the proposals of Sestius for his recall did not go quite far enough (*Att.* 3.20.3, 3.23.4). When he wrote his brother about his offer of help, he said that most people had expected him to be angry with Sestius and that his prompt support had made him look extremely indulgent and generous (*Q Fr.* 2.3.5). In his next letter to his brother (2.4.1), he reports that he leaned over backward to warrant a reputation for generosity, despite the defendant's unreasonableness ("perversitas") and hard-to-please ("morosus") temperament. We do not know what reason Cicero had for anger, but it seems likely that Sestius had been a difficult client, possibly offering Rome's greatest advocate unwanted advice on how to manage the case. Sestius's literary efforts were notoriously inept, as not only Cicero (*Fam.* 7.32.1; *Att.* 7.17.2) but also Catullus (poem 44) attest.

The man who made the original *postulatio* on 10 February 56 was an M. Tullius (Cic. *Q Fr.* 2.3.5). Of him, we hear nothing more, so he either lost out in the *divinatio* or served as *subscriptor* without being mentioned by Cicero in his defense speech or elsewhere. The chief prosecutor, as it turned out, was P. Albinovanus, mentioned as a *pontifex minor* in 57 (Cic. *Har. resp.* 12).[1] There was more than one prosecutor ("accusatores," *Vat.* 3), and one of the other participants, presumably a *subscriptor*, was an otherwise unknown T. Claudius. This none too distinguished prosecutorial team was strengthened by the participation of the much better known P. Vatinius (tribune of the plebs in 59), whose role in the trial permitted Cicero to speak of the formal prosecutors as tools of Vatinius ("a te accusatores esse instructos et subornatos" [the prosecutors had been instructed and coached by you], 3), with the additional elaboration by Cicero to the effect that not only did Vatinius advise the prosecutors but Clodius supported them (". . . alter tuis consiliis, illo tamen adiuvante" [. . . the other at your suggestion, but with his assistance], 41). A Clodian role is supported by the Bobbian scholiast (125St), who says that Clodius accused "Sextius [*sic*] de vi," having set up P. Albinovanus as the head of the prosecution ("inmisso velut principe delationis P. Albinovano" [with Publius Albinovanus having been inserted as the chief of the prosecution]). In chapters 8 and 9, we have seen other examples of attempts to discredit the prosecutors by claiming that they are tools of someone else, and we will see another such example in chapter 12.[2] The formal role of Vatinius was as a witness (*Vat.* 3), but as we will see in this chapter, he comes to play a much more important role in the prosecution than a witness normally would. Even if we distrust Cicero's characterization of Vatinius's role in the *Pro Sestio* or the *In Vatinium,* we possess reliable evidence that Vatinius did attack Sestius: Cicero, in a letter to his brother, refers to "Vatinium, a quo palam oppugnabatur" [Vatinius, by whom he was being openly attacked] (*Q Fr.* 2.4.1).

The prosecution effort was riven by disputes on two fronts: who should prosecute and what criminal statute provided the best grounds for attacking Sestius. Vatinius attacked Albinovanus from the beginning as a *praevaricator,* someone not engaged in a bona fide effort to obtain a conviction ("quem praevaricatorem esse ab initio iudicasses" [whom you from the beginning had judged to be in collusion with the defense], *Vat.* 3). According to Cicero, in the course of the whole trial—including a *postulatio* or *divinatio,* the appearance of Vatinius as a witness, and the day before Cicero attacked him in the *In Vatinium*[3] —Vatinius contradicted himself, on the one hand providing evidence that T. Claudius had discussed the case with him, that Albinovanus had discussed it with him at his house, and that he had afforded Albinovanus copies of otherwise unobtainable speeches of P. Sestius, yet on the other hand claiming hardly to know Albinovanus and not to have spoken with him about the prosecution of Sestius or anything else. But as Pocock points out,[4] these so-called inconsistencies may have a logical explanation. Vatinius may have been making the points (a) that he did not know Albinovanus and therefore had no confidence in him and (b) that in general Albinovanus was a "nobody." When Albinovanus had won the position of *nominis delator,* however, Vatinius passed on to him copies of some of Sestius's speeches and cooperated with the prosecution in other ways. The prosecution's conduct confirmed Vatinius's initial doubts, possibly weakening its case by justifying Milo's violence as opposed to Sestius's (see discussion later in this chapter), and at some point, Vatinius decided to denounce the prosecution for *praevaricatio.*

The other issue on which Cicero tried to embarrass the prosecution was a controversy over whether *vis* was the best charge on which to prosecute

Sestius. Speaking before the time when Cicero delivered the *In Vatinium*, Vatinius said that he had not thought that *vis* was an appropriate charge to use against Sestius (41). With hindsight, since we know that Sestius was unanimously acquitted on the *vis* charge, the wisdom of his objection seems obvious. Vatinius may have been concerned that Sestius's allegedly violent actions were so similar to Milo's, when in 57 B.C. both used the office of tribune to try to get Cicero recalled, that Sestius would be protected by the approval that Milo was attracting. Even Vatinius himself had praised Milo in this trial, despite the fact that in the trial of Milo (probably a *iudicium populi* [TLRR no. 266, n. 2]), still ongoing at the time of this trial (*Sest.* 144), he had testified against the defendant (*Vat.* 40).[5] Possibly, Albinovanus had argued that the procedural advantages provided by a *vis* prosecution—in getting space on a court calendar that, in this year, was unusually crowded—outweighed this drawback.[6] Just as Vatinius held his reservations about Albinovanus in check throughout most of the trial, so he held his reservations about the charge in check, until it seemed clear to him that the prosecution was doomed, at which time he attempted to retrieve the situation by violently denouncing the prosecutors, as well as the defense *patroni* and the defendant.

The issue of *praevaricatio* may help us understand the nature of the *oratio in Vatinium*. The circumstances of this speech have been debated, especially whether Vatinius really did deliver a continuous speech to which Cicero responded with the extant speech.[7] There is ample internal evidence in the *In Vatinium* that Vatinius had made a speech, to which Cicero was responding. Cicero says that he had attacked Vatinius "paulo ante" (*Vat.* 1), possibly the day before, and this would have been in response to testimony that Vatinius had delivered the day before (3), in which he had minimized the relationship he had with the prosecutors and the role he played in their planning. The next day, after L. Gellius Publicola had testified (*Vat.* 4), an enraged Vatinius attacked Cicero in what Cicero seems to describe as a continuous speech ("cum multa . . . diceres . . ." [when you said many things . . .], *Vat.* 41), to which Cicero responded in kind (*Vat.* 5–10). Cicero says in the *In Vatinium* that after he has given this speech, Vatinius will be allowed to respond to it (*Vat.* 40).

As Pocock points out,[8] such internal evidence is not conclusive. Either if Vatinius had not delivered a continuous *oratio* in this trial or if Cicero had never responded to a speech by Vatinius, Cicero could have inserted false references to these prior events to enhance the verisimilitude of a speech that he composed and published later. However, as Pocock also notes,[9] there is also later, external evidence of a speech by Vatinius to which Cicero replied (Macrob. *Sat.* 2.1.12; cf. 2.3.5, as well as, according to Pocock, Quint. *Inst.* 5.7.6).[10] Cicero himself, in a letter to Lentulus (*Fam.* 1.9.7), provides the strongest evidence that his speech was an *interrogatio*, because he labels it as such while describing it as a total attack on Vatinius's tribunate of 59, a description that fits sections 13–32 (out of forty-one sections). He goes on to mention three points—the first made by Vatinius in his speech, the second and third made by Cicero in his. Although Meyer (1919, 135 n. 1) has challenged the correspondence between this account and the published speech (thus arguing that the published version was quite different from the orally delivered version), Pocock has convincingly argued that the first and third items do correspond to what we know from our version of the *In Vatinium*, and the second point could have appeared in a lacuna between sections 4 and 5. The three points are (1) Vatinius said in his testimony that Cicero had succumbed to Caesar's success and was beginning to be his friend, (2) Cicero responded that he preferred the fate of Bibulus to all of Caesar's triumphs and victories, and (3) Cicero declared that the people who forced him into exile were the same people who prevented Bibulus from leaving his house. Pocock argues that the first point could have been made by Vatinius in his speech, the second could have appeared in the missing section between sections 4 and 5, and the third point is alluded to in sections 5 and 22.[11] He suggests that Vatinius obtained permission, presumably from the praetor, to make a statement.

> If it be argued that it is not the part of a witness to make speeches in the course of a case, the reply is that it seems no more improbable that Vatinius should have obtained leave to make a statement, as his personal honour had been assailed and *the interests of justice compromised* [my italics], than that he should have been allowed to sling abuse at his cross-examiner.[12]

In the phrase I have italicized, Pocock may have provided a key insight to the understanding of this unusual rhetorical event, wherein a witness delivered a continuous speech, followed by defense rebuttal and witness counterrebuttal.

The legal point that Vatinius made in his speech was that the prosecutors were colluding with the defense, so that the jury was not hearing a proper presentation of the case against the defendant (*Vat.* 3, 40, 41).[13] By analogy with the *lex repetundarum* (line 56), it is likely that after this trial, if *praevaricatio* could be shown to have taken place, the original verdict would be voided, the case would be reheard, and a new verdict would be rendered.[14] But it is very likely that the judicial officials, praetors and *iudices quaestionis*, were reluctant to grant permission for cases to be retried, especially in the crowded courts of 56 B.C. Two alternative procedural possibilities should be considered. First, it is possible that some or all of the statutes whereby *quaestiones perpetuae* were established did not rule out a special hearing to take place in the middle of the trial, so that the question of prosecutorial misconduct could be immediately adjudicated and a true verdict rendered. Second, the praetor might have been persuaded that the circumstances in this case were in some way extraordinary and that in this case, on an exceptional basis, a special hearing should be granted. If either of these possibilities were the case in 56 B.C., the speech by Vatinius, the response by Cicero (the *In Vatinium*), and Vatinius's response to Cicero's speech could have constituted a trial within a trial, to settle the question of *praevaricatio*.[15]

Although we have no evidence of such a hearing in the late Republic, we do have an example of the second procedural possibility occurring around the year A.D. 100. Pliny the Younger (*Ep.* 3.9) writes about a set of trials that revolved around the alleged extortion of Classicus, the governor of Baetica.[16] Casta, the wife of the former governor, was prosecuted, and a witness accused Norbanus Licinianus, one of the Spanish representatives, of collusion. Pliny, who was serving as prosecutor, speculates that Norbanus either was angry at being compelled to testify or had been corrupted by one of the defendants to damage the case. Pliny explains that the law provided that a *praevaricatio* hearing should occur after the trial, because the good faith of prosecutors can be best judged from their handling of the whole case. But in this case, general indignation against someone associated with the reign of Domitian overwhelmed the letter of the law. Despite Norbanus's protestations that a future date for the hearing should be set and the charges against him laid out, the matter was heard at once, and he was found guilty (not only of *praevaricatio* in this trial but of *calumnia* in others) and was relegated to an island. When the court returned to the trial of Casta, Pliny tried to use this verdict against her, but she was acquitted nonetheless—in an unprecedented combination of a verdict of innocence for the defendant and a verdict of guilty for a member of the prosecutorial team adjudged to have colluded with her (3.9.28–34).[17]

This sequence of legal events occurring about a century and a half later than the trial of Sestius directly supports the possibility that the praetor allowed a hearing to take place in the middle of the trial to deal with Vatinius's charge of *praevaricatio* between Albinovanus and Cicero. But the evidence does not rule out the possibility that the republican laws regularly allowed a trial within a trial and that the statute referred to by Pliny as stipulating that a *praevaricatio* hearing should be held off until the end of the trial ("est lege cautum ut reus ante peragatur, tunc de praevaricatione quaeratur" [it has been legally prescribed that first legal proceedings are carried through regarding the defendant, and then there is an investigation about collusion], *Ep.* 3.9.30) refers to a later, possibly Augustan, reform, perhaps designed to prevent the use of such a hearing as a stalling tactic. Although the epigraphic *lex repetundarum* contains nothing about holding such a *praevaricatio* hearing before a verdict is rendered, nothing in it rules out that possibility. Line 75 establishes a procedure for calling back the original jurors to judge *praevaricatio* after the criminal trial was over (intelligently allowing for the fact that some of the original jurors may have died), but that clause does not preclude the possibility that a no longer extant clause of the law also allowed for a *praevaricatio* (or *calumnia*) hearing before the verdict was given in the main trial. Whether such a hearing was ordinary or extraordinary, it would not be surprising if the jurors much preferred to judge the matter of prosecutorial misconduct during the main trial, rather than being forced to return to the matter months or even years later. All in all, a hearing on *praevaricatio* would account not only for the trio of speeches in the middle of the *interrogatio* but also for the fact that Vatinius, in his first speech, attacked both Albinovanus and Cicero, the two men he was accusing of colluding together. It would also account for the dissension that sprang up among those who had participated in the prosecution in some role: for example, L. Aemilius Paullus (consul in 50), a prosecution witness, immediately began to threaten a prosecution of Vatinius (Cic. *Q Fr.* 2.4.1).

The speakers for the defense were Cicero, Hortensius, Crassus, and C. Licinius Calvus (*Schol. Bob.* 125St). In the *Pro Sestio*, Cicero refers to the fact that other speakers have answered the individual charges ("Sed quoniam singulis criminibus ceteri responderunt . . ." [But since the other speakers have answered each individual charge . . .], 5), allowing Cicero to expatiate on the defendant's fine character. He twice refers to Hortensius's contribution, first rather generally (3), then specifying that Hortensius spoke about the tribunate of Sestius in such a way as to provide a model of political activity for Rome's youth (14). Pompey himself entered the city to deliver a *laudatio* for Sestius (Cic. *Fam.* 1.9.7), though he held imperium at the time and probably needed a special dispensation (see Shackleton Bailey, *CLF,* 1:309, 392).

Since Hortensius and the other *patroni* had dealt with the actual charges, Cicero makes almost no reference to them in his *Pro Sestio.* Indeed, it is all too easy to list his specific references to the prosecutors' speeches:

1. "'Atqui vis in foro versata est'" ["And yet violence came frequently to the Forum"] (77). There was violence in the forum, starting with an abortive attempt on 23 January 57 to vote on a bill that called for Cicero's recall.

2. "... [accusator] qui P. Sestium queritur cum multitudine in tribunatu et cum praesidio magno fuisse ..." [... [the prosecutor], who complains that Publius Sestius during his tribunate was with a throng and a large bodyguard ...] (78). The prosecutor complained that as tribune in 57, Sestius went around accompanied by a retinue and a large bodyguard. This charge is amplified: "'Homines ... emisti, coegisti, parasti'" ["You bought, collected, and prepared men"] (84). The implication here is that those who surrounded Sestius were not friends, clients, and other voluntary supporters but mercenaries for hire.

3. "'At nondum erat maturum; nondum res ipsa ad eius modi praesidia viros bonos compellebat'" ["But it was not yet the proper time; the situation itself was not yet forcing good men to protective measures of this sort"] (84). Conceding the necessity to use force at some point, the prosecution claimed that Sestius used it before it was required. The prosecution may have claimed that Sestius, by his premature use of force, compelled his opponents to arm themselves; thus, he would have initiated violence rather than reacted to it.

4. Cicero notes that Sestius's conduct has been unfavorably contrasted with that of Milo, his colleague in the tribunate of 57 (86–87). Both used a bodyguard, but if we can believe Cicero, the prosecution approved of Milo's but disapproved of Sestius's (90), arguing that Milo used a combination of *ius* (law) and *vis* (92).

5. Cicero argues against the claim that Sestius represented the interests of a "natio optimatium" [breed of *optimates*] (96, 132).[18] The
prosecution's implication probably was that Sestius promoted
the interests of a narrow faction of Romans who were trying to
take control of the state.

Overall, the prosecution painted a grim picture of the violence that had
overtaken the Roman Republic. It tried to anticipate the argument that
force was necessary to meet force, by arguing that Sestius had resorted to
violence early on and had therefore instigated it rather then checked it, and
by contrasting Sestius with Milo—the former as being part of the problem,
the latter as being in some way part of the solution or at least acting within
his legitimate rights, possibly the right of self-defense. Thus, the prosecution avoided a hard-line stand based on the letter of the law, which would
have held that all violence was wrong, even if it was retaliation or self-
defense; it favored a more moderate position that there was a right way and
a wrong way to use force. In political terms, it probably hoped to make
those jurors who were sympathetic to Milo and the forces that supported
Cicero's recall feel that they could vote to condemn Sestius without
renouncing their political beliefs.

Cicero does not deny that his client had raised an armed force—a
"manus" [band] and "copiae" [troops] (*Sest.* 84)—nor does he argue (as he
might have been able to, and perhaps Hortensius did so) that his client did
the deed but did so legally. In rhetorical terms, he presents not a conjectural
issue (*non feci*) or a legal (*legitima*) issue (*iure feci*) but a juridical issue, of
the assumptive type, based on *translatio criminis* (the crimes of Clodius
necessitated the course of action chosen by Sestius) and on the *comparatio*
(any violence was justified by a greater good, the welfare of the state).[19] To
neutralize the prosecutors' arguments, he uses the concessions granted by
them to ridicule them for inconsistency. What is the difference, he asks,
between Milo's and Sestius's conduct (86, 87)? How is Milo's bodyguard
different from Sestius's? he queries (90). At the same time, he tries to associate his opponents with Clodius's indictment of Milo for violence in a
iudicium populi (*Sest.* 95; *TLRR* no. 266). Cicero glides over the distinction
that Milo made use of the courts as well as violence, maintaining that both
tribunes were following the same policy, without necessarily imitating each
other in every respect (*Sest.* 92; cf. *Schol. Bob.* 125St).

When the prosecution threw the abusive phrase *natio optimatium* in the face of the defense, Cicero rolled the dice and attempted to turn a liability into an asset for his client. His discussion of the *optimates* and *populares* (96–143) is the most famous section of the speech. This section and, indeed, the whole speech in general are often studied as an expression of Cicero's own political ideas, a declaration of Cicero's political philosophy,[20] defending a union of all loyal Roman citizens, the *consensus omnium bonorum*, and making a resounding case for *cum dignitate otium* (peace with honor).[21] It has also been interpreted as a statement in which Cicero positioned himself within the constellation of the political figures of his time, especially in opposition to Caesar.[22] Stockton interprets one passage in the *Pro Sestio* (not cited, but apparently section 141), where Cicero says that it is preferable to die in defense of the Republic than to attack and seize it, as a comparison between Bibulus and Caesar to the detriment of the latter.[23] Yet in one passage where Cicero does mention both of the consuls of 59 B.C. (*Vat.* 21–22), he takes pains to tone down his praise of Bibulus ("non dicam bene de re publica sentientem" [I will not say that he had good views about the state]), albeit in a way that expresses as much sarcasm toward Vatinius as possible and to protect Caesar ("clementissimi atque optimi viri" [a most merciful and fine man]) from criticism by claiming that many of the acts committed in Caesar's name were actually done at the initiative of the tribune. Even Gruen, who in general believes that "an attack on Vatinius' tribunate could be read in no other way than an indirect critique of Caesar's consulship," takes note of several passages in the *In Vatinium* (13, 15, 22, 29, 38–39) where Cicero distinguishes between the former consul, now proconsul, and the tribune.[24] Mitchell maintains that the jurors would not attribute the legislative program of Vatinius, as described by Cicero in these two speeches, to Caesar;[25] and as Mitchell points out, Clodius and the consuls of 58 B.C. come under much more direct attack than Caesar or any of the triumvirs.[26] Cicero emphasizes the role Sestius tried to play in persuading Caesar to take up Cicero's cause, and while he does not claim that his entreaties enjoyed great success, his implication is that Sestius had some influence with Caesar (*Sest.* 71). It would hardly make sense for Cicero to imply this association between Caesar and his client if the rest of Cicero's speech portrayed Caesar as an utter scoundrel.

What was the involvement of Crassus in this trial? Can it be used to uncover a "triumviral" stance on Sestius? It probably cannot. As Tatum points out, Crassus was "at once a tireless and indiscriminate advocate and a nimble politician."[27] No overwhelming obstacle presented itself to this distinguished *patronus* to compel him to remove himself from this field of battle, where he could display his skills and ingratiate himself with Sestius's many and influential supporters.[28]

Cicero may well have been glad to have an opportunity to preach—not only to the jurors but to the *corona* standing around and ultimately to the reading public—on the glories of the cause that had defeated his enemies and brought him back from exile, into what he hoped (in vain, as it turned out) would be a position of respect and leadership. As far as I know, nothing he says in the *Pro Sestio* contradicts either his general views on politics or his assessment of the current political situation, though he may have had mental reservations about his generous comments toward his inconstant supporter Pompey, considering Pompey's tardy efforts to bring about Cicero's recall (*Sest.* 67).[29] But this was a situation where Cicero's inclinations and his client's interests coincided. As it happened, Cicero was not called on in this trial to choose between expressing his own views and performing his duty, as an advocate, to help his client. His duty as advocate was the paramount consideration.[30] That the *corona* was bigger than Cicero had ever previously not only witnessed in a trial (36) but addressed must have pleased him, in part because, as a performer, he must have loved an audience; in part because he was happy to have a platform from which to speak about the political situation; and in part because, as he implies to the jurors, the size of the crowd justified his description of his travails at the hands of his enemies: by linking the jurors' alleged desire to hear his story and the crowd's similar desire (evidenced by the fact that they are present, by their own volition), Cicero exploits the crowd to influence the jury.

Cicero made an excellent speech to get his client acquitted, possibly the best possible speech, to judge by the unanimous verdict of acquittal. Mitchell correctly characterizes the description of the trial that Cicero sent to his brother (*Q Fr.* 2.4.1): "There is not the slightest hint in this account that he was concerned in the trial with anything other than the discharge of his duties as an advocate and grateful friend." As Mitchell says, historians should place more weight on that letter than on Cicero's programmatic account written two years later to Lentulus.[31] The political content of Cicero's *Pro Sestius* and *In Vatinium,* both on general issues about the management of the Roman Republic and in terms of judgment on specific individuals, is part of an overall strategic plan to secure an acquittal for Sestius.

The prosecution threw down the phrase *natio optimatium* because it believed that it could exploit a considerable body of feeling at Rome that held that a group of incorrigible naysayers had been blocking public business since 59 B.C. out of a misguided conviction of their own superiority. The prosecution wanted to portray the defenders of Sestius as members or followers of this "breed." In other words, it wanted the jury to judge the defendant by his defenders and to associate those defenders with a group of politicians who, it believed (with some justification), would not attract the support of the majority of jurors—that is, the group of diehard opponents of the so-called triumvirs. Cicero exploits the political side of the trial that the prosecution has opened up with its use of the pejorative term "breed of *optimates*." He turns the tables on his opponents by making it as inclusive as possible, exploiting the root *optimus* in the word *optimates*. By the end of his speech, the jurors might well have thought it an insult not to be associated with this group. Cicero thus blunts the divisive thrust of the word and transforms it into an instrument of inclusion.

The prosecution's references to the events of the previous three years, starting with 59, allow Cicero to recall to the jurors the indignities suffered by his client as he fought for the *"optimate"* cause. The fact that Vatinius bitterly attacked Cicero gave him the perfect opening to justify his own conduct and that of his allies. If Cicero could make it appear that the prosecution against Sestius had been launched to attack Cicero, not Sestius (*Sest.* 31), Cicero's actions could be drawn into the trial, and he would gain an opening to expatiate on them. The Bobbian scholiast (125St) is right to argue that although Cicero seems to many to wander from the subject in the *Pro Sestio*, the entire speech is germane to his purpose—though, as Cicero clearly recognizes (*Sest.* 119, 123), it errs on the side of exhaustiveness. The political slant that the prosecution (unwisely, as it turned out, but understandably) introduced into the trial allows Cicero to avoid questions of fact and law relating to *vis*—subjects that, to judge by his silence on them and his lack of reference to the defense offered by Hortensius and Crassus, were better left unmentioned for the defendant's sake.

Cicero defended a man accused of *vis* by denouncing *vis*, employing the logic that Sestius and his supporters had suffered more from *vis* than had the alleged victims. By the time they finally heard about Sestius again, later in Cicero's speech (*Sest.* 144), the jurors must have been tempted to see the trial as a referendum on civil unrest, as Cicero wanted them to, rather than on the past conduct of the defendant in relation to the *vis* statute. The outcome of this referendum was that all votes were cast in favor of "cum dignitate otium" (98), with no votes cast to condemn Sestius (Cic. *Q Fr.* 2.4.1).

CHAPTER TWELVE

In M. Caelium Rufum

The trial of M. Caelius Rufus has received eternal notoriety from what must certainly be Cicero's most popular forensic speech, a seemingly lighthearted effort whose éclat has been enhanced by the fact that republican Rome's most popular poet today, Catullus, wrote obsessively about the person whom Cicero would like us to believe is the central, though hidden, character in the trial. But the sources' literary acclaim does not guarantee their historical importance. On the one hand, this trial can be viewed as a minor episode in the use of trials for nonjudicial purposes, when a young prosecutor sought revenge on Caelius for his dogged persistence in prosecuting the young prosecutor's father, even in the face of an acquittal that had just been handed down. The prosecutor may well have thought that the failure of the recent prosecution mounted by Caelius, combined with Caelius's disreputable personal and political background and a widely shared perception that he was implicated in unsavory and illegal acts, held out the promise of a relatively easy victory. On the other hand, the trial can be viewed as an important chapter in a struggle over control of Egypt, an area that, although it was not ruled by Rome as a province, constituted the last major area over which Rome exercised nonprovincial hegemony, a land of enormous wealth that was to provide, in the next generation, a base of power whose seizure consolidated a takeover of the whole Roman Empire. Finally, this trial may represent the "fortuitous"[1] confluence of these personal and political factors.

When Caelius was tried in 56, Rome's relationship to Egypt was attracting keen public interest. The Ptolemaic king of Egypt, Ptolemy XII Auletes, had been expelled by an Alexandrian populace angry over the loss of Cyprus to the Romans. He first took refuge with Pompey at his Alban villa (Cic. *Rab. Post.* 6; Dio Cass. 39.14.3) and then went on to Ephesus (Dio Cass. 39.16.3). Pompey, Gabinius, and Lentulus Spinther were viewed as possible generals to lead an army to reinstate the deposed monarch.[2] On the other side, an Alexandrian legation, led by the philosopher Dio, came to Rome to plead against the return of Auletes. But according to Dio Cassius (39.13.2), the king successfully destroyed the legation by arranging for the murder of legates on their way to Rome by hiring assassins and neutralized other opponents through fear or bribes.[3] The philosopher Dio was murdered, and Cicero, in his defense of Caelius, acknowledges not only that Dio was murdered but that the king took responsibility for the deed (*Cael.* 23). Given the importance of Egypt, this homicide was a matter of state, something Roman jurors would not wink at. The importance of Rome's relationship with Egypt must have been one reason why Caelius was a tempting target, since, as we shall see, he was implicated in this murder, as well as in the harassment of other members of the legation.

Caelius's personal reputation and political background were two more reasons why a prosecutor might have calculated that he could succeed in convicting him. Personally, people thought that Caelius was a rake. Politically, he had been attracted into an alliance or at least a dalliance with Catiline. The facts of the case and the character of the defendant coincided to make the prosecution of Caelius an eminently winnable case.

There were willing prosecutors, and although they lacked rhetorical eminence, they had reason to think that they could be successful. The chief prosecutor was a young man whose father had been prosecuted that year by Caelius for *ambitus,* and Caelius was in the process of prosecuting the father a second time. Two minor figures assisted the young prosecutor, P. Clodius (not likely to be the distinguished orator famous as the archenemy of Cicero)[4] and L. Herennius Balbus. In retrospect, we know that an alliance of two of Rome's most distinguished advocates, Cicero and Crassus, aided by the oratorical talent of the defendant himself, would defeat these prosecutors. But the prosecutors can be excused for not predicting, when they brought their case, that Cicero would come to the aid of a defendant who had been connected not only to Catiline but also to a sibling of Clodius!

The *nominis delator* was L. Sempronius Atratinus. Although he rates a listing in *ORF* (no. 171), he was only seventeen years old at this time, if Jerome (*Chron.* II 143g Schoene) can be believed. Atratinus depended on an aged rhetor, L. Plotius Gallus (*ORF* no. 97), to provide him with his speech for this case.[5] Cicero treats Atratinus "patrie" [paternally], as Quintilian says (*Inst.* 11.1.68), or in Craig's even better phrase, "with avuncular condescension."[6] Cicero could not claim that Atratinus was acting out of empty malice: he had to grant him the exercise of filial duty, for Caelius had unsuccessfully prosecuted his father[7] (*TLRR* no. 268) and was preparing to do so again (*TLRR* no. 269; *Cael.* 1). Cicero claims not to object to the actions of the nominal prosecutors, such as Atratinus, who are only doing their duty in defending their associates ("suos," *Cael.* 21), and Caelius patronizingly compliments Atratinus on the hesitation he showed in attacking Caelius's character (8)—implying, of course, that his charges are false.[8]

Most scholars agree that the P. Clodius who assisted as *subscriptor* in the prosecution was not the famous P. Clodius Pulcher but a less notorious P. Clodius.[9] Cicero's dismissal of his speech is so peremptory—he calls this Clodius just a ranter (*Cael.* 27)—that it is hard to avoid the surmise that it presented material damaging to Caelius. Austin (*Pro Caelio³*, 155–56) is probably right that Cicero's ironic description of P. Clodius as "amicus meus" [my friend] (*Cael.* 27), as vague as it is, would not be apt if he were addressing his archenemy and that Cicero's prosopopeia of the famous Clodius (36) is hardly consistent with a role for him in the trial—although, as Austin points out (*Pro Caelio³*, 156), on the day when Cicero made his speech, Clodius, as aedile, would have been holding the Ludi Megalenses (*Cael.* 1, *Har. resp.* 22–26). Heinze admits that it is possible, even if remarkable, that the famous Clodius gave a speech on the first day of the trial but was absent from the trial on the second day (4 April).[10] Dorey concludes that the Clodius involved in this trial was a nonentity whom Clodia had persuaded to appear to make it appear that her family supported her, but it could be true instead—or as well—that the role of this prosecutor was to provide authority to some of the prosecution statements about Caelius that related to the Clodii, such as statements about the rent paid by him as tenant to P. Clodius Pulcher (*Cael.* 17).[11]

The other *subscriptor* who spoke for the prosecution was L. Herennius

Balbus, whom Cicero describes as his "familiaris". [friend] (*Cael.* 26). He is mentioned twice in connection with Bestia: once with respect to the formerly close ties between Bestia and Caelius (26) and once to the effect that it was Caelius's renewed prosecution of Bestia in 56 that caused Herennius to come forward as a member of the prosecution team (56). Though he did not refute the points of P. Clodius, Cicero takes the trouble to refute the points made by Herennius, and it is possible that Herennius was a mature, experienced speaker who could compensate for the youth of Atratinus and the obscurity of P. Clodius. Gotoff contrasts Cicero's full response to Herennius's speech (Cicero portrays Herennius as the *pertristis patruus* (severe uncle) of comedy and himself as the indulgent father) with his curt treatment of Clodius's speech, and he rightly suggests that Cicero's purpose was to divert attention away from the latter to the former.

> If we suspect that it was not the style but the content of Herennius' speech that had left its mark on the judges, may we not wonder whether the brevity with which Cicero deals with Clodius' speech represents an even larger diversion?[12]

The speakers for the defense were Caelius himself, Crassus, and Cicero. Caelius and Crassus spoke before Cicero (*Cael.* 18, 23, 45). At this point, Cicero and Crassus require no introduction. We know Caelius more directly than almost any other Roman of the period, principally because of the engaging and irreverent letters (contained in Cicero's *Epistulae ad familiares*) sent by him to Cicero when the latter was governing Cilicia (51/50 B.C.), as well as from this speech and possibly from references to him in the poetry of Catullus.[13] His political career was successful; he was curule aedile in 50 (possibly having served as quaestor in 58 or 57) and peregrine praetor in 48, the year in which he died as a result of the civil war.[14] His participation in his own defense was undoubtedly not perfunctory, since he was one of Rome's best speakers (Cic. *Brut.* 273), though he was not known for his moderation; his prosecutions attracted more acclaim than his defenses (Quint. *Inst.* 6.3.69; Tacitus [*Dial.* 25] describes him as "amarior" [rather biting]).[15] As Cicero's speech shows, his personality and behavior made him vulnerable to charges in which excessive exuberance played a role.

In his defense of Caelius, Cicero uses the device of attributing an unseen and illegitimate motivating force to the prosecution. That force is an upstart individual who does not know his or her own place. Cicero so portrayed Chrysogonus in the *Pro Sexto Roscio Amerino* and Sassia in the *Pro Cluentio*. In the *Pro Caelio*, he alleges that the manipulator is Clodia, cast by Cicero as the scorned libidinous woman whose fury has no limits.[16]

Although Cicero alludes to this theme at the very beginning of his speech (". . . oppugnari opibus meretriciis" [. . . is being attacked by a prostitute's wealth], *Cael.* 1), he develops it only gradually, letting it reach a crescendo by the end of the speech. His overall purpose is twofold. First, he uses it to try to discredit the prosecution as a tool in the hands of a woman and thereby to persuade the jurors, who were of course all males, to put up resistance to potential indirect manipulation of themselves by not only a woman but a woman of ill repute. A statute that should be used for momentous affairs of state is being exploited, he claims, to satisfy the desires and whims[17] of a woman.

> Quae lex ad imperium, ad maiestatem, ad statum patriae, ad salutem omnium pertinet . . . hac nunc lege Caeli adulescentia non ad rei publicae poenas sed ad mulieris libidines et delicias deposcitur. (70)

> [The law that is relevant to the power, the grandeur, the condition of the state, and the welfare of all . . . under this law Caelius's youth is now summoned not to the state's punishments but to a woman's desires and delights.]

Cicero argues that just as the jurors who judged the case of Sex. Cloelius should not have allowed the defendant to be "acquitted by a woman's favor," so these jurors should not let Caelius be "sacrificed to a woman's lust."[18] Second, Cicero attacks Clodia to discredit her in advance in case she will be brought as a witness on the charges of *aurum* and *venenum* ("gold" and "poison"; see discussion later in this chapter), matters in which she was an actual or at least potential participant. Like Chrysogonus in the trial of Roscius of Ameria and like Sassia in the trial of Cluentius, she is attacked by Cicero as if she were a prosecutor, which she is not, but unlike those two, whom the prosecutors in those trials had no reason to bring into the trial, Clodia might well have played a meaningful—albeit subsidiary—role, as a prosecution witness.[19]

Cicero's abuse of Clodia is related to two reasons for blackening her reputation. First, in this way, Cicero can attack the prosecution without attacking the actual prosecutors, who, by Roman standards, are admirably suited to their task: P. Clodius can speak for the Clodian gens and about the wrongs Caelius has done to it; L. Herennius Balbus is possibly the experienced orator who can competently express the facts of the case, with a dose of personal indignation over Caelius's treachery; and Atratinus is the young and innocent dutiful defender of his biological father. These men, Cicero claims, are dupes in the hands of a woman: "Non enim ab isdem accusatur M. Caelius a quibus oppugnatur; palam in eum tela iaciuntur, clam subministrantur" [For Marcus Caelius is not accused by the same people who attack him; the spears are openly thrown against him, but they are being secretly furnished] (*Cael.* 20).[20] But even though the abuse against Clodia begins, at least by implication, early on in the speech, it is only well past the halfway point that Cicero actually claims that this woman has fabricated a charge, the murder of Dio (". . . utrum temeraria, procax, irata mulier finxisse crimen . . . videatur" [. . . whether you think, on the one hand, that an irresponsible wanton virago of a woman has preferred a false charge], 55; trans. Austin). Her motive was to get revenge on Caelius for having broken off a sexual liaison with her: "sin autem iam suberat simultas, exstincta erat consuetudo, discidium exstiterat, hinc illae lacrimae nimirum et haec causa est omnium horum scelerum atque criminum" [*if, on the other hand, jealousy was already latent, if their intimacy had been brought to an end, if a rupture had occurred, well, well—then the cat is out of the bag*, and this is the reason for all these alleged crimes and charges] (61; italicized words from Austin's translation). The jurors can be expected to scorn Clodia for her extramarital—or since she is a widow, postmarital—affair, but not Caelius for the dalliance of an *adulescens*.[21] In any case, Cicero has turned the jurors' attention away from filial duty, to which they are bound to feel sympathetic, toward feminine fury, which they can be expected to wish to oppose.

Second, his characterization of her not only as a sexually promiscuous woman but as a *meretrix* is related to her qualifications as a witness. Prostitutes were not qualified to testify, at least not under the later *lex Iulia de vi*, which referred to "quaeve palam quaestum faciet feceritve" [a female prostitute present or past] (Callistratus *Dig.* 22.5.3.5; trans. Honoré, ed. Watson).[22] Although Cicero does not argue for a legal disqualification of Clodia in a literal sense, he creates a very concrete and specific *infamia* for her. The theme of *meretrix* reoccurs in phrases throughout the speech ("opibus meretriciis" [the wealth of a prostitute], *Cael.* 1; "vicinitatem meretriciam" [the neighborhood of a prostitute], 37; "meretriciis amoribus" [affairs with prostitutes], 48; "meretricia vita" [the life of a prostitute], 49; "meretricio more" [in the manner of a prostitute], 57).²³ Cicero argues that Clodia is not an ordinary prostitute whose sexual activity serves as a way to earn money but a prostitute so consumed by sexual passion that it rules her, "non solum meretrix sed etiam proterva meretrix procaxque" [not only a prostitute but a lascivious and lewd one] (49).²⁴ Cicero applies additional epithets to signify her sexual promiscuity ("amicam omnium" [everyone's girlfriend], 32; "temeritas ac libido" [boldness and lust], 34; "ex inimica, ex infami, ex crudeli, ex facinerosa, ex libidinosa domo" [from a hostile, disgraced, cruel, criminal, and lustful house], 55). A recurrent theme in Cicero's speech is Baiae, which, although a geographical term, clearly carries an implication of sexual vice, as Las Vegas does today. Cicero refers to "libidines, amores, adulteria, Baias, actas, convivia, comissationes, cantus, symphonias, navigia" [orgies, flirtations, misconduct, trips to Baiae, beach parties, dinner parties, drinking parties, musical entertainments and concerts, boating picnics] (35; trans. Austin) and identifies Clodia as "cuius in hortos, domum, Baias iure suo libidines omnium commearent" [a woman to whose grounds, house, estate at Baiae, there was an automatic right of way for every lecherous person] (38; trans. Austin), and he mentions "Baiae denique ipsae" [finally, Baiae itself] (47; trans. Austin). Cicero is clearly describing something about sexual promiscuity when he says sarcastically that Clodia's agents might possibly have been able to gain entrance to the Senian baths in street clothes, if Clodia had made her usual "farthing deal" with the gatekeeper of the baths ("nisi forte mulier potens quadrantaria illa permutatione familiaris facta erat balneatori" [unless, naturally, that influential lady, doing the usual farthing deal, had turned into a crony of the bathman], 62; trans. Austin). His use of the word *quadrantaria* echoes Caelius's reference to Clodia as a *quadrantaria Clytaemestra* (Quint. *Inst.* 8.6.53), implying that her husband, Metellus Celer, had suffered the same fate as Agamemnon. Thus, Cicero is recalling the rumor that Clodia had poisoned Celer (59–60). The use of *quadrantaria* carries two implications, both of which are insulting to Clodia, and neither exclusive of the other. He might be referring to a custom of hers of paying the men's fee to gain admittance into the baths, rather than the higher women's fee;²⁵ he might be suggesting that her usual price for sexual intimacy is the absurdly low *as*, in other words, that she is a "two-bit whore"; or both insults could apply.²⁶

Other sources record remarks made about Clodia that, while insulting, imply quite a different image of her. According to this portrayal, she was much more calculating and in control of herself. Quintilian (*Inst.* 8.6.53) cites (as a hard-to-understand riddle) a description Caelius applied to Clodia in his prosecution speech against her: "in triclinio coam, in cubiculo nolam" [a Coan woman in the dining room, a Nolan woman in the bedroom]. Hillard (1981) has unlocked the riddle as follows. The word *Coan* sounds like *Coam,* which refers to a method of producing an almost transparent silk, to be used for sexually provocative clothing.[27] Nola was a Campanian city that was proverbially difficult to take by siege, and its name sounds like *nolam,* meaning "no thank you." Caelius implied by these two connected phrases that Clodia was a "tease" (and he, of all people, had been in a position to know), that is, that while she made herself enticing at the dinner table, she was not available in the bedroom.[28] Thus, she was far from being a lascivious prostitute who was willing to sell herself for a pittance. Indeed, Plutarch's version of the *quadrantaria* story (*Cic.* 29) says that a lover fooled her into accepting copper in place of silver.[29] According to this picture, she charged a good price, a price enforced by her ability to say no.

Cicero's emphasis on Clodia as the catalyst for the prosecution overwhelms whatever role other members of her family may have played in it. Cicero interjects a gratuitous reference to Clodius as her husband or brother (*Cael.* 32) and to their joint action in saving Sex. Cloelius (78), and his emphasis on the *domus* as the source of the charge of murdering Dio (55) suggests the involvement of more than just Clodia. The presence of P. Clodius as *subscriptor* presumably shows some involvement of the Clodian family in the case but is hardly evidence of a major commitment by that family.[30] We do not know enough about this Clodius to speculate on the extent or meaning of his participation in the trial. Cicero claims, disingenuously, that the effect of his long-standing quarrel with Clodia's brother makes him more reticent to attack her. He then immediately takes advantage of the various meanings of *amicus* and its cognates to sully Clodia's sexual morality.[31]

But what does the sordid, titillating saga of the romance between Caelius and Clodia really have to do with the prosecution, as opposed to the defense? Unlike Chrysogonus in the trial of Roscius of Ameria and unlike Sassia in the trial of Cluentius, Clodia is not just a red herring brought in by the defense to distract the jurors from the real issues in the case. She was mentioned by the prosecution—though, I will argue, in a less prominent way than Cicero's speech might lead readers to think. Cicero says that the prosecutors have hurled accusations of personal impropriety against Caelius and have said that, in so doing, they were acting with the approval of Clodia (*Cael.* 35). That they did say so should be accepted as true, since Cicero would look foolish if he attributed to the prosecution a statement that they had never made in a speech that the jurors had heard just the day before. Moreover, Balbus elaborated a formal charge involving Clodia (51)—that Caelius used gold borrowed from Clodia to try to have Dio poisoned—and Clodia could have been expected to offer testimony on that point. The prosecution's case made Clodia a logical prosecution witness.[32]

It might be thought that the prosecution brought in the personage of Clodia in one more way, that is, by comparing Caelius to Jason and thereby, by implication, comparing Clodia to Medea.[33] Austin (*Pro Caelio*[3], 69, on *Cael.* 18) is cautious: "Possibly Atratinus had said that Caelius had won his golden fleece and kept it . . . , deserting his Medea, though certainly this afforded an obvious means of retort." The retort would be that if Caelius had been intimate with Clodia the way Jason was with Medea, Clodia was not a respectable woman, so her testimony should not be believed. That is the line that Cicero does in fact take, so the question is, why would Atratinus fall into such an obvious trap? I argue that while Atratinus did compare Caelius to Jason, the "Medea" in his comparison was not Clodia at all but Ptolemy Auletes. I argue that Cicero, however, exploited Atratinus's allusion to Medea, which had already been echoed by Caelius and Crassus, to portray Clodia as a "fallen woman" and a sorcerer.

Fortunatianus (3.7 = Halm, *Rhet. Lat. Min.* 124) quotes Atratinus as calling Caelius a "pulchellum Iasonem" [pretty little Jason]. Two elements of the comparison are clear enough. First, Caelius, like Jason, is disloyal: Caelius was Bestia's friend and supported his candidacy for the praetorship, but he then turned around and prosecuted him.[34] Atratinus may be referring to rewards that Caelius would have obtained from a successful *ambitus* prosecution of Bestia, just as Jason stood to benefit from his betrayal of Medea by marrying the daughter of the king of Corinth.[35] Second, Jason got the Golden Fleece, and Caelius, the prosecution charged, was part of a conspiracy to take huge bribes from Ptolemy so that Roman foreign policy would be corrupted and Ptolemy restored to the throne. The charge that he got gold from Clodia (*Cael.* 30) is relevant only in the sense that Caelius is portrayed by Atratinus as a greedy person, so it would stand to be more plausible that he would have plotted to get gold from Clodia. But although it might seem obvious that Clodia is the implied "Medea" in the comparison (since, like Medea, she was seduced and abandoned), a glaring difference between the two women is evident, which makes the comparison at best ineffective and at worst meaningless. Medea, the Pontine sorceress, is an outsider in Greece, and that foreign status makes Jason's rejection of her particularly disastrous, since she now lacks a protector. But Clodia came from one of the most noble families in Rome—in fact, a patrician family—and was the daughter of a consul (Ap. Claudius Pulcher, consul in 79), not to mention the widow of Q. Caecilius Metellus Celer (consul in 60), who was also her cousin.[36] Cicero makes use of her lofty background as a stick to beat her with, when he has Ap. Claudius Caecus (censor in 312, consul in 307 and again in 296) berate her for her sexual transgressions (34) and for bringing dishonor to the family name. Even if Atratinus was foolish enough to want to cast her as the pitiful woman who has been seduced and abandoned, her position was by no means as desperate as Medea's. We need to look elsewhere for an analogue to Medea.

It is clear that the defense seized with enthusiasm on the legend of Jason as something that it could exploit for its own ends. In some speech, Caelius used the phrase "Pelia cincinnatus" [a Pelias in curls] (cited at Quint. *Inst.* 1.5.61), and the occasion may have been his speech *pro se* in this trial.[37] The point of the comparison is that the prosecution was trying to destroy Caelius, as Pelias wished to destroy his half brother's son Jason. In explicating the comparison, Münzer[38] notices an additional similarity: Herennius Balbus had addressed Caelius as a strict paternal uncle (*Cael.* 25), and Pelias was the paternal uncle of Jason. Crassus picks up the theme, quoting the first line of Ennius's *Medea exul,* "utinam ne in nemore Pelio . . ." [would that in a Pelian grove [the timber] had not . . .], as an elaborate way of expressing regret that someone made a voyage. Cicero's reference to this passage in Crassus's oration makes it clear that this is a way of regretting the voyage of Ptolemy from the foreign city of Alexandria to Rome and that it has nothing to do with Clodia: "Quo loco possum dicere id quod vir clarissimus, M. Crassus, cum de adventu regis Ptolemaei quereretur" [At this point I can say what that very illustrious man, Marcus Crassus, [said] when he was complaining about the arrival of King Ptolemy] (18).[39] We can presume that Crassus expressed regret that Ptolemy had come to Italy because of all the troubles that his trip caused the Romans, and Crassus may have at least implied that Ptolemy did Rome a favor by leaving for Ephesus. Since the defense does not deny that Dio was murdered but claims that the perpetrator was Ptolemy (at least through agents) and not Caelius, it can afford to go along with the popular opinion that Alexandria and its dynastic struggles were a nuisance for Rome. I argue that Cicero shrewdly alters the *comparanda* by going on to cite the continuation of the Ennian passage, picking out, from the following eight lines, the phrases "Nam numquam era errans . . ." [For never a straying mistress . . .] and "Medea animo aegro, amore saevo saucia" [Medea, wounded with a sick heart and savage love . . .].[40]

I argue that the point Atratinus wished to make was that Caelius had enriched himself from Ptolemy, who serves as the Medea figure in the analogy. Like Medea, who came to Jason's country (Greece), Ptolemy voyaged to Caelius's country (Italy). Just as Medea had found favor in Jason's eyes, Ptolemy had found favor in the eyes of Caelius, in the sense that Caelius was at that time allied to Pompey,[41] who favored Ptolemy, letting him stay at his Alban villa (Cic. *Rab. Post.* 6).[42] But just as Medea was rejected by Jason and forced to leave his home, so Ptolemy could be pictured as having suddenly been deserted by Pompey—and, implicitly, by Caelius—and forced to leave the Alban villa for Ephesus. (In fact, we do not know what precisely led Pompey to determine that his guest would be better off in Ephesus, but the prosecution could claim that the reason for his departure was betrayal by Pompey and his followers.)

Two objections might be made to this exegesis of Atratinus's allusion to the legend of Jason and Medea. The first is the difference in gender between Medea and Ptolemy. But Atratinus would not have shied away from attributing effeminacy to Ptolemy, just as his attribution of the adjective *pulchellus* to Jason mocks Caelius for the same characteristic.[43] In fact, Cicero (*Leg. Man.* 22) had compared Medea to Mithridates—though clearly that comparison had the advantage that both were from Pontus. The second objection might be that Atratinus had no motive for creating sympathy for Ptolemy, since he was attacking the murderers of Dio and thereby arraying himself against Ptolemy. Such an objection misconceives the ancient reaction to the character of Medea, who, although pathetic, was the murderer of her own children, hardly a sympathetic character. In fact, murder is something that Medea and Ptolemy have in common, since Cicero says that Ptolemy has freely admitted to his part in the murder of Dio (*Cael.* 23). In conclusion, Atratinus meant to show that Ptolemy was seduced and abandoned by Caelius and Pompey, as his flight to Ephesus showed; that characterization was designed to bring disgrace on Caelius, without rendering Ptolemy in a sympathetic light. Atratinus had no intention of casting Clodia as the "Medea" in this drama, and therefore it probably never occurred to him that just by alluding to the story of Jason and Medea, he was giving the defense an opening to discredit his potential witness Clodia as a promiscuous strumpet. His was a youthful error. Cicero, as we have seen, exploited this opening offered him and broke open the prosecution's case.

Cicero's speech is relatively rich in references to what his opponents had said, and these references have furnished the basis for extensive scholarly discussion in the twentieth century. One of the focal points of this discussion has been which of these points represented formal charges and which involved character attack. Cicero refers specifically to this distinction.

Sed aliud est male dicere, aliud accusare. (*Cael.* 6)

[Defamation and accusation are entirely different.] (trans. Austin)

Omnia sunt alia non crimina sed maledicta, iurgi petulantis magis quam publicae quaestionis. "Adulter, impudicus, sequester" convicium est, non accusatio. (30)

[All the other things are not accusations, but insults, *more suited to some loutish brawl rather than to a court of justice.* "Adulterer, profligate, bribe depository" is abuse, not accusation.] (The italicized words are from Austin's translation.)

We should accept this distinction as one that a Roman jury understood, even while we recognize that Cicero—to whom *iurgia petulantia* were well known, in the giving as well as the receiving—stresses the distinction in the interest of his client, whom the prosecutors, especially Herennius Balbus, had, as I shall show shortly, subjected to a withering barrage of character attack. In this circumstance, Cicero clearly wanted the jurors to take a very legalistic line, as opposed to considering the whole character of the defendant to judge the plausibility of the charges against him.

Even if the jurors did adopt the stance Cicero preferred, we still need to define what a legalistic line was in the context of Roman legal procedures. These procedures did not include the presentation of a formal bill of indictment, which the prosecution was required to prove; or, to express this caveat more cautiously, the evidence is insufficient to allow us to presuppose such a bill of indictment.[44] Rather, it appears that the standard of legal inclusion grew out of the statute that established the *quaestio* in which the case was being tried, and in the case of Caelius, the statute was the *lex Plautia* (or *Plotia*) *de vi.*[45]

It is this law—or rather confusingly, its predecessor—that Cicero invokes as the governing rule (or set of rules) in the trial. Any allegation involving *vis*, as defined by the *lex Plautia*, was relevant to the case.[46] All other matters, whether they involved violations of other statutes or violations merely of Roman *mores* (i.e., unethical conduct) can be viewed as an attack on the character of the defendant, an attack that was relevant to the verdict only so far as it rendered the allegations of *vis* more plausible. For example, it could be argued that an individual who lacked sexual control was more likely to attack foreign ambassadors than one who conformed to Roman sexual *mores.* But it was up to the jury to draw the line between *crimina* and *maledicta,* since the presiding magistrate did not issue a charge to the jury before it reached its decision.[47] The opposing advocates could only recommend to the jury where they should draw that line.

Despite the controversy that Cicero's speech has engendered among scholars of the twentieth century, his oration actually provides a relatively clear picture of what the three prosecutors had said. It is useful to draw the distinction between *vis* charges and other *maledicta.* The latter fall into eight categories.[48]

First, the prosecution noted that Caelius's father was of low status and that M. Caelius senior was in some way "parum splendidus" [insufficiently illustrious] (*Cael.* 3). Cicero counters that there is no disgrace in holding equestrian status (4), thereby undoubtedly trying to turn the equestrian jurors against the prosecution. He is probably distorting what the prosecution actually said, which may have been that the defendant was living above his station.[49] Also, as Austin notes (*Pro Caelio*[3], 97), Cicero portrays the father as the *senex* (old man) of comedy by describing him as "parcus" [thrifty] and "tenax" [close-fisted] (*Cael.* 36), thus interpreting his apparent stinginess in a less negative way.

Second, the prosecution charged that Caelius showed little respect for his father (*Cael.* 3). He lived apart from him, having left the paternal home to take up residence in the Palatine, a fashionable area. The prosecution must have wanted this address to seem an extravagance that endangered the paternal finances, although Cicero claims that this was just a good way to be near the Forum.[50]

Third, the prosecution maintained that Caelius's fellow townsmen, the Interamnates Praetuttiani,[51] disapproved of him (*Cael.* 5). Cicero counters that they selected him as a *decurio* (local senator) and honored him in other ways and have sent a delegation of senators and knights to the trial as *laudatores* (eulogists).

Fourth, the prosecution stated that Caelius supported Catiline (*Cael.* 10–15). This statement is clearly true, as Cicero does not try to deny it. He tries to limit the damage by claiming (a) that Caelius supported Catiline only when Catiline was campaigning in 63 for the consulate of 62, not beforehand, during Catiline's previous campaigns and extortion trial (*TLRR* no. 212), and not thereafter, during the actual *coniuratio* (conspiracy), and (b) that many good citizens were enticed by Catiline's charms— even, almost, Cicero himself (*Cael.* 14). Cicero argues that Caelius's prosecution of C. Antonius (consul in 63; *TLRR* no. 241), in part "coniurationis accusatio(ne)" [an accusation of conspiracy] (*Cael.* 15), clears him from suspicion of participation, although Cicero would certainly reject the converse—the reductio ad absurdum that Cicero's defense of Antonius rendered Cicero suspect of complicity.

Fifth, the prosecution charged that Caelius was guilty of *ambitus* and of other electoral abuses described by the words *sodales* (companions) and *sequestres* (agents) (*Cael.* 16). Linderski has shown that this kind of campaign abuse had already been the target of a senatus consultum on 10 February 56 (Cic. *Q Fr.* 2.3.5) urging the passage of a law on the subject, with the same penalties as the *vis* law, and that this senatus consultum led to the passage of the *lex Licinia de sodaliciis* in 55 B.C., as an addition to Cicero's own *lex Tullia de ambitu*. Since the *lex Licinia* was not passed until 55 B.C., no statute constraining the activities of *sodales* and *sequestres* for illicit campaign practices was on the books at the time of the trial of Caelius (April 56). Whereas the activity described by the prosecutors of Caelius could have constituted a formal *crimen* in a trial held under the appropriate statute in 55 and thereafter, this statute had not yet been passed in 56. Therefore, Cicero can claim in the *Pro Caelio* that it has been introduced in this case merely to blacken the defendant's character.[52] Cicero's response is that someone who had been involved in bribery would never accuse someone else of the same crime, as Caelius had twice done to Bestia. In point of fact, that is exactly what the *ambitus* laws seem to have been designed to encourage, by giving rewards to those convicted of bribery who informed on their partners in crime.[53] Moreover, Austin (*Pro Caelio*[3], 65, on *Cael.* 16) may well be right to suggest that the occasion the prosecutors set forth for the crime might have been Bestia's candidacy for the praetorship of 57,

which Caelius had supported (*Cael.* 26). Other possibilities have been suggested, and they are not mutually exclusive, since Caelius could have been
involved in bribery on more than one occasion. Heinze refers to the
pontifical elections mentioned in section 19,[54] and Drexler suspects that the
occasion might have been Catiline's campaign in 63 for the consulate of
62.[55] We also cannot rule out the suggestion of Sumner that the prosecution
complained about the defendant's own campaign for the quaestorship.
This suggestion depends on Sumner's dismissal of Pliny the Elder's birth
date for Caelius (82 B.C.; *HN* 7.165)—Sumner establishes his birth date as
not later than 87—and on acceptance of Caelius's standing for the
quaestorship at the normal date, either in 59 for 58 or in 58 for 57.[56] This
campaign would predate the trial by several years.

Sixth, the prosecution reported that Caelius had gone deeply into debt
and had failed to produce accounts, as the prosecution had requested (*Cael.*
17). Cicero attributes the brevity of his own reply to the charge's lack of sub-
stance, but he may have had little he could say by way of defense. The three
points he does make are (a) that Caelius, as a *filius familias* (son under
paternal authority), does not keep accounts; (b) that he made no *versura*
(loan), which means not that he did not contract debts but that he did not
contract new debts to pay off old ones (see Austin, *Pro Caelio*[3], 66, ad loc.);
and (c) that his annual rent is not thirty thousand sesterces but ten thousand. Crook concludes that Cicero is exaggerating Caelius's lack of income
and that he probably received an annual allowance.[57] If this is the case,
either he must have entered into transactions, or his father must have done
so on his behalf, and if Caelius does not have the records because he is *in
patria potestate* (under paternal authority), would not his father have them?
If his father is not producing them, perhaps there was a real father-son
conflict, substantiating the second item of character disparagement already
mentioned.

Seventh, the prosecution charged Caelius with disloyalty. He betrayed
Bestia, whom he had supported for the praetorship but then prosecuted
unsuccessfully for bribery, and now he had started a second prosecution
despite the failure of the first (*Cael.* 1, 16, 26, 56, 76, 78). Herennius asserted
that he would not have launched this prosecution if Caelius had not refused
to accept the verdict of his first prosecution of Bestia, attempting to try him
again on the same grounds (56). Disloyalty may also have been imputed to
Caelius for having turned against Clodia.

Impudicitia (unchastity) is the final character fault that the prosecution

attributed to Caelius, and the name of Clodia is of course intimately connected with this allegation. With the seven other character flaws, it is clear
that the prosecution used them against Caelius and how it used them, but
in the matter of Caelius's sexual morality, scholars have disagreed sharply
about how the prosecutors presented this side of Caelius's character to the
court, specifically about the extent to which they tried to use Caelius's previous sexual relationship with Clodia against him.

The prosecutors impugned the *pudicitia* (chastity) of Caelius and portrayed him as debauched. Herennius specifically attacked him at length on
grounds of "luxuries," "libido," "vitia iuventutis," and "mores," as well as
lecturing him on "incontinentia" and "intemperantia" (respectively,
extravagance, lust, vices of youth, character, self-indulgences, and licen-
tiousness [*Cael.* 25]). Later (44), Cicero denies the following signs of vice in
his client: "luxuries," "sumptus," "aes alienum," and "conviviorum ac lus-
trorum libido" (respectively, extravagance, lavish expenditures, debts, *passion for guzzling and debauchery*, 44; italicized words from Austin's translation). Clear evidence of this charge comes from a passage in Caelius's
speech cited by Quintilian (*Inst.* 1.6.29), in which he attempts to stretch the
word *frugi* (thrifty) to his own character: ". . . ut cum M. Caelius se esse
hominem frugi vult probare, non quia abstinens sit (nam id ne mentiri quidem poterat), sed quia utilis multis, id est fructuosus, unde sit ducta frugalitas" [as when Marcus Caelius wants to prove that he is a *homo frugi*, not
because he is temperate (for he could not even make that false statement),
but because he is useful to many people, that is, *fruitful*, from which *frugality* has been derived].

Cicero's treatment of Caelius's relationship with Clodia has formed the
basis of several interesting studies of Cicero's skill in reversing the charge of
impudicitia onto the prosecution's witness, Clodia, while at the same time
protecting Caelius as having, at most, allowed himself the privilege of youth
in sowing some wild oats. The most original contribution to this debate
comes from Geffcken (1973), who shows that Cicero uses the stereotypes of
Roman comedy (Caelius as the young lover, Clodia as both the strumpet
and the *miles gloriosus*, and Herennius as the censorious, puritanical old
man) as a way of both reminding the jurors what they are missing during
the Ludi Megalenses (Games of the Great Mother) and minimizing the
damage that Caelius's dalliance with Clodia does to his reputation, while
exaggerating the *infamia* that Clodia ought to suffer as a result. In Craig's
words, Cicero is walking a tightrope.[58] Stroh finds Cicero so successful in

walking this tightrope that he claims that the prosecutor had never mentioned the love affair between Caelius and Clodia and that there was no common knowledge of such an affair, if it occurred at all.[59] He is reacting to the view of Heinze that the love affair had occurred and was well known at Rome, although the prosecutors avoided any reference to it.[60] Austin (*Pro Caelio*[3], 86, on *Cael.* 30) takes the view that Cicero would not have mentioned it if Herennius had not already done so and that Herennius, unwisely as it turned out, calculated that he could use it to discredit Caelius without discrediting his witness Clodia.

In the midst of all this scholarly discussion, it is important to focus on our primary source, Cicero's *Pro Caelio*,[61] and its key passages, sections 35 (stressed by Reitzenstein)[62] and 50, in which Cicero makes it clear that the prosecutors, in saying what they did about "libidines, amores, adulteria, Baias, actas, convivia, comissationes, cantus, symphonias, navigia" (35, cited and translated earlier in this chapter), asserted that they did so with the approval of Clodia and that Clodia can be expected to testify (i.e., "in forum deferri iudiciumque" [be brought into the Forum and into court], 35). It would be rash to assume that Clodia will testify only about her love affair, because clearly the prosecution has accused Caelius of far more scandalous conduct than a sexual relationship with the widow of a consular, and it is conceivable that she could testify to these far worse excesses without having to admit that she participated in them. However, Cicero asserts that the prosecutors have announced that Clodia will serve as a "testem eius criminis" [witness to this charge] (50), where the last offense mentioned ("cum hac si qui adulescens forte fuerit" [if by chance a young man should be with her], 49) is the love affair between Caelius and Clodia. He wants to persuade the jurors that any woman who can testify to such matters must have been intimately involved in them, a line that he develops in purple passages about Baiae (38, 47, 49). But if we can distance ourselves from Cicero's language, we can see that Clodia could testify to, for example, notorious goings-on at Baiae without confessing to her participation in them.

Indicative of the prosecutorial line are three references to Caelius as a *familiaris* of Clodia: "Cur aut tam familiaris fuisti ut aurum commodares, aut tam inimica ut venenum timeres?" [Why have you been so friendly [with Caelius] that you lend him money, or so hostile that you fear poison?], 33); " Si tam familiaris erat Clodiae quam tu esse vis . . ." [If he was as intimate with Clodia as you make out that he is . . .], 53; trans. Austin); "si

enim tam familaris erat mulieris quam vos voltis . . ." [For if he was so intimate with the woman as you [prosecutors] make out that he is . . .], 58).
Even when applied to a relationship between a man and a woman, the term
familiaris can imply a nonsexual relationship, as, for example, when Cicero,
writing to Atticus (*Att.* 15.11.2), describes Servilia, the mother of Brutus, as
Atticus's *familiaris* (cf. Nep. *Att.* 11.4). It is very likely that the prosecution
charged that just as Caelius had betrayed Bestia, so now he was turning on
his former protectress Clodia.

Cicero was only following on the heels of Caelius, who appealed to the
jurors' lowest instincts by regaling them with a story, too improper for
Quintilian (*Inst.* 6.3.25) to explicate, involving a *pyxis* (*Cael.* 69), a tightly
fitting jar suitable for medicines, poisons, and other liquids.[63] This obscure
reference should probably be connected with the *unguenta* (unguents)
mentioned in an earlier passage that sums up and downplays the importance of the accusations of *impudicitia* that Herennius had hurled against
Caelius.

> Tibi autem, Balbe, respondeo primum precario, si licet, si fas est
> defendi a me eum qui nullum convivium renuerit, qui in hortis
> fuerit, qui unguenta sumpserit, qui Baias viderit. (27)

> [But I first humbly respond to you, Balbus, if I may, if it is right that
> a man is defended by me who has refused no dinner invitation, who
> has been in a park, who has used perfumes, who has gone to see
> Baiae.]

Here we see some of the highlights of the prosecution attack: "convivium"
refers to Caelius's friendship with Bestia ("cenasse" [dined], 26); "hortis" to
the presence of Clodia and Caelius in the same park (36), possibly her park
by the Tiber; "unguenta" to his use of perfume (a commonplace of personal attack).[64] Of course, Baiae is mentioned. It is likely that Herennius
attacked Caelius for his use of *unguenta*, Caelius retorted with the story
about the *pyxis* and linked it to Clodia in some way that discredited her,
and Cicero then reminded the jury about it one more time. The connection
between the *pyxis* and *unguenta* cannot be asserted with certainty, but if
there is no connection, we are left with an anomaly, namely, that whereas
Cicero elsewhere in the speech deals with the banquets, parks, and Baiae
mentioned in section 27, he never says anything about perfume.

It is obvious that Cicero tries to put Clodia in the worst possible light, and one of the ways he blackens her reputation is to exaggerate the seclusion that would be expected of a widow from a prominent Roman family in the late Republic. Granted that it was not proper for a freeborn Roman woman to engage in sexual relations with anyone other than her husband, it was shocking neither that the widow of a consular from Rome's most elite family would lend money to a male friend who told her that he needed it to help with the expense of providing games, possibly for someone else (*Cael.* 53), nor that he might have some dealings with her slaves without her knowledge. The prosecution had alleged that Caelius used (or perhaps tried to use) Clodia's slaves to poison Dio, presumably behind their mistress's back, and Cicero tries to capitalize on this scenario by claiming that it implies that the slaves were excessively *familiaris* with their mistress and that she allowed them to run free in her household. Unless this was the case, Cicero says, Caelius could not have been so *familiaris* with the slaves as to draw them into the plot. The prosecution must have claimed that Caelius had tried to corrupt Clodia's slaves to his nefarious purpose—attempting to corrupt another's slaves is a cardinal sin in a slaveholding society—and that her only fault was her naive trust in her young friend. In general, Wiseman describes Roman attitudes more accurately than Caelius's advocate did, when Wiseman writes that with Clodia's father dead and the relatives willing not to exert their authority, "she could do pretty much as she liked."[65] Widows were generally expected to remarry,[66] and that process must have involved some circulation in society. To summarize, the prosecution may have had good reason to put forward Clodia as a credible witness to persuade the jury that Caelius led a wild life, although, with hindsight, we can see that it was a serious mistake.

Seven allegations of actual violations of the *vis* law were made against Caelius.[67] Just as Cicero makes relatively clear the character allegations against his client, so he makes the actual charges relatively clear, even though he deals only briefly with those already covered by Crassus (*Cael.* 23).[68] To gauge the worth of each charge, it is useful to describe each *crimen* separately and then see how Cicero tries to refute it.

First, Caelius was charged with assault on a senator during pontifical elections (*Cael.* 19). This is a clear example of a public disturbance. Cicero belittled the charge by implying that if it were genuine, the senator would have come forward independently and immediately, rather than waiting and coming to court as a witness in a trial of someone else. These elections

must have been held after the restoration of pontifical elections in 63 (Dio
Cass. 37.37.1) and no later than 57, since Cicero's comments on the tardiness
of the trial would hardly have made sense if these were the elections of 56.
The senator in question may have been Q. Fufius Calenus (tribune of the
plebs in 61), since one manuscript tradition contains the rubric "DE TESTE
FUFIO" [ABOUT THE WITNESS FUFIUS], which would indicate an
abridgement Cicero made in the published speech.[69] Cicero here follows
the advice later given by Quintilian (*Inst.* 5.7.23) on how to discredit witnesses: if there is only one, he or she is not credible for that reason, and if
there are many, they constitute a conspiracy. Cicero derides the prosecutor
for, in effect, having located and persuaded to testify a senator who had
been attacked by the defendant in the course of public business. If we can
assume that Cicero always used the best possible defense, it seems very
likely that Caelius's actions were indefensible.

Second, Caelius was charged with sexually molesting wives returning
from a banquet at night (*Cael.* 20). Other than to mock their husbands, the
prospective witnesses, as "nocturni testes" [night-bird witnesses] (trans.
Austin) and for not already having obtained public redress, Cicero has no
response to make to this charge, and this kind of crime was typical of Rome
late at night.

Crassus had been responsible for answering the next three charges
(*Cael.* 23). Third, Caelius was implicated in "seditiones Neapolitanae" [dis-
turbances at Naples] (23). We do not know what Caelius is supposed to
have done in Naples. Heinze suggests that Caelius was involved in a local
disturbance without political significance.[70] If that is true, the disturbance
could have been related to the theme of Baiae, on which, as I have shown
elsewhere in this chapter, the prosecution expatiated. It also could have had
something to do with the presence of legates from Alexandria in the Bay of
Naples (cf. the fourth charge).[71] Fourth, Caelius was charged with attacking
the Alexandrian legation at Puteoli. This clearly involves public business.[72]
Fifth, Caelius was charged with doing something wrong to the goods of a
certain Palla. Quintilian, in justifying Cicero's strategy of defending Caelius
against the slander on his character rather than the actual charges, mentions this charge (which Caelius himself had attempted to refute in his
speech) as if it were very important to the case—perhaps the most important charge—and somewhat separate from "totam de vi causam" [the
whole question of violence] (or possibly the most glaring instance of *vis*):
"tum deinde narret de bonis Pallae totamque de vi explicet causam, quae

est ipsius actione defensa?" [should he then tell about the goods of Pallas and unfold the whole plea concerning violence, which has been defended in his own speech?] (*Inst.* 4.2.27). It should not be considered surprising that *vis* could be related to property, for there could easily be an overlap between *vis* and property crimes. According to Marcianus (*Dig.* 48.6.5.1), in the *lex Iulia de vi publica,* as interpreted by Antoninus Pius, "si de vi et possessione vel dominio" [if concerning violence and possession or ownership], the charge of *vis* took precedence.[73] Callistratus (*Dig.* 48.7.7) relates a ruling that *vis privata* can involve matters other than wounding, and specifically that even a creditor who seizes a debtor's property without first going before a *iudex* (judge) is committing *vis.* Ciaceri, however, ingeniously suggests that this charge could refer to violence committed on an estate (*bona*) belonging to Palla.[74]

The final two charges involved *aurum* (money) and *venenum* (poison). Sixth, Caelius was charged with borrowing money from Clodia to bribe Lucceius's slaves to murder Dio when he was a guest at the house of Lucceius (*Cael.* 23–25, 51–55); seventh, the prosecution charged that Caelius then bribed the slaves of Clodia to murder their mistress (57). Cicero twice characterizes these accusations as the real charges (30, 51), and he contrasts them with mere "convicia" [reproaches] (30), such as charges of adultery, sexual immorality, and receiving money for distribution as bribes. Since these two charges have evidently been assigned to him for refutation, his discussion of them is fairly full, from which we can extrapolate the sequences of events that the prosecution had presented to the court.

Cicero attempts to brush aside the sixth charge by saying (a) that Ptolemy had admitted responsibility for the murder of Dio and (b) that Asicius, who was accused of complicity (*TLRR* no. 267), was acquitted. Caelius takes the point of view that whether Asicius was really innocent or had been acquitted only through *praevaricatio* (collusion), his case is totally separate from that of Asicius (*Cael.* 24). But it was equally true that the acquittal of Asicius in no way cleared Caelius or anyone else, and given that Ptolemy would not have tried to kill Dio himself, the question remained, who was working with Ptolemy to get rid of Dio? Cicero claims, in an elliptical passage, that the brothers Titus and Gaius Coponius feel the same way about the relationship of the Asicius trial to this trial; it is clear that their name has been mentioned (though Cicero does not say whether by the prosecutors or by a previous defense speaker), and Cicero raises the possibility that they will be called to testify ("si producti erunt" [if they are brought forth as witnesses]).[75] Dio had stayed at the house of Titus Coponius, probably moving there after Lucceius's house no longer seemed safe,[76] so the brothers were probably well disposed toward Dio. But we really do not know what their testimony was going to be if they were indeed summoned, and neither did Cicero when he delivered his speech.

The prosecution claimed that Caelius borrowed gold from Clodia ostensibly to help defray the cost of games but really to persuade the slaves of Lucceius to murder their master's guest, Dio (*Cael.* 53). Cicero's main defense is that Lucceius has submitted written testimony to the effect that this did not happen (55), and Cicero says that he can bring him forward as a witness (54). Since Lucceius was morally responsible for the welfare of his guest and legally responsible for the conduct of his slaves, the self-interest of his testimony is evident.[77] Other than appealing to Lucceius's deposition, Cicero uses the same fallacious argument that he uses in the *Pro Roscio Amerino* (see chap. 8), the argument that a multiplicity of possibilities rules out any one of them. Cicero argues that Caelius might have met with the slaves in person or through an intermediary; he maintains that the former course of action would be dangerous, and he notes that no intermediary has been named (*Cael.* 53). Cicero claims it is for the sake of brevity (54) that he does not deal with such issues as motive, place, opportunity, complicity of others, or reasonable expectation of avoiding detection, but the reader suspects that he is less concerned about taxing the jurors' patience than about revealing the weakness of the defense. The prosecution may have had a very plausible argument: that Caelius, as a wastrel and *filius familias,* needed to borrow the money from someone to bribe the slaves. One wonders why Ptolemy would not have been able to bankroll the plot. But he may have had reasons for wanting to avoid a direct connection. An attempted murder could well be construed as *vis,* even if it also constituted a violation of the *lex Cornelia de sicariis et de veneficiis,* and it made sense to use it as a charge against Caelius in a *vis* case, especially given the procedural reasons for choosing that court (see the introduction to part 3).

According to the prosecution, Caelius, having failed to arrange for Dio's murder through the slaves of Lucceius, tried to arrange for Clodia's murder through her own slaves by persuading them to poison her (*Cael.* 57). The prosecution maintains that Caelius even procured a slave on whom to test the poison and determined that it was sufficiently lethal (58). Cicero attacks this charge in two ways, neither of which is convincing. First, he claims that Caelius had no motive to poison Clodia. He dismisses the possibility that Caelius was trying to avoid repayment of the loan incurred by himself for the murder of Dio, by asking (without answering) whether she was demanding the return of the money (56). Whether or not she had demanded her money back around the time of the alleged attempt on her life, she might have done so eventually. One might think that Cicero could have argued that in the event of her death, her heirs could have tried to collect the debt in any case, and thus that her liquidation would have done Caelius no good. But the prosecutors had precluded that argument by saying that she lent the money without a witness (31), simply taking it from her money chest ("armarium," 52), and that her heirs thus probably would have found it very difficult to collect on the debt. Cicero also dismisses the possibility that Caelius wanted to kill Clodia to get rid of a potential witness to his plot against Dio. Cicero states that no one prosecuted Caelius until he prosecuted someone else, citing Herennius's statement that he would not have prosecuted Caelius had Caelius not brought Bestia into court a second time (56). But, we may object, that report, even if true and not just a rhetorical flourish, in no way demonstrates that no one would have prosecuted Caelius if only he had refrained from prosecution. In a trial of Caelius for the attempted murder of Dio, Clodia's evidence would be crucial for the prosecution.

Having inadequately dealt with motive, Cicero then turns to the question of means. Here again, he uses a multiplicity of opportunities to cast doubt on all of them. The prosecutor alleged that Caelius had tried to use the slave of Clodia to accomplish the deed. Cicero responds that it would be very risky to use the slave of another person (but this must have been a common technique, despite the risk). Cicero tries to take advantage of the supposedly close relationship that these slaves had with their mistress (ridiculing Clodia as a mistress who allows the slaves to take over the management of the household), by using that relationship as a reason why Caelius would have known that they would have reported to their mistress the attempt to corrupt them (*Cael.* 57). If Caelius really did try to corrupt Clodia's slaves, the simple fact is that they were loyal to their mistress, as slaves were supposed to be, and reported the attempt to her. At this point, Cicero raises five standard questions regarding the plot ("ubi quaesitum est [venenum], quem ad modum paratum, quo pacto, cui, quo in loco traditum" [Where was the poison obtained? In what way was it supplied? In what manner, to whom, and in what place was it handed over?], 58), but he then avoids providing even the pretense of answers to them, by digressing on the tragedy of the death of Metellus Celer and insinuating that his widow, Clodia, was the cause of it (59–60).

According to the prosecutors, after Clodia found out about the plot to poison her, she set up a sting operation to unmask Caelius (*Cael.* 61–69). The prosecutors claimed that Caelius gave the poison to P. Licinius, whom Cicero describes as "pudens adulescens et bonus" [a decent and fine young man] (61)—a description suspect in its blandness and lacking credibility, since it was clearly designed to cast doubt on the prosecutors' claim. Caelius, the prosecutors said, arranged for Clodia's slaves to pick up the poison from Licinius at the Senian baths. Clodia instructed her slaves to play along with Caelius, while she arranged for friends to witness the transfer of the poison from Licinius to her slaves. Cicero says in his speech that these witnesses have not been named, but it is clear that he thinks that they may appear, because he pours ridicule on them and on their handling of the encounter. They hid in the baths but jumped out from hiding a little too soon, so that Licinius was able to pull the *pyxis* containing the poison back in time and flee (67).[78]

This is exactly the kind of trap that Cicero describes in the *Pro Cluentio* as providing ironclad evidence of poisoning (see chap. 9), but here he ridicules the episode as a broad comedy staged by Clodia (*Cael.* 64). His objections (63–69) are:

a. the witnesses would either be in the forecourt (*vestibulum*) of the baths or inside, in which case they would have to have disrobed;

b. if the witnesses had succeeded in seizing Licinius after he had handed over the box of poison, he could have raised a hue and cry and denied any association with the box;

c. the witnesses would have been suspects for the very crime they intended to view, yet they could not have seen the transfer from inside the baths;

d. it is implausible that the witnesses were unable to apprehend Licinius;

e. the witnesses are friends of Clodia and, therefore, the sort of dandies whose word is worthless; and

f. the manumission of the slaves who helped Clodia by reporting the plot shows that they were freed (1) so that they would help frame Caelius with their testimony, (2) to avoid their being tor-

tured into giving testimony, or (3) to reward them for the many
services rendered by them to their mistress.

All of these arguments are unconvincing. As to point *a*, it hardly seems
impossible that fully clothed men were able to go from the *vestibulum* into
the *apodyterium* (disrobing room) and, rather than disrobing, simply wait
there. Points *b* and *c* reveal how Cicero exploits the inherent problem in
any such trap, which is really designed to prove two things, both that the
criminal (in this case, Licinius) is in possession of poison and that he is
intending to hand it over to someone else. Seizing the criminal before he
hands it over proves the possession but not the transfer, whereas seizing
him after the transfer proves the transfer but not his prior possession.
Points *b* and *c* also suggest that the witnesses may have run a risk of implicating themselves in a crime that they only intended to view. The risk noted
by point *d* may explain the failure of the sting operation: they jumped out
too soon because they were afraid of ending up in possession of the poison.
That they were all inside the baths, rather than surrounding Licinius (presumably to avoid detection by him), made it more difficult to catch him. As
to point *e*, if the witnesses' association with Clodia disqualifies them as witnesses in court, the same applies to Caelius. Finally, as to point *f*, manumit-
ting the slaves was a natural reward for their loyalty, after that loyalty had
saved Clodia's life.

When describing the ironclad case that Cluentius had against Scamander and Fabricius (in 74 B.C.), Cicero had implied that this kind of trap can
provide irrefutable evidence. With two differences, everything almost two
decades later is the same: there was a secret meeting to transfer the poison,
witnesses lay in hiding, they watched the exchange, and they seized the
money and the poison. The differences are, first, that no exchange of
money seems to have been involved in the incident in the Senian baths and,
second, that Licinius, unlike Scamander, got away with the poison. Still, it
seems that this kind of trap was a very good way of providing a modicum of
physical evidence to substantiate a poisoning charge. Although the incident
in the Senian baths could have led to a prosecution under the *lex Cornelia
de sicariis et veneficiis,* there were clear procedural reasons for bringing this
charge into a *vis* prosecution. The public aspect of this particular act of
attempted violence lay in the fact that it may well have constituted an attack
on a witness, who would have thereby been involved in public business. So
both the *aurum* and the *venenum* charges were appropriate to this court.

The seven charges made against Caelius were all relevant to the charge of *vis*, and Cicero's rebuttal of them is so weak as to make them seem more plausible. If we add to this inherent weakness of the defense case the fact that the defendant possessed a reputation as a violent wastrel who had even slipped into the ranks of the Catilinarians, the success of the defense against justifiably confident prosecutors appears all the more remarkable. It is likely that the jurors in this case did indeed sit as spectators to a comedy more amusing than any offered at the games that they were missing.

CHAPTER THIRTEEN

Conclusion

e cannot know for sure what factors did or did not move jurors in Roman trials. The answer may be different for each trial. The "inartificial proofs" (mainly testimony and documents) and the "artificial proofs" that the speakers on the two sides presented may not have always determined the outcome. The jurors may have been swayed by the personal prestige of the defendant or lack thereof or by the prestige or rhetorical skills of the prosecutors and advocates in comparison with each other. They may have been swayed by political factors, especially as an air of crisis came to pervade the Roman Forum toward the end of the fifties B.C.

Cicero, when he appeared for the defense and also when he prosecuted Verres, spoke as if his arguments and evidence would affect the verdict, and his adversaries appear to have presented similar kinds of arguments as he did, as if those arguments too could sway the jury. Riggsby (1997, 244) is right to assert that an advocate had to follow a "strategy of truth"; that is, an advocate had to give the jurors a reason or reasons to vote the desired way. Perhaps it was not always the case that the best reason or set of reasons would carry the day and that personal or political factors would predispose a juror to vote in a certain way and would thus affect the result. But the prosecutors and the *patroni* had to present some justification for the verdict—condemnation or acquittal—that was the goal of their opposing efforts.

Whereas it might have been sufficient for the defense to undermine the prosecution case with doubts without advancing a coherent version of what had or had not happened, the prosecutor needed to present a coherent story to the jurors, showing what acts had been committed by the defendant and how those acts constituted a violation of the statute according to which the trial was being conducted. This story would be all the more convincing if the prosecutor could portray the defendant as a wicked person and, better yet, a person with the vices that would naturally lead him to commit the crimes with which he was charged.

To accomplish his goals, the prosecutor needed to assemble evidence, which he described in his speech, caused to be read into the record (in the case of documentary evidence), or presented through witnesses after he and opposing counsel had spoken. Different kinds of cases required different kinds of evidence. For crimes of physical violence, it was difficult to produce a large quantity of hard evidence. There might be eyewitness accounts, but often the eyewitnesses were slaves, whose testimony was not considered reliable and could sometimes be prevented by purchase of the slave. Therefore, motive and character had to bear the weight of the prosecution's case. Crimes of electoral misconduct, by their very nature, involved large numbers of people, some as active participants and many more as passive recipients of largesse. Therefore, the prosecutor had to prevail on some of these people to provide information, even though few—if any—of them felt themselves personally victimized by the electoral misconduct; on the contrary, they had probably profited from it in financial terms. The prosecutor had to discover these people, persuade them to come forward, and assemble their evidence into a compelling picture. Extortion cases, involving as they did large—often huge—sums of money and witnesses from a foreign, often distant part of Rome's empire, required the greatest organizational effort from the prosecutor. He had a limited span of days to go to the affected province, collect the necessary documents (especially financial records), locate the right witnesses, persuade them to come to Rome, and then, in what amounted to almost two separate trials, present all those witnesses and documents in a way that the jurors could understand as they listened. Moreover, the prosecutor's goal was not just to get a conviction but also to secure financial restitution for the victims of the defendant. The prosecutor was rarely lucky enough to have as his defendant an ex-governor who had alienated absolutely everyone, Roman citizen and noncitizen alike, in his province, so the prosecutor had to contend with recalcitrant witnesses and municipalities, as well as those who testified on behalf of the defendant. All this had to be accomplished under intense pressure of time, generally within one calendar year, not only because of legal limits, but also because memories could quickly grow stale and because the track of evidence could quickly grow faint.

The prosecutor was often a relatively young man, and although he would normally seek the assistance of others as *subscriptores,* their efforts had to be managed and coordinated. In the eleven trials that form the core of this book, the advocate on the other side was Cicero, who, except in the trial of Roscius of Ameria, when he was still a beginner, was Rome's leading orator. Moreover, the defendants in these eleven trials were all people of some stature, at least *domi nobiles* and often Roman nobles. They had some base of support, and in this critical time, they mustered all their resources to ward off disaster. Given the nature of the various punishments prescribed by the statutes that established *quaestiones perpetuae,* the defendants' very civic existence and often their personal wealth were at stake. They had everything to lose if they were condemned, and they had nothing to gain by halfhearted measures. The jurors held in their hands the defendants' lives as the defendants knew them.

In each of these trials, the prosecutor was fighting a desperate foe aided by a master forensic strategist and tactician. A strong case was required for victory. To make the case, the prosecutor could not choose a tack from among evidence, law, rhetorical brilliance, and his own personal prestige. Many or all of these ingredients of a successful prosecution had to be assembled and combined to achieve victory. Moreover, this chemistry had to take place without compromising the jurors' feeling of importance as the arbiters of the case. If they felt in any way that they were being manipulated by the prosecutor, the opposing *patronus* would be sure to arouse in them animosity against the crafty orator who, he would claim, was using rhetorical tricks to make them serve as his instrument in the ruin of their fellow citizen. Art had to conceal art.

Most and perhaps all of the prosecutors whose efforts have been discussed in this book failed to put all the pieces of victory together. They must have thought that they had a real chance of securing a condemnation, since they were private citizens who were under no obligation to prosecute cases, they were looking for renown or revenge, and they would gain little of either if the defendant was acquitted. But in most or all of these cases, the task was too difficult for them. Still, we should try to acknowledge the magnitude of that task and recognize the strengths, as well as the weaknesses, of the cases for which they spoke, even if these prosecutors failed to achieve victory.

Appendixes

List of *Crimina*

T his list contains a summary of the formal *crimina* against the defendants in the eleven trials discussed in this book. The criterion for inclusion is that the charge be an action that constitutes a violation of the statute under which the trial was being held. Violations of other statutes or of Roman standards of personal morality are not included. Where the charge is preceded by a question mark, there is doubt about whether the charge constituted a formal charge according to this criterion.

M. Fonteius, *lex Cornelia de repetundis*

1. ?debt reduction as quaestor in 84 B.C.
2. accepting bribes in road contracts
3. duties on wine
4. ?management of war with Vocontii
5. ?management of winter camps

L. Valerius Flaccus, *lex Cornelia* (?) *de repetundis*

1. collection of ship money
2. "Mithridaticum crimen"
3. extortion from the cities of Acmonia, Dorylaum, and Temnos
4. ?interference in arbitration decision involving Heraclides

5. ruling (?) against Lysanias on debt
6. malversation of funds collected to honor the defendant's father
7. using imperium to gain the inheritance of Valeria
8. rulings as governor against M. Aufidius Lurco and Decianus
9. charging a fee for approving a tax-farming contract for Falcidius
10. confiscation of Jewish money destined for Jerusalem

M. Aemilius Scaurus, *lex Iulia de repetundis*

1. "frumentarium crimen"
2. ?murder of Bostar

C. Rabirius Postumus, *lex Iulia de repetundis*

no *crimen* (recovery of ten thousand talents paid by Ptolemy to Gabinius)

L. Licinius Murena, *lex Tullia de ambitu*

1. electoral offenses in the campaign for consulate of 62 B.C.
    a. payments to hire people to meet the candidate
    b. payments to hire a retinue
    c. payments to tribes for gladiatorial games and dinners

Cn. Plancius, *lex Licinia de sodaliciis*

1. *coitio* in the first election for aedileship of 55 B.C. (?)
2. *coitio* in the second election for aedileship of 55 B.C. (?)
3. ?vote fraud in the second election

Sex. Roscius of Ameria, *lex Cornelia de sicariis et de veneficiis*

1. murder of the defendant's father

A. Cluentius Habitus, *lex Cornelia de sicariis et de veneficiis*

1. "judicial murder" of Oppianicus senior
2. poisoning of C. Vibius Cappadox
3. attempted poisoning of Oppianicus junior, leading to the death of Balbutius
4. poisoning of Oppianicus senior through the agency of M. Asellius

P. Cornelius Sulla, *lex Plautia de vi*

1. involvement in the "First Catilinarian Conspiracy" of 66 B.C.
2. involvement in the Catilinarian conspiracy of 63 B.C.
    a. contacts with the Allobroges
    b. falsification of *tabulae publicae* on interrogation of the Allobroges
    c. plot to murder Cicero and others
    d. procurement of gladiators in support of Catiline

e. sending P. Sittius to Further Spain to support Catiline

f. incitement of inhabitants of Pompeii to join Catiline

g. attempt to use force to pass a law that retroactively weakened the penalties of the *lex Calpurnia de ambitu*

P. Sestius, *lex Plautia de vi*

1. violence in the Roman Forum beginning in January 57 B.C.
2. use of a bodyguard
3. premature use of force

M. Caelius Rufus, *lex Plautia de vi*

1. assault on a senator at pontifical elections
2. molestation of *matronae*
3. causing sedition at Naples
4. attack on an Alexandrian legation at Puteoli
5. wrong done to goods of Palla (or on estate of Palla)
6. attempted murder of Dio at house of L. Lucceius
7. attempted poisoning of Clodia

Witnesses and Documents against Verres

his appendix contains lists of all specific individuals who, according to the second *Verrines*, testified for the prosecution in the case against Verres (including legates from specific communities who did so) and a list of the documentary evidence that Cicero caused to be read at the trial. The purpose is threefold: (1) to demonstrate the organizational effort required of Cicero in conducting this prosecution, (2) to demonstrate the role of evidence (in the form of testimony and documents) in the trial, and (3) to provide a factual basis for an argument that the second *Verrines* accurately reflect what happened in the first *actio*. To the extent that I have left out references to "multi iurati" [many people under oath] and similar vague references, this list underrepresents the number of witnesses. I have included documents that Cicero claims to have seen and that he cites, even if he does not say that he has entered them into the official record. The spelling of names of people and places follows Shackleton Bailey's *Onomasticon to Cicero's Speeches* (1988). Passages from the second *Verrines* showing that someone was a witness or that a document was placed in evidence are cited. For most witnesses, Cicero makes it clear with a verb in the past tense or future tense whether the witness had been heard in the first *actio* or would be heard in the second. In the few instances in which he uses present tenses, guesses

have to be made as to the *actio* in which the witnesses spoke. I regret that I
omitted some witnesses from the first *actio* in *TLRR;* I have marked these
here with an asterisk (*). In *TLRR,* I did not list witnesses planned for the
second *actio,* since that hearing was never held.

WITNESSES IN THE FIRST *Actio*

Citation	Name	Subject
2.156; 3.108, 114	Andro of Centuripae	extortionate tithe collection
1.14; 5.73, 156	M. Annius*	execution of a Roman citizen
3.74, 4.50	Apollodoros Pyragrus of Agyrium	extortionate tithe collection
4.53	Archagathus of Haluntium*	forced sale of silver and bronze
3.129	Archonidas of Helorus*	suicide of Tyracinus of Helorus
3.105	Artemidorus of Aetna*	extortionate tithe collection
2.156, 3.108	Artemo of Centuripae*	extortionate tithe collection
2.23	L. Caecilius	dispute over a legacy
2.23	Q. Caecilius Dio	dispute over a legacy
1.52	Charidemus of Chios	damage to the sanctuary of Juno and to Samos
5.133	Cleomenes of Syracuse	illegal exemption from naval duty
2.103	Cn. Cornelius Lentulus Marcellinus (consul in 56)*	granting of a trial in absentia
4.53	"	forced sale of silver and bronze
5.165	M. Cottius	crucifixion of P. Gavius, a Roman citizen
5.165	P. Cottius	crucifixion of P. Gavius, a Roman citizen
4.38	Diodorus of Melita	improper prosecution
1.139	L. Domitius Ahenobarbus (consul in 54)	award of contract as praetor
5.15	Eumenidas of Halyciae*	judicial extortion
1.128	Cn. Fannius (*eques Romanus*)	receipt of bribe as praetor
1.14, 5.155	L. Flavius (*eques Romanus*)	execution of T. Herennius
5.15	"	judicial extortion
2.23	L. Fufius Calenus	dispute over a legacy
2.13, 5.47	C. Heius of Messana	construction of a *navis oneraria* (cargo ship)

4.16, 27	"	seizure of statues, tapestries
2.66	Heraclius of Centuripae*	annulment of an arbitration award
2.15	Heraclius of Syracuse	judicial extortion
4.70	"homines e conventu" of Syracuse (citizens of the Syracuse district)	seizure of *vasa* (vessels), *candelabrum* (lampstand)
1.139	M. Iunius*	award of contract as praetor
3.105–6, 4.114	*legati* (legates) from Aetna	extortionate tithe collection
3.73, 120; 4.114	*legati* from Agyrium	extortionate tithe collection
2.120, 4.114	*legati* from Catina	sale of offices, extortionate tithe collection
2.120, 4.114	*legati* from Centuripae	sale of offices, extortionate tithe collection
2.120	*legati* from Halaesa	sale of offices
4.114, 5.133	*legati* from Herbita	extortionate tithe collection
4.104	*legati* from Melita	despoiling of temple
2.120	*legati* from Panhormus	sale of offices
2.119	C. Licinius Sacerdos (praetor in 75)*	receipt of bribes in trial
5.165	Q. Lucceius of Regium	crucifixion of P. Gavius, a Roman citizen
1.93	Publicius Malleolus, his mother, and his grandmother	accounts relating to *tutela* (guardianship) over Malleolus when Verres was proquaestor in 80 B.C.
2.23	T. Manlius or T. Manilius[1]	dispute over a legacy
2.80	Q. Minucius (*eques Romanus*)	receipt of a bribe in a trial
4.62, 70	"	seizure of *vasa, candelabrum*
3.109	Mnasistratus of Leontini*	extortionate tithe collection
2.119	M. Modius (*eques Romanus*)	receipt of a bribe in a trial
4.113	Nicasio of Henna	seizure of images of Ceres and Victory
4.113	Numenius of Henna	seizure of images of Ceres and Victory
5.163, 165	C. Numitorius	crucifixion of P. Gavius, a Roman citizen
1.127	L. Octavius Ligus (senator?)	improper judgment as praetor
2.23	"	dispute over a legacy

Citation	Name	Subject
1.127	M. Octavius Ligus (senator)	improper judgment as praetor
5.120	Onasus of Segesta*	burial of Heraclius
4.46	L. Papinius (*eques Romanus*)*	seizure of *emblema* (embossed work)
5.116, 122	Phalacrus of Centuripae	naval malfeasance
3.80	Philinus of Herbita*	extortionate tithe collection
4.29, 50	Phylarchus of Centuripae	purchase of silver
5.90, 122	Phylarchus of Haluntium*	naval malfeasance
2.23	Sex. Pompeius Chlorus	dispute over a legacy
2.102	"	granting of a trial in absentia
2.102	Cn. Pompeius Theodorus	granting of a trial in absentia
2.102	Posides Macro of Solus	granting of a trial in absentia
5.158	people from Regium	crucifixion of P. Gavius, a Roman citizen
2.119	Cn. Sertius (*eques Romanus*)	receipt of a bribe in a trial
4.92	Sopater of Tyndaris	torture
1.14, 5.147	L. Suettius (*eques Romanus*)*	deaths of Roman citizens in quarries
1.128	Q. Tadius	receipt of bribes as praetor
2.23	M. Terentius Varro Lucullus (consul in 73)	dispute over a legacy
1.71	P. Tettius	riot at Lampsacum
1.139	" [2]	award of contract as praetor
4.113	Theodorus of Henna	seizure of images of Ceres and Victory
2.119	Q. Varius	receipt of a bribe in a trial
5.158	people from Vibo Valentia*	crucifixion of P. Gavius, a Roman citizen
1.71	C. Visellius Varro (*tribunus militum* in 80–79)*	riot at Lampsacum
1.45	?	theft of gold from temple of Minerva at Athens

WITNESSES IN THE SECOND *Actio*

Citation	Name	Subject
3.103	people from Agrigentum	extortionate tithe collection
3.200	Artemo of Entella	extortionate tithe collection

3.97	C. Cassius Longinus (consul in 73)	extortionate tithe collection
5.15	Cn. Cornelius Lentulus Clodianus (consul in 72, censor in 70)[3]	judicial extortion
2.175	*decumani*	destruction of records injurious to Verres
5.154	P. Granius	execution of freedmen, theft of ship and cargo
5.10	"homines e conventu" of Lilybaeum	judicial extortion
4.70	"homines e conventu" of Syracuse	seizure of *vasa, candelabrum*
3.63	M. Lollius Q.f.	extortionate tithe collection
3.200	Meniscus of Entella	extortionate tithe collection
4.92	Poleas of Tyndaris	seizure of statue of Mercury
4.80	people from Segesta	seizure of image of Diana
3.200	Sositheus of Entella	extortionate tithe collection
3.166	P. Vettius Chilo	interest received on public funds lent out

DOCUMENTS CITED

Citation	Document	Subject
1.92	*codex* (account book) of C. Publicius Malleolus	accounts relating to *tutela* over his ward when Malleolus was quaestor in 80 B.C.
2.104, 107; 3.41	codex of Verres	trial of Sthenius (71 B.C.)
5.54	*commentarius* (minutes) of Verres	release of Messana from obligation to supply grain
5.56	decree of Verres	release of Netum from obligation to supply grain
1.106, 110, 113, 116–17	edict of Verres	Verres as urban praetor in 74 B.C.
1.117; 2.33–34; 3.26, 37	edict of Verres	Verres as governor of Sicily in 73–71 B.C.
3.45	*epistula* (letter) of L. Caecilius Metellus (consul in 68) to communities of Sicily	Verres as propraetor of Sicily in 70 B.C.
3.123–28	*epistula* of L. Caecilius Metellus (consul in 68) to consuls, (urban?)	sales of tithes

	praetor, and urban quaestors; Metellus as propraetor of Sicily in 70 B.C.	
3.154–57	*epistula* of Timarchides (freedman and *accensus* of Verres) to Q. Apronius	on protecting Verres in 71 B.C.
1.83, 84	*epistula* of Verres to C. Claudius Nero (praetor in 81, governor of Asia in 80)	riot at Lampsacum
5.50	*foedus* (treaty) with Tauromenium	exemption from obligation to furnish ship to Rome
5.50	*foedus* with Messana	obligation to furnish ship to Rome
3.117	(*lex*) *decumae venditae* (tithe contract)	sales of tithes in Leontini under C. Norbanus (consul in 83) as governor of Sicily in 87 B.C.
3.83	*lex decumis vendundis* (tithe contract)	sales of tithes in Sicily under Verres
1.143, 146, 148	*lex operi faciundo* (contract for service)	contract for repairs on temple of Castor
2.183	*libelli* (papers) of L. Canuleius	records of *publicani* in Sicily
1.96, 99	*lites aestimatae* (damages) against Cn. Cornelius Dolabella (praetor in 81)	result of extortion trial in 78 (for Dolabella's acts as governor of Cilicia in 80–79; *TLRR* no. 135)
3.92	*litterae* (letter) of Verres	to Segesta, allows *vadimonium promittere extra forum* (citing outside of the district)
5.43	*litterae* of Verres	illegal exemption from naval duty
5.56	*litterae* of Verres	exemption of Netum from obligation to supply grain
3.167	*litterae* from P. Vettius Chilo, P. Servilius, and C. Antistius, *magistri* of a company of *publicani*	to L. Carpinatius
3.74	*litterae publicae* (public letter) of Agyrium	extortionate tithe collection
3.89	*litterae publicae* of Amestratus	extortionate tithe collection

3.173, 175	*litterae publicae* of Halaesa	extortionate tithe collection
3.102	*litterae publicae* of Hybla	extortionate tithe collection
3.85	*litterae publicae* of Lipara	extortionate tithe collection
3.102	*litterae publicae* of Menaenum	extortionate tithe collection
5.43	*litterae publicae* of Messana	illegal exemption from naval duty
4.79	*litterae publicae* of Segesta	seizure of statue of Diana
3.120	*litterae publicae* of *civitates* of Sicily	census of *aratores*
5.147	*litterae publicae* of Syracuse	prison record showing imprisonment of Roman citizens in quarries
4.92	*litterae publicae* of Tyndaris	seizure of statue of Mercury
3.93	*nomen* (entry) of Diocles Phimes of Panhormus	extortionate tithe collection
1.150	*nomina* (entries) of Habonius[4]	contract for repairs on temple of Castor
1.128	*nomina* of Q. Tadius	receipt of bribes as praetor
1.57	*rationes* (accounts) of P. Servilius Vatia Isauricus (consul in 79)	accounts from proconsulate in Cilicia (77–74 B.C.)
1.36, 37, 98	*rationes* of Verres	accounts as quaestor (84 B.C.)
1.98	*rationes* of Verres	accounts as legate (80–79 B.C.)
2.100	resolution of ten tribunes	banishment of Sthenius (71 B.C.)
1.37	senatus consultum	regarding accounts?
2.95	proposed senatus consultum	in absentia trials of people in provinces on capital charges
3.100	senatus consultum of Imachara	DE TRIBUTO CONFERUNDO
4.143 44	senatus consultum of Syracuse	eulogy of Verres
4.12	*tabulae* (records) of Heius of Messana	sale of statues
4.31	*tabulae* of Q. Tadius[5]	Verres' use of Cornelius Tlepolemus and Hiero of Cibyra
2.187, 189–91	*tabulae* of *publicani*	alteration of financial records
1.60	*tabulae* of Verres senior	personal accounts

1.60	*tabulae* of Verres	personal accounts up to 73 B.C.
5.10	*tabulae* of Lilybaeum	judicial corruption
3.99	*tabulae* of Thermae	extortionate tithe collection
1.156	*tabulae hominum honestissimorum* (records of very honorable men)	evidence in trial of Q. Opimius (*tribunus plebis* in 75; *TLRR* no. 157)
1.79, 84	*testimonium* of Verres	Verres as legate in Cilicia (80 B.C.), at trials of Philodamus and Artemidorus
5.61	*testimonium civitatum*	illegal exemption from naval duty
3.83	*testimonium publicum* of Acesta	extortionate tithe collection
3.106	*testimonium publicum* of Aetna	extortionate tithe collection
3.74, 5.133	*testimonium publicum* of Agyrium	extortionate tithe collection, illegal exemption from naval duty
3.89, 5.133	*testimonium publicum* of Amestratus	extortionate tithe collection, illegal exemption from naval duty
5.133	*testimonium publicum* of Henna	illegal exemption from naval duty
5.133	*testimonium publicum* of Herbita	illegal exemption from naval duty
3.100	*testimonium publicum* of Imachara	extortionate tithe collection
3.85	*testimonium publicum* of Lipara	extortionate tithe collection
5.43	*testimonium publicum* of Messana	illegal exemption from naval duty
5.133	*testimonium publicum* of Netum	illegal exemption from naval duty
3.99	*testimonium publicum* of Thermae	extortionate tithe collection
3.87	*testimonium publicum* of Tissa	extortionate tithe collection
5.133	*testimonium publicum* of Tyndaris	illegal exemption from naval duty

Notes

CHAPTER 1

1. On this topic of the rhetorical schools, see Quint. *Inst.* 7.4.36.

2. Translations are mine, unless otherwise indicated.

3. On Cestius and on the date of the younger Cicero's governorship, see Kaster's commentary in Suetonius Tranquillus 1995, 327–29.

4. See *Inst.* 3.6.93 and 10.1.23, where Quintilian makes it clear that Brutus's speech was written "exercitationis gratia" [for the sake of practice], although Cornelius Celsus mistakenly believed that it was actually delivered.

5. This criterion enables me to avoid the trial of C. Rabirius (*TLRR* no. 221) in 63 B.C., which took place in a *iudicium populi* (trial before the people), and the trial of Milo (*TLRR* no. 309) in 52 B.C., which occurred in a *quaestio extraordinaria* (special court). The first is the most difficult of all trials to understand in legal terms, and Cicero's published speech in the second is probably farthest removed from the delivered version.

6. See Ayers 1950. Pierpaoli (1997) has described the speech of Ser. Sulpicius Rufus in the trial of Murena; references to his article occur in chap. 6 of the present book. In the category of works that examine some of these trials from a non-Ciceronian perspective, I should also mention the fictional creations of Steven Saylor, three historically convincing mystery novels based on, respectively, the *Pro Roscio Amerino,* the *Pro Caelio,* and the *Pro Milone: Roman Blood* (1991), *The Venus Throw* (1995), and *A Murder on the Appian Way* (1996), all published by St. Martin's Press. Saylor narrates the events surrounding these three trials from the point of view of a detective called Gordianus the Finder. I refrain from discussing Saylor's reconstruction of events, so as not to lessen the enjoyment of future readers of these novels.

7. Ayers 1950, 1–3.

8. For that reason, when I cite a section number without any accompanying title, the section citation is to that speech. Unless otherwise indicated, the Oxford Classical Text has been followed for Cicero's orations, except the *Pro Sulla,* for which Berry's text has been used, and the *Pro Caelio,* for which Austin's text has been used.

9. This analysis is based on trials listed in *TLRR.* Although there could be disagreement about the precise numbers, the overall picture is indisputable. Of course, it is possible that the extant sources do not provide a representative sample of the actual trials that took place during this period.

10. This statement is based on the criminal trials listed in *TLRR.* I calculate 108 condemnations and 105 acquittals between 149 and 50 B.C., but I concede that there can probably be no agreement about the exact numbers, since the verdict, and sometimes even the occurrence of the trial, is often doubtful. The overall picture, however, is that verdicts could go either way.

11. See Crawford 1984, 15.

12. The crucial attack came from P. A. Brunt (1965).

13. Riggsby (1999) makes important progress in this direction with his comprehensive coverage of Ciceronian forensic speeches and the trials in which they were delivered.

14. Riggsby (1995a, 249) calls this "appropriation" and "reversal."

15. Crook 1995, 197.

16. This section is meant to provide a general overview, rather than presenting original conclusions, and provides only a sketch of a very complex topic. See Greenidge 1901, 456–76; Bianchini 1964; Alexander 1977, 98–130, 200–22; Alexander 1985; David 1992, 497–589; Santalucia 1997.

17. Fantham (1997, 120–21) writes: "Many a young man made his name by accusing a public figure. . . . it was virtually a duty for a young Roman to lay a charge if there was a family vendetta and to prosecute the man who had laid charge against his father."

18. Quintilian (*Inst.* 7.4.34) lists *industria, vires,* and *fides* (respectively, "energy," "force," and "trustworthiness") as the criteria by which the prosecutor was chosen.

19. See Alexander 1982, 154.

20. See Greenidge 1901, 479. Quintilian (*Inst.* 6.4.5) says that some orators compensated for weak speeches by their performance in the *altercatio.*

21. The locus classicus is Polyb. 6.14. For an overview of Roman capital punishment and exemptions from it, see Bauman 1996, 14–19. I shall refer to the defendant as masculine, because I deal in this book with no female defendants, and they cannot have been common in the *quaestiones perpetuae,* the standing criminal courts. However, it might have been possible to prosecute a woman before one of these courts, especially on a charge of poisoning. In these courts, the defendants were always citizens.

22. Professor Richard A. Epstein of the University of Chicago Law School explained this dichotomy in his remarks as a discussant at the conference "Law Courts and the Mediation of Social Conflict in the Ancient Mediterranean World" held on 30 March 1996 at the University of Chicago. I thank him for permission to paraphrase his remarks. Gotoff (1986, 123) implies that defense speeches are likely to be somewhat disjointed: "It is a truism for trial lawyers, universally ignored by Ciceronian scholars, that the defense

advocate will argue where and what he thinks will be most effective and will treat the opposition arguments in the manner that he thinks he can best control and manipulate."

23. Some kind of presumption of innocence is implied by the fact that it took a majority to convict, so a tie vote resulted in acquittal (*lex repetundarum,* line 55).

24. It may be objected that Quintilian's views are not really relevant, since he wrote in the first century A.D., well after the late Republic. But his *Institutio oratoria* are based to such a large extent on examples drawn from Cicero's works, as is shown by an *index locorum,* that his work can be said to reflect the oratory of the late Republic, although seen from a later point of view. I analyze his views first because they are generally more cogently expressed and more profound than those of the earlier rhetorical writers, but there are no major disagreements between him and these authors on the matters discussed by me here. However, Axer (1998) questions Quintilian's reliability as an interpreter of Cicero's rhetorical theory and practice.

25. *Inst.* 4.1.36 reads, "Id tamen totum respondenti facilius est quam proponenti, quia hic admonendus iudex, illic docendus est" [All this is, however, easier for the person who answers the charge than the person who presents it, because the former must remind the judge, whereas the latter must instruct him]. The construction *hic . . . ille* does not always mean "the latter . . . the former"; it can mean the opposite, as it does here. For this use, see *TLL* (vol. 6.3, fasc. 15, col. 2716, line 57), which cites also for this usage Quint. *Inst.* 3.10.1, 6.1.21, and 6.2.21. The *OLD* (s.v. "hic," no. 11), notes that *hic* can refer to "the one with whom the context is primarily concerned."

26. In the *Partitiones oratoriae* (117), Cicero advises prosecutors as to how they can strengthen the effectiveness of the witnesses they present.

27. We do not know of any passage where Cicero says precisely that it is easier to prosecute than to defend. Cousin's note in the Budé edition (Quintilian 1975–79, 3:248–49) explains that "quod Cicero saepe testatur" [what Cicero often gives evidence of] refers to the fact that Cicero spoke much more often for the defense than for the prosecution, as he implies at *Div. Caec.* 1. But this would explain Quintilian's comment only if Cicero's attraction to the role of defense speaker can best be explained by its greater difficulty compared to speaking for the prosecution.

28. For a discussion of the authorship and dating of the *Rhetorica ad Herennium,* see Pina Polo 1996, 70–72. Caplan's introduction to his Loeb edition of that work ([Cicero] 1954, xxv–xxvi = Caplan 1970, 16–17) dates it to the years 86–82 B.C. and says that it is likely, though not certain, that Cicero's *De inventione rhetorica* (discussed shortly in text) was composed before it.

29. An introduction to Cicero's rhetorical works is provided by Kirby (1997, 14–18).

30. Cf. Apsines' *Art of Rhetoric* 1.31 (Apsines 1997, 85), where the author presents the argument that no jury ought to pity someone who has evaded conviction on previous charges and, instead of reforming, has again committed a crime.

31. See Kurke 1989, 186–88.

32. Cic. *Brut.* 260. Douglas (*Brutus,* 190) translates this term "an habitual prosecutor of long standing."

33. The italicized words are the translation supplied by Douglas (*Brutus,* 107).

34. See Stroh 1975, 31–54: "Exkurs: Zur These Jules HUMBERT und dem Problem der schriftlichen Redaktion von Cicero Gerichtsreden." Zetzel (1994) has recently

voiced agnosticism on the connection between spoken and published speeches, although he does imply that such a connection exists.

All this can be taken one stage further. The speeches that we have are not the speeches Cicero delivered, but the texts of those speeches that he chose to publish later. Whether they are close to the original speeches is unimportant and impossible to determine; but they are representations of genuine speeches, and meant to be taken as such.

Laurand's (1928) treatment of this problem in his chapter "Les discours prononcés par Cicéron et les discours publiés" (1–23) is very sensible and useful. Classen (1985, 1–13), in his discussion of the subject, raises two more points besides the relationship between the delivered and published versions of a speech, which he argues must have been somewhat different: (1) corruptions in the written version and (2) the necessity to see even the published version as something meant to be read and heard aloud, not laboriously studied word by word. See also M. von Albrecht, "M. Tullius Cicero, Sprache und Stil," *RE* Suppl. 13 (1973): 1246–1347.

35. Riggsby 1999, 178. Stroh (1975, 53) voices a similar point of view: "Nicht die wirklich gehaltene Rede muß publiziert werden, sondern die Rede, wie sie wirklich gehalten sein könnte" [It is not the speech as actually delivered that must be published, but the speech as it could actually be delivered]."

36. Vasaly 1993, 10.

37. Stroh 1975, 45 n. 62.

38. On *commentarii*, see Premerstein, "Commentarii," *RE* 4 (1900): 727; Marshall 1985, 298.

39. I interpret the *principium* here to be the equivalent of an exordium, since the latter was delivered from a (memorized) prepared text (Quint. *Inst.* 4.1.1).

40. See Schanz-Hosius 1:405. Aulus Gellius (*NA* 1.7.1, 13.21.16) cites Tiro's edition of the *Verrines* as authoritative.

41. "Cum iam rebus transactis et praeteritis orationes scribimus, num irati scribimus?" [When, after the business has been settled and is in the past, we write out speeches, we do not do so in anger, do we?] (*Tusc.* 4.55).

42. "... pleraeque enim scribuntur orationes habitae iam, non ut habeantur." See Douglas, *Brutus*, 79, ad loc.

43. Shackleton Bailey, *CLA*, 5:351, on Cic. *Att.* 13.32.3.

44. It has been suggested to me that these four senators might have served to provide quality control by comparing their four versions of the text. This is a possible procedure, but the production of four separate texts just for the purpose of ensuring accuracy seems excessive.

45. See Berry, 219. Settle (1963, 276–77 n. 20) suggests that the story related by Plutarch may be an elaboration of Cicero's statement about the four senators. This view is followed by Marshall (1987, 733). McDermott (1972, 272) makes the same suggestion, although his treatment of the incident does not bring out the fact that the incident related by Plutarch took place two days after the testimony of the Allobroges and the conspirators.

46. Mentz 1931, 372.

47. P. Groebe ("M. Tullius Tiro," *RE* 2.7 [1948]: 319) puts the year of Tiro's birth in

103 B.C., three years after Cicero's. But Shackleton Bailey (*CLA*, 3:231) questions whether, if this were the case, Cicero would have still referred to him as an *adulescens* in 50 B.C. (*Att.* 6.7.2, 7.2.3).

48. See Mentz 1931, 371–72, 385–86.

49. Since the *Second Philippic* was never actually delivered, that episode is not an example of the process of editing a speech for publication after its delivery. On the practice of sending drafts to friends and acquaintances (and only to them) for their comments, see Starr 1987, 213. Starr notes that small wafers of red wax were sometimes affixed to the manuscript to show where corrections were needed (see also Shackleton Bailey, *CLA*, 6:273; Cic. *Att.* 15.14.4, 16.11.1).

50. Shackleton Bailey dates *Att.* 13.44 to "28 (?) July 45." Interestingly, about twenty-six days before (if Shackleton Bailey's dating of *Att.* 13.20 is correct), Cicero had already refused to make an addition to the text of the speech (*Att.* 13.20.2), on the grounds that the text was already being circulated. But he makes clear that this addition would have been a change he did not want to make in any case.

51. See Gotoff's commentary on Cicero's Caesarian speeches (Cicero 1993, 174–75).

52. See Habinek 1998, 106–8, "Maintain a Personal Relationship."

53. This is the interpretation suggested by Shackleton Bailey (*CLA*, 2:183).

54. Riggsby 1995b, 124.

55. Marshall 1985, 229, on Asc. 62.4.

56. Riggsby 1995b, 124. On the Pliny passage, see the discussion later in the present chapter.

57. Humbert 1925, 46–50; Kumaniecki 1970, 8.

58. Stroh 1975, 38–39.

59. Marshall 1987.

60. Settle 1963, 271–73.

61. He writes "quoque in prooemio" [even in the introduction] because that part of the speech was prepared carefully in advance.

62. Our (published) text is 105 sections in length. The *Pro Ligario* and the *Pro rege Deiotaro*, both described as *oratiunculae* (respectively, at *Att.* 13.19.2 and *Fam.* 9.12.2), are thirty-eight and forty-three sections in length, so an *oratiuncula* is not necessarily totally negligible in size.

63. See Millar 1964, 46–55, especially 49.

64. See Crawford 1984, 210–18, no. 72, for more fragments and *testimonia*. Clark presents in his edition (Cicero 1895, 29) the argument that a passage that some editors have included in the published *Pro Milone* (33) belongs instead to the delivered speech.

65. See Lintott 1974, 74. For an opposing view, see Settle 1963, 276–77. On the *Acta Diurna*, see Baldwin 1979.

66. Marshall 1987, 731.

67. For a refutation of Settle's view that the no longer extant text of the original *Pro Milone* was in fact a forgery that fooled Quintilian and Asconius, see Stone 1980, 88. Crawford (1984, 211 n. 4) rightly points out the skepticism expressed by Settle about his own arguments.

68. Kennedy 1972, 276–77.

69. Millar (1998, 9) uses a passage from Valerius Maximus (5.9.2) as support for potential difference between the delivered speech and the "disseminated" text. Valerius

Maximus says that when Hortensius disseminated the text of a speech, he retained a witticism that he had employed in the delivered speech. As Millar notes, Valerius Maximus implies that Hortensius could have omitted the witticism but decided not to. This passage does not record an actual discrepancy between the two versions but does suggest that such a discrepancy would have been possible.

70. Moreau (1980, 235–36) suggests that Cicero's original speech on behalf of Murena against charges of *ambitus* had contained a section defending Clodius's involvement in Murena's campaign for the consulate of 62 and that Cicero had suppressed this section when he edited and published the speech several years later, when Cicero and Clodius were enemies. Tatum (1999, 58–59) finds this explanation attractive.

71. See *TLRR* no. 368; Crawford 1994, 7–18.

72. See Austin, *Pro Caelio*³, 70–71, ad loc.

73. Kurke (1989, 82 n. 266) points out that the joke by which Cicero secured an acquittal for his client Flaccus was already in ancient times no longer present in the published speech. However, as Kurke notes, the joke could have been made during the examination of witnesses (discussed later in chap. 3).

74. Stroh 1975, 51–53. Crawford (1984, 9) rightly emphasizes the reasons why Cicero might decide not to publish a speech, particularly the desire to avoid giving offense to men of influence or causing them embarrassment.

75. It might be argued that Cicero's publication of the *Pro Milone* constitutes a contrary example, since many readers would know that it was quite different from the speech that Cicero actually delivered. However, if one holds that this speech was an exception because Cicero was not able to deliver the speech that he had planned to give and instead delivered a speech that was substantially different, the rationale for Cicero to publish the original speech and for the public to read it would be that he thereby afforded his readers an opportunity to read the "real" speech, that is, the speech he intended to deliver but that no one had ever heard. In the other trials, he did deliver the speech he intended, and that would be the one that his readers would want to obtain.

76. Ayers (1950, 46) notices that Hortensius's interjected protests on testimony are mentioned only in the first two speeches (Cic. 2 *Verr.* 1.71, 151; 2.156; possibly 2.24), and he concludes that Hortensius eventually lapsed into silence as Cicero went through his witnesses. But I argue that this imbalance reflects Cicero's presentation of witnesses, not Hortensius's growing stupefaction. Hortensius did not protest against the witnesses' testimony relating to the final three speeches because very little of that was actually presented in the first *actio* and of course, because as the trial turned out, Hortensius never had an opportunity to hear the other witnesses. Therefore, this fact noted by Ayers corroborates the thesis that the speeches of the second *Verrines* provide accurate information about what was said in the first *actio*.

77. Gotoff 1986, 123. Of course, this rule does not apply to the *Verrines*, where Cicero is speaking for the prosecution.

78. Harris 1995, 15–16.

79. The quotations are from Gruen 1995, 264–65, 288–89, 298. Gruen writes in a previous work (1968b, 6), "Conviction or acquittal was more often an index of political power than a testimony to the effectiveness of legal argument." Gruen (1968b, 6) also states that the fact that a trial can be labeled as "political" does not mean that the defendant is innocent. I am encouraged not only that Riggsby (1997) agrees that trials have

something to do with laws and legally relevant evidence but also that he, like me, thinks the question worth asking. He cites as proponents of the irrelevance of law Zetzel (1994), who argues that rhetorical effrontery won over juries, and Swarney (1993), who agrees that the outcome of a trial was decided by a clash of social reputation and prestige.

This section of the present chapter is based on a talk entitled "What Do Roman Trials Have to Do with Roman Law" that I presented to the University of Cincinnati Classics Graduate Student Association in 1995.

80. Gotoff 1993, 293.

81. Zetzel 1994, 449.

82. Gotoff 1993, 293 n. 16, 296 n. 26.

83. Riggsby (1997) has also thought it worthwhile to discuss this question, in a slightly different form ("Did the Romans believe in their verdicts?"), and his answer is similar to mine. He writes (1997, 237), "The problem has been a tendency to underestimate drastically the 'relevance to the case' of many of Cicero's arguments."

84. In his *Rhetorica* (1354a–b), Aristotle decries and at the same time accepts the appeals to emotion that an orator needs to use in most trials and contrasts this situation to trials before the more exclusive and therefore, in his view, the more rational Areopagus. For this passage, see Wallace 1989, 124, with more discussion of the difference between ἔξω τοῦ πράγματος and εἰς τὸ πράγμα. Cf. εἰς αὐτὸ τὸ πράγμα ἐρεῖν [to speak to the point at issue] (Ps.-Arist. *Ath. Pol.* 67.1; trans. von Fritz and Kapp). See, in the Attic orators, Antiphon 6 [*On the Chorus Boy*] 9 and Demosthenes 57 *Eubul.* 7, 59, 60. For Aristotle's discussion of the use of laws in rhetoric, see *Rh.* 1375a–b. Harris (1994) makes the case that the law did play an important role in Athenian trials and that law and rhetoric were not incompatible.

85. See Arist. *Rh.* 1376a–1377a for other inartificial proofs, such as contracts, witnesses, torture, and oaths; see also Ps.-Arist. *Rh. Al.* 1432 a–b.

86. The starting point of research on this subject is Solmsen 1941, as well as Solmsen 1938. More recent scholarship sees the connection as more indirect than Solmsen did: see Fantham 1973; Fortenbaugh 1988; Kennedy 1994; and Schütrumpf 1994. Douglas (1973, 95–102) advances some common-sense considerations on the relationship between Greek rhetorical theory and Cicero's rhetorical works, arguing "for a Greco-Roman intellectual background still sufficiently alive to undergo modification and development" (101).

87. This discussion of the role of character is based on a talk entitled "The Legal Relevance of *ethos* in Roman Forensic Oratory," presented by me to the American Society for the History of Rhetoric in November 1997. On the importance of character in Roman oratory, see also May 1988; Kurke 1989, 118–22. It is useful to distinguish arguments based on the character of the defendant from those based on the character of the speaker.

88. Berry (1990, 204), reviewing May 1988, cautions that the idea that character is a constant may have been a convenient one for orators to exploit, rather than one that was universally held.

89. Thierfelder (1965, 390) writes: "Der normale Fall is also, daß der Anwalt auf Grund der Möglichkeit, die der alt-ererbte Patronatsbegriff bietet, das Gewicht seiner Persönlichkeit zu Gunsten des Klienten in die Waagschale wirft. Das Gewicht einer Persönlichkeit wird zu verschiedenen Zeiten verschieden sein" [The normal situation is

therefore that the advocate throws his weight as an individual in the scales on behalf of the client on the basis of the possibility that the long-inherited concept of the patronage offers. The weight of one individual will be different at different times].

90. Fantham (1997, 121) writes: "The Roman public played as large a part in these trials as the formal jury." Millar (1998, 217–18) and Tatum (1999, 15) agree.

91. I presented this analysis in a paper entitled "Legal Technicalities in Roman Oratory," delivered at the annual meeting of the American Philological Association in December 1995. Riggsby (1997, 243 n. 24) accepts my conclusion. See Alexander 2000, 61–62.

92. Frier 1985, 29; for the date of the trial, see 45–46.

93. Riggsby 1997, 243–44.

94. As I mentioned earlier in this chapter, Quintilian here seems to be thinking of witnesses called by the prosecution, perhaps because only the prosecutor had the right to compel witnesses to appear.

95. See Cic. *Rosc. Am.* 55–57; Tac. *Ann.* 4.30.2; Crook 1995, 138–39.

96. See n. 27.

97. See Quint. *Inst.* 6.3.69 on Caelius. Other examples are in Cicero's *Brutus:* M. Brutus (130), L. Caesulenus (131), and C. Rusius (260).

98. Kurke (1989, 191 n. 244) makes this point.

99. See Alexander 1982, 153–64. Frier (1994, 212), in his review of Lintott 1992, describes this feature of the *lex repetundarum* as an "oddity," implying that it cannot be used as a model by which to understand other laws. Challenging my interpretation is the note for this passage in *Statutes* (1:106), which argues that a supplement can be supplied whose "implication would be that an offence was what a man did to a particular claimant or group of claimants." The note continues, "if his act damaged others who had not yet sued, this clause does not prevent them from suing; for *their* claim was a different *res,* even if only one act lay behind it." My difficulty with this interpretation involves the phrase *nisei quod postea fecerit* in the *lex repetundarum;* this phrase would be quite redundant if the trial related only to specified acts, which clearly would not be things done afterward. See also, in the present book, chap. 9, n. 24.

100. The evidence presented here is in accord with the conclusions of Santalucia (1997) in an article in which he attacks the findings of Giuffrè (1994). Santalucia argues on the basis of Quint. *Inst.* 3.10.1 that a trial could take cognizance of several charges of the same type, as in the case of extortion. He disputes Giuffrè's interpretation of Cic. *Clu.* 97, where Cicero describes how the prosecutor of Bulbus for *maiestas* (*TLRR* no. 160) brings in extraneous material about Bulbus's activities as a juror in the *iudicium Iunianum* (*TLRR* no. 149) to establish the defendant's bad character, not as a formal charge. Santalucia shows that the reference to *tabulae publicae* (*Clu.* 62) pertains not to an official list of charges presented by the prosecutor but rather to the official record of the testimony presented in the trial. Finally, he argues that Cic. *Inv. rhet.* 2.58–59 refers to a special case where the prosecutor has claimed *parricidium,* thus gaining the procedural advantages of an earlier trial and harsher punishment, but has failed to substantiate *parricidium* in the actual trial (see discussion of the case later in this chapter and in chap. 9).

101. On the Augustan adultery law, see Treggiari 1991, 277–98. Treggiari describes the crime as "odd" and the law as "anomalous" (298).

102. See Mommsen 1899, 129 n. 8.

103. See Alexander 1982, 159; Wlassak 1917, 10–11.

104. See Alexander 1982, 159–60. The text of Asconius here is lacunose: see Lintott 1968, 114–15; Marshall 1985, 211, ad loc.

105. Giuffre 1994, 361. See n. 100.

106. See Alexander 1982, 160–61; Santalucia 1997, 408.

107. See Greenidge 1901, 463; Bianchini 1964, 43–44.

108. Santalucia 1997, 413.

109. It might be objected that raising a legal issue of this sort would have worked against the defendant, showing him to be the sort of person who took refuge in a legal technicality. Reliance on legalisms did pose this risk, but a device that I call the "repudiated technicality" allowed the *patronus* to deal with it (see Alexander 2000). When defending Rabirius Postumus, Cicero argues that charges that had not been put forward at the earlier main trial cannot be introduced in the *litis aestimatio* or in a *quo ea pecunia* hearing (see chap. 5 in the present book). His ability and willingness to make this technical argument supports the notion that defense speakers would have argued that charges not mentioned in the *inscriptio* should not be raised in the trial, if it were possible to do so.

110. See *lex repetundarum*, line 34. There were some restrictions on who could be summoned as a witness, including one (but only one) advocate for the defendant (*lex repetundarum*, lines 32–33). See Sherwin-White 1982, 26. On *testes voluntarii*, see Quint. *Inst.* 5.7.9.

111. Cicero's defense of Roscius may provide some contrary evidence. See chap. 8.

112. Of course, some trials had more than one *actio*, so by the second *actio*, the defense attorney would have had more time to react to the charges. That the defense lawyer depended on the prosecutor to explain the charges accounts for Hortensius's frustration over Cicero's speech against Verres in the first *actio*. He said he could not defend his client, because he had not heard the charges presented, except for one lapidary sentence at the end of the speech (Cic. 1 *Verr.* 56): "Dicimus C. Verrem, cum multa libidinose, multa crudeliter in civis Romanos atque socios, multa in deos hominesque nefarie fecerit, tum praeterea quadringentiens sestertium ex Sicilia contra leges abstulisse" [We say that Gaius Verres, when he has committed many wanton and cruel acts against Roman citizens and allies, when he has committed many foul acts against gods and men, has furthermore illegally made off with forty million sesterces from Sicily]. This approach best explains Hortensius's expression of frustration to which Cicero refers in the speeches of his second *actio* (2 *Verr.* 1.24). If one believes, as I have argued (Alexander 1976), that Hortensius actually made a response to Cicero's speech in the first hearing, Cicero is referring to something that Hortensius actually said in court; if, as Brunt (1980, 279–80 n. 44) believes, Hortensius made no reply, Cicero is imagining what Hortensius would have said if he had replied, since the fiction of the speeches of the second *actio* is, of course, that the case is continuing to go forward—thus, that Hortensius responded in the first hearing, witnesses were called, a *comperendinatio* (adjournment prescribed by law) took place, and now the court has reassembled. Brunt holds that the reply of Hortensius to Cicero mentioned by Quintilian (*Inst.* 10.1.23) must have been a mere literary composition or else a speech delivered at the *litis aestimatio*.

113. See Stroh 1975, 231 and n. 16; Alexander 1982, 161; Riggsby 1999, 17.

114. See Kunkel 1963, 764; Stroh 1975, 37–38 n. 27. The evidence is very well summarized in Kurke 1989, 72 n. 237.

115. See Mommsen 1899, 426; Woodman and Martin's commentary in Tacitus 1996, 152.

116. It appears that a fixed ratio existed between the maximum times for each side. The most common such ratio is 2:3 (prosecution to defense), but the earliest specific evidence dates only from the *lex Pompeia de vi* of 52 B.C. (Asc. 36C; Tac. *Ann.* 3.13; Plin. *Ep.* 4.9.9; Dio Cass. 40.52.2). The *lex coloniae Iuliae Genitivae* CII.33–36 (*Statutes,* 1:409, no. 25) contains a 1:2 ratio. See Stroh 1975, 37–38 n. 27; Sherwin-White 1985, 167; Kurke 1989, 72–73 n. 237.

117. See *MRR* Suppl., 43, based on Marinone 1965–66.

118. For discussion and examples of this phenomenon, see Tac. *Dial.* 34.6–7; Apul. *Apol.* 66; Alexander 1977, 37–40; David 1983; David 1992, 541–42.

119. On the significance of this change in the extortion prosecutor from victim to representative of the victims, see Serrao 1956. The importance of Serrao's findings is stressed by Badian (1962, 204 = Seager 1969, 10).

120. The involvement of the Metelli in Sicilian affairs might be justified by their patronal status with relationship to the island, if we can believe Pseudo-Asconius (187St). Indeed, about a decade before, two members of the family had begun to prosecute an ex-governor of Sicily for extortion (*TLRR* no. 131). However, they abandoned the prosecution, and Nicols (1981) argues that the scholiast is mistaken, confusing forensic *patrocinium* with the kind of patronal status created by *deditio in fidem* (surrender). On the other hand, it is somewhat misleading to cite the *lex repetundarum* (lines 9–12), as Nicols does, to illustrate forensic *patrocinium,* since by the time of this potential trial, the prosecutor in an extortion case was no longer legally termed a *patronus* for the plaintiffs. For some ties between the Metelli and Sicily, see Badian 1984, 296, 302.

121. See Mitchell's commentary on 2 *Verr.* 1 (Cicero 1986, 8–9); Marinone 1950.

122. By this strategy, Cicero also put Hortensius in an untenable position. If he replied with a *perpetua oratio,* he would seem to be confirming Cicero's analysis of the defense strategy; moreover, before he tried to refute the charges against his client, he would have to frame them, thereby tending to confirm them. He evidently protested against this unfairness (see n. 112). Brunt (1980, 279–80 n. 44) writes,

> As Cicero's opening speech on 5 August (I [Verr.] 31) set out none of the evidence on which he relied, Hortensius could make no useful reply in the first *actio;* it would have been imprudent to anticipate the detailed charges.

Hortensius's reply was therefore minimal, and he did not even cross-examine the witnesses in the first *actio* (Cic. 2 *Verr.* 3.41).

123. The testimony of witnesses can be particularly crucial in proving judicial bribery (Cic. 2 *Verr.* 2.119).

124. See Schmitz 1989 on the personal qualities of witnesses.

125. One wonders whether the law imposed a similar obligation to listen to the pleaders' speeches. The inscription is too lacunose here to tell.

126. See Ayers 1950, 137 n. 29.

127. Those who disapprove strongly of any departure from the truth on the part of advocates may be shocked to read Quintilian's warning that the risk of treachery is espe-

cially great when witnesses have promised to give false evidence; such witnesses may feel guilty and change their minds. Sticklers for the truth may take some comfort, however, from his warning that false evidence is easier to refute than true (*Inst.* 5.7.13–14).

128. Münzer ("Tullius" no. 26, *RE* 2.7 [1939]: 823–24) estimates his age as eighteen to twenty years old.

129. On this point, see Alexander 1982, 157–58. See also Tac. *Ann.* 3.13.1; Woodman and Martin's commentary in Tacitus 1996, 153. Quite possibly, before being granted official powers of investigation, the prosecutors made an effort to find out as much as they could about the defendant's misdeeds at Rome or nearby in Italy.

130. Metellus also tried to cancel the demolition of statues of Verres and his son that had been decreed by the senate of Centuripa (Cic. 2 *Verr.* 2.161–64).

131. Brunt (1980, 281 n. 50) cites the parallel of the favor that Cicero, as governor of Cilicia, showed his predecessor Ap. Claudius (Cic. *Att.* 6.2.10; *Fam.* 3.10.1, 5).

132. Dilke 1980. Since Cicero had served as quaestor in the western part of the province, his ties were weaker in the eastern part.

133. Classen 1980.

134. These prefaces are introductory in nature and do not claim to present original findings on their subjects.

PART 1

1. For discussions of extortion, see Mommsen 1899, 705–32; Venturini 1979; Lintott 1981; Sherwin–White 1982; Alexander 1984; Lintott 1992, 10–33; Santalucia 1994, 197–98; Bauman 1996, 22–24; Riggsby 1999, 120–29.

2. See Alexander 1984, especially 536–39.

3. See Lintott 1992, 29.

4. For a concise discussion of the identity of the epigraphic law, see Lintott 1992, 166–69; Riggsby 1999, 121. For recent editions with commentary, see Lintott 1992, 88–169; *Statutes*, 1:65–112, no. 1. See also Griffin 1973a, 121–23.

5. See chap. 3.

6. Cicero (*Clu.* 104) says that P. Septimius Scaevola was assessed damages in a *litis aestimatio* on the count of accepting bribes as a juror, although the actual trial related to other charges (see *Clu.* 116; *TLRR* no. 172). See Venturini 1979, 84; Riggsby 1999, 217 n. 22.

7. See Alexander 1984, 532; Bauman 1996, 24.

8. Riggsby 1999, 123.

9. Macer (*Dig.* 48.11.7.3) does say that homicide committed even in the absence of money could be grounds for punishment, but he says this in a section where he is talking about the imperial practice in his own day ("hodie"), during which, he makes clear, offenders were punished "extra ordinem" [under imperial jurisdiction].

10. It seems clear that conviction for extortion in the Republic did not necessarily cause the loss of *caput*. It is controversial whether the reason that those convicted of extortion went into exile was that the damages assessed rendered them bankrupt and therefore *infamis*. See Strachan-Davidson 1912, 2:1–15; Sherwin-White 1949.

11. See Frederiksen 1966, 128, with sources.

12. See Luraschi 1983, Alexander 1985.

CHAPTER 2

1. C. Iulius Victor (Halm, *Rhet. Lat. Min.* 400.13).

2. Gruen 1971, 12. Shatzman (1975, 63) also makes the point that Verres' crimes are distinctive in their scale but not in quality.

3. Since Fonteius served in Macedonia in 77 (*Font.* 44), he cannot have come to Gaul before 76. He must have been stationed in Gaul by 74, because Pompey's troops wintered there in 74/73 when Fonteius was governor. If Fonteius had started his service in Gaul in 76, he probably would have been gone by 74, so the two remaining possibilities for the start of his service there are 75–73 and 74–72. Badian (1966, 911–12) argues strongly for the latter alternative, on the ground that Q. Caecilius Metellus Pius (consul in 80), while waging a campaign in Spain, wintered in Gaul in 75/74 (Plut. *Sert.* 21), yet Cicero fails to mention him as someone whom Fonteius had aided. Badian maintains that even if Metellus were a hostile witness, Cicero would not have ignored him in his speech. This argument *ex silentio* is unconvincing for three reasons: first, the speech we have is fragmentary; second, it is only one of two speeches that Cicero delivered at this trial; and third, Cicero clearly adopts in the *Pro Fonteio* a strategy of ignoring hostile testimony, rather than trying to refute it. Hermon (1993, 262 n. 13) also voices skepticism in her note on the chronology. Broughton (*MRR* Suppl., 93) argues that both 75–73 and 74–72 are possible dates for Fonteius's command.

4. See *MRR* 1:437.

5. See *MRR* 2:24, 25 n. 13.

6. See Wiseman 1971, no. 479; Nicolet 1966–74, vol. 2, no. 386. He was married to the sister (Cic. 2 *Verr.* 3.168) of T. Vettius Chilo, quaestor in 72 and 71 under Verres (*MRR* Suppl., 43, 219), and of P. Vettius Chilo (Nicolet 1966–74, vol. 2, no. 386), who appears as a witness in the trial (Cic. 2 *Verr.* 3.166). The duty of the *divisores* was to make distributions to fellow tribe members. Originally, these were legitimate gifts, but by the late Republic, they were often bribes. See Taylor 1949, 67; Adamietz's commentary in Cicero 1989, 195; Kunkel and Wittmann 1995, 83 n. 102; Tatum 1999, 26.

7. Cic. 2 *Verr.* 1.35. See Wiseman 1971, 104; *MRR* Suppl., 218. On Verres' desertion of Carbo, see also Cic. 2 *Verr.* 3.178.

8. His father by adoption was the second cousin of Verres' successor in Sicily, L. Caecilius Metellus (consul in 68); Cicero complains about his interference with the prosecution's collection of evidence in Sicily (2 *Verr.* 2.64, 3.122). See chap. 1 in this volume.

9. But in another work (*Orat.* 129), Cicero describes Verres as a *familiaris reus* (a client who is a friend) to Hortensius.

10. Yet also in the *Verrines* (1 *Verr.* 47), Cicero describes Verres as having neither "gratia" nor "cognatio."

11. Gruen (1971) has challenged the contention of Ward (1968) that Fonteius was prosecuted as part of a Metellan counterattack on a Pompeian faction that had instigated the prosecution of Verres. As governor in Gaul, Fonteius had aided both Metellus Pius and Pompey in their campaigns in Spain against Sertorius, and one would expect Cicero to parade Pompey's support for his defense of Fonteius if Pompey had played a key role in it. However, one should not rule out the possibility that Cicero referred to Pompey's support in a missing section of this speech or in his speech in the other *actio* of this trial. The controversy is well summarized by Crawford (1984, 56).

12. See *MRR* Suppl., 157; Wiseman 1971, no. 320.

13. Badian's comments (1984, 264) on Q. Fabius Sanga, a patron of the Allobroges in 63, are relevant to his identity and status. Badian's skepticism is warranted as to whether a mere client of the noble Fabii could inherit their *clientela,* especially when some of them were alive. I cannot agree with Münzer's comment ("Fabius" no. 26, *RE* 6 [1909]: 1747) that the way Cicero speaks of Fabius demonstrates that he was not of the patrician Fabii. On the contrary, it seems to rule out the possibility that he could have been of Gallic origin, because Cicero would certainly have used that origin as a basis for mocking him and his participation in the prosecution. See Clemente 1974, 151; see 99–162 for a very useful commentary on the *Pro Fonteio.*

14. The order of events in a trial was (1) speech for the prosecution, (2) speech for the defense, (3) prosecution witnesses and cross-examination by defense, and (4) defense witnesses and cross-examination by prosecution. In extortion cases, after the *lex Servilia (Glauciae)* of the late second century introduced compulsory *comperendinatio* (Cic. 2 *Verr.* 1.26), the rule was to repeat the whole series one more time. Therefore, when Cicero is delivering the extant *Pro Fonteio,* the prosecution would have already had one opportunity to present witnesses.

15. With the phrase "dux Allobrogum ceterorumque Galliorum" [leader of the Allobroges and of the other Gauls] (*Font.* 46), Cicero may exaggerate the power of Indutiomarus; while Indutiomarus may have led his own people, it is doubtful that the Gallic tribes were united in submitting to the leadership of any one person.

16. See chap. 1 for advice from rhetorical handbooks on the handling of witnesses. On the rhetorical stereotype of the Gauls as prone to giving false testimony and hostile to Rome, see Vasaly 1993, 193–94.

17. See Badian 1968a, 24, 98 n. 32. Sumner (1973, 94–97) argues forcefully for 118 as the date when L. Licinius Crassus (consul in 95) and Cn. Domitius Ahenobarbus (consul in 96) served as *duumviri coloniae deducendae* (members of the commission of two for founding a colony) for the foundation of Narbo. Broughton (*MRR* Suppl., 118) provides a survey of the chronological controversy. On the Via Domitia, see G. Radke, "Viae publicae Romanae," *RE* Suppl. 13 (1973): 1667–84.

18. See Badian 1966, 904.

19. Another view is that by this restriction, the Romans made the Gauls more dependent on importing Italian wine and thereby could drive a harder bargain with the Gauls in the import of metals and slaves (see Tchernia 1983, 100). Such a trade could well have benefited the city of Massilia, which was in a position to play the middleman.

20. There were, in addition, private citizens who traveled to Rome on their own account to help Verres, whom Cicero dismisses as very unimportant individuals from minor and depressed towns (2 *Verr.* 2.14). One other town, Leontini, failed to support Cicero in his prosecution, because, according to Cicero, none of the people of that town, with one exception, owned any land, and therefore none of them could suffer from Verres' agricultural exactions. In fact, Cicero claims that they benefitted from Verres' actions (2 *Verr.* 3.109), although he does not explain how. On Verres' support in Sicily, see chap. 1 in the present book; Dilke 1980; Classen 1980.

21. Badian (1972, 108) draws the parallel in succinct terms.

Verres showed what could be done by intervening in the sale of locally sold taxes; and, profiting by the vast independent powers of the governor, a man might even get away with introducing new taxes and apparently collecting them on his own authority—and, no doubt, at least partly for his own benefit.

Badian continues (153 n. 117),

> This seems to be what Fonteius did in Gaul (Cic. *Font.* 19f. (unfortunately incomplete)), quite apart from some shady dealings over road contracts, which recall Verres (ibid. 17f.).

Badian also draws a parallel between Verres and Ap. Claudius Pulcher, Cicero's predecessor in Cilicia.

22. This change allows us to date the trial to 69, or, rather, to establish 69 as the earliest possible year in which the trial could have taken place, since the *lex Aurelia* was passed in the final months of 70, as we see from the fact that at the time of the trial of Verres, it was still a bill that threatened senators. See Clemente 1974, 146, on *Font.* 26, though it is section 36 that refers specifically to the mixed composition of the jury (evidently combining *tribuni aerarii* with the *equites*).

23. On the role of the *vita ante acta* and allegations arising from it, see chap. 1.

24. In fact, Ebel (1975) argues that the province of Transalpine Gaul was organized by Pompey, just before Fonteius's governorship; that Fonteius was still in the process of creating an ordered province; and that the necessary measures that he took created the disaffection among the native Gauls that led to his prosecution:

> . . . Fonteius directed military operations against at least some Gauls, the Vocontii being specifically mentioned; he confiscated lands and cleared them by force; he requisitioned supplies of all kinds and money as well; he called up cavalry for service in other wars; he ordered the refurbishing of the Via Domitia. He rigidly controlled the circulation of money and provided winter quarters for a large Roman army. In doing all this, he seems to have been careful to avoid offending Roman citizens and non-Gallic allies in the province. On the other hand, virtually every important Gallic tribe sent witnesses against Fonteius at his trial. On the whole, the description of Transalpina which Cicero presents is not one of an organized province, but rather one in the process of being organized. (366)

Another account of the historical background to the speech can be found in Hackl 1988.

25. I have discussed this question in Alexander 1982, 158.

26. Ryan (1996a) argues that this date for his quaestorship is almost certain.

27. The amount is disputed, as either 23,000,000 or 3,200,000, and it is not clear from this fragment whether the sum pertains only to his quaestorship or also to his office of *monetalis* (see Clemente 1974, 107). See also Alexander 1982, 158.

28. See Clemente 1974, 103–6.

29. This is the exegesis of Jouanique (1960). On this subject, see also Clemente 1974, 105; Piazza 1987, 289–91.

30. See Bulst 1964, 335; Badian 1967, 187–89; Barlow 1980, 216.

31. See *MRR* 2:91, 95; Clemente 1974, 160.

32. See *MRR* 2:78.

33. For Centuripa, see Cic. 2 *Verr.* 2.120, 4.114; for Agrigentum, 3.103, though it is not clear that this is an official delegation.

34. Münzer ("Fonteius" no. 7, *RE* 6 [1909]: 2842) argues that this man could not have been related to the defendant as brother, because Cicero would have mentioned this. More probably, the prosecutor had used the kinship to discredit any defense claim that C. Fonteius had acted independently of the defendant, and Cicero avoids reminding the jurors of this point.

35. I have copied the order of punctuation of the Oxford Classical Texts edition. But the question mark in the sentence "Tu mihi ita defendas . . ." must refer to the whole sentence, not just to the part within the quotation marks.

36. It is likely that Cicero's description reflects the relative importance of this charge in the prosecutor's speech. Of course, Cicero is quite capable of distorting his opponents' speeches, in particular with regard to the relative importance of the charges, as I argue in the case of the prosecution speech against Cluentius (see chap. 9). But here Cicero's stress on the prosecutor's intention would probably make the jurors aware of such a distortion, since they had just recently heard the prosecutor's speech. In the *Pro Cluentio,* in contrast, Cicero does not claim to tell his audience what the prosecutor said about the relative importance of the charges.

37. The text is preserved in Amm. Marc. 15.12.4. An alternative reading is "quod illi venenum arbitrabantur" [that after this the Gauls will drink wine mixed with water, which they once thought poison]. Tchernia (1983, 93) provides a good paraphrase:

> . . . granted, the tax affects our products. But in reality it only operates against the Gauls. So those drunkards have to pay more for their wine, do they? There is a perfectly simple way for them to make up for the increase caused by the Fonteius taxes: instead of drinking their wine neat, they should mix it with water, as do all civilized people.

Laet (1949, 83) may be wrong to suggest that these new duties hindered this profitable trade, since the demand seems to have been so inelastic (i.e., a price increase did not deter the Gauls from purchasing the product).

38. See Posidonius no. 67 Edelstein and Kidd; Diod. Sic. 5.26.3 (reporting that the Gauls were willing to trade a slave for an amphora of wine); Polyb. 2.19.4; App. *Celt.* 7. See also Clemente 1974, 100.

39. Hdt. 6.84; see also Plato *Leg.* 637E.

40. See chap. 1, "The Delivered Speech and the Published Speech."

41. For help with the geography, readers may wish to turn to Rivet 1988 (70 n. 42; 122; 139; 120, fig. 7) and to G. Radke, "Viae publicae Romanae," *RE* Suppl. 13 (1973): 1667–84.

42. Clemente 1974, 136.

43. Hermon 1993, 282–90.

44. Clemente 1974, 131–32. As Laet (1949, 81) suggests, this group could have been the tax farmers mentioned by Cicero (*Font.* 19): Titurius, Porcius, Munius, Servaeus, and C. Annius.

45. Clemente 1974, 137–38.

46. See *MRR* 2:104; *MRR* Suppl., 162.

47. On the matter of repaying debts according to the terms of the *lex Valeria* (see discussion earlier in this chapter), Cicero claims to have complete enough records to demonstrate his client's innocence (*Font.* 3–4). Of course, this charge pertains to events

at Rome. Cicero mocks his opponent for failing to make use of records right at Rome and instead pursuing evidence in the wilds of Gaul.

48. The parallel with Hortensius's decision not to cross-examine Cicero's witnesses in the trial of Verres is striking (see chap. 1, n. 122).

49. Apparently, Massilia sent to the trial only a formal resolution of support, rather than actual *legati:* "... vos autem absens orat atque obsecrat ut sua religio, laudatio, auctoritas aliquid apud vestros animos momenti habuisse videatur" [. . . and now [the people of Massilia], though absent, beg and beseech you that their sense of obligation, their good reputation, and their influence seem to have carried some influence on your minds] (*Font.* 14). Interestingly, Messana, too, failed to send a delegation in support of Verres.

50. D.-G. 6:356 n. 6.

51. Heinze 1909, 981 n. 2 = 1960, 116 n. 50.

52. Cicero writes of extortion law, "Haec lex socialis est" [This law relates to the allies] (*Div. Caec.* 18). This does not necessarily show that only non-Romans could bring an action under extortion laws.

53. I was wrong in *TLRR* (no. 186, n. 4) to accept the notion that his relocation to Naples could possibly be construed as evidence that he was condemned and went there in exile. After Naples became a *municipium* in 89 B.C., this right of exile (recorded at Polyb. 6.14.8) would no longer have been available. See D'Arms 1970, 155; Berry, 167.

54. Drumann (D.-G. 5:357) says that Fonteius was acquitted. David (1992, 803) writes, "En 69, il est édile plébéien, défend sans doute avec succès M. Fonteius, préteur en 76–75, accusé *de repetundis*" [In 69, he is a plebian aedile, and defends, doubtless successfully, M. Fonteius, praetor in 76–75, who was accused of extortion], yet he writes in the accompanying note (806 n. 15), "L'acquittement de M. Fonteius est probable" [The acquittal of M. Fonteius is probable]. Münzer ("Fonteius," no. 12, *RE* 6 [1909]: 2845) says, "Der Ausgang des Prozesses ist unbekannt" [The outcome of the trial is unknown], and his judgment is followed by Ciaceri (1926–30, 1:91) and Karl-Ludwig Elvers (*Neue Pauly* 4 [1998]: 587).

CHAPTER 3

1. The grandfather served as *monetalis* (moneyer) in 140 B.C. according to Crawford's dating (1974, 1:262–63, no. 228). The reason for his lack of success in obtaining office could be an early death. Hayne (1978) paints a picture of the family as being in decline and prone to alienate those with whom they came in contact.

2. See chap. 1, n. 73; n. 83 in the present chapter.

3. As Kurke (1989, 40–42) points out, it is somewhat puzzling that the praetor of 63 had not run for the consulate of 60, 59, or even 58. He suggests that Flaccus's conduct in Asia might have eliminated his hopes for the consulate. Kurke's dissertation provides an outstanding exegesis of the trial of Flaccus, covering many points of detail in a complete yet concise manner.

4. The one area of the defendant's past life that Laelius may have touched on is Flaccus's actions against the Catilinarian conspiracy in 63. Kurke (1989, 85–87) draws this conclusion from protests preserved in fragments about the execution of the conspirators (*Schol. Bob.* 95St). This tactic, he suggests, opened the way for Cicero to expatiate on his and Flaccus's joint glory in suppressing the conspiracy.

5. On the contrast between the prosecutor's reliance on Flaccus's conduct as governor in Asia and Cicero's emphasis on his whole career, see Kurke 1989, 6–8.

6. Cicero refers to the trial at *Att.* 2.25.1, dated by Shackleton Bailey possibly to September 59. Although Shackleton Bailey (*CLA*, 1:405) concludes that the trial must have taken place shortly before this letter was written, it is better to take the letter as written after Hortensius spoke in the first *actio* but before Cicero spoke in the second (see Taylor 1950, 48; Kurke 1989, 69 n. 220, 71, 76).

7. See Oost 1956, 27. On the use of *hac*, see Hofmann 1965, 2:407. I am grateful to my colleague John T. Ramsey for alerting me to the significance of the word order in this passage. On whether this law was in fact an extortion law, see *Schol. Bob.* 97St; Du Mesnil, 40–42; Mommsen 1899, 393 n. 2; Greenidge 1901, 485 n. 3; Webster, *Pro Flacco*, 66.

8. See Val. Max. 8.1 *absol.* 10; *MRR* 2:188; Magie 1950, 2:1243.

9. For arguments that the trial of Flaccus was held under the *lex Cornelia*, see Kleinfeller, "Repetundarum crimen," *RE* 1A (1920): 607; Venturini 1979, 323 n. 3; Kurke 1989, 55 n. 170. For arguments that it was held under the *lex Iulia*, see Du Mesnil, 41–42; Bergmann 1893, 9, 19; Webster, *Pro Flacco*, 111; Greenidge 1901, 476 n. 9, 501.

10. Du Mesnil (38) makes the argument that the limitation of the prosecution speeches to a total of six hours (Cic. *Flac.* 82) is identical to the limit set by the *lex Iulia de repetundis* (Plin. *Ep.* 4.9.9). But we do not know when this limit was first set; see Sherwin-White 1985, 167, on Plin. *Ep.* 2.11.14, and 2 *Verr.* 1.25, 32. Zumpt (1871, 235–36) maintains that the *lex Cornelia de repetundis* must have stipulated a less restrictive limit than the six hours mentioned in the *Pro Flacco*, which he believes was delivered in a trial held under the *lex Iulia de repetundis*, but his reasoning seems based on the questionable premise that on the basis of the published *Verrines*, we can estimate how long Cicero spoke against Verres. See also Mommsen 1899, 428 n. 5.

11. See Cic. *Vat.* 27; Weinrib 1970, 430–31; Du Mesnil, 36–37; Oost 1956, 27–28.

12. See *MRR* Suppl., 116.

13. Kurke (1989, 56 n. 174) provides an excellent overview of the evidence regarding the identity of the *subscriptores* in this trial.

14. See Badian 1956, 95; Sumner 1973, 120.

15. See Sumner 1973, 81–83.

16. Conversely, personal enmity could also be viewed as an asset in a prosecutor, in that it guaranteed his good faith.

17. See Cic. *Flac.* 70, 74; Nicolet 1966–74, 2:781–83.

18. Kurke (1989, 71 n. 231) perceptively notes a division of labor between Laelius and Decianus. Laelius handled the charges for which Greeks and Jews served as witnesses, while Decianus, who had lived in Asia for many decades in the Roman community there, handled charges for which Roman citizens provided the evidence.

19. Schöll 1896, 388. Webster (*Pro Flacco*, 56) leans toward this solution.

20. See Austin, *Pro Caelio*³, 156. The name also appears in a vexed reading containing a comment of Asconius (34C) on the *Pro Milone*; see Marshall 1985, 173. This possibility is mistakenly omitted in *TLRR*.

21. Münzer, "Cornelius" no. 69, *RE* 4 (1900): 1262; "Laelius" no. 6, *RE* 12 (1924): 411; "Valerius" no. 79, *RE* 2.8 (1955): 35.

22. Valerius Maximus goes on to relate that this Valerius supported his attackers and hated his defenders to the extent that he made Balbus his sole heir.

23. Schöll 1896, 387–88.

24. Shackleton Bailey (1988, 28) defends the cognomen *Caetra*.

25. See Classen 1985, 180–81 n. 2, which contains a brief discussion of the identity of the *subscriptores*.

26. Macrobius (*Sat.* 3.13.3) tells the amusing story that Hortensius once asked to reverse the usual order so that he could irrigate his plane tree (with wine) at his villa in Tusculum. We do not know in connection with which trial this incident occurred. It is possible that this anecdote came from a prosecutor, when he tried to make fun of Cicero and Hortensius on seeing that they were not speaking in the usual order.

27. Münzer ("Valerius," no. 179, *RE* 2.8 [1955]: 34) writes: "Doch wichtiger war vielleicht, daß die Triumvirn in V. ein Mitglied der widerstrebenden Nobilität unschädlich zu machen wünschten" [It was perhaps still more important that the triumvirs wanted to render harmless in V[alerius Flaccus] a member of the opposing nobility]. Gruen (1995, 290–91) posits a quarrel between Pompey and Flaccus, which led to support for him from the antitriumviral party and opposition to him from the triumviral party:

> . . . Pompeius Magnus stood behind the prosecution. . . . Flaccus, of old patrician stock, had been a Pompeian legate in the Mithridatic war. There had evidently been a falling-out. In the year of the triumvirate that fact contained political implications. The opponents of the triumvirs turned out in force to buttress Flaccus' defense. . . . The case mirrors accurately the new political lineup inspired by the coming of the triumvirate.

28. Epstein 1987, 109–11.

29. If the *esset* in this text, the reading of the scholiast, is correct, the text reports an impression that had spread throughout Asia, not a fact, and Cicero is clearly implying that it is a false impression.

30. Flaccus served under Servilius in Cilicia in 78–76 and under Metellus Creticus in Crete in 68–67 (*Flac.* 6, 30, 100; *MRR* Suppl., 212). In 66 B.C., a Lucius Flaccus served with Pompey (Dio Cass. 36.54.2–3). If this is the same Flaccus, we see that the commander/subordinate relationship did not guarantee loyalty. That Cicero fails to mention Flaccus's service under Pompey may indicate that some ill will grew out of that contact. See *MRR* 2:156 n. 3.

31. Cicero (*Flac.* 14) writes, "Pompei autem auctoritas cum apud omnis tanta est quanta esse debet, tum excellit in ista provincia quam nuper et praedonum et regum bello liberavit" [Moreover, not only is the prestige of Pompey as great in everyone's eyes as it ought to be, but it also is preeminent in that province that he has recently freed from war both against pirates and against kings].

32. Mitchell (1991, 122 n. 72) writes, "Pompey's opposition can be explained by the fact that he had unusually close ties to Asia (*Flac.* 14) and he had a duty to look out for the interests of his clients."

33. I agree with Kurke (1989, 55 n. 171) that Laelius cannot have been collecting evidence for several years as an official *accusator*.

34. Shatzman (1975, 427) provides the following summary of the charges against Flaccus (quoted here verbatim):

   a. collecting moneys for ship building;
   b. confiscating several hundred thousand sesterces collected by Jews to be sent to Jerusalem;

c. charging 50 talents for approving a contract of tax-farming (Flacc., 90–3);

d. taking money which had been collected in Tralles for games in honour of his father, the consul of 86 (Flacc., 56–7);

e. exacting 206,000 drachmas from the town of Acmonia, and a similar sum from one of its citizens;

f. taking the inheritance of Valeria, his freedwoman.

35. In the Milan fragment, Cicero describes Asia as "sollicitata," "concitata," or "coacta" (i.e., as acting under, respectively, incitement, provocation, or compulsion). Yet he admits that he, too, brought witnesses to Rome in an official capacity, from Sicily when he prosecuted Verres ("ego testis a Sicilia publice deduxi" [I officially summoned witnesses from Sicily], *Flac.* 17), a statement borne out by the text of the *Verrines* (2 *Verr.* 4.137–49). I am interpreting the word *publice* as meaning "officially," not as meaning "at public expense." Both translations are given for the word in the *OLD,* but there is no evidence in the *Verrines* that the Roman government paid a *viaticum* to the prosecution witnesses. Kurke (1989, 197 n. 263) interprets the word *publice* to mean that either the Roman state or the Sicilians funded travel for witnesses.

36. "... non Asiae testibus, sed accusatoris contubernalibus traditus" [... delivered not to the witnesses from Asia but to the prosecutor's lodgers] (frag. xii *apud Schol. Bob.* 97St). In the Oxford Classical Texts edition, Clark reads "accusatoribus contubernalibus."

37. The Bobbian scholiast (98St) glosses this phrase as referring to the poor, citing Cic. *Cat.* 2.21 as a parallel. The poverty of these witnesses is also mentioned in the Milan fragment ("per egentissimos testis" [by means of the neediest witnesses]) and at *Flac.* 6 ("qua egestate" [with what poverty]).

38. Ayers (1950, 43) draws a comparison between Cicero's criticism here of the relationship between the prosecutors and their witnesses, on the one hand, and Hortensius's complaint that Artemo spoke more like a prosecutor of Verres than like a witness against him (Cic. 2 *Verr.* 2.156). However, I cannot agree with Ayers that this statement implies that Artemo was in league with the prosecution. Perhaps Hortensius's point was that Artemo was not so much providing information (as a witness does) as drawing conclusions from it (like a prosecutor).

39. See Quint. *Inst.* 5.7.5; Vasaly 1993, 198–205. Vasaly shows how Cicero here contrasts Greek *levitas* with Roman *gravitas,* a point made also by Kurke (1989, 166 n. 161). Kurke (163–77) covers both Cicero's "*ad gentem* attack" in the *Pro Flacco* and his use of this technique more generally. As Kurke points out (168), Cicero contrasts their testimony with the self-restraint showed by Roman witnesses (*Flac.* 10–11), even though they are hostile prosecution witnesses.

40. The explanation of the difference is, as Kurke (1989, 73 n. 239) implies, that they answer the prosecutor's questions at length but become taciturn during the cross-examination.

41. Shackleton Bailey (1988, 69) corrects Münzer ("Mithridates" no. 36, *RE* 15 [1932]: 2215) for attributing the name *Mithridates* to this witness.

42. On this witness, see discussion later in this chapter. As prosecutor, Cicero expressed concern about the subornation of his witnesses. When prosecuting Verres, Cicero complained that the consul-elect for 69, Q. Caecilius Metellus, tried to pressure the Sicilian witnesses (1 *Verr.* 27–28; see Kurke 1989, 74).

43. Webster (*Pro Flacco,* vi, 110), suggesting that Laelius made this charge at the

beginning of the second *actio,* reconstructs the order of events as follows: in the first *actio,* Laelius spoke, then Decianus; in the second, Laelius made his charge and was followed by L. Herennius Balbus, the "Lucceius" of *Flac.* 83 (see discussion of this "Lucceius" earlier in this chapter), who charged that Flaccus had tried to bribe him to desert the case for two million sesterces. Kurke (1989, 76) suggests that Balbus was compelled to finish Decianus's presentation with inadequate preparation, which prompted Cicero to mock Balbus's lack of rhetorical polish (*Flac.* 83).

44. For example, according to Cicero (1 *Verr.* 40), Verres often said that he kept the profits of his first year as governor of Sicily for himself, the profits of the second year to pay his *patroni* and *defensores,* and the profits of the third year to bribe the jury.

45. Kurke (1989, 297), within his general discussion (295–306), notes (on the basis of *Flac.* 31 and 33) that the specific complaint may have been the requisition of rowers.

46. "'Minuis,' inquit, 'gloriam Pompei'" [He [Laelius] says, "You are lessening Pompey's glory"] (*Flac.* 28).

47. Cicero responds to this under the third heading, that of accounting, rather than under the second, that of need.

48. Cicero points out that two quaestors in 61 collected money for a navy to patrol the seas around Italy (*Flac.* 30). S. Mitchell (1979, 17) points out that if we accept a manuscript reading identifying one of these quaestors as "P. Sestullius," Cicero's reference makes sense; this quaestor was connected with family members who were causing trouble for Flaccus in this case, "whose actions were no less (and no more) culpable than those of Flaccus himself." Broughton (*MRR* Suppl.) does not comment on the possibility that the quaestor of 61 was a Sestullius.

49. See Kurke 1989, 304.

50. Cicero does complain about the fact that Verres cannot substantiate his claim that the Mamertines built him a cargo ship with his own personal funds (2 *Verr.* 5.47).

51. Kurke (1989, 154–57) discusses the testimony of individual witnesses.

52. See Geyer, "Mithridates" no. 15, *RE* 15 (1932): 2205.

53. Badian (1980, 471–72) and Shackleton Bailey (1988, 89) accept the conclusion of S. Mitchell (1979) that the correct reading is "Sestullius," rather than "Sextilius."

54. See Kurke 1989, 223–28.

55. See Kurke 1989, 229–32.

56. Webster (*Pro Flacco,* 81, ad loc.) points out a parallel at Cic. 2 *Verr.* 5.48, where the Mamertines pay money to Verres under the heading "Public Works." On the charges from Temnos, see Kurke 1989, 232–36.

57. See Kurke 1989, 269–75.

58. The office of *sitones* would be another possibility. For the dates, see *MRR* Suppl., 215, on P. Varinius (1). It is somewhat surprising that Cicero would have been so dismissive of the rank of *sitophulax.* However, the state's role in storing grain was not as prominent in the Greek East as at Rome, though it was more highly developed in the Hellenistic East than in classical Greece (see Gallant 1991, 181). Cicero may well be understating the social importance this position betokens for Heraclides. Garnsey (1988, 73) writes, "This [*sitophulax*] and the very common post of Grain Commissioner, *sitones,* or an equivalent, circulated among the more wealthy and public-spirited members of each community."

59. Only two sections later (*Flac.* 49), we learn that the arbiters were appointed by

Flaccus. Cicero evidently does not wish to make it clear to his listeners how the suit of Hermippus against Heraclides is related to the prosecution of Flaccus.

60. On the legal background to this dispute, see Kupisch 1974; on the historical and legal background, see Zehnacker 1979.

61. See Kurke 1989, 277–78. It may have been unusual for Cicero to know in advance about witnesses who had not yet spoken. The explanation here is probably that Decianus, having deserted the prosecution side, has reported to the defense counsel information that they otherwise would not have.

62. See Venturini 1979, 354–60; Kurke 1989, 244–55.

63. *Flac.* 59. Cf. 56, "recuperata est multis post annis" [it was recovered many years later].

64. Brennan (1992, 142 n. 113), in his authoritative study, determines that the elder Flaccus was governor in Asia in 95 and/or 94. See also Sumner 1973, 82; Sumner 1978a, 148; *MRR* Suppl., 212. Kurke (1989, 244 n. 110) points out that the money would have been collected when the elder Flaccus was governor, not in 86, when Mithridates was in control and when the father, accompanied by his son, went to Asia.

65. The people of Smyrna passed a decree in honor of Castricius when he died (75 B.C.); this suggests that the dispute may have been between Smyrna and Tralles and that Castricius in some way took the side of the former.

66. Ulp. *Dig.* 47.2.10 reads, "Cuius interfuit non subripi, is actionem furti habet" [A person who had an interest in the thing not being stolen has the action for theft] (trans. Jameson, ed. Watson). See also Gai. *Inst.* 3.203–7; *Inst. Iust.* 4.1.13–17. A standard example is a cleaner who, having received payment to clean clothing, has it stolen from his keeping; since, as long as the cleaner is financially solvent, he can be sued by the owner of the clothing, the cleaner has an interest that the clothing not be stolen, even though he does not own it.

67. Craig (1993, 173) groups this dilemma with those that he characterizes in the following way: "Dilemma can serve to begin a line of argument with the appearance of invincible reasoning."

68. See Marshall 1969, 267–69. This *inimicitia* was caused in turn by a suit that the father of Decianus had unsuccessfully brought against the father of Flaccus (*TLRR* no. 78).

69. Webster (*Pro Flacco*, 101) suggests that she was the freedwoman of either his father or his grandfather. But Cicero implies that she was *ingenua* (freeborn). On this charge, see Marshall 1975a; Kurke 1989, 255–66.

70. This passage has given rise to a debate between Watson and Treggiari about the power of *usus* to create a *manus* marriage—which, both scholars agree, had become relatively rare by this time—and about whether the rules changed in the first century B.C. Watson (1967, 20–23) argues that the approval of the woman's tutors was necessary for *usus* to create a *manus* marriage, that the *trinoctium* (an interval of three nights away from the marital home) was no longer necessary to prevent it, and that this situation was an innovation of the early first century B.C. Treggiari (1991, 20) argues that the same traditional rule applied in 59 B.C. as before; the approval of the father or guardians was required for *usus* to be created, and the *trinoctium* was employed to prevent the creation of a *manus* marriage that for some reason was no longer wanted.

71. Cicero argues: "Omnibus (tutoribus) ergo auctoribus; in quibus certe Flaccum

fuisse non dices" [Therefore it was done with the approval of all the guardians; but you will surely not say that Flaccus was among them] (*Flac.* 84); "Nihil istorum explicari potest, nisi ostenderis illam in tutela Flacci non fuisse. Si fuit, quaecumque sine hoc auctore est dicta dos, nulla est" [None of these things can be accounted for unless you show that she was not in the guardianship of Flaccus. If she was, whatever dowry was declared without his approval is void] (86). On this case, see Rauh 1993, 246–47.

72. See Linderski 1974, 472 = 1995, 271; *MRR* Suppl., 29; *TLRR*, 123 n. 9.

73. As Vasaly (1993, 71) points out, Cicero praises the people of Apollonis of Lydia, since they are testifying for his side in the case, and contrasts them with the other Greeks ("a Graecorum luxuria et levitate remotissimi" [totally alien from the extravagance and the irresponsibility of the Greeks], *Flac.* 71). On Cicero's use of Greek witnesses who are testifying on behalf of his client, see Kurke 1989, 177–84.

74. For the date, see Webster, *Pro Flacco*, 98.

75. Marshall (1969, 267–70) provides a very clear exegesis of this incident (see also Kurke 1989, 279–92). Marshall argues that it was primarily Decianus who initiated legal proceedings before the authorities, both Greek and Roman. From Cicero's awkward account of the decision of Globulus in 63 ("Apud P. Globulum, meum necessarium, fuisti gratiosior. Utinam neque ipsum neque me paeniteret!" [You were more influential with my friend Publius Globulus. I wish that neither he nor I had come to regret that!] (*Flac.* 76), it is clear that Globulus ruled in favor of Decianus. (Marshall describes this ruling as "auspicious"; in fact, Decianus may have thought that he had finally obtained his goal.) The easiest scenario is as follows: when Decianus made no headway with Greek officials, he, as Marshall suggests, took his case to the Roman governor in 64 and was turned down; in 63, he renewed his case and received a favorable ruling from the new governor; as a result, the Apollonians appealed to the Senate in that year, which issued a decree supporting their case; they then brought the matter to the next year's governor, Flaccus, and he issued a ruling in their favor and against Decianus. The prosecution presented in evidence a letter written by Quintus Cicero, the successor to Flaccus, which seems (the manuscript is corrupt here) to refer to a woman and to Quintus's generous response to her; this might be the mother-in-law of Amyntas, who is said by Cicero to have fallen under the control of Decianus.

76. Webster (*Pro Flacco*, 104, ad loc.) points out that in 61, the Asian taxes were contracted by the censors at Rome (*Att.* 1.17.9), and he interprets the phrase "Globulo praetore" (*Flac.* 91) as indicating that the taxes were let by the praetor. His explanation (relying on Dio Cass. 37.9.4) is that the tribunes in 64 hindered the censors from carrying out their normal duties. However, the ablative absolute could indicate merely the time when this happened.

77. On Falcidius's charge, see Kurke 1989, 236–42. When the tithes had already been sold and could not be resold, Verres enacted new regulations, which, according to Cicero, were clearly designed to create the need to bribe Verres to circumvent them (2 *Verr.* 3.51). Cicero also explains (3.71–72) that farmers were forced to pay a bonus (*lucrum*) to the *decumanus* (tithe collector) Apronius, and Cicero very strongly implies that at least some of this extra money went to the governor: "Apronio, deliciis praetoris, lucelli aliquid iussi sunt dare. Putatote Apronio datum, si Apronianum lucellum ac non praetoria praeda vobis videbitur" [They were ordered to give a small something extra to Apronius, the governor's darling. You shall think that it was given to Apronius, if it

appears to you that this was Apronius's something extra and not plunder for the governor]. (See also 3.99, 153.) One man at Syracuse and, later, a Roman knight went as far as to challenge Apronius in a formal *sponsio* to deny that he had often said that he and Verres were partners in the tithes (3.132, 135–141). Interestingly, Cicero argues that "capere et conciliare pecunias" [to take and obtain funds] is extortion whether the governor uses his power to get money for himself or for someone else (3.71). Just as Cicero argues as defense *patronus* that the alleged victim did not have to pay the governor out of his capital ("de vivo," *Flac.* 91), so he claims as prosecutor that the victim could have made the necessary payment only by doing just that (2 *Verr.* 3.118). He also complains of small *accessiones* (surcharges) that farmers were forced to pay, on the order of two or three thousand sesterces (2 *Verr.* 3.118).

78. If Frederiksen (1966, 132) is right that a pound of gold was worth about six thousand sesterces, the Jewish gold for the year could have amounted to a figure on the order of two million sesterces.

79. On the temple tax, see Smallwood 1976, 124–25. Wardy (1979, 601–6) argues convincingly that there is no reason to believe that the opinions expressed by Cicero about the Jews represent his personal opinion. She argues that they follow the pattern of *improbatio testium* (discrediting of witnesses), and she points out that Cicero says much the same sort of thing about Gallic witnesses in the *Pro Fonteio* and about Sardinian witnesses in the *Pro Scauro* and that he also attacks Greeks and Asiatics who were not true Greeks in the *Pro Flacco*. Rutgers (1994, 64) argues that this view is preferable to that of Williams (1989, 780), who maintains that Cicero's portrayal of the Jews as constituting a cohesive and unruly crowd expresses a consistent Roman view of the Jews.

80. See also Kurke 1989, 293–95.

81. Cicero says, "Exportari aurum non oportere cum saepe antea senatus tum me consule gravissime iudicavit" [The Senate often before decreed very sternly that gold should not be exported, and especially when I was consul] (*Flac.* 67). See Marshall 1975b, 150. Smallwood (1976, 126–27) favors the prosecution argument; she believes that the Jews had been granted a permanent exemption from the senatus consultum regarding the outflow of precious metals and that Flaccus was acting ultra vires. Wardy (1979, 609) makes the intriguing suggestion that the governor's prohibition may have been legal but that the Jews were protesting against his seizure of their money. She suggests that Flaccus had captured and confiscated the money for the Roman treasury because some Jews had tried to evade the edict by smuggling out the gold. She supports this suggestion by pointing out that Cicero mentions only four Asiatic towns where the money was seized (Apamea, Laodicea, Adramytium, and Pergamum) and that these were not towns with large Jewish populations, like Smyrna, Ephesus, and Miletus.

82. Marshall (1975b, 152–54) points out (on the basis of Cic. *Q Fr.* 1.1.25) that the Asian cities were suffering from debt in this period and could not afford outflows of precious metals and that Pompey's import of vast amounts of booty from the East into Rome may have exacerbated the problem.

83. Marshall 1975b, 142–43. Macrobius (*Sat.* 2.1.13) writes, "atque ego, ni longum esset, referrem in quibus causis, cum nocentissimos reos tueretur, victoriam iocis adeptus sit; ut ecce pro L. Flacco, quem repetundarum reum ioci opportunitate de manifestissimis criminibus exemit" [And, if it were not tedious, I would recall in what trials he achieved victory by jokes when he was defending the most guilty defendants, as, for

example, on behalf of Lucius Flaccus, whom he saved from the most open-and-shut charges by the right joke at the right time]. Magie (1950, 379–80) says that the evidence against Flaccus was weak but that Cicero's evasions and reliance on prejudice against Greeks lead to the suspicion that Flaccus was guilty.

CHAPTER 4

1. Shackleton Bailey (*CLA*, 2:216) convincingly defends the view that this refers to part of the case, since six advocates spoke for the defense. Cicero apparently wishes to emphasize the partial scope of his defense; while it was not unusual for him to speak with another *patronus,* the presence of six *patroni* was unusual, and Cicero may have wished to emphasize the limits of his role in this case.

2. The entry for this trial (no. 295) is longer than any other in *TLRR*, with the exception of the entry for Cicero's prosecution of Verres (no. 177). See Bucher 1995, 398 n. 4.

3. Douglas (*Brutus*, 194) suggests that this might be the same as the impressive orator C. Valerius Triarius, described by Cicero at *Brut.* 265 (cf. *Fin.* 1.13), since he is often mentioned either as C. (rather than P.) or without praenomen, as if there was only one important Valerius Triarius. Asconius's characterization of the prosecutor of Scaurus as "adulescente parato ad dicendum et notae industriae" [an eloquent and energetic young man] (18C; trans. Squires) supports the suggestion of Douglas. If this suggestion is accepted, the prosecution team seems somewhat more impressive.

4. The father is C. Valerius Triarius. Shackleton Bailey (1991, 45) argues that he is also the quaestor of 81, rather than his brother, Lucius. His view is accepted by Broughton (*MRR* Suppl., 214–15). The evidence that he served in Sardinia comes from the *Pro Scauro,* where a Sardinian to whom he gave citizenship is mentioned (29), as well as from Asconius (19C) and from Zorzetti's reading of Iulius Exuperantius 6 (Exuperantius 1982, 8). He went on to serve with Lucullus in the East (73–67 B.C.). See Volkmann, "Valerius" no. 363, *RE* 2.8 (1955): 233.

5. She was a uterine half sister to Cato the Younger, being the child of Livia and her first husband, Q. Servilius Caepio, while Cato was the child of Livia and her second husband, M. Porcius Cato. For their family tree, see Münzer 1920, 282; Syme 1939, table II, "The Kinsmen of Cato"; Courtney 1961, 153. Aulus Gellius (*NA* 13.20) records a disquisition by C. Sulpicius Apollinaris on this family.

6. There is dispute about the cognomen. For references, see Marshall 1985, 123–24. A connection with the Claudii Pulchri would make political sense, since C. Claudius Pulcher was a potential rival of Scaurus for the consulate of 53 and since it was not legally possible for two patricians to hold that office together (*Schol. Ambros.* 275St). But, as Rawson (1977, 349) notes, "it would be hard to show a parallel for the use of a patron's name in this way, though double *nomina* are not rare in Oscan Italy." Moreover, as Courtney (1961, 154) points out, by the time of the trial (summer 54), C. Claudius Pulcher had already committed himself to a third year as governor of Asia (*Scaur.* 35); see Broughton 1991, 24 n. 41. However, it is possible that he had committed his services as a *subscriptor* before the governor of Asia withdrew himself from contention for the consulate of 53.

7. He is possibly also the quaestor of 50. Gruen (1995, 333 n. 107) suggests he was a

relative of the L. Marius who, as tribune of the plebs in 62, worked with his colleague Cato in passing legislation.

8. Cicero also had reason to avoid a frontal attack on Ap. Claudius, because he had just that year been reconciled to him after a period of enmity over the actions of his other brother, C. Clodius Pulcher, and Cicero's return from exile through the agency of Pompey (Quint. *Inst.* 9.3.41), whose son was married to Appius's daughter (Cic. *Fam.* 3.10.10) by this time, if Tatum (1991b) is right that the marriage took place in the aftermath of the meeting at Luca in 56. See Cic. *Q Fr.* 2.11.3 and Shackleton Bailey, *CLQf,* 193; Cic. *Fam.* 1.9.4 and Shackleton Bailey, *CLF,* 1:314.

9. See Epstein 1987, 53. I do not agree with Epstein that Cicero was also referring to himself as a predecessor to Appius, in that he held the consulate in 63 and Appius in 54.

10. Marshall (1985, 150–56) provides a cogent and succinct description of those who appeared for the defense, as well as a sober analysis of the interpretations that have been put forward to explain this concatenation of individuals.

11. See Sumner 1973, 147–48.

12. If this omission is not due to modesty, it can be attributed to Cicero's decision not to deal with living orators (*Brut.* 251).

13. Cicero describes a peroration of Clodius as "sane disertus" [really eloquent] (*Att.* 4.15.4). His reputation for eloquence is attested by Velleius Paterculus ("disertus," 2.45.1) and Plutarch (πλούτῳ καὶ λόγῳ λαμπρός [illustrious in wealth and speech], *Caes.* 9.1). See Tatum 1999, 41, 262 n. 46. For the argument that Cicero allows bias to enter into his assessment of oratory, see Tatum 1991a; see p. 369 for Tatum's estimation of Clodius's oratory.

14. Marshall (1985, 128–29) does not class Clodius and M. Valerius Messalla Niger among those "at the top of the oratorical profession." However, Clodius was an experienced and effective speaker, and if we judge Messalla by Cicero's description of him in the *Brutus* (246), he provided very solid service as an advocate.

15. It would be unwise to draw conclusions about Cicero's personal likes and dislikes from his participation in this case, for in this year, he yielded to pressure to defend Gabinius in an extortion trial (*TLRR* no. 303). His source of information on conditions in Sardinia was his brother Quintus, who served as legate there under Pompey in 56 B.C., as Cicero notes in the *Pro Scauro* (39).

16. See Marshall 1985, 153. Hortensius persuaded Cato to divorce Marcia and let him marry her (Plut. *Cat. Min.* 25) and was associated with the Servilii Caepiones through marriage; see Münzer 1920, 346, for a reconstruction of the relationship. For a family tree of the Catones, see Syme 1939, table II; for a family tree for Brutus, see Hallett 1984, table IV.

17. He and the defendant were uterine half brothers, sharing Caecilia Metella as mother. He proclaimed his intention to have a bodyguard of three hundred men, after what he claimed was an assassination attempt against him by Scaurus's rivals (Asc. 20C).

18. On the cognomen *Lepidus,* see Shackleton Bailey 1988, 11–12.

19. On this individual (suffect consul in 34) and the Memmii in general, see Sumner 1973, 85–90.

20. Gruen 1995, 335 n. 117.

21. Marshall 1985, 155. This point is conceded by Courtney (1961, 155).

22. The seminal attack on the prosopographical approach is contained in Brunt 1988, especially 351–81 (chap. 7, *"Amicitia"*), 382–442 (chap. 8, *"Clientela"*).

23. Gruen 1969a, 316. Gruen views these events as reflecting a historical change more in quantity than in quality.

24. Marshall 1976–77, 129–30.

25. Milo twice tried to prosecute Clodius for *vis* in 57 (*TLRR* nos. 261–62). Clodius successfully tried to escape the trial by getting himself elected to the aedileship (Dio Cass. 39.7.3), and Milo must have hoped that a conviction would prevent Clodius's election. That the elections of 57 were delayed by violence meant that because of a lack of quaestors, a jury for the trial could not be constituted if the letter of the law was followed, and Milo was unsuccessful in his attempt to have an exception made (Dio Cass. 39.7.4). On the trials of 57, see Clark's commentary on the *Pro Milone* (Cicero 1895, 37); Tatum 1999, 196.

26. The condemnation in 113 of C. Porcius Cato, consul in 114 (*TLRR* no. 45), did not render him *infamis*, though, since he had just held the consulate, election to office was hardly an issue.

27. Weinrib (1971, 149) writes, "The last clause indicates that a politician achieved security from the judicial process only when he formally entered upon his magistracy, not when he won election." Weinrib 1971 is related to Weinrib 1968.

28. Weinrib 1971, 149 n. 8.

29. The higher magistrates (with imperium) were definitely immune from prosecution, and the lower magistrates may have in practice enjoyed the same immunity. See Kunkel and Wittmann 1995, 259–60. However, it has to be conceded that there might have been a difference between initiating a trial against a magistrate and continuing a trial that had begun when the current magistrate was only a candidate or magistrate-designate.

30. Scholars have noted the parallel with Catiline's situation in 66 B.C. He was also prosecuted during an election campaign. Judging by Asconius's account (89C), however, there were some slight differences in the order of events. First, the people from the province, in this case Africa, complained in the Senate about Catiline's conduct. Then, he declared his candidacy: "Professus deinde est Catilina petere se consulatum" [Catiline then declared his wish to stand [for the consulate]], Asc. 89C; trans. Squires). Then, the consul Volcacius called a *consilium* to decide whether to accept his candidacy. Asconius implies that the issue was the extortion complaint, although there may not have been at this point an actual prosecution under the *lex Cornelia de repetundis*. However, the reason Sallust gives for the rejection of Catiline's candidacy is that Catiline had not made his declaration in time: "Post paulo Catilina pecuniarum repetundarum reus prohibitus erat consulatum petere, quod intra legitumos dies profiteri nequiverat" [A little later, when Catiline was charged with extortion, he was prevented from seeking the consulate because he had not been able to make his declaration within the legal time period] (*Cat.* 18). Sumner (1965, 228–29), followed by Stockton (1971, 74 n. 19), McGushin (1977, 124–28), and Ramsey (1982, 124–25, 128–29), has argued convincingly that the reason Volcacius refused to let Catiline stand at the supplementary election in 66 for the consulate of 65 was that he had not declared his candidacy for the original election in 66 for the consulate of 65. T. N. Mitchell (1979, 223 n. 93) remains unconvinced, arguing that it is implausible that Catiline would have abstained from participating in the first, regular election that year and then run in the second, supplementary election.

31. For bibliography, see Marshall 1977; *MRR* Suppl., 10; *TLRR*. If Asconius is saying that all three elements that the prosecutors feared would happen in this trial were present in the prosecution of the father (extortion trial, beginning of magistracy before end of trial, and subsequent command), Marshall has a strong case for an extortion trial on the basis of the propraetorian command, rather than the proconsular command.

32. See Gruen 1995, 337. As we saw before in this chapter, it was common for magistrates-designate (after the election, of course) to be prosecuted for *ambitus* and other electoral offenses.

33. Cicero does include a short section on Scaurus in his speech ("pauca de Scauro" [a few things about Scaurus], *Scaur.* 22).

34. Two fragments of *Pro Scauro* after section 45 (fragment l, preserved in Quint. *Inst.* 5.13.40, and fragment m, preserved in Cic. *Orat.* 223–24) seem to reflect this accusation about the columns. This theme of personal luxury manifested in artistic splendor occurs, of course, at 2 *Verr.* 4.

35. For references, see Marshall 1985, 120.

36. See Plin. *HN* 36.113–15. Pliny also relates that items were moved after the games to Scaurus's Tusculan villa, for use there, and that his servants were so enraged by his extravagance that they burned down the villa, which was valued at thirty million sesterces.

37. Cicero later uses the unanimity of witnesses as grounds for discrediting their testimony, arguing that it shows a conspiracy: "Etenim fidem primum ipsa tollit consensio, quae patefacta est compromisso Sardorum et coniuratione recitata" [For first their credibility is destroyed by their very agreement, which was revealed when the pact and conspiracy of the Sardinians was read out] (*Scaur.* 38).

38. For Verres' cruelty, see 2 *Verr.* 5.106, 112–21, 123, 142, 145, 159–63. For his sexual excesses, see 5.27–28, 30–31, 34, 38–40, 63, 81, 86, 94, 100; for his excesses specifically with married women, 5.34, 81–83, 133, 137. Cicero implies that these charges were not directly relevant to the trial but that these excesses created a climate whereby Verres might extort money illegally, as for exemption from providing rowers and soldiers (2 *Verr.* 5.133) or plundering ships of their cargo (5.145–46, 154).

39. In what must strike us as a singularly unpersuasive piece of argumentation, Cicero tries to suggest that since she is unlikely to have read works by Greek philosophers, such as Plato and Pythagoras, who praise death (although they forbid suicide), she is unlikely to have killed herself to save her honor (*Scaur.* 4–5).

40. In the *Pro Sex. Roscio Amerino* (18–19), Cicero similarly suggests that the fact that Mallius Glaucia, a freedman and a client of T. Roscius Magnus (but clearly not Roscius's freedman, as the names show), immediately set out from Rome and very quickly reached Ameria to report the death of Roscius senior to T. Roscius Capito suggests strongly that the freedman was part of a plot between Magnus and Capito. But one can just as well argue that it would be natural for a freedman to inform other members of the family when a catastrophe had struck one of them. However, in the case of the death of Roscius, Cicero tries to make capital out of the fact that Mallius had not gone directly to the victim's closest relative, his son and Cicero's client (see chap. 8).

41. Quintilian (*Inst.* 5.7.5) writes, "gentium simul universarum elevata testimonia" [the testimonies of whole peoples all together have been discounted].

42. Cicero argues, "Nunc est una vox, una mens non expressa dolore, sed simulata, neque huius iniuriis, sed promissis aliorum et praemiis excitata" [Now there is one

voice, one attitude, not forced out by grief, but feigned, and provoked not by the defendant's wrongdoing, but by the promises and rewards of others] (*Scaur.* 41). It is hardly surprising that the witnesses were victims who hoped to regain the money that had been extorted from them. Cicero might be referring to the legal *praemia* that the law may have offered to the one person, possibly Aris, who was most responsible for the success of the prosecution (see Alexander 1985, 20–21).

43. Within two years of this judicial vindication, Scaurus was convicted under the *lex Pompeia de ambitu* (*TLRR* no. 319) and went into exile.

CHAPTER 5

1. Ramsey 1980, 329–30.

2. The trial of Rabirius took place during the winter months (*Rab. Post.* 42). Lintott (1974, 67–68) expresses skepticism that the extortion trial of Gabinius could have been completed by the end of 54 (given the holidays in the autumn) or before late 53 (given the lack of elected magistrates for the first part of 53). According to Lintott's view, the trial of Rabirius could have taken place only in late 53. Klodt (commentary in Cicero 1992, 33–34) considers Lintott's argument plausible and puts the trial at the beginning of 52, and Berry supports Klodt's view in his review of her work (1996, 206). But legal arguments might be able to save the earlier date for the trials of Gabinius and Rabirius: trials were sometimes completed in the fall, as Klodt points out; the epigraphic extortion law provides for an expedited procedure for extortion trials after 1 September (*lex repetundarum*, line 7); it was possible to appoint someone to preside over a trial in the absence of magistrates (Fantham 1975, 443); and Ramsey (1980, 330) shows that a trial held under a *quo ea pecunia pervenerit* clause could be completed very quickly. Fascione (1974) provides an introduction to the trial of Rabirius.

3. There is one piece of evidence that Cicero had previously defended Gabinius in the sixties (*TLRR* no. 380), in a passage where he claims that the consuls of 58 had not come to his aid in order not to appear partisan, since Cicero was related to Piso through his son-in-law C. Calpurnius Piso (quaestor in 58), a relative of the consul, and since he had previously defended the other consul, Gabinius: "sed veriti sunt ne gratiae causa facere viderentur, quod alter mihi adfinis erat, alterius causam capitis receperam" [for they [the consuls] feared that they would seem to be acting out of favoritism, because one was my in-law, and I had taken on a capital case for the other] (*Red. pop.* 11). However, Gruen (1995, 527) argues, "Cicero would hardly have avoided mention of Gabinius' ingratitude if he had, in fact, defended him in the past." Crawford (1984, 263–64), while she does not accept Guerriero's (1936) contention that the passage is not genuine, doubts the existence of such a trial, arguing that Cicero's statement about it is as ironic as his claim that his son-in-law was related to the consul of 58. In any case, Crawford is right to point out (263 n. 3) that Cicero says only that he accepted the case, not that he actually argued it through to a verdict. Nisbet, in his commentary on the *In Pisonem* (Cicero 1961, 189 n. 1), suggests that the word *causa* in Cicero's statement may refer to a threat to prosecute Gabinius after his tribunate of 67. I am inclined to accept the possibility of such a trial. An argument from silence is doubly weak if one discordant voice is eliminated, and it is conceivable that there were reasons why Cicero did not want to recall his services to Gabinius, which, in any case, may have been rather minimal, if the

case was aborted early. Berry (1992, 110), in his review of *TLRR*, writes, "The authenticity of Cic. *Red. Pop.* is not in question, and the prose rhythm of the disputed passage is characteristically Ciceronian. I therefore see no need to doubt that the trial occurred."

4. See Shackleton Bailey 1991, 82. A useful biography of C. Rabirius Postumus is Siani-Davies 1996; see especially 221–29 for the events relating to this trial. However, White (1995) casts doubt on the generally accepted analysis of the family tree, first advanced by Dessau (1911).

5. Cicero says, "Iubet lex Iulia persequi ab eis ad quos ea pecunia quam is ceperit qui damnatus sit pervenerit" [The Julian law stipulates seeking restitution from those people into whose hands money taken by the condemned defendant has come] (*Rab. Post.* 8). On the legal basis of the trial, see Klodt's commentary in Cicero 1992, 40–51.

6. The epigraphic extortion law, generally taken to be the Gracchan *lex Acilia,* did not contain the *quo ea pecunia pervenerit* provision. Mattingly's arguments to the contrary (1970, 162–63) have been refuted by Sherwin-White (1972, 87–91) and Lintott (1992, 147).

7. This point is noted by Ramsey (1980, 329 n. 27).

8. Besides this case, our main model for the *quo ea pecunia pervenerit* procedure comes from a letter of Caelius to Cicero in 51 B.C. (Cic. *Fam.* 8.8.2–3), describing a prosecution of M. Servilius in 51 B.C. (*TLRR* no. 339). See Sumner 1973, 146; Shackleton Bailey 1961, 86; Shackleton Bailey, *CLA*, 3:264, on Cic. *Att.* 6.3.10. The confused verdict reveals the obscurity of the *quo ea pecunia pervenerit* procedure, which confused the presiding magistrate.

9. See Alexander 1984, 528–29. For sources on the *quo ea pecunia pervenerit* provision, see Lintott 1992, 28 n. 58.

10. Between the Gracchan law and the law of Glaucia, another extortion law was briefly in force, the *lex Servilia (Caepionis).* (For sources, see *MRR* 1:533.) Besides the fact that it transferred the juries from the *equites* to the senators, we do not know anything about its provisions, although it may have introduced *divinatio* (see Lintott 1981, 188; Lintott 1992, 167; in the present book, chap. 1, n. 119).

11. This amount equals 60,000,000 denarii or drachmas or 240,000,000 sesterces (*Rab. Post.* 21). This bribe is also mentioned by Appian (*Syr.* 51) and Plutarch (*Ant.* 3).

12. For purposes of comparison, Verres was accused of having extorted forty million sesterces, resulting in damages of either one hundred million or, possibly more precisely, eighty million sesterces (Cic. 1 *Verr.* 56; *Div. Caec.* 19); see Sherwin-White 1949, 8, incorrectly stated in Alexander 1984, 528. It is possible that Gabinius was assessed damages for more than the bribe from Ptolemy. He was heartily disliked in his province of Syria, by both the inhabitants and the Roman *publicani* there (Cic. *Q Fr.* 2.12.2; Cic. *Prov. cons.* 9; Cic. *Sest.* 93; Dio Cass. 39.56.1). See n. 19 in the present chapter; Badian 1972, 109. Dio Cassius (39.55.5) vaguely says that Gabinius was convicted for more than one hundred million drachmas. Ciaceri (1918, 215–17) argues that Cicero's silence on this score demonstrates that the extortion that Gabinius had allegedly committed in Syria was not an issue in his trial and that these charges reflect the anti-Gabinian tradition that Cicero started and nurtured. But as Fantham (1975, 441) argues, it is quite possible that Memmius did present these charges in the trial of Gabinius but dealt in the trial of Rabirius with only the matter in which Rabirius had been involved, that is, the restoration of Ptolemy and the payment of the ten thousand talents. If it is correct that the

prosecution could go after any damages in the *quo ea pecunia pervenerit* procedure, regardless of whether the defendant had been involved in the extortion leading to those damages, Memmius ought to have been able to seek even more from Rabirius. But he may have believed that he would be lucky to recover just the ten thousand talents.

13. Shatzman 1971, 368–69. Shatzman provides an account of the struggle over the Egyptian succession, its connection to Roman politics, and, specifically, the role of Rabirius.

14. One talent was equal to six thousand drachmas. One drachma was roughly equal to one Roman denarius. One denarius was equal to four sesterces, and therefore a talent was roughly equal to twenty-four thousand sesterces.

15. There was a rumor circulating in Puteoli by 22 April 55 that Ptolemy had been restored (Cic. *Att.* 4.10.1). Since Puteoli was the main port for ships coming from the East to Rome, it would be the natural place to pick up the latest news from Egypt.

16. Ciaceri (1918, 221) argues that the prosecutor's claim only that ten thousand talents had been promised to Gabinius shows that the money was not actually paid. Although at the trial of Gabinius, the Alexandrine witnesses denied that Gabinius received the money (*Rab. Post.* 34), Gabinius claimed not that he had not received the money but that he acted "rei publicae causa" (20), and Ptolemy claimed not that he had given Gabinius no money but that he had given him no money except for military purposes ("nisi in rem militarem," 34). It seems likely that Ptolemy did pay the money, but to his treasurer Rabirius to hand over to Gabinius, and that the Alexandrine witnesses charged that Rabirius had never transferred it to Gabinius ("'At habet et celat,'" 38). The matter would have been difficult to determine, because what was in question was not the physical transfer of bags of coins but the appropriate entries in the accounts that Rabirius was keeping—a debit for the king and a credit for the Roman general.

17. Ptolemy's annual revenue is given as either 6,000 talents (Diod. Sic. 17.52.6) or 12,500 talents (Cicero *apud* Strabo 17.1.13 [C 798]). See Klodt's commentary in Cicero 1992, 38 n. 77.

18. We do not know that this sum was actually paid in its entirety. However, Jolliffe (1919, 26) goes too far in saying that all the evidence points to Gabinius's failure to collect the whole amount. No evidence bears on the question, other than that Gabinius was condemned on the extortion count and therefore had probably received at least something.

19. A recently published papyrus (*P. Med.* inv. 68.53) contains what appears to be a protest against the activities of Rabirius Postumus as the *dioecetes* of the king. See Balconi 1993, with discussion of the trial of Rabirius; 1994.

20. Cicero poses a false dilemma at this point, claiming that one needs to know whether this commission was in addition to the base amount or deducted from that amount. He argues that it is unlikely that an extra one thousand talents would have been added by Ptolemy to the already heavy burden of ten thousand talents and that it was implausible that someone as greedy as the prosecution had made Gabinius out to be would have voluntarily given up one thousand of his ten thousand talents. Neither proposition is convincing; there is nothing to say that the king would have exacted ten thousand talents from his subjects but not eleven thousand or that Gabinius would necessarily have been unwilling to let a competent agent deduct a commission (see Ciaceri 1918, 210). Moreover, Cicero's analysis excludes the middle possibility that Rabirius was

required to "kick back" part of his commission to Gabinius. The third book of the second *Verrines,* with its detailed accounting of the various fees relating to the requisition of grain that the Sicilians had to pay, provides parallel situations. Throughout it, Cicero relates the *lucrum* that various *decumani* were allowed to make on their activity, beyond the basic tithe that they were collecting. In particular, he spotlights the role of Quintus Apronius, whose profits (referred to with the diminutive *lucellum* with heavy sarcasm) Cicero particularly decries. Nowhere in his speech does Cicero seem to concern himself greatly with the final destination of this extra money. He decries the four percent deduction from payments to the Sicilian towns that was made to pay the *scribae,* pointing out that they already received a salary (2 *Verr.* 3.181–87). Elsewhere, however, he implies that the *decumani* shared their profits with Verres. He decries as a heinous crime the *societas* between Verres and them (3.130, cf. 144) and, more specifically, claims that Verres did receive profit from the sale of the tithes. That explains why, he says, Verres wanted to make sure that the sale went to Apronius, who was popularly called "tuus procurator" [your [sc. Verres'] agent] doing "tuum negotium" [your [sc. Verres'] business] (3.149–52). This echoes a possibility that Cicero has already raised (3.112), namely, that Apronius said he failed to keep records either because he had discarded them as incriminating himself or because he was not conducting his own business—that is, that he was really working for Verres. In the third speech of 2 *Verrines,* Cicero implies that Verres is ultimately responsible for whatever impositions are visited on the Sicilians, without seeming to find it necessary to clarify at each point whether a particular exaction would find its way into Verres' pockets or whether he allowed his lieutenants to keep something for themselves.

I do not agree with Klodt that the prosecution of Rabirius is aimed at recovering only the one thousand talents (see Klodt's commentary in Cicero 1992, 56–57 and 41: "Auf die Rückgabe dieser 1000 Talente lautete die Anklage" [The charge was for the return of these 1000 talents]).

21. The two sides might have debated whether a commission that Rabirius subtracted from money paid by Ptolemy before he gave it to Gabinius should be reckoned as money that had gone from Gabinius to Rabirius. The defense may have argued that it had never reached Gabinius and therefore could not have been transferred from Gabinius to Rabirius, whereas the prosecution could have argued that, for all intents and purposes, a certain sum of money was delivered to Gabinius, with a portion of that sum then going to Rabirius.

22. Mommsen (1899, 732) points out (citing Plin. *Ep.* 3.9.17) that the money can be collected even from legitimate creditors who have collected money from the defendant.

23. This statement refers to the *lex Iulia repetundarum,* which is the law governing this trial.

24. See Watson 1968, 24–31; 1975, 155.

25. Yaron 1967, 215–25.

26. Klodt's commentary in Cicero 1992, 161–62.

27. See Mommsen 1899, 732 n. 4; Ciaceri 1918, 207.

28. Of course, it is perfectly plausible that someone who generally practiced conspicuous consumption would conceal his wealth if that was the best or only way to preserve it.

29. Cicero also tries to disassociate Rabirius from the now condemned Gabinius as

much as possible by arguing that Rabirius had acted to restore Ptolemy under the authority granted by the Senate not to Gabinius but to P. Cornelius Lentulus Spinther, consul in 57 and proconsul in Cilicia in 56 (*Rab. Post.* 21).

30. On Alexandrian mimes, see Świderek 1954. Their performances were considered to be indecent, to a greater or lesser degree (Plut. *Quaest. conv.* 712e; Val. Max. 2.10.8).

31. Cf. the use of the term *insulsitas* at Cic. *Brut.* 284 and the translation of Douglas (*Brutus,* 210, ad loc.), "tastelessness." The emphasis here seems to be on the Alexandrians' blatant inconsistency.

32. See Ciaceri 1918, 203–4; Mommsen 1899, 732 (cf. 729).

33. See *MRR* Suppl., 181. On the question of Rabirius's possible senatorial standing in the forties, see Sumner 1971, 254; Shackleton Bailey, *CLF,* 1:495, on Cic. *Fam.* 2.16.7.

34. Caesar provided financial support to many people who suffered financial reverses as a result of Rabirius's troubles arising from loans made to Ptolemy (*Rab. Post.* 41). Suetonius (*Iul* 54) says that Ptolemy had contracted a large debt, six thousand talents, to Caesar and Pompey, possibly in 59 B.C. Plutarch (*Caes.* 48) reports that Caesar, in his occupation of Egypt after Pharsalus, claimed that the Egyptian king's father, Ptolemy Auletes, had owed him 17,500,000 drachmas; Plutarch reports that Caesar had remitted a large part of that debt to Ptolemy's children but demanded 10,000,000 drachmas as repayment (see Gelzer 1968, 247). The larger sum is close to three thousand talents and could represent Caesar's share of the six thousand talents that Ptolemy had contracted as a debt to Caesar and Pompey in 59 B.C. (I owe this observation to my colleague John T. Ramsey.) See Ciaceri 1918, 214 n. 2; Butler's note in Suetonius Tranquillus 1982, 114. In the mid-fifties, Crassus was trying with difficulty to compete with the largesse of his fellow triumvirs (see Badian 1968a, 82). Ciaceri (1918, 240, 242) argues that Crassus in general supported the activities of Gabinius, but Fantham (1975, 431) argues that Crassus had been hostile to Gabinius. Dio Cassius (39.60.1) says that Crassus supported Gabinius in 55 partly out of deference to his fellow consul Pompey and partly because he received bribes from Gabinius. On the enormous wealth of the triumvirs, see Badian 1968a, 76–92.

35. On Cicero's willingness—or lack thereof—to publish unsuccessful speeches, see Crawford 1984, 15.

PART 2

1. See Mommsen 1899, 865–77; Kunkel 1963, 744–45, Linderski 1961a = 1995, no. 16; Linderski 1985 = 1995, no. 9; Adamietz 1986; Bauerle 1990; Lintott 1990; Cloud 1994, 515–17; Santalucia 1994, 192, 197, 200 n. 155, 202 n. 162; Berry, 167–68; Yakobson 1999; Riggsby 1999, 21–27. In the present book, I have discussed some of the legal questions regarding *ambitus* and *sodalicia* in the chapters on, respectively, the trials of Murena and Plancius, since we have only one speech of Cicero for each of these crimes.

2. See Patterson 1985, 29.

3. Cloud 1994, 517.

4. See Linderski 1985, 91 = 1995, 111.

5. See Dio Cass. 36.38.1. Other sources are Asc. 69C, 88C; Cic. *Clu.* 147; Cic. *Mur.* 46, 67. For the political situation, see Griffin 1973b. The *lex Calpurnia* contained no provisions against *divisores,* as the tribune Cornelius was proposing (see Griffin 1973b, 208; Marshall 1985, 261).

6. See Dio Cass. 37.29.1; Cic. *Mur.* 3, 5, 67; Cic. *Vat.* 37; Cic. *Planc.* 83.

7. See Linderski 1985, 92 = 1995, 112; Bauman 1996, 29–30.

8. On the basis of *Mur.* 47 and 54, Adamietz notes (in Cicero 1989, 195) that the *lex Tullia* contained tougher penalties against the *divisores*. Cicero says that Sulpicius called for this change in the *ambitus* law and that the Senate established this change unwillingly ("non libenter"). Cicero emphasizes the senatorial reluctance so as to explain Sulpicius's unpopularity, but Cicero's *lex Tullia* seems to have incorporated this provision.

9. See Linderski 1985, 92 = 1995, 112.

10. See Cloud 1994, 517.

CHAPTER 6

1. The reading "filius" is not secure. See Shackleton Bailey 1979, 257.

2. See Münzer, "Sulpicius," no. 96, *RE* 4A (1931): 861. Shackleton Bailey's certitude that the *subscriptor* is not the son of the chief prosecutor (1979, 257–59; see also 1988, 90) evidently did not persuade Syme (1981, 424). Adamietz, in his commentary on the *Pro Murena* (Cicero 1989, 11–12) agrees with Shackleton Bailey that he was a relative, but not the son, of the main prosecutor.

3. On the spelling of the nomen, see Sumner 1971, 254 n. 26; Sumner 1973, 144; Sumner 1978b, 161; Shackleton Bailey 1991, 37–38; Shackleton Bailey 1988, 80; *MRR* Suppl., 172; Broughton 1991, 39 n. 15.

4. I agree with Pierpaoli (1997, 235 and n. 18) that Servius Sulpicius must have served as *nominis delator*, with Cato as *subscriptor*.

5. For testimony on Cato's abilities as an orator, see *ORF* no. 126; Douglas, *Brutus*, 97.

6. Adamietz states (in Cicero 1989, 16), on the basis of *Mur.* 10 and 48, that Hortensius spoke before Crassus. While that conclusion is plausible, we cannot be sure.

7. Already by the time of Pliny the Younger (*Ep.* 1.20.7), the text read this way.

8. Ayers (1953–54, 253 n. 10) is right to dismiss the suggestion of Husband (1916–17, 108–9) that this phrase could refer to charges against bribery agents. Husband (109) makes the interesting suggestion that they may have been liable under the *lex Calpurnia de ambitu* and may have testified to secure immunity under the law. It would certainly be consistent with *ambitus* laws to provide such a reward for providing information against others (see Alexander 1985, 28). But it is debated whether the final outcome of the confused events of 67 was a law that held *divisores* liable, although it was recognized that no *ambitus* law would be effective without such a provision (see Cic. *Corn. apud* Asc. 74–75C; McDonald 1929, 204; Griffin 1973b, 197 n. 15; Marshall 1985, 246, 261).

9. This kind of dispute, if it did occur, would have been analogous to the issue relating to the judicial bribery that took place in the trial of Oppianicus in 74 (*TLRR* no. 149), where there was no question that judicial bribery had occurred, and there Cicero (*Clu.* 9) has to fight the presumption that it had occurred in favor of the side that won, that is, the prosecution.

10. See Taylor 1949, 64; Staveley 1972, 169. The author of the *Commentariolum petitionis* underscores the importance of the knights, whom he associates with *adulescentes*, especially for Cicero (33). The weight that should be placed on the relevant passage from the *Commentariolum petitionis* depends on the authorship of this document, whether it

was written by Cicero's brother, Quintus (as it purports to be), by a contemporary, or by a later writer. For a discussion of this question, see Nardo 1970, 3–55; David et al. 1973.

11. For a general overview of electoral bribery, see Lintott 1990; my discussion of *ambitus* in the introduction to part 2 in the present book.

12. See Nicolet 1966–74, 2:979. Pinarius became the brother-in-law of Clodius, and Cicero was delighted in 56 when Pinarius died (*Att.* 4.8a.3).

13. She was probably his kinswoman Licinia (*Mur.* 73); see Münzer, "Licinia," no. 185, *RE* 13 (1927): 498.

14. This is not Murena himself: see Syme 1955b, 137, accepted by *MRR* Suppl., 123.

15. See Gruen 1995, 223 n. 56; Lintott 1990, 9. Kinsey (1966b) asks why the prosecution used offenses against this *senatus consultum*, which involved the interpretation of the *lex Calpurnia,* as charges against the defendant, if the *lex Tullia* had superseded the *lex Calpurnia* by the time of the trial. I agree with Classen's explanation (1985, 166 n. 190) that the prosecution wanted to take advantage of the fact that Cicero was the author of both the *lex Tullia* and the *senatus consultum,* as a way to tax him with inconsistency. That this decree was passed at the behest of all the candidates ("omnibus postulantibus candidatis," *Mur.* 68), presumably including Murena, must have given the prosecution another stick with which to beat the candidate: he had demanded a severe interpretation of the law but had violated the law as interpreted in this way.

16. Ayers (1950, 124) suggests that Cato argued that the passage of this *senatus consultum* showed that the Senate believed that not only Catiline but also Murena was guilty of violating its provisions. But, as Ayers points out, its wording was conditional. He advances as a parallel the senatorial judgment that Cluentius should be punished for judicial murder if he had violated the relevant statute (Cic. *Clu.* 136), a decree that some saw as a senatorial judgment that Cluentius was guilty, even though it, too, was phrased in a conditional way. However, the situations are slightly different, in that the decree mentioned in the *Pro Murena* was passed during the election campaign, might have been meant as a warning to all the candidates, and so to some extent related to future activities, whereas the decree relating to Cluentius, passed after the infamous trial in which he served as prosecutor, referred to activities that were already completed. Moreover, no one could have doubted that that decree referred to Cluentius alone.

17. For a similar argument in the judicial context, see n. 9 in this chapter; chap. 9. Cicero (*Clu.* 64) argues that the long shot in the trial of Oppianicus in 74 was the defense, since two previous cases (*TLRR* nos. 147–48) had gone for the prosecution; therefore, it was the defense, not the prosecution, that felt it had to resort to bribery. I agree with Riggsby that Adamietz is wrong in classifying this kind of attack as legally irrelevant slander against the candidate. The argument that the defeated candidate was actually a stronger candidate than the victor is logically related to the claim that the victor engaged in bribery, since that claim explains how he managed to win the election, as Adamietz says (in Cicero 1989, 111). However, like Riggsby (1999, 47–48), I do not agree with Adamietz (1986, 117; also in Cicero 1989, 29) when he suggests that the comparison of the candidates' merits was justified by the idea that the jury was "redoing" the election as a proxy for the Roman people: "Die Aufgabe der Richter bestand in den Ambitus-Fällen nicht so sehr darin, zu einem 'schuldig' oder 'nicht schuldig' zu gelangen, sondern zu klären, welcher der Kontrahenten in höherem Maße geeignet war, das Amt zu bekleiden" [The task of the judges consisted, in *ambitus* cases, not so much in arriving at a "guilty" or "not guilty," but to settle which of the opponents was to a higher

degree fit to hold the office]. This point of view is countered by Cicero himself (*Planc.* 8) with the argument that it sets the jurors over the assemblies, as Riggsby points out, and Cicero clearly expects his audience of jurors to disagree with this point of view.

18. This ranking not only was a matter of pride but also was related to the outcome of the election, especially when many candidates were competing for an office with many seats. For a description of the *renuntiatio* (official returns), see Staveley 1972, 177–81.

19. For a summary of recent discussion of the date, see *MRR* Suppl., 123.

20. Cicero says, "Pater enim fuit equestri loco, avus nulla inlustri laude celebratus" [For your father was of equestrian rank, and your grandfather's praises were not famously sung] (*Mur.* 16). Nicolet (1966–74, 2:1028–29) suggests that Cicero's phrase "equestri loco" implies that the previous generation was also equestrian. But Kunkel (1967, 25) holds that the grandfather of the prosecutor was perhaps still a senator, and scholarly opinion leans strongly in that direction: see Syme 1955a, 69; Shackleton Bailey 1988, 90–91. See also Leeman 1982, 208; Pierpaoli 1997, 240 n. 35.

21. Cicero's summarizing apothegm on the *peculatus* court is "cui placet oblivisci-tur, cui dolet meminit" [The winner forgets, the loser remembers] (*Mur.* 42).

22. Ryan (1994) argues convincingly that *Mur.* 47 should be read, "promulga-tionem legis Maniliae flagitasti" [You demanded the promulgation of the Manilian law], and that it refers to a law, annulled by the Senate, that would have allowed freed-men to be registered in all tribes.

23. See Ayers 1953–54, 253 n. 19, for similar usage of this term at Cic. *Cat.* 2.23, *Pis.* 22, and *Off.* 1.150.

24. See Leeman 1982, 205.

25. See Leeman 1982, 195.

26. For a contradictory view, see Leeman 1982, 227. Shackleton Bailey maintains that this Murena could be A. Terentius Varro Murena, the consul's son by birth, but Münzer argues that the fact that Cicero refers to him as Varro Murena or Varro (*Fam.* 13.22.1) suggests that this is someone else. On the name, see also McDermott 1941, 256–57; Treggiari 1973, 253–57; Shackleton Bailey 1991, 84–85.

CHAPTER 7

1. Gruen (1995, 230) argues that Crassus wanted to deprive others of some of the tactics that Pompey and he had used to gain the consulate of 55.

2. The story that the clothing of the presiding consul Pompey was splattered with blood at the aedilician elections—much to the shock of his wife, Julia, on his return home—is found or referred to in several sources: Val. Max. 4.6.4; Plut. *Pomp.* 53.3; Dio Cass. 39.32.2; App. *B Civ.* 2.17. See Linderski 1971, 284 = 1995, 118.

3. For the latter's place on the *stemma* of the Cassi Longini, see Sumner 1973, 50–51.

4. For such expressions of friendship voiced by the *patronus* for the prosecutor, see Craig 1981, especially 35 (on the trial of Plancius).

5. Craig 1981, 35 n. 14.

6. Craig 1981, 35–36 n. 15.

7. Laterensis also boasts of his lack of rhetorical training, by pointing out that he never was at Rhodes—unlike, of course, his opponent Cicero (*Planc.* 84).

8. Linderski develops the analysis of Kroll (1937, 136). For the argument that Hort-

ensius's speech the day before was delivered in the Senate as a commentary to the ongoing trial, see D.-G. 3:94, 6:47 n. 2; V. Mühll, "Hortensius" no. 13, *RE* 8 (1913): 2478; Taylor 1964, 25 n. 41. Taylor states that there is no evidence Hortensius appeared in court on behalf of Plancius. Malcovati lists neither speech in *ORF*.

9. See the references in *MRR* 2:197.

10. To make room for them in that office, Taylor (1964) moves the aedileship of L. Aemilius Paullus (consul in 50) to 56 and argues that in 55, M. Nonius Sufenas was not curule aedile but praetor.

11. Sumner 1971, 249 n. 12.

12. I am not convinced by Sumner's claim that because Pompey is mentioned by Cicero as the presiding magistrate over the first election (see the end of this note) but not over the second (*Planc.* 49), he did not preside over the second election, and therefore that the second election must have taken place after the year 54 had begun. Cicero is trying to demonstrate the reliability of the election results in the first election, since his client was victorious, and for that reason, he brings Pompey's prestige into play. Of course, Cicero might have wanted to do the same for the second election, whose results he also wants to uphold, but perhaps Pompey would not have wished to be reminded of the part that he played in them, since they, too, were, according to Cicero, controversial. Taylor (1964, 13–17) has shown that the consul to whom Cicero refers as the "harum ipsarum legum ambitus auctor" [champion of these very bribery laws] (*Planc.* 49) is not the *lator* (proposer), Crassus, but the laws' champion, Pompey.

13. Broughton, *MRR* Suppl., 158.

14. Crawford 1974, 1:454–55, no. 431.

15. A letter from Cicero to his brother, Quintus (Cic. *Q Fr.* 3.1.11), in which Cicero discusses his recent publications shows that already by some time in September he had produced his *Pro Plancio* in written form. The Ludi Romani were intimately connected with the office of curule aedile (Livy 6.42.12). It is interesting to see how Cicero capitalizes on a prosecutor's attempt to neutralize a possible Ciceronian argument by anticipating it. Laterensis said he was trying to prevent a trial from taking place at the same time as the Ludi Romani because Cicero would then be able to carry on about *tensae* (ceremonial chariots), as he had done before on behalf of aediles; in response, Cicero abjures discussing *tensae* with a *praeteritio* (pretended omission) that probably made the issue more memorable than if he had been the one to introduce the subject (*Planc.* 83).

16. Linderski (1971, 284 = 1995, 118) accepts Taylor's (1964) conclusion that the aedileships of Plancius and Plautius occurred in 55.

17. Shackleton Bailey (*CLA*, 2:211–12) argues that Messius was curule aedile in 55. This would obviously affect Taylor's (1964) reconstruction, since room would have to be made for Messius among the curule aedileships.

18. Taylor 1964, 23–25. Linderski (1971, 302 = 1995, 136) would add a prosecution of Sufenas in 54 for *ambitus* committed in his campaign for the praetorship of 55. See also Gruen 1995, 147–48, 313–22.

19. See Linderski 1961a, 116–18 = 1995, 214–16, 649.

20. For the chronology of the electoral campaigns in this year, see Linderski 1971, 286 n. 32 = 1995, 120. Taylor (1964, 24 n. 34) argues that the trial *de sodaliciis* of Messius, whom she classifies as a plebeian aedile in 55 and thus elected in 56 (before the passage

of the *lex Licinia*), shows that the statute had a retroactive force. But see n. 17 in the present chapter.

21. Sumner's own warning against arguments from silence (see, in the present book, chap. 12, n. 56) are salutary in this context as well.

22. M. Valerius Messala, consul in 53, was prosecuted under this law in 51 for his campaign for the consulate of 53. See Shackleton Bailey, *CLF*, 1:385, for explanation of the delay.

23. This article is summarized in Shackleton Bailey, *CLQf*, 178.

24. Gruen (1995, 229–30) maintains that the triumvirs prevented the passage of the *senatus consultum* into law in 56, when they wanted to push through the election of Pompey and Crassus to the consulate, but that in 55, having secured their electoral objectives, Crassus proposed a similar measure, which was passed into law. Linderski (1985, 93–94 = 1995, 113–14, 638–39) agrees with this analysis.

25. See Linderski 1961a, 116 = 1995, 214 ("Gesteigerter"). Mommsen (1899, 217) speaks of "schwerer Ambitus."

26. A clear analysis of what we know about this statute can be found in Bauerle 1990, 74–82. Staveley (1972, 204) is maybe too harsh on the *lex Licinia* when he writes, "Cicero's successful defence of his client, Plancius, suggests that the legislation was comparatively ineffective." To judge by a slightly larger sample than one trial, we know of two *sodalicia* prosecutions that were successful (*TLRR* nos. 311, 331), two that were not (*TLRR* nos. 292–93), and one whose outcome we do not know (*TLRR* no. 289). It may have taken prosecutors a few years to learn how to manage a case under this law.

27. See Mommsen 1899, 872 n. 2; Lintott 1990, 9.

28. The combination of the words *decuriare* and *conscribere* also occurs in Cic. *Sest.* 34, and only slightly different words occur in Cic. *Dom.* 13. For a discussion of this vocabulary, see Linderski 1961a, 114–15 = 1995, 212–13.

29. See Mommsen 1899, 874. Caelius (*apud* Cic. *Fam.* 8.2.1) comments that M. Valerius Messalla Rufus, having been acquitted for *ambitus* (*TLRR* no. 329), faces a *maius periculum* under the *lex Licinia de sodaliciis* (*TLRR* no. 331). Dio Cassius (39.37.1) speaks of πικρότερα ἐπιτίμια (heavier penalties) passed at this time for those who committed bribery. Mommsen (1899, 872 n. 2) misinterprets this passage to mean that Dio thought the law focused on force rather than money; Lintott (1990, 9) seems to follow Mommsen's interpretation. Rather, Dio is criticizing the triumvirs' hypocrisy in acting as if their seizure of power by force was less blameworthy than the acquisition of office by bribery. This passage in fact implies that Dio did not believe that violence and voter intimidation were the objects of this law, and there is indeed no evidence that they were.

30. See Mommsen 1899, 875.

31. See Staveley 1972, 205; Yakobson 1999, 151. See especially Bauerle 1990, 9–12, for a clear explication of the debate on *coitio*.

32. The text reads, ". . . lege Licinia, quam M. Licinius Crassus, Cn. Pompei Magni collega, in consulatu suo pertulit, ut severissime quaereretur in eos candidatos, qui sibi conciliassent <sodales> ea potissimum de causa, ut per illos pecuniam tribulibus dispertirent ac sibi mutuo eadem suffragationis emptae praesidia communicarent" [. . . under the *lex Licinia*, which M. Licinius Crassus, the colleague of Cn. Pompeius Magnus, carried in his consulate so that a very strict trial would be held against those candi-

dates who had won over companions [?] for themselves, especially on the ground that they distributed money through them to the tribe members and jointly shared the same protections of purchased votes with each other]. Taylor (1949, 64) writes that in the late Republic, *coitio* was classified as an electoral malpractice. See Bauerle 1990, 96 n. 150, for an analysis of the evidence.

33. Hall (1964, 289) explains the consequences of multiple votes for multiple seats, citing not only the election of Plancius but also Cic. *Tog. Cand. apud* Asc. 85C. That a candidate was declared elected when he received 50 percent of the tribal vote plus one meant that the outcome of the election depended somewhat on the order in which results were announced from each tribe. As Staveley (1972, 179–80) shows with an arithmetical example, winning was possible for candidates who did not carry the largest number of tribes or who would not have done so if every group had been permitted to record its vote. Because the order of announcing the voting results from each tribe could be crucial, the order was sometimes decided by lot (see Taylor 1966, 81; Staveley 1972, 181; Rosenstein 1995, 43). See also Marshall 1985, 284–85.

34. Staveley 1972, 205.

35. When he presents a list of illicit ways to pursue wealth, Cicero mentions "intercessiones pecuniarum in coitionibus candidatorum" [guarantees of money in the alliances of candidates] (*Paradoxa Stoicorum* 46). However, alternative readings for "intercessiones" here are "intercidas" (?) or "inpensas" (meaning "expenditures"). See Birt 1930; Molager's Budé edition (Cicero 1971, 150).

36. See David's contribution to David et al. 1973, 277, citing Asc. 75C on the attempt made by *leges* and senatus consulta to distinguish between useful and harmful *collegia*. See Venturini 1984, 799–804, on the relationship between the concepts of *vis, ambitus,* and *sodalicia,* charges of which, as Venturini shows on the basis of Asc. 38C, could all arise from the same set of facts. Hall (1964, 302 n. 144) notes that Asconius's description of the *coitio* surrounding the election for the consulate of 63 (83C) indicates that it was not illegal. But, of course, this occurred before the passage of the *lex Licinia*, which may have been designed to counter such activity.

37. The scholiast's phrase "ac sibi mutuo eadem suffragationis emptae praesidia communicarent" (*Schol. Bob.* 152St; see n. 32 in the present chapter) suggests two candidates' joint efforts to buy a vote for each, yielding two votes for the price of one or at least for less than the two votes would have cost separately.

38. See Alexander 1985, 27–28.

39. Yakobson 1999, 51.

40. Some manuscripts read "excitarent."

41. On this meaning of *puncta* (votes), see Hall 1964, 298 and n. 134; Staveley 1972, 175–76.

42. Craig 1990, 76, n. 6.

43. This provision seems to be reflected in the *lex Malacitana;* see Bruns 1909, no. 30, col. 2 sec. 56. It clearly deals with a tie number of *suffragia,* that is, group votes (e.g., tribes), not individual *puncta* within a tribe. See Rosenstein 1995, 43–44.

44. Cicero argues that it is implausible that Plancius and Plotius, having done very well in the first election, would have been less willing to give away the vote of their own tribe in the second. But the agreement in the first election may have been part of a larger deal to eke out the maximum gain from the resources at their command, and when the

first election revealed their front-runner status, they may have decided to eschew trickery and simply to gather in as many votes as they could. Moreover, they may have believed that their agreement applied only to the first election, not to the second, which, of course, they had had no reason to foresee would occur.

45. Craig 1990, 76 n. 6.

46. As Craig (1990, 76 n. 6) points out, Venturini (1984, 795–96) fails to deal with it.

47. Two possible technicalities in the law might have protected Laterensis against such a prosecution. First, the fact that a candidate would have "thrown" a tribe to a rival may have been grounds for prosecuting only the "giver," not the "receiver." (Admittedly, it is hard to believe that Laterensis had not agreed to give something back in return.) Second, perhaps no one other than the defeated candidates could have brought an action under this law; that is, only injured parties may have had standing to prosecute. Thus, Laterensis may have been sure that Plancius would not have been allowed to launch a counterprosecution. In any case, it seems very plausible that the law was drafted in such a way as to encourage members of an illegal coalition to inform on each other, given that they possessed the inside knowledge to launch an effective prosecution; for example, they may have obtained immunity if they did so. Cf. such a provision in the case of electoral bribery, which also inherently involves a combination of several people. See Alexander 1985, 27–29.

48. So argues Grimal, in his Budé edition of the *Pro Plancio* (Cicero 1976, 99 n. 1).

49. At this point, individual jurors would have to be found from the three selected tribes, and it seems from Cicero's protests that the prosecutor had a right to pick particular individuals from those tribes. Cicero complains that the defense ought to have been allowed to reject five jurors but that it was denied this right (*Planc.* 40). It is not clear how jurors were selected out of the tribes, especially in the case of senators, since, as Greenidge points out, it might have been difficult to find enough senatorial jurors from a given tribe. See Mommsen 1899, 217; Greenidge 1901, 453–56.

50. See Linderski 1961b, 310 = 1995, 334, no. 31; Gruen 1995, 231.

51. On the use of the phrase *in crimen vocari* to mean "be drawn into a trial [of someone else]," see chap. 10, n. 31.

52. See Wiseman 1971, nos. 312, 321, 324; Nicolet 1966–74, vol. 2, nos. 263, 273, 275. On the *novitas* (status as a "new man") of Plancius, see also Syme 1939, 88–89.

53. See Cic. *Att.* 1.17.9; Grimal's commentary in Cicero 1976, 80 n. 2.

54. See *MRR* Suppl., 116.

55. Cicero's argument against provincial service is the same as that Cato used against Murena (see chap. 6 in the present book).

56. See *MRR* Suppl., 191.

57. One might have thought that candidates from distinguished families would enjoy an advantage particularly when running for more minor offices, since voters with ignorance of or lack of interest in a campaign might be expected to vote for candidates with greater name recognition. But for the purposes of his case, Cicero puts more stress on the campaign than on the background of the candidate, emphasizing the importance of demonstrating an eager desire to be elected to the position. It seems strange to a modern reader that Cicero could argue at the same time against both high birth and merit as the criteria for obtaining office, since we see an opposition between birth and merit. But Cicero's audience would have seen high birth as a form of merit.

58. For an analysis of how Cicero diverts the attention of his audience from his support of the triumvirs to his supposed embarrassment at the conflicting claims of *gratia* to Laterensis and Plancius, see Craig 1990.

59. If Sumner's reconstruction of the chronology were correct, we could be sure of Plancius's acquittal, since the trial would have taken place before he held office and since a conviction would have meant that he would not hold office. However, since Taylor seems to be correct in arguing that the trial followed his year of office, we cannot be so sure. In favor of acquittal, we must therefore rely on the fact, cited by Gelzer (1969, 200) in this regard, that Cicero's speedy publication of this speech, along with his defense of Scaurus, suggest a successful outcome (see Cic. *Q Fr.* 3.1.11).

60. Gelzer 1969, 199.

61. Syme (1939, 89) writes: "It was no part of Cicero's policy to flood the Senate with municipal men and capture for imported merit the highest dignity in the Roman State. . . . He desired that the sentiment and voice of Italy should be heard at Rome—but it was the Italy of the post-Sullan order, and the representation, although indirect, was to be adequate and of the best, namely his own person."

PART 3

1. On laws relating to homicide and violence, see Mommsen 1899, 629–66; Kunkel 1963, 741–42; Lintott 1968, 107–24; Ferrary 1991; Cloud 1994, 520–24; Santalucia 1994, 118–25; Riggsby 1999, 50–55, 79–84.

2. Cloud (1994, 523) attributes the lower status of this court to the inferior standing of its defendants.

3. See Jones 1972, 58; 128 nn. 86, 87.

4. On the name of this statute, see Cloud 1968; Riggsby 1999, 200 n. 1. Santalucia (1994, 118 n. 44) objects to this title, on the grounds that it is illogical to juxtapose the name of the criminals (*de sicariis*) with the name of the crimes (*de veneficiis*).

5. See Kunkel 1962, 64–67; Cloud 1969; Cloud 1994, 522.

6. See Bauman 1996, 30–32.

7. See Cloud 1994, 524.

8. See Jones 1972, 58.

CHAPTER 8

1. Landgraf (191–92, ad loc.) shows that the plural in Cicero's phrase "domus uxor liberique" need not be taken literally (see Gell. *NA* 2.13; Shackleton Bailey, *CLF,* 2:416; *OLD,* s.v. "liberi"; Gamberale 1995, 436–38), so there is no problem in the fact that Roscius senior had only one child at Ameria.

2. In fact, Cicero claims that Roscius was the most fervent pro-Sullan in the vicinity: "praeter ceteros in ea vicinitate eam partem causamque opera, studio, auctoritate defendit" [more than anyone else in the neighborhood he defended that side and cause with his effort, zeal, and prestige] (*Rosc. Am.* 16). This runs contrary to Badian's analysis (1984, 247): "At Ameria, the leading family of the Roscii was divided against itself, with the senior Roscius apparently cautiously neutral and his more daring relatives eager in support of Sulla."

3. Magnus is described as a "cognatus" [kinsman] (*Rosc. Am.* 87), and the same was almost certainly true of Capito. Stroh (1975, 55 n. 2) argues rightly that Cicero's wording at *Rosc. Am.* 96 implies that Capito was a relative of the murdered man. Cicero complains that T. Roscius Magnus sent a messenger announcing the murder to Capito, rather than to "tot propinqui cognatique optime convenientes" [so many relatives and kinsmen who were on excellent terms with him]. Stroh argues that Cicero would have clearly stated that T. Roscius Capito was not related to the victim if that were the case; his failure to do so means that he wants us to infer from his statement that Capito was a *cognatus non optime conveniens.* Kinsey (1985, 189 and n. 4) describes Capito as "possibly a relation," arguing, "Cicero's reference to *propinqui cognatique optime convenientes* might be taken to imply that Capito possessed none of these attributes."

4. To avoid confusion, I refer to the father as "Roscius senior," to the son as "Roscius junior," to T. Roscius Magnus as "Magnus," and to T. Roscius Capito as "Capito."

5. According to Plutarch (*Sull.* 32), Catiline obtained the retroactive proscription of his own brother, whom he had killed before the end of the civil war. Whether or not the story is accurate, it testifies to the belief that some individuals were proscribed after their death.

6. Plutarch (*Cic.* 3) provides the figures of two thousand drachmas (evidently a mistake for two thousand sesterces, or four times too high [see Garzetti's commentary in Plutarch 1954, 10, ad loc.]) as the sale price and 250 talents (or six million sesterces, the same figure as Cicero provides) as the real value. Frier (1985, 11 n. 25) doubts the figure of six million sesterces for thirteen *fundi* (estates), about 460,000 sesterces on average, which far exceeds figures for other *fundi.* However, these farms must have been choice agricultural real estate, since almost all of them bordered the Tiber River.

7. See Kinsey 1967, 64–67. Aulus Gellius (*NA* 15.28.3; cf. Quint. *Inst.* 12.6.4) specifically dates the speech to 80. For relevant sources, see Landgraf, 8–11. Bauman (1996, 30) argues that Roscius, if convicted, actually faced the prospect of the traditional punishment for parricide, which was to be sewn into a leather sack with a dog, a monkey, a snake, and a rooster and thrown into a sea or river.

8. Some time after this case, Erucius again served as a prosecutor opposed to Cicero, and Cicero called him an imitator of the great orator M. Antonius (Quint. *Inst.* 8.3.22; *TLRR* no. 368).

9. He may be the Ericius who served as *tribunus militum* under Sulla at Chaeronea (Plut. *Sul.* 16, 18). The name *C. Erucius* appears in one Italian inscription (*CIL* 11.4800) and one inscription from Delos containing the name of someone who was probably a freedman (Münzer, "Erucius" no. 2, *RE* Suppl. 3 [1918]: 441). For the nomen, whose origins may lie in northern Italy, see Schulze 1904, 112 n. 3, 170, 411 n. 1.

10. Landgraf (45, on *Rosc. Am.* 17) writes that Cicero is trying to discredit the upcoming testimony of Magnus, whereas Stroh (1975, 57 n. 7) and Schmitz (1985, 34) maintain that there is no evidence for this view.

11. See Landgraf, 203, on *Rosc. Am.* 104.

12. See Landgraf, 45.

13. Ayers 1950, 14 and 137 n. 29.

14. This information was contained in *Rosc. Am.* 132; although it falls in a lacuna in the text, the gist seems to be provided by the scholiast (*Schol. Gron.* D 314–15St).

15. This point is noted by Stroh (1975, 58). Ciaceri (1926–30, 1:22 n. 4) argues that Capito was put on the delegation because he was a client of Chrysogonus (*Rosc. Am.* 106). But at least according to Cicero's account, their intention was to approach Sulla directly (*Rosc. Am.* 25), and it was Chrysogonus who made the effort to sidetrack them.

16. I cannot agree with Kinsey (1980, 176) that *Rosc. Am.* 19, unlike *Rosc. Am.* 96, fails to state that Mallius went first to Capito; this is the clear implication of the fact that he went first not to the son but to his "enemy" Capito.

17. See Kinsey 1980, 176. The father had put Roscius junior in charge of managing most or all of the farms and, furthermore, had allowed him to keep the proceeds from some of them ("Quid? si constat hunc non modo colendis praediis praefuisse sed certis fundis patre vivo frui solitum esse . . ." [What? If it is established that the defendant was not only in charge of farming the estates but that he was accustomed to enjoy the profits from certain farms while his father was alive . . .], *Rosc. Am.* 44). Depending on how scattered these farms were, it may have been difficult (especially in the early morning hours) to find out exactly where Roscius was at the time.

18. "Cisiis" (*Rosc. Am.* 19) is the accepted reading, although some manuscripts and the scholiast (*Schol. Gron.* D 305St) have "cissis." One would expect the singular form *cisio;* perhaps Cicero uses the plural to exaggerate the degree of preparation, with transport supplied in relays (see Landgraf, 51, ad loc.).

19. Cicero avoids specifying the person who conveys this information, by using passives without an agent ("res defertur, magnitudo pecuniae demonstratur, bonitas praediorum . . . huius inopia et solitudo commemoratur" [the matter is reported, the amount of the money is shown, the quality of the farms . . . and the defendant's defenselessness and isolation are mentioned], *Rosc. Am.* 20–21). He then moves to an active verb in the third-person plural ("demonstrant" [they show]) and says that the conspiracy was, at that point, entered into ("societas coitur" [the partnership is formed], 21), consisting of individuals whom we have already met. He fortifies that impression by naming Chrysogonus, Magnus, and Capito as the three people who ended up in possession of the confiscated property.

20. See Kinsey 1980, 177 and n. 5. Frier (1985, 1–27) provides an excellent description and analysis of such a *controversia,* one not very far from Ameria and in which the disturbances caused by Sulla and their consequences also played a part. It led to the lawsuit (probably in 69 B.C.) in which Cicero delivered the *Pro Caecina.* Frier shows that it was possible for such a dispute to exist for a period of time without immediately turning into a legal struggle: "During this time these actors had used private law mainly as a means to an end that was predominantly non-legal in character; though they doubtless gave at least passing consideration to the legal implications of their conduct, law was kept more or less to the 'back region' of their interactions, while the 'front region' was dominated by their social and economic purposes. In such interactions there was room for a considerable tolerance of legal ambiguity; the actors did not have to concern themselves continuously with the possibility of lawsuits and how they might fare in them" (28–29). See also the quote of Frier in chap. 1 of the present book.

21. This account is contained in a long sentence that switches from historical presents to historical infinitives (*Rosc. Am.* 110); according to Landgraf (210), it does so for the sake of *variatio.*

22. Kinsey 1985, 192, 194.

23. Cf., for example, *Cael.* 4. For references, see Austin, *Pro Caelio*³, 49; Alexander 1993, 255 n. 45.

24. Some friends and *cognati* had supported Roscius to the extent of advising him to flee to Rome for support (*Rosc. Am.* 27).

25. Cf. *Rosc. Am.* 59: ". . . quod antea causam publicam nullam dixerim" [. . . because I have never before defended a criminal case]; Cic. *Brut.* 312: "prima causa publica pro Sex. Roscio dicta" [my first criminal case, defending Sextus Roscius].

26. Later (*Rosc. Am.* 124), Cicero refers to the dangers that Chrysogonus and "alii plures" [several others] unnamed (presumably including Sulla himself) will feel themselves insulted ("laesos") if he brings up the role of Chrysogonus; he claims he does not fear the anger of Chrysogonus, but he leaves the implication that he should be concerned about what the others think.

27. See Sumner 1973, 131.

28. See Sumner 1973, 131. Sumner notes that Niger could have been born as late as 102, if there was a "patrician" *cursus*.

29. Cicero states several times (*Rosc. Am.* 18, 81, 92, 94) that Roscius was never at Rome, as if there can be no argument on that point. Erucius must have been happy to concede that Roscius junior never went to Rome as a general rule, since he uses that as an argument to show his father's dislike of him (see the next paragraph in the present chapter). As Stroh (1975, 59 n. 19) points out, saying that Roscius stayed in Ameria is not quite the same as saying that at the precise time of the murder, he was not at Rome but at Ameria. However, I cannot agree with Stroh's further point here that Cicero's failure to mention Roscius junior specifically by name as someone to whom Mallius Glaucia could have brought the news of his father's death signifies that Cicero felt he could not claim that Roscius junior was definitely in Ameria at the time of the murder. The phrase Cicero uses at *Rosc. Am.* 96, "Cum Ameriae Sex. Rosci domus uxor liberique essent" [When Sextus Roscius had at Ameria a home, wife, and children], makes the desired point that many people would have been better choices for recipients of the bad news than Capito; Cicero is not claiming that Mallius Glaucia should have necessarily gone directly to the location where Roscius junior was to be found the day after the murder.

30. Cicero attempts to turn this argument on its head with the claim that such a "horrida incultaque vita" [rough and uncouth life] provides a likely environment for innocence, not for "maleficia" [crimes] (*Rosc. Am.* 75). For discussion of contrary commonplaces on rural life and character, see Vasaly 1985; Vasaly 1993, 156–72; Riggsby 1995a, 245–46.

31. See Landgraf, 162, 223–24, ad loc.

32. Erucius did not mention him in his speech (*Rosc. Am.* 60).

33. Such damage is evidenced by Ulp. *Dig.* 48.18.7, which sets limits on torture so that the person tortured will be "salvus" [safe and sound]. Clearly, the risk of physical injury was real, as is shown by Cicero's account (even allowing for exaggeration) of the torture of three slaves (*Clu.* 176–77; see chap. 9 in this volume). This is possibly what Kinsey (1985, 191) alludes to when he writes, "there may have been respectable reasons for refusing to submit possibly valuable slaves to this ordeal." (Cicero scoffs at the idea that the slaves of Roscius senior—"homines paene operarios, ex Amerina disciplina patris familiae rusticani" [little more than laborers, products of the training at Ameria by a rural head of household] [*Rosc. Am.* 120]—would have any value to the elegant

Chrysogonus, disregarding the fact that the paterfamilias Roscius spent most of his time at Rome and might well have wanted around him slaves that met the urban standard of refinement.) I do not agree with Kinsey that the possible unreliability of evidence gathered through torture (Ulp. *Dig.* 48.18.1.23) would have justified withholding the slaves' information because torture had to be applied to slaves when they were examined (see Cic. *Mil.* 58; Buckland 1908, 87–88). Magnus argued that slaves should not be examined against their masters; Cicero responded that Roscius is no longer their master (*Rosc. Am.* 120). However, later jurists ruled that a slave could not be interrogated to provide evidence against his or her former master (Paul. *Dig.* 48.18.18.6), and Chrysogonus may have relied on such an opinion if it was current already in the late Republic.

34. Contrary to Cicero's protestations, Roscius junior must have been enough of a man of the world to arrange this. As Craig (1993, 36) remarks, "A man who would come to Rome and stay in the house of Caecilia, a woman related to both of the consuls-elect, would not be completely ignorant of how events might be made to happen in the City."

35. Craig (1993, 34–36) argues that this conforms to Quintilian's definition of dilemma at *Inst.* 5.10.69, where Quintilian uses the example of the *Pro Vareno* as showing that the defense offers the prosecution two possibilities, each of which is damaging to the prosecution ("deinde utraque facit accusatori contraria" [he then renders both detrimental to the prosecution]). But in the *Pro Roscio,* most of the alternatives presented are quite consistent with the prosecution's case that the defendant is responsible for the murder of his father, even if he did not commit it with his own hand; as Craig points out, the alternatives presented are not so much impossible as unsubstantiated. Classen (1982, 168–70) describes, with copious citation of examples, how Cicero often confuses his audience with a barrage of questions and, without really grappling with the issues raised, creates the appearance of refuting the claims of the opposition.

36. "Denn wenn auch nur eine Möglichkeit vorhanden war, den Freispruch des Angeklagten hinzustellen als motiviert nicht durch seine erwiesene Unschuld, sondern durch sein Recht, den proskribierten Vater zu töten, so blieb einerseits das Odium des Vatermordes auf Roscius haften und alle weiteren Schritte zugunsten seiner Restitution wurden aufs äußerste gehemmt; und anderseits war die Gültigkeit der Proskription von der Gegenpartei damit so gut wie zugegeben, und auch von diesem Gesichtspunkt aus waren dann den Freunden des Roscius die Hände gebunden, Chrysogonus blieb unangefochten im Besitz seines Raubes: dies, und nichts anderes, war eben der Zweck seiner Anklage" (Heinze 1909, 961–62 = 1960, 99–100). Gelzer (1969, 19) seems to accept this solution or at least does not dispute it.

37. Ayers (1950, 22), in his discussion of this whole problem (17–23), advances the possibility that the prosecution might have argued that Roscius killed his father before he was proscribed, in which case his property might have been confiscated as someone who was killed *in adversariorum praesidiis.* For that reason, Cicero could say, "quo in numero Sex. Roscius non est" [to which group [the proscribed] Sextus Roscius does not belong] (*Rosc. Am.* 126). If this were the case, the confiscation of property might be legal, but the killing would not be legal. However, as Ayers concedes, this solution runs up against the fact that Roscius senior was killed at Rome, not in enemy territory, as Cicero immediately points out (126), completing the dilemma.

38. Quintilian admits that many people believe it is inconsistent to use both arguments and that therefore anyone who does so will not be believed. But he maintains that

different people are moved by different arguments and, thus, that it is wise to use both (*Inst.* 4.5.14). He argues that denial of the facts is always the stronger defense (3.6.10). Cicero's reliance on that argument in this case is consistent with Quintilian's (later, of course) recommendation.

39. For the technique of a simulated division between the wishes of the client and the words of the *patronus,* see Kennedy 1968 (at 431–32, Kennedy discusses *Rosc. Am.* 143); Thierfelder 1965, 388–89; May 1981; Alexander 2000.

40. It will become clear that I am not willing to take this argument as far as the Heinze/Stroh theory does.

41. It is possible that this anecdote was added to the speech by Cicero when he edited it for publication. But we cannot rule out the possibility that Cicero had the presence of mind to improvise this summary of Erucius's demeanor while he was delivering the speech or that Cicero possibly had an inkling of what Erucius's reaction would be and was prepared to describe it if it turned out as he expected.

42. Jones 1972, 58–59. See n. 44 in the present chapter.

43. Cloud 1994, 523. I find the first point more convincing than the second, in support of which Cloud adduces the fact that Cicero, while serving as praetor over the extortion court, argued a case before the *quaestio de sicariis et veneficiis.* It does not seem persuasive to compare presiding over one court with speaking as an advocate before another, since the one activity did not preclude the other. I cannot reconcile Cloud's agreement with Jones that some courts had "lower status" with Cloud's denial, at the same time, that the "overall prestige" of some courts was greater than others.

44. Fannius had served as *iudex quaestionis* over this court before (*Rosc. Am.* 11). The view that he served in this capacity in 81 (having been plebeian aedile in 83) and then as praetor over the same court in 80 has been altered, in view of the redating of a coin issued by him and his fellow aedile L. Critonius to 86 B.C. (see Crawford 1974, 1:367, no. 351; 1:78). He could have served as *iudex quaestionis* any year between 85 and 81 (see *MRR* Suppl., 78, 90).

45. See Badian 1962, 230; *MRR* Suppl., 74–75. Badian (1970, 12) cites *Rosc. Am.* 139 as evidence that by the time of the trial, some semblance of constitutional rule must have been restored: "Dum necesse erat resque ipsa cogebat, unus omnia poterat; qui postea quam magistratus creavit legesque constituit, sua cuique procuratio auctoritasque est restituta" [While it was necessary and the situation demanded it, one man had power over everything; after he created magistracies and established laws, each person's responsibility and influence was restored to him]. Badian is supported by Twyman (1976, 87), who points out (88) that this passage, even if it is the result of later editing for publication, is not likely to misrepresent the original political character of the speech: "It would not serve Cicero's presumed purpose in revision—depicting himself as a courageous foe of tyranny—to insert in the speech a passage admitting (by implication) that Sulla was no longer dictator." Badian's interpretation of the course of Sulla's rule, from dictator in 81 to consul in 80 to private citizen in 79, is now generally accepted.

46. Pareti (1953, 3:640 n. 2), who dates the trial to 79, points out that at *Rosc. Am.* 131, Cicero describes the era when Sulla held sole power as having occurred in the past. He minimizes the bravery shown by Cicero, since Sulla had already abdicated. However, if we date the trial to the previous year, we should be less reluctant to "sopravvalutare" [overrate] the courage shown by Cicero, even if Sulla was by now consul and no longer dictator.

CHAPTER 9

1. Much has been written about the trial of Cluentius and Cicero's speech. In addition to the bibliography cited in Alexander 1982 (162 nn. 55, 56), see Kirby 1990 (and works cited there on p. 8); Giuffrè 1993; Giuffrè 1994; Pugliese 1994; Riggsby 1999, 66–78.

2. The civil law speeches, in comparison, often offer a wealth of detail about life in Italy outside of Rome, as Frier (1985) shows in his analysis of the background to the trial in which Cicero delivered the *Pro Caecina*.

3. For a discussion of the alternatives *Attius* or *Accius*, see Nicolet 1966–74, 2:792–93, Shackleton Bailey 1991, 4; Solin 1987, 596. The name *Attius* is attested in Pisaurum (see Münzer, "T. Accius" no. 1a, *RE* Suppl. 1 [1903]: 6). Opinion is leaning toward acceptance of *Attius*.

4. Moreau (1983, 112 and n. 105) convincingly argues that Oppianicus junior began working on the prosecution as soon as he legally could, that is, when he reached the age of seventeen (in 69 B.C.); Moreau maintains that this was a normal age when a young man could be engaged and, thus, that Sassia got Oppianicus junior engaged in the same year to her daughter, Auria. It may have been considered quite honorable for a wife or other female relative to avenge the prosecution and execution of a male relative by assisting those who went to court against the former prosecutor who had secured the conviction: see Plin. *Ep.* 9.13.5; Lendon 1997, 46.

5. On Hermagoras, see Kennedy 1963, 303–19.

6. Tacitus (*Dial.* 19) characterizes Hermagoras's work as "aridissimus."

7. This description of στάσις theory is taken from Kennedy 1963, 307–8.

8. The section of the Via Flaminia that connected Ancona and Brundisium went through Larinum. See G. Radke, "Viae publicae Romanae," *RE* Suppl. 13 (1973): 1574.

9. See Torelli 1973, 347.

10. For the geographical background, see Barker, Lloyd, and Webley 1978; Dyson 1992, 74.

11. Shackleton Bailey (1988, 9) states that the nomen is *Abbius*, not *Albius*. See also Boyancé's introduction to his Budé edition of the *Pro Cluentio* (Cicero 1953, 9 n. 1); Nicolet 1966–74, vol. 2, no. 1 (a Roman knight). I have not found any support for Torelli's suggestion (1973, 348–49) of *Gabbius*.

12. See Torelli 1973, 336–43.

13. Torelli (1973, 342) and Dyson (1992, 71) suggest that the purpose of this reform may have been to contribute to a power base for the new regime of Oppianicus, as part of Sulla's reorganization of the *municipia*. Dyson (74) puts forward the possibility that small farmers may have declined in status as agricultural land was turned over to pasturage and that Oppianicus championed the Martiales to appeal to this group. However, citizens of the town who saw their economic and political power declining may have been the most jealous of their own rights and the least receptive to the admission of new citizens.

14. Torelli (1973, 342–43) suggests that Sulla's death may have sparked this assertion of traditional rights.

15. See Stewart 1995, 74; Stewart's article outlines the importance of regional Italian interests in the Roman politics of the sixties, as well as the Roman elite's difficulty in coming to terms with those interests. See also Tatum 1997, 496–97.

16. Ramsay, in his commentary (Cicero 1889, 174–75, on *Clu.* 47), rejects attempts to alter the text so as to avoid the situation where Scamander had both the poison and the money in his hands at the same time. He points to the force of *Clu.* 49 and 53 (cf. 50, 56), in which it is said that Scamander had the poison, as well as the money, when he was seized. "Venenum esse deprehensum" [Poison was detected] (50) was the leitmotif of the prosecution of Scamander: "The money without the poison would have been no proof of guilt at all" (Cicero 1889, 177). Classen (1985, 50) argues that Cicero's misleading summary of this affair much later in the speech, when he is summarizing the crimes of the elder Oppianicus ("manifesto deprehensus sit" [he was detected in the act], *Clu.* 125), demonstrates Cicero's unreliability on this matter, but I do not agree that this glib statement that Scamander was "caught red-handed" reduces the credibility of Cicero's more detailed earlier account of the sting operation.

17. Classen (1985, 49 n. 97) is aware of this difficulty: "Daß Diogenes (der Sklave des Cluentius) das Gift mitbrachte, um es Scamander zu verkaufen, damit dieser dann Cluentius vergiftete, wird man vollends nicht annehmen oder gar behaupten können; sowohl Ciceros eigene Worte (47; 61: *per servum medici*) wie auch jede Wahrscheinlichkeit sprechen dagegen: Denn Scamander hätte sich das Gift besser aus einer anderen Quelle beschafft als gerade aus dem Sklaven des Mannes, den er töten wollte. . ." [One will not be able to assume entirely or indeed assert that Diogenes (the slave of Cluentius) brought along the poison in order to sell it to Scamander, so that the latter would then poison Cluentius; not only Cicero's own words (47; 61: *per servum medici*) but also every likelihood speaks against this. For Scamander could have better procured the poison from another source than precisely from the slave of the man whom he wanted to kill . . .]. Classen goes astray here in not realizing that, although Cluentius, by the time of the nocturnal meeting, had purchased the slave Diogenes from the doctor Cleophantus, Scamander would not yet have known of this purchase. If he had, he would have undoubtedly suspected that the scheme had been uncovered.

18. In fact, the vote was close, in a sense. In another speech (*Caecin.* 29), Cicero says that Oppianicus could not have been convicted if there had been just one less vote for condemnation. There were thirty-two votes, so seventeen "guilty" votes (50 percent [of the total vote] plus one) were needed for condemnation (*Clu.* 73). Five were cast for acquittal (76). Possibly, there were seventeen votes for condemnation and ten *non liquet*. If one of the "guilty" votes had shifted to acquittal, there would have been only 50 percent for conviction, which would not have sufficed. See Ramsay's commentary in Cicero 1889, 18 n. 2. This calculation is based on voting rules that mean either that a *non liquet* vote has the same effect as a vote for acquittal or, if there is a difference in the effect of the two, that the difference is presumably that *non liquet* votes above a certain percentage (33 percent in the *lex repetundarum*, line 49) will force a *comperendinatio* (compulsory adjournment), in which case the magistrate will pronounce *amplius* (again)—a real possibility, as *Caecin.* 29 shows—rather than an acquittal.

19. Moreau (1983) provides a very detailed account of marriage relationships at Larinum, extracting as much information as possible from the references scattered throughout the *Pro Cluentio*, leading to profound conclusions.

20. Moreau 1983, 120.

21. That Cicero does not describe the outcome of this action suggests that the other side, led by Oppianicus senior, may have prevailed in that struggle.

22. I agree with Pugliese (1994, 250), arguing against Giuffrè (1993, 191), that at issue here is not whether there is a presumption of innocence or guilt toward the accused. The questions are rather the extent to which the jurors should weigh only the defense arguments and whether they should be willing to import arguments of their own into their consideration.

23. On the name, see Shackleton Bailey 1988, 14. It is interesting that the prosecutor had not mentioned this incident, but Cicero claims that he knows that testimony to this effect is on the way (*Clu.* 163).

24. That is what the *lex repetundarum* (line 56) seems to have stipulated, and many features of later criminal trials are consistent with—and none are totally inconsistent with—the proposition that the later Republic criminal statutes acted in this fashion. I wish to stress that I am referring to violations of the law under which had been established the *quaestio* that was judging the case. Classen (1985, 107), in a *Korrekturzusatz* (correction addendum), claims that my 1982 article makes no distinction between reproaches and formal charges. He has evidently misunderstood my argument there, since he thinks that it leaves unanswered the question "warum es überhaupt verschiedene *quaestiones* gibt, wenn alle möglichen Vergehen ohne jeden Unterschied in einem Prozess als Anklagepunkte vorgebracht werden können" [why there are after all different *quaestiones,* if all possible crimes can be brought forward as counts of prosecution in one trial without any distinction]. On the contrary, my view stresses the importance of the statute under which the trial was conducted as the central criterion of relevance:

> It is the contention of this article that accusations against a defendant in a *quaestio* fall into three categories: 1) violations of the law of that *quaestio;* 2) violations of another law; and 3) violations of social norms. Accusations in the first category—*all* those accusations, whether or not they have ever been presented to the authorities before the trial—are relevant. Those in the second and third categories are irrelevant and should only influence the jurors to the extent that they corroborate the accusations of the first category. (Alexander 1982, 102)

Actually, the distinctions drawn by me are not very different from Classen's own analysis (1985, 111) in which he distinguishes between relevant charges (under the statute of a particular court) that the prosecutor has specified to get permission to bring a case, charges under that statute that should be punished according to the spirit of the law, those that are punishable under other statutes, and violations of moral standards. I differ only in that I do not believe that the prosecutor was restricted to only those statutory violations specified by the prosecutor in the *legibus interrogatio* (interrogation according to the laws), and I think that it would have been up to the jurors to decide whether to follow the letter or spirit of the statute in terms of which violations they would consider as covered by that statute. See also Classen 1972, 2–3.

25. Meyer (1978) presents a similar interpretation of these lines. Frier (1994), in his review of Lintott 1992, implies that the *lex repetundarum* may be idiosyncratic in its treatment of multiple claims against a single person. Lintott (1992, 30–31) provides a picture of the workings of the epigraphic law whereby an extortion trial "was expected to embrace any possible damage to any victim (even perhaps in different regions or provinces) up to the time of the trial," and he argues that "the impression we get from cases under later *repetundae* laws" is that "prosecutors deliberately accumulated every charge possible." See also *Statutes,* 1:106.

26. Cloud (1994, 514) emphasizes the inclusion by prosecutors of charges that, though based on law, were irrelevant to the particular *quaestio* before which the trial was taking place: "Prosecutors tackled the problem of multiple charges by introducing matter that was strictly speaking irrelevant to the charge they were actually bringing." Cloud (n. 110) supports his view by arguing that in the trial of Caelius, the prosecution introduced murder charges (the sedition at Naples and attacks on the Alexandrian ambassadors) that were irrelevant since they had taken place beyond Rome and a one-mile-wide band around it, as well as charges of murder inside Rome (Dio and the alleged plot against Clodia) that should have been brought under the murder law, not under the *vis* law. But although Jones (1972, 82) leans toward the view that murder outside of Rome was handled by municipal courts throughout Italy—Jones (n. 250) considers the trial of T. Cloelius or Cloulius of Terracina (Cic. *Rosc. Am.* 64; *TLRR* no. 367; see Shackleton Bailey 1988, 36) to be the only doubtful case—it seems clear that in the trial of Cluentius, the prosecution charged the defendant with having poisoned Oppianicus senior when he was in exile and therefore outside of Rome (*Clu.* 169–75). On the second point, the prosecution could have reasonably argued that homicide is a form of *vis* and that it could be prosecuted under the *vis* law as well as under the *lex Cornelia de sicariis et veneficiis*. So while it is true that prosecutors brought up matters that related to statutes other than that under which a particular trial was being held (my second category listed in n. 24 in the present chapter), I would not give as much emphasis to this practice as Cloud does.

27. See chap. 1, n. 109.

28. Giuffrè 1994, 363. On this point, Giuffrè is convincingly challenged by Santalucia (1997, 409–13). See chap. 1, "Advantages for the Prosecution."

29. Ryan (1996b, 196–97) notes that the trial of Atilius took place after the trial of Oppianicus (*Clu.* 88). I regret that my brevity of expression at *TLRR* no. 160 can convey the impression that n. 1 of no. 162 is to be applied in its entirety to no. 160 and that no. 160 could have taken place at a time prior to the *iudicium Iunianum*. The connection is that the three trials mentioned in 1 *Verr.* 39 (those of C. Herennius, C. Popillius, and M. Atilius Bulbus) do not have to be linked to the praetorship of Verres in 74 B.C.

30. Ryan (1996b, 199) dates Gutta's conviction to the period between 70 and 66.

31. On the praenomen, see Shackleton Bailey 1988, 79; Ryan 1996b, 198 n. 17.

32. These are *TLRR* nos. 154 and 170. Ryan (1996b, 201) shows, on the basis of *Clu.* 103, that the outcome of no. 154 was definitely an acquittal, not "uncertain" as I wrote. He shows, on the basis of *Clu.* 103 and 108, that it must be dated to a time after 10 December 74, perhaps in 73. Therefore, the information in *Clu.* 103 that I misapplied to no. 170, specifically acquittal in the first *actio*, should be moved to no. 154.

33. Classen (1972, 3–4 and nn. 8–9) deals with this question but does not consider it important.

34. See Alexander 1982, 162 n. 57.

CHAPTER 10

1. Reams (1986–87) and Berry (appendix 1, pp. 320–21) have shown that there are no grounds for rejecting Dio Cassius's statement (36.44.3) that P. Cornelius was the nephew of L. Cornelius Sulla. My debt to Berry's lucid and very helpful commentary

will be obvious to the readers of this chapter; it has greatly facilitated my study of the *Pro Sulla,* not least in those areas wherein my conclusions differ from his.

2. For a concise description of the provisions of the three *ambitus* laws of the Ciceronian era, with sources, see Berry, 167–68.

3. See Cic. *Off.* 2.29; Dyck 1996, 405–6. In this sense, this Sulla was similar to Chrysogonus and his cronies, though the bond of kinship must have put him much closer to the center of power than the bond of emancipation and patronage did for Chrysogonus. See chap. 8 in the present book.

4. At the time of the trial, L. Manlius Torquatus junior was an *adulescentulus* (Cic. *Fin.* 2.62). If he was praetor in 49, as Caesar says (*B Civ.* 1.24.2–3), then he probably was born in 89, but Shackleton Bailey (*CLA,* 4:342–43) objects that he is not described as praetor in 49 in Cic. *Att.* 8.11b.1 (or in 9.8.1), so Sumner (1973, 139–40) is willing to consider 90 as an alternative. Sumner also points out that if Badian (1964, 151–52) is right that patricians could skip the aedileship, 88 and 87 are possible birth dates for Torquatus junior. Thus, in 66, Torquatus junior reached the age of no older than twenty-four and no younger than twenty-one.

5. The senior Torquatus not only was one of the two defeated candidates in the first consular election in 66 (for 65) but was, like Sulla, a patrician. Since there could be no more than one patrician consul, the original election of Sulla had meant his defeat, and the conviction of Sulla created an opening for him.

6. Cicero's statement (*Sull.* 90) that electoral competition, rather than *inimicitiae,* had drawn both of them ("vos") to the case ("ad causam") shows that both participated. Some scholars believe that the son played the lead role of *nominis delator,* but there is no reason to believe that he was anything other than a *subscriptor;* Asconius (75C) and Dio Cassius (36.44.3) state that the father prosecuted his opponent, and in my view, the two relevant passages from Cicero's works (*Sull.* 49–50; *Fin.* 2.62) do not decisively contradict them (see Ramsey 1982, 129 n. 33; Alexander 1985, 26 n. 20; Alexander 1999). For the opposing view, see Marshall 1985, 261–62; Berry, 4–5 n. 21. On the basis of what we know about some previous legislation, it appears likely that Torquatus junior could have been awarded a *praemium* for the successful prosecution, even if he served in a subordinate role, as long as he was judged the person most responsible for the conviction (see Alexander 1985, 21–22).

7. This is the suggestion of Wiseman (1965), emending "Mallius" at Cic. *Att.* 1.16.16 to "Manlius." See Berry, 187, ad loc.

8. See Nicolet 1966–74, 2: 853, no. 117.

9. Münzer ("Cornelius" no. 19, *RE* 4 [1900]: 1255) suggests that he may have created immunity for himself, but this is hard to square with Cicero's statement that he received no *praemium.*

10. Berry (24) notes, "The prosecution had been able to base their case on their fathers' supposed knowledge of the events concerned." Of course, there was no possibility that the Torquati possessed inside knowledge of the conspiracy. For the motive of Cornelius junior, see n. 25 in the present chapter.

11. Berry (153, 151) suggests that in reality Cicero was miffed at having been excluded from the *consilia* of Torquatus when the latter was consul in 65 and that Hortensius took over the refutation of the so-called First Catilinarian Conspiracy of 66 by default, because Cicero was clearly better qualified to deal with the genuine conspiracy of 63.

12. The Torquatus who made this remark was probably the son, although his father also had Epicurean leanings (Cic. *Fin.* 1.39), and Hortensius's retort could have been directed against either the father or the son. Gellius's description of this speaker as "subagresti homo ingenio et infestivo" [a man with a somewhat crude and charmless nature] (*NA* 1.5.3) does not square with Cicero's praise of the younger Torquatus's "gravitas" [dignity] and "integritas" [uprightness] in the *Brutus* (265), but it is not impossible that both characterizations relate to the same person. For a possible connection to Catullus 61 and 68A, see Münzer, "Manlius," no. 80, *RE* 14 (1928): 1205; Wiseman 1974, 103; Berry, 26.

13. See Berry, 211.

14. Berry, 211.

15. See Berry, 216.

16. See chap. 1 for discussion of this claim.

17. Gabba 1961, 92. Berry (206) says that the word *contubernalis,* meaning literally "sharer of the same tent" and thus "close friend," could refer to mutual attendance on a senior in, for example, military or educational contexts.

18. Berry, 216. For other sources, see *MRR* 2:173.

19. See Sall. *Cat.* 26.5 (*consulibus*); Plut. *Cic.* 14; Dio Cass. 37.29.2–5. At *Sull.* 51, Cicero uses the word *caedem.*

20. Berry, 233.

21. Berry, 233.

22. *Sull.* 52 reads, "Sed quoniam Cornelius ipse etiam nunc de indicando dubitat, ut dicitis . . ." [But since Cornelius himself is even now hesitating about informing, as you say . . .]. For the reading, see Berry, 236, ad loc.

23. See Berry, 155, on *Sull.* 12.8.

24. Berry, 236.

25. Gruen (1995, 284) suggests that Cornelius was perhaps trying to gain some improvement in his father's condition by participating in the prosecution, but the little we know about the rewards for informing against the Catilinarians (Sall. *Cat.* 30.6) mentions, for informers of free status, immunity only for informers themselves, as well as two hundred thousand sesterces. *Ambitus* laws enabled a condemned man to overturn some of the effects of his conviction by prosecuting others for the same crime (see Alexander 1985, 28), but we do not know of such a provision in the *quaestiones perpetuae de vi,* although a *quaestio extraordinaria de vi* may provide one example (see Cic. *Att.* 2.24.4; Cic. *Vat.* 26; Alexander 1985, 31). In any case, the son was serving as prosecutor—which is precisely Cicero's point.

26. On the relationship, see Berry, 2, 241.

27. See *MRR* 2:170.

28. We know that they were held in 60 (Cic. *Vat.* 32; Dio Cass. 37.51.4). Such a long interval between death and funeral games is not unheard of; see Marshall and Baker 1975, 227 n. 31.

29. Berry, 243–44, ad loc.

30. Berry (245) suggests that Cicero's phrase "ad ferramenta prospicienda" (literally, "to scout out hardware") is a euphemism "to soften the fact that Sulla's freedman did assemble arms." But, as Berry points out, the word *ferramenta* had also been used by Cethegus—who claimed to collect arms as a hobby ("se semper bonorum ferramento-

rum studiosum fuisse," Cic. *Cat.* 3.10)—as a cover for procuring *gladii* and *sicae* for the coming revolution (see also Cic. *Cat.* 3.8), whereupon he was exposed to ridicule by Cicero's revelation of the letter he had written to the Allobroges. One can well imagine that this euphemistic phrase had become a standing joke—as "gun collector" might be today if someone tried with that phrase to explain away a cache of weapons stored for a planned uprising—and that rather than being a euphemism that would protect the person engaged in finding weapons, it made him look somewhat ridiculous. According to this interpretation, Cicero is using this language to mock the Catilinarians and remind the listeners of his own anti-Catilinarian credentials, without admitting that this "arms collecting" provided any credibility to Cornelius senior as a witness against Sulla.

31. Sittius was probably not directly involved in this trial, for the phrase *in crimen vocari* can be used to mean "be drawn into a trial [of someone else]"—as in *Sull.* 61, where the phrase is used of the Pompeiani, who are not actual defendants in the trial of Sulla but are the subject of accusation in it. Shackleton Bailey (*CLF*, 1:323), commenting on the passage in Cicero's letters, also concludes that this was not an actual trial of Sittius where Cicero conducted the defense (correcting Gruen 1995, 285 n. 94), arguing that Cicero would have then mentioned this trial in the *Pro Sulla*. I agree with Shackleton Bailey's conclusion but not with his reasoning, since the fact that Sittius had been prosecuted, even if he was acquitted, might have been damaging to Cicero's current client, Sulla.

32. Sallust (*Cat.* 21.3) asserts the involvement of Sittius in the Catilinarian conspiracy, with an army in Spain, along with C. Calpurnius Piso in Hither Spain.

33. On the *annona*, see Cic. *Dom.* 11. Heurgon (1950, 375–76) suggests the possibility that Sittius was involved in the grain trade with Cirta but that the trial was *de vi*. As Gruen (1995, 285 n. 94) points out, there is no evidence for this point of view; in fact, Appian (*B Civ.* 4.54) talks of a civil suit: Σίττιος ἐν Ῥώμῃ δίκην ἰδίαν οὐχ ὑποστὰς ἔφυγε [Sittius, not resisting a private suit at Rome, fled]. See also Dio Cass. 43.3.1. Berry (1992, 110), in his review of *TLRR*, correctly points out the omission of this trial.

34. Berry, 232, 245–50.

35. Shackleton Bailey, *CLF*, 1:323.

36. Syme 1964, 100–101. Syme argues that Sallust has retrojected this much later military activity back into the sixties.

37. See Berry, 245. Berry (247, on *Sull.* 56.2) regards this defense as decisive.

38. Berry (248, 250) argues that Cicero's phrase "praediis deminutis" (*Sull.* 56), implying sale of some assets, provides more reliable testimony than his phrase "omnis suas possessiones" (58).

39. See Berry, 245.

40. Berry, 248.

41. Cicero's wording at *Sull.* 60 implies that even the colonists realized the justice of Sulla's settlement (see Berry, 253, on *Sull.* 60.11). On the colony at Pompeii, see Hampl 1952, 65–66.

42. Wiseman 1977.

43. This is probably the father-in-law of Rullus, mentioned by Cicero (*Leg. agr.* 2.69, 3.3) as having reaped enormous amounts of land from the Sullan proscriptions. See the commentary of Nisbet and Hubbard in Horace 1978, 2:167–68; Gabba 1976, 202 n. 187; Brunt 1971, 303 n. 8. This background is similar to Sulla's (discussed earlier in the present chapter).

44. Berry (167–68, 260–61) provides sources and citations to modern scholarship on the development of *ambitus* penalties. The two main sources are *Schol. Bob.* 78–79St (on *Sull.* 17) and Dio Cass. 36.38.1, 37.25.3.

45. See Marshall 1985, 245–46, ad loc. Lintott (1968, 133) says that a *derogatio* was merely an exhortation from the Senate to a magistrate to bring a certain measure before an assembly.

46. For the development of *ambitus* legislation, see also Gruen 1995, 212–24.

47. Reams (1986–87, 305) shows that L. Caecilius Rufus was the son of a Caecilius Rufus born from the marriage of P. Sulla's mother to a Caecilius Rufus who married her after her first husband, the dictator's brother, had died. See also Berry, 1, 258–59.

48. Stone 1998.

49. For a family tree, see Berry, 2, fig. 1.

50. See Berry, 267.

51. See Berry, 265–66.

52. Ramsey 1982, followed by Berry (271–72).

53. See Sumner 1965.

54. Berry (273–74) explains that "fere" is to be taken with "omnibus" in *Sull.* 69, and he emphasizes that the word *fere* here implies less in the way of omission than does the English word *almost*. Nevertheless, the word *fere* does imply that some charges have not been dignified with a refutation, possibly because they are either valid or at least irrefutable.

55. See Berry, 232.

56. Ramsey (1999, 724–25) also takes issue with Berry's evaluation of the strength or weakness of Cicero's various rebuttals. Ramsey argues that Cicero does in fact follow the practice of slipping his weaker points between the stronger or more impressive arguments that Cicero wants the jurors to remember. However, Ramsey says that Cicero was "on firmer ground" in his rebuttals of the Sittius charge and the charge of recruiting gladiators.

57. See Berry, 21–22. Berry (20) quotes with approval the statement of Gruen (1995, 284) that Cornelius "added little adornment to the cause," but it would be surprising if such a nonentity were entrusted with presenting five out of eight charges.

58. See Berry, 11 n. 62.

59. Berry, 34.

60. Berry, 35–36.

61. Berry, 38.

62. See Gell. *NA* 12.12.2–4, corroborated by Cic. *Att.* 1.16.10, where it is clear that this purchase by Cicero has attracted criticism. See Berry, 31.

63. Berry (40–41) makes a good case that he did not.

64. See Dyck 1996, 405–6; Berry, 1, 13. On the date of the composition of the *De officiis*, see Dyck 1996, 8–10.

CHAPTER 11

1. Shackleton Bailey (1991, 5–6; 1988, 13) points out that *Albinovanus* is a *gentilicium* and therefore that this person cannot be amalgamated with M. Tullius, even if the lat-

ter's praenomen were in fact *P.* Cicero (*Har. resp.* 12) and the Bobbian scholiast (125St) provides the praenomen *P.* for Albinovanus.

2. Pocock (131) is right that we have no evidence of any assistance provided to the prosecution by Clodius. Tatum (1999, 206–7) also minimizes the role of Clodius.

3. Pocock (136–37) identifies four stages prior to the altercation between Vatinius and Cicero: (1) the proceedings before the actual trial ("ab initio" [from the beginning]); (2) Vatinius's presentation of information ("paullo ante imprudens indicasti" [a little before you incautiously informed]); (3) evidence presented by Vatinius on that same occasion, that is, the day before the delivery of Vatinius's speech and Cicero's response (which was the *In Vatinium*), that is, "hesterno die [or "heri te" in Maslowski's Teubner text] pro testimonio" [yesterday in your [Vatinus's] testimony] (*Vat.* 3); and (4) on that day, a violent attack on Vatinius by Cicero (*Vat.* 1.). The second stage involved *indicium* (informing) as opposed to *testimonium* (testimony).

4. Pocock, 140.

5. Tatum (1999, 206) suggests that the prosecution's praise of Milo may indicate that Vatinius was right to claim that the prosecution was colluding with the defense.

6. A possible reason why Clodius used a *iudicium populi* to prosecute Milo— besides "*popularis* archaism" (see Lintott 1968, 199)—was the crowded docket in the *quaestiones.*

7. Pocock (3–5, 134–36) defends the authenticity of the speeches by Vatinius and Cicero, whereas Gundel ("Vatinius," *RE* 2.8 [1955]: 505) leaves the matter in doubt. Since *ORF* does not contain an entry for Vatinius, Malcovati may not have believed that Vatinius really delivered a speech and that Cicero really responded in a speech of his own.

8. Pocock, 4.

9. Pocock, 135 n. 3.

10. Pocock, 136. Quintilian does not say that Cicero delivered a separate *actio* against Vatinius. Quintilian is writing here about how speeches are published, not about how they are delivered. If one looks at the whole section (*Inst.* 5.7.3–6), which is part of a discussion of witnesses, we see that Quintilian first makes the distinction between the *actio* and the *interrogatio*. He then says that in the speeches, one often presents arguments first about the credibility of witnesses in general and then about the credibility of certain classes of witnesses. Finally, he says that the orator sometimes attacks certain individuals and that in very many speeches, we read a kind of attack either incorporated into the defense ("insectationis genus et permixtum defensioni") or, sometimes, published separately ("separatim editum"), as in the attack on the witness Vatinius. This analysis would be consistent with either of two possibilities: either (1) Cicero attacked Vatinius in the original (orally delivered) *Pro Sestio* but published it separately, or (2) Cicero delivered a separate speech against Vatinius and could have incorporated it into the published *Pro Sestio* but instead left it in its original, freestanding form.

11. Pocock, 196–97. Albini (1959, 177–78) also argues for the authenticity of the speech as we have it, maintaining that both Cicero's reply to Vatinius's criticism of his attempt to reconcile with Caesar and the other two points cited in the letter to Lentulus could have occurred between *Vat.* 4 and 5. Moreover, he argues, it would do no good for Cicero to delete in a published version critical references to Caesar, because Caesar could obtain the original.

12. Pocock, 136.

13. See Pocock, 140–42.

14. See also *lex agraria,* line 38 (*Statutes,* 1:117, no. 2); *lex de provinciis praetoriis,* Cnidos copy, col. V, line 34 (*Statutes,* 1:244, no. 11).

15. These speeches evidently were still classified as constituting the *interrogatio* (Cicero uses the term *interrogatio* to describe his speech [*Vat.* 40; *Fam.* 1.9.7]), and the fiction of question-and-answer is implied at the end of the *In Vatinium* ("Sed ut aliquando audiamus, quam copiose mihi ad rogata respondeas, concludam iam interrogationem meam" [But that we may at some point hear how full your answers are to my questions, I will end my examination] [40]; "Extremum illud est quod mihi abs te responderi velim . . ." [The final point on which I would like to receive an answer from you is . . .] [41]), as well as by the multitude of questions (generally rhetorical) employed in the speech. Of course, if the main issue here was *praevaricatio,* an offense that involves the defense as well as the prosecution, one would hardly have expected Cicero to have recalled this issue in his letter to Lentulus.

16. For the chronology, see Sherwin-White 1985, 231.

17. Claudius (*FIRA* 1:44) proposed that prosecutors who failed to appear in court should be found guilty of *calumnia* on the spot. See Momigliano 1932, 132; Levy 1933, 213 = 1963, 418–19; Levick 1990, 118; Lintott 1992, 130. Claudius had the reputation for sometimes giving peremptory legal judgments (Suet. *Claud.* 15).

18. To make it clear that the prosecution had raised the issue of the *optimates,* Cicero uses the phrase "natio optimatium" with the phrases "sic enim dixisti" [for so you said] and "ut dixisti" [as you said] in these two passages, as well as "quam tu 'nationem' appellasti" [whom you have called a "breed"] in *Sest.* 97.

19. See *Schol. Bob.* 125St. For *relativum, relatio criminis,* or *translatio criminis,* see Cic. *Inv. rhet.* 2.78; *Rhet. Her.* 1.25. For *compensatio* or *comparatio,* see Cic. *Inv. rhet.* 2.72; *Rhet. Her.* 1.25.

20. Cf., for example, Meyer 1919, 135 n. 2 ("eine politische Broschüre"); Wood 1988, 62 ("primarily a manifesto"); Badian in *OCD³,* s.v. "Publius Sestius" ("optimate manifesto").

21. The classic explication of this phrase is Wirszubski 1954 (= Seager 1969, 183–95).

22. Pocock (5–7) argues that despite Cicero's claims to separate Caesar from Vatinius (*Vat.* 13, 15), his attack on the tribunate of Vatinius would necessarily be seen as an attack on Caesar. Smith (1966, 172) states that the issue in the *Pro Sestio* "was between Caesarism and Ciceronianism," and Fuhrmann (1992, 100) says that the attacks against Vatinius "hit the triumvirate on whose behalf he had acted, and Caesar in particular."

23. Stockton 1971, 205–6. Stockton may be interpreting this passage in light of a remark by Cicero in his letter to Lentulus, "dixi me M. Bibuli fortunam, quam ille adflictam putaret, omnium triumphis victoriisque anteferre" [I said . . . that I thought M. Bibulus' sad plight (as Vatinius regarded it) preferable to any man's Triumphs and victories] (*Fam.* 1.9.7; trans. Shackleton Bailey). Note, however, that Shackleton Bailey (*CLF,* 1:309) does not find any such statement in our texts of the *Pro Sestio* or the *In Vatinium.*

24. Gruen 1969b, 91 n. 94. Gruen implies that these passages were added in the published version of the speech.

25. Mitchell 1969, 311. For an opposing point of view, see Tatum 1999, 207.

26. Mitchell 1991, 174.

27. Tatum 1999, 206.

28. Marshall (1976, 121) writes, "Crassus realised that there was no point in continuing opposition now that Cicero was back; he might even work with him in the hope that he could be made useful."

29. See the sources cited by Mitchell (1969, 314 n. 46).

30. Therefore, I cannot agree with Thierfelder's formulation (1965, 400) that Cicero's digression on the *optimates* should be viewed as an example of the phenomenon "daß Cicero in manchen Fällen über das Prozeßdienliche hinausging" [that in many instances Cicero went beyond what was useful to the trial], if Thierfelder means that Cicero served himself rather than his client. The digression is a logical part of Cicero's *refutatio* against the prosecution case and thereby serves his client; this observation of mine does not deny that Cicero's praise of the *optimates* may also accord with or even advance his own political beliefs. Thierfelder also states that all this is fundamentally important to the case, citing the scholiast (*Schol. Bob.* 125St) to this effect, and if the previously quoted statement from Theirfelder means only that Cicero speaks at greater length and more explicitly on the *optimates* than the case demands (see Thierfelder 1965, 406), I cannot prove Thierfelder wrong, since it is hard to estimate how effective an abbreviated speech would have been compared to the extant version.

31. Mitchell 1969, 308–9.

CHAPTER 12

1. Gruen 1995, 307.

2. See Wiseman 1994, 391–92; see also 373. For a description of Egyptian affairs that related to the trial, see Tatum 1999, 194–96.

3. Strabo (17.1.11 [C 796]) puts the responsibility for these actions on Pompey himself.

4. Even Cicero has praise for a peroration of Clodius as "sane disertus" (*Att.* 4.15.4). See Tatum 1999, 41, 262 n. 46.

5. Suetonius (*gramm. et rhet.* 26.2) says that Gallus was ridiculed by Caelius in this trial as a "hordearius rhetor," that is, a "barley-bread"—therefore, "cut-rate" or "ersatz"—rhetorician. Suetonius's use of the verb *dictasse* implies that Atratinus was, in Kaster's phrase, "a mere schoolboy parroting his teacher." See Kaster's commentary in Suetonius 1995, 295–97, ad loc. At some point in his long career ("nam diutissime vixit" [for he lived to an advanced age], Suet. *gramm. et rhet.* 26.2), Gallus coauthored a book about gesture in oratory (Quint. *Inst.* 11.3.143).

6. Craig 1981, 34. See also Picheca 1980.

7. It is generally accepted that this was L. Calpurnius Bestia, whom Cicero had successfully defended against Caelius in February, though not necessarily in the pending trial involving the same two principals and the same kind of charge. See Münzer 1909; Austin, *Pro Caelio*³, appendix VI, pp. 154–55, 157; Badian 1968b, 5; Shackleton Bailey 1991, 90; Broughton 1991, 35–36.

8. Syme (1939, 269) says that Atratinus spent a "dissipated youth in the circle of Clodius." I do not know what evidence there is for this assertion other than Cicero's

statement, addressing Atratinus, that anyone of Atratinus's age lies open to the kind of charges that he made against Caelius. This statement may be designed to plant in the jurors' minds a suspicion that Atratinus is also guilty of uncontrolled behavior, but it is too vague to allow us to draw that conclusion.

9. So argues Heinze (1925, 196). Arguing for identification are Münzer (1909, 140 n. 2) and Reitzenstein (1925, 32).

10. Heinze 1925, 196 n. 3. It is possible that a *patronus* was present for only part of the trial. In two works (*De or.* 2.313; *Brut.* 207), Cicero decries the bad consequences of the practice of having many *patroni* speak for the defendant. In the *Brutus*, he implies that some of the defense speakers replied to a prosecution case that they themselves had not heard. This is not precisely the same as a *patronus* delivering his part of the defense case and then not staying for the rest of the case. However, Cicero's following complaint— that when several *patroni* speak, it can happen that each one begins the case anew and that the different speeches are not properly coordinated (*Brut.* 208)—makes it seem more likely that a defense speaker might deliver his speech one day and not reappear the next day to hear his colleagues on the defense team. The same could also have been true of multiple prosecutors.

11. Dorey 1958, 175 n. 3.

12. Gotoff 1986, 131. Herennius reappears briefly as someone who summoned into court slaves connected with the trial of Milo in 52 (Asc. 34C), though questions about punctuation make it doubtful exactly what his exact role was (see Austin, *Pro Caelio*[3], 78; Marshall 1985, 173; *TLRR* no. 307). Whether he is related, as Gruen (1995, 307) suggests, to the C. Herennius who helped arrange for the transfer of Clodius into plebeian status (Cic. *Att.* 1.18.4, 1.19.5) must be a matter for speculation.

13. See Austin, *Pro Caelio*[3], appendix III, pp. 148–50.

14. See Sumner 1973, 146–47; *MRR* Suppl., 44.

15. For a brief biography, see Austin, *Pro Caelio*[3], v–xiii.

16. For a sober biography of the real Clodia, see Skinner 1983.

17. Cicero's phrase is "libidines et delicias," translated as "depraved caprice" by Austin (*Pro Caelio*[3], 133, ad loc.).

18. These are Austin's translations (*Pro Caelio*[3], 140) of "absolutum muliebri gratia" and "libidini muliebri condonatum" (*Cael.* 78).

19. Dorey (1958) also reaches this conclusion.

20. Here, I differ with Stroh (1975, 257 n. 70), who argues that while the contrast in *Cael.* 20 between "accusare" and "oppugnare" might seem to recall the same contrast in *Cael.* 1, where it is clear that Clodia attacks him "opibus meretriciis," Clodia cannot be meant as the unseen attacker in section 20, because Cicero goes on to give grudging praise to those who defend their associates or stand up for themselves when injured and because he could not describe Clodia in this manner. Stroh argues that the word *accusare* is being used for those who are going to testify against Caelius. I agree that the witnesses (and, I would add, the *nominis delator* and the *subscriptores*) are those by whom "palam in eum tela iaciuntur" [spears are openly thrown at him] (*Cael.* 20). But when we look at the flow of the argument, we see that Cicero is trying to persuade the jury to dismiss the testimony of a senator who claims that Caelius attacked him and of other men who say that he attacked their wives when they were returning home from a banquet (20). Since Cicero apparently cannot deny the charges, he resorts to a com-

monplace about the unreliability of witnesses (22) and the ease with which their testimony can be distorted. He argues that witnesses can be manipulated ("in voluntate testium . . . quae facillime fingi" [on the inclinations of witnesses, which can be very easily shaped]). Even if they are sincere in their accusations, notes Cicero, they are being used by others, and these manipulators are the people by whom "clam subministrantur" [[the spears] are secretly furnished] (20), one of whom could well be Clodia. Of course, if Clodia really did think that Caelius had tried to poison her, she could justifiably class herself among those who Cicero describes as follows: "laesi dolent, irati efferuntur, pugnant lacessiti" [when hurt they feel grief, when angered they cry out, when provoked they fight] (21). In reality, then, if she was going to appear as a witness, her actions and enmity were open to view, not hidden. I agree with Stroh that Heinze (1925, 215), Drexler (1944, 16), and Austin (*Pro Caelio³*, 72, on *Cael.* 21.7) are wrong to associate Cicero's phrase "in eos quibus gloriosum etiam hoc esse debet" [against those to whom even this [prosecution] should be praiseworthy] specifically with the Clodii, since I think that he is referring to the potential witnesses who are going to testify to their injuries and those of people associated with them. As Stroh points out, Cicero later (*Cael.* 68) implicitly denies an alliance between Clodia and other Clodii. We could better evaluate the role of the Clodii if we knew more about the *subscriptor* P. Clodius.

21. He was not really so young, since he was about thirty (born in 87; see later in this chapter and n. 56). For the double standard, see Craig 1994–95, 413–14.

22. This proscription is cited by Mommsen (1899, 403 n. 1), Dorey (1958, 178 n. 3), Wiseman (1985, 85), and Bauman (1992, 70–71).

23. Bruun (1997) has ingeniously found a connection to brothels and Clodia in Cicero's reference to the Aqua Appia of Appius Claudius Caecus (*Cael.* 34), on the basis of a quotation of a speech from Caelius six years later (in Frontin. *Aq.* 76.1–2) and on the basis of a clause found at this point in the *Pro Caelio*: "ut ea [aqua] tu inceste uterere" [so that you might use it [water] unchastely]. He argues that Cicero is reminding his audience about a common practice of illegally diverting water to brothels and that he is implying that Clodia is misappropriating publicly supplied water for her brothel. Butrica (1999a, 1999b) responds that the clause in the *Pro Caelio* could also refer to washing the mouth after fellatio and that prostitutes customarily used water for douching after sexual intercourse.

24. The custom that the Roman prostitute and convicted adulteress wore the same male dress, the toga, may suggest that the Romans or at least Roman men perceived a connection between the two groups of women. See Marquardt 1886, 44 n. 1.

25. A *quadrans* was the usual bath fee for men, and references to it and its derivatives were easily associated with the bath fee ("quadrante lavatum" [to wash for a farthing], Hor. *Sat.* 1.3.137; "res quadrantaria" [a matter of a farthing], Sen. *Ep.* 86.9), even without context (Mart. 3.30.4)—just as Americans still associate a dime with the price of a phone call. To pay a *quadrans* was to act like a man (Juv. 6.447), since women paid more (cf. the *lex metalli Vipascensis* [Bruns 1909, no. 112, lines 22–23]).

26. Williams (1994, 78–79) points out the double implication of Cicero's phrase "quadrantaria Clytemnestra" (that Clodia was no better than a prostitute and that she had poisoned her husband) and finds a parallel in Greek. Austin (*Pro Caelio³*, 171), in his supplementary note, suggests that Mart. 3.93.14, which pictures the *balneator* admitting to his baths tomb-frequenting (thus, probably the lowest-level) prostitutes after he has

extinguished his lamp (presumably, after the closing hour), suggests another implication of the passage. McDermott (1970, 41–42) suggests a reference to Clodia's status as "quarta" [fourth] among five sisters as another source of the epithet's relevance.

27. The word also recalls *coire*, meaning "to engage in sexual intercourse." See Wiseman 1985, 44.

28. This interpretation of the second riddle quoted by Quintilian from Caelius fits with the first enigmatic phrase that he cites from the same source, "quadrantariam Clytaemestram" (see the preceding paragraph in the present chapter). Clytemnestra was, in her own way, very alluring when she met Agamemnon in public upon his return from Troy, but she was considerably more hostile to him in private, where she killed him.

29. It is possible that the lover who played this trick on her was the mysterious Vettius of Cic. *Cael.* 71 (see Austin, *Pro Caelio*[3], 134 ad loc.; Wiseman 1985, 38–39).

30. Dorey (1958, 175 n. 3) writes: ". . . it is inconceivable that, had Clodia's family been giving their official sanction to the prosecution, they would not have selected some more weighty and responsible representative. It seems that he was some nonentity whom Clodia had induced to appear to give the impression that she had the support of her family." Of course, this interpretation of Clodian tactics is dependent on the premise that P. Clodius is not P. Clodius Pulcher (see discussion earlier in the present chapter).

31. *Cael.* 32 reads, "nec enim muliebris umquam inimicitias mihi gerendas putavi, praesertim cum ea quam omnes semper amicam omnium potius quam cuiusquam inimicam putaverunt" [for I never thought that I would have to carry on a feud with a woman, especially with one who everyone has always thought was everyone's girlfriend rather than anyone's enemy].

32. We do not know whether she ever appeared as one. It is possible that she never appeared as a witness because Cicero's vilification of her was so effective that her testimony would have been more damaging to the prosecution than to the defense.

33. A comparison between Clodia and Medea can be found in Volpe 1977 (317–18):

> Atratinus evidently began by calling Caelius a "pretty little Jason" (*pulchellum Iasonem*) while Caelius retorted that in that case Atratinus must have been a "curly-haired Pelias" (*Pelia cincinnatus*). (Note: The joke rests on the charge that Caelius tried to steal the gold of Clodia and then deserted her as Jason had taken the golden fleece with the aid of Media [*sic!*] and then deserted her. Pelias was an opponent of Jason and tried to dethrone him.) Crassus carried on the mythological reference by quoting a passage of Ennius' *Medea exsul* in reference to the embassy of Dio. Cicero topped everyone, deliberately distorting the passage "to entertain his audience" by referring to Clodia as the "Media of the Palatine" (*Palatinam Medeam*), a particularly biting retort since Media had poisoned her children to be with her lover, Jason, and Clodia's husband had died mysteriously—Cicero insinuates by poisoning—immediately prior to her affair with Caelius.

The Medea legend was well known at Rome. According to Jocelyn's commentary in Ennius 1967 (346), besides Ennius's *Medea exul,* Cicero knew of Pacuvius's *Medus* and Accius's *Medea.* On the treatment of Medea in Roman drama, see Arcellaschi 1990.

34. *Cael.* 26 reads, "fuisse meo necessario Bestiae Caelium familiarem, cenasse apud eum, ventitasse domum, studuisse praeturae" [that Caelius had been a friend to my associate Bestia, that he had often dined at his home, that he had frequently visited his house, and that he had supported his bid for a praetorship].

35. For rewards for prosecutors, especially in *ambitus* cases, see Alexander 1985, 28–29.

36. For a family tree of the Claudii, see Wiseman 1985, 16–17.

37. So Kaster's commentary in Suetonius 1995 (296) is correct: "Caelius' phrase *Pelia cincinnatus,* prob. applied to Atratinus."

38. Münzer 1909, 136 n. 3.

39. Gardner's Loeb edition (Cicero 1958, 428 n. a) mistakenly says that Crassus's point in citing the Ennian passage was "to show what a calamity it was that the deputation led by Dio had ever reached Italy." This differs from what Cicero says (". . . cum de adventu regis Ptolemaei quereretur" [. . . when he was complaining about the arrival of King Ptolemy], *Cael.* 18). Volpe (1977, 317–18) makes the same mistake.

40. Salzman (1982) makes the case that since the trial was being held during the Ludi Megalenses, the jurors would naturally have associated Clodia, the older woman, with the Magna Mater, while they would have associated Caelius, the handsome but unfaithful younger man, with Attis. Just as the Magna Mater punished Attis by castration, so Clodia would be seen as trying to punish Caelius through the prosecution. If the jurors would have made this association, they would have done so under the influence of Cicero, since he was the speaker who claimed that Clodia was behind the prosecution.

41. This was evident by the time of the trial, though it may not have been so at the time of the association. See Wiseman 1985, 67.

42. See Wiseman 1985, 59, 67.

43. As Austin notes (*Pro Caelio³,* 69, on *Cael.* 18), Caelius retorted with the same theme by describing Pelias/Atratinus as "cincinnatus" (cited at Quint. *Inst.* 1.5.61). Effeminacy was a prime charge in ancient invective; for example, Cato expressed scorn for the Third Mithridatic War as one fought with "mulierculae" [little women] (*Mur.* 31), as a way to dismiss the accomplishments of Murena in it (see chap. 6 in this volume). The term *pulchellus* was clearly insulting, and even *pulcher* could have the same connotation, as Servius (*Ad Aen.* 3.119) explains in connection with Lucil. 1.16; see Münzer 1909, 137, 136 n. 3.

44. See Alexander 1982, especially 153–64; chap. 1 in this volume, "Advantages for the Prosecution."

45. There was also a *lex Lutatia de vi,* passed by Q. Lutatius Catulus, probably in 78 B.C. when he was consul, in the context of the uprising of Aemilius Lepidus, and Cicero refers to that statute (*Cael.* 70) in language that seems to suggest that the trial of Caelius was being held under it. However, as Hough (1930, 143) points out, Cicero's point is to contrast the seriousness of the threat that law was designed to counter with the allegedly nugatory charges brought against Caelius. The date of the *lex Plautia* (or *Plotia*), probably a successor to that law, is unknown. There were two laws passed by a tribune called Plautius or Plotius in 70, and this could be a third (see *MRR* 2:130 n. 4). The law must have been passed by 63, when a prosecution under it was begun against Catiline (*TLRR* no. 223). For a full discussion, see Lintott 1968, 109–23. For the current standing of the question, see Cloud 1994, 524; Cloud maintains that we do not know what different

types of *vis* the two laws covered, if there was such a distinction. See also the introduction to part 3 in the present book. One would expect that any statute that established a *quaestio publica*, as both of these did, pertained to offenses that affected the res publica, not just private interests. This was the case with the charges against Caelius, since violence against a legation to the Roman Senate was at issue.

46. To be more precise, to the extent that we can judge by the analogy of the *lex repetundarum* (line 56), if Caelius had previously been tried on a *vis* charge (regardless of whether the verdict was guilty or innocent), no actions of his that had occurred prior to that first trial would have been admissible in this case. However, to judge by Cicero's description of his client's previous career, he had never before been charged with *vis*. See Alexander 1982, 142–50.

47. For a more activist interpretation of the role of the presiding magistrate in a *quaestio perpetua*, see Bauman 1996, 25–26.

48. Cicero has a personal interest in defending Caelius against these personal attacks, since he served as his mentor in the period from 66–64 (*Cael.* 10) and was therefore somewhat responsible for the formation of his character.

49. See Austin, *Pro Caelio*³, 46.

50. See Riggsby 1995a, 246.

51. On the reading of the name, see Austin, *Pro Caelio*³, appendix II, pp. 146–47.

52. See Linderski 1961a = 1995, no. 16, 204–17, 647–49. Shackleton Bailey (*CLQf*, 178) expresses agreement with Linderski's findings and summarizes them in his comment on *Q Fr.* 2.3.5.

53. See Alexander 1985, 28–29.

54. Heinz 1925, 212.

55. Drexler 1944, 13.

56. See Sumner 1971, 248. Sumner points to the passage (*Cael.* 18) in which Cicero specifically states that in 59, Caelius was of an age to run for office. Cicero's silence about this office does not concern Sumner, and Sumner's stricture on the argument from silence (248 n. 11) deserves quotation:

> The argument from silence is, as usual, treacherous. Cicero's failure to mention Caelius' quaestorship could have various explanations: e.g., it had been dealt with by the previous speakers, M. Crassus and Caelius himself, and was not relevant to Cicero's line of defence; or Cicero preferred not to discuss it, seeing that in 58–57 Caelius had been closely associated with Cicero's enemy P. Clodius.

See also Sumner 1973, 146–47. Broughton (*MRR* Suppl., 44) is inclined to agree with Sumner, although he is troubled by Cicero's failure to mention this office in his speech.

57. Crook 1967, 120.

58. Craig 1994–95, 413.

59. Stroh 1975, 243–98.

60. Heinze 1925, 228, 245–48.

61. I accept the current commonly held view against Catullus 77.1 as referring to M. Caelius Rufus. See Wiseman 1969, 56–60; Stroh 1975, 297–98.

62. Reitzenstein 1925, 32.

63. For this conundrum, see Wiseman 1969, 56–60.

324 Notes to Pages 235–37

64. Cicero castigates Catiliniarians as people "qui nitent unguentis, qui fulgent purpura" [who glisten with perfumes, who gleam with purple (*Cat.* 2.5). Use of *unguenta* was one of the signs of excessive luxury. Scipio Africanus (*apud* Gell. *NA* 6.12.5) lists the daily use of perfumes first as one characteristic among many that mark the *cinaedus* (this term, which can mean "catamite," often refers to an effeminate man or a man living a luxurious life). See also Sen. *Ep.* 86.11, 13; 108.16; 122.3; Sen. *Dial.* 7.7.3. Ulpian (*Dig.* 15.3.3.6) cites Labeo's description of "ad luxuriae materiam" [luxury items], first of which are *unguenta,* along with "si quid ad delicias vel si quid ad turpes sumptus sumministravit" [things for titillation or vicious practices] (trans. Weir, ed. Watson). Perfumes were associated specifically with *comissationes* (drinking parties), with which the prosecutors taunted the defendant (*Cael.* 35); see Hug, "Salben," *RE* 2.1 (1920): 1855.

65. Wiseman 1985, 51.

66. See Treggiari 1991, 500. Treggiari argues that Clodia filled the role of the "stereotypical merry widow, free to love where she would and happy in the control of her life and fortune," although she also believes that Clodia opened herself to the imputation of behaving like a courtesan. Wiseman (1969, 58–59) sums up the realities of the situation in this way, in connection with Catullus's Lesbia, whichever of the three sisters Clodiae she was:

> . . . she [Clodia Metelli] had herself been given in marriage to a great politician (all the Clodiae had consular husbands), and since her own family lacked the funds to match their ambition, it is hard to imagine her and her sisters being left unproductively single for very long after death and divorce had sundered them from Lucullus, Marcius Rex and Metellus Celer. . . . What is surprising is not the notion that the Clodiae might have remarried, but the fact that Clodia Metelli had evidently not yet done so at the time of the *pro Caelio,* three years after Metellus Celer's death.

67. Austin (*Pro Caelio*[3], 69) classifies the first two allegations not as *crimina* but as "Caeli diffamatio," but they seem to fall within the *vis* law, as I will explain, and therefore to be *crimina.* Neither of these two charges are found in Austin's appendix V (pp. 152–54) or in Lintott (1968, 111), and I missed the second in *TLRR* (no. 275).

68. Cicero's speech would lead us to believe that the refutation of charges was delegated not to Caelius but to Crassus. However, Quintilian (*Inst.* 4.2.27) implies that one of the reasons why Cicero does not and should not deal with the *crimina* (specifically *veneficium*) without thoroughly discussing the character issues is that Caelius has already defended himself against the *crimina*: "tum deinde narret de bonis Pallae totamque de vi explicet causam, quae est ipsius actione defensa?" (quoted with translation later in this chapter). Quintilian had evidently read the speech of Caelius, as is implied by his praise of Caelius's moderation, suitable for a defendant whose *caput* was in danger (11.1.51)—though Caelius had a reputation for a grand style, which he gained in three prosecutions (Cic. *Brut.* 273; cf. Quint. *Inst.* 6.3.69).

69. The authenticity of this rubric has been questioned; see Austin, *Pro Caelio*[3], 70–71, on *Cael.* 19.

70. Heinze 1925, 201.

71. Craig (1994–95, 411) writes, "The charges against Caelius were all connected to

his role in interfering with a group of Alexandrian ambassadors (thus the charges *de seditionibus Neapolitanis, de Alexandrinorum pulsatione Puteolana,* and perhaps *de bonis Pallae,* all in sec. 23)."

72. As Heinze (1925, 201) and Lintott (1968, 112 n. 1) point out, the *lex Iulia* forbade those with imperium from attacking *legati.* However, I do not agree with Lintott that Ulp. *Dig.* 48.6.7 supports this point, since I believe that the passage mentions *legati,* along with *oratores comitesve,* as potential perpetrators rather than victims.

73. See also Callistratus *Dig.* 5.1.37.

74. Ciaceri 1930, 11–12. It has also been suggested that Palla is a female relative of Atratinus by marriage: see Austin, *Pro Caelio*³, 74, on *Cael.* 23; Wiseman 1974, 120–21. But Wiseman (1985, 68 n. 76) now believes that this is Πώλλα, a man. Shackleton Bailey (1988, 74) favors the reading "Palla."

75. We may be justified in inferring from the conditional nature of the clause that Cicero is raising the possibility that the prosecution would call them as witnesses, since we may presume that Cicero knew whom the defense was going to call.

76. See Heinze 1925, 222 n. 1.

77. For *testimonium per tabulas datum* (testimony given in writing), see Austin, *Pro Caelio*³, 116–17, on *Cael.* 55. If no testimony was to be obtained from the slaves of Lucceius, the reason could have been that he had not given permission (perhaps to spare them the torture that this examination would have required), but the exercise of that right was limited in this period to testimony against a slave's master (see Buckland 1908, 88) and would therefore imply that the prosecution case implicated Lucceius in some way, at least for his failure to prevent the plot, if not for active complicity.

78. Hollis (1998) argues that Cicero here (*Cael.* 67) alludes to a tragedy, *Equus Troianus.*

APPENDIX 2

1. See Shackleton Bailey 1988, 65.

2. For the identification of this witness with the one mentioned at 2 *Verr.* 1.71 and for his status, see Shackleton Bailey 1988, 92–93.

3. It is more obvious that he is going to be a witness if the correct reading is "dicet" than if it is "dicit."

4. Shackleton Bailey (1988, 83) prefers the manuscript reading "Rabonius."

5. On the praenomen, see Shackleton Bailey 1988, 91.

Works Cited

Adamietz, Joachim. 1986. "Ciceros Verfahren in den Ambitus-Prozessen gegen Murena und Plancius." *Gymnasium* 93:102–17.

Afzelius, Adam. 1942. "Zwei Episoden aus dem Leben Ciceros." *CM* 5:209–17.

Albini, Umberto. 1959. "L'orazione contro Vatinio." *PP* 14:172–84.

Alexander, Michael C. 1976. "Hortensius' Speech in Defense of Verres." *Phoenix* 30:46–53.

———. 1977. "Forensic Advocacy in the Late Roman Republic." Ph.D. diss., University of Toronto.

———. 1982. "Repetition of Prosecution, and the Scope of Prosecutions, in the Standing Criminal Courts of the Late Republic." *CA* 1:141–66.

———. 1984. "Compensation in a Roman Criminal Law." *University of Illinois Law Review*, 521–39.

———. 1985. "*Praemia* in the *Quaestiones* of the Late Republic." *CP* 80:20–32.

———. 1990. *Trials in the Late Roman Republic, 149 B.C. to 50 B.C.* Phoenix Supplement 26. Toronto: University of Toronto Press.

———. 1993. "How Many Roman Senators Were Ever Prosecuted? The Evidence from the Late Republic." *Phoenix* 47:238–55.

———. 1999. "The Role of Torquatus the Younger in the *Ambitus* Prosecution of Sulla in 66 B.C., and Cicero *De finibus* 2.62." *CP* 94:65–69.

———. 2000. "The Repudiated Technicality in Roman Forensic Oratory." In *Lex et Romanitas: Essays for Alan Watson*, ed. Michael Hoeflich, 59–72. Studies in Comparative Legal History. Berkeley: Robbins Collection Publications.

Apsines. 1997. *Art of Rhetoric*. In *Two Greek Rhetorical Treatises from the Roman Empire: Introduction, Text, and Translation of the Arts of Rhetoric Attributed to Anonymous*

Seguerianus and to Apsines of Gadara, ed. Mervin R. Dilts and George A. Kennedy. *Mnemosyne* Supplement 168. Leiden: Brill.

Arcellaschi, André. 1990. *Médée dans le théâtre latin d'Ennius à Sénèque.* Collection de l'école française de Rome 132. Rome: École française de Rome.

Asconius Pedianus, Quintus. 1990. *Commentaries on Five Speeches of Cicero.* Ed. and trans. Simon Squires. Wauconda, IL: Bolchazy-Carducci.

Axer, Jerzy. 1998. "A Reasonable Doubt: Cicero and Quintilian's Testimony." In *Dissertatiunculae Criticae: Festschrift für Günther Christian Hansen,* ed. Christian-Friedrich Collatz et al. 195–200. Würzburg: Königshausen and Neumann.

Ayers, Donald M. 1950. "The Speeches of Cicero's Opponents: Studies in *Pro Roscio Amerino, In Verrem,* and *Pro Murena.*" Ph.D. diss., Princeton University.

———. 1953–54. "Cato's Speech against Murena." *CJ* 49:245–53.

Badian, E. 1956. "P. Decius P.f. Subulo: An Orator of the Time of the Gracchi." *JRS* 46:91–96.

———. 1984. *Foreign Clientelae (264–70 B.C.).* 1958. Reprinted with corrections, Oxford: Clarendon.

———. 1962. "From the Gracchi to Sulla (1940–59)." *Historia* 11:197–245. Reprinted in Seager 1969, 3–51.

———. 1964. *Studies in Greek and Roman History.* Oxford: Blackwell.

———. 1966. "Notes on *Provincia Gallia* in the Late Republic." In *Mélanges d'archéologie et d'histoire offerts à André Pignaniol,* ed. Raymond Chevallier, 2:901–18. Paris: S.E.V.P.E.N.

———. 1967. "The Testament of Ptolemy Alexander." *RhM,* n.s., 110:178–92.

———. 1968a. *Roman Imperialism in the Late Republic.* 2d ed. Oxford: Blackwell.

———. 1968b. "The Sempronii Aselliones." *PACA* 11:1–6.

———. 1970. "Additional Notes on Roman Magistrates." *Athenaeum,* n.s., 48:3–14.

———. 1972. *Publicans and Sinners: Private Enterprise in the Service of the Roman Republic.* Ithaca: Cornell University Press.

———. 1980. "A *Fundus* at Fundi." *AJP* 101:470–82.

Balconi, Carla. 1993. "Rabirio Postumo dioiketes d'Egitto in *P. Med.* inv. 68.53?" *Aegyptus* 73:3–20.

———. 1994. "Rabirio Postumo dioiketes d'Egitto: Prima testimonianza papiracea." In *Proceedings of the Twentieth International Congress of Papyrologists, Copenhagen, 23–29 August, 1992,* collected by Adam Bülow-Jacobsen, 219–22. Copenhagen: Museum Tusculanum Press.

Baldwin, Barry. 1979. "The *acta diurna.*" *Chiron* 9:189–203.

Barker, Graeme, John Lloyd, and Derrick Webley. 1978. "A Classical Landscape in Molise." *PBSR,* n.s., 33:35–51.

Barlow, Charles T. 1980. "The Roman Government and the Roman Economy, 92–80 B.C." *AJP* 101:202–19.

Bauerle, Ellen A. 1990. "Procuring an Election: *Ambitus* in the Roman Republic, 432–49 B.C." Ph.D. diss., University of Michigan.

Bauman, Richard A. 1992. *Women and Politics in Ancient Rome.* London: Routledge.

———. 1996. *Crime and Punishment in Ancient Rome.* London: Routledge.

Bergmann, A. 1893. *Einleitung in Ciceros Rede für L. Valerius Flaccus.* Jahresbericht des

Königlichen Gymnasiums mit Realklassen zu Schneeberg 543. Schneeberg: Druck von C. M. Gärtner.

Berry, D. H. 1990. Review of May 1988. *JRS* 80:203–4.

———. 1992. Review of Alexander 1990. *CR*, n.s., 42:109–10.

———. 1996. Review of Cicero 1992 et al. *JRS* 86:201–7.

Bianchini, Mariagrazia. 1964. *Le formalità costitutive del rapporto processuale nel sistema accusatorio romano.* Milan: Giuffrè.

Birt, Th. 1930. "Zu Ciceros *Paradoxa* 46." *Philologus,* n.s., 39:100–101.

Brennan, T. Corey. 1992. "Sulla's Career in the Nineties: Some Reconsiderations." *Chiron* 22:103–58.

Broughton, T. Robert S. 1951–52. *The Magistrates of the Roman Republic.* 2 vols. Philological Monographs of the American Philological Association 15. Cleveland: American Philological Association.

———. 1986. *The Magistrates of the Roman Republic.* Vol. 3 Supplement. Atlanta: Scholars.

———. 1991. *Candidates Defeated in Roman Elections: Some Ancient Roman Also-rans.* Transactions of the American Philosophical Society, vol. 81, part 4. Philadelphia: American Philosophical Society.

Bruns, Karl Georg, ed. 1909. *Fontes Iuris Romani Antiqui.* Ed. Otto Gradenwitz. 7th ed. Tübingen: Mohr.

Brunt, P. A. 1965. "'Amicitia' in the Late Roman Republic." *PCPS,* n.s., 11:1–20. Reprinted with revisions in Brunt 1988, 351–81.

———. 1971. *Italian Manpower, 225 B.C.–A.D. 14.* Oxford: Clarendon.

———. 1980. "Patronage and Politics in the *Verrines.*" *Chiron* 10:273–89.

———. 1988. *The Fall of the Roman Republic and Related Essays.* Oxford: Oxford University Press.

Bruun, Christer. 1997. "Water for Roman Brothels: Cicero *Cael.* 34." *Phoenix* 51:364–73.

Bucher, Gregory S. 1995. "Appian *BC* 2.24 and the Trial *de ambitu* of M. Aemilius Scaurus." *Historia* 44:396–421.

Buckland, W. W. 1908. *The Roman Law of Slavery: The Condition of the Slave in Private Law from Augustus to Justinian.* Cambridge: Cambridge University Press.

Bulst, Christoph Meinhard. 1964. "'Cinnanum Tempus': A Reassessment of the 'Dominatio Cinnae.'" *Historia* 13:307–37.

Butrica, James L. 1999a. "Using Water 'Unchastely': Cicero *Pro Caelio* 34 Again." *Phoenix* 53: 136–39.

———. 1999b. "Using Water 'Unchastely': Cicero *Pro Caelio* 34 Again—Addendum." *Phoenix* 53:336.

Caplan, Harry. 1970. *Of Eloquence: Studies in Ancient and Mediaeval Rhetoric.* Ed. Anne King and Helen North. Ithaca: Cornell University Press.

Ciaceri, Emanuele. 1918. *Processi politici e relazioni internazionali: Studi sulla storia politica e sulla tradizione letteraria della repubblica e dell'impero.* Ricerche sulla storia e sul diritto romano 2. Rome: Nardecchia.

———. 1926–30. *Cicerone e i suoi tempi.* 2 vols. Milan: Dante Alighieri di Albrighi.

———. 1930. "Il processo di M. Celio Rufo e l'arringa di Cicerone." *Atti della Reale Accademia di archeologia, lettere, e belle arti* (Naples), n.s., 11:3–24.

Cicero, Marcus Tullius. 1883. *Ciceros Rede für L. Flaccus.* Ed. Adolf Du Mesnil. Leipzig: Teubner.

———. 1889. *Pro Cluentio.* Ed. William Ramsay and George G. Ramsay. 2d ed. Oxford: Clarendon.

———. 1895. *Pro T. Annio Milone ad Iudices Oratio.* Ed. Albert C. Clark. Oxford: Clarendon.

———. 1926. *A Commentary on Cicero In Vatinium, with an Historical Introduction and Appendices.* Ed. L. G. Pocock. London: University of London Press.

———. 1931. *Pro L. Flacco Oratio.* Ed. T. B. L. Webster. Oxford: Clarendon.

———. 1953. *Discours.* Vol. 8, *Pour Cluentius.* Ed. Pierre Boyancé. Paris: Budé.

———. 1958. *Pro Caelio. De Provinciis Consularibus. Pro Balbo.* Trans. R. Gardner. Cambridge, MA: Harvard University Press.

———. 1960. *Pro M. Caelio Oratio.* Ed. R. G. Austin. 3d ed. Oxford: Clarendon.

———. 1961. *In L. Calpurnium Pisonem Oratio.* Ed. R. G. M. Nisbet. Oxford: Clarendon.

———. 1965–70. *Cicero's Letters to Atticus.* Ed. D. R. Shackleton Bailey. 7 vols. Cambridge: Cambridge University Press.

———. 1966. *Brutus.* Ed. A. E. Douglas. Oxford: Clarendon.

———. 1971. *Les Paradoxes des stoïcens.* Ed. Jean Molager. Paris: Budé.

———. 1976. *Discours.* Vol. 16, part 2, *Pour Cn. Plancius* Ed. Pierre Grimal. Paris: Budé.

———. 1977. *Epistulae ad familiares.* Ed. D. R. Shackleton Bailey. Cambridge: Cambridge University Press.

———. 1978. *Cicero's Letters to his Friends.* Trans. D. R. Shackleton Bailey. 2 vols. New York: Penguin Books.

———. 1980. *Epistulae ad Quintum fratrem et M. Brutum.* Ed. D. R. Shackleton Bailey. Cambridge: Cambridge University Press.

———. 1986. *Verrines II.1.* Trans. T. N. Mitchell. Warminster: Aris and Phillips.

———. 1989. *Pro Murena.* Ed. Joachim Adamietz. Texte zur Forschung 55. Darmstadt: Wissenschaftliche Buchgesellschaft.

———. 1992. *Ciceros Rede* pro Rabirio Postumo, *Einleitung und Kommentar.* Ed. Claudia Klodt. Beiträge zur Altertumskunde 24. Stuttgart: Teubner.

———. 1993. *Cicero's Caesarian Speeches: A Stylistic Commentary.* Ed. Harold C. Gotoff. Chapel Hill: University of North Carolina Press.

———. 1995. *Orationes in P. Vatinium testem et pro M. Caelio.* Ed. Tadeusz Maslowski. Scripta quae manserunt omnia 23. Stuttgart and Leipzig: Teubner.

———. 1996. *Pro P. Sulla Oratio.* Ed. D. H. Berry. Cambridge Classical Texts and Commentaries 30. Cambridge: Cambridge University Press.

[Cicero]. 1954. *Ad C. Herennium: De ratione dicendi (Rhetorica ad Herennium).* Trans. Harry Caplan. Cambridge: Harvard University Press.

Clark, A. C. 1927. Review of Humbert 1925. *CR* 41:74–76.

Classen, C. Joachim. 1972. "Die Anklage gegen A. Cluentius Habitus (66 v. Chr. Geb.)." *ZSS* 89:1–17.

———. 1980. "Verres' Gehilfen in Sizilien nach Ciceros Darstellung." *Ciceroniana,* n.s., 4:93–114.

———. 1982. "Ciceros Kunst der Überredung." In *Éloquence et rhétorique chez Cicéron,* ed. W. Ludwig, 149–92. Entretiens sur l'antiquité classique 28. Geneva: Fondation Hardt.

———. 1985. *Recht-Rhetorik-Politik: Untersuchungen zu Ciceros rhetorischer Strategie.* Darmstadt: Wissenschaftliche Buchgesellschaft.

Clemente, Guido. 1974. *I Romani nella Gallia meridionale (II–I sec. a. C.)*: Politica ed economia nell'età dell'imperialismo. Bologna: Pàtron.

Cloud, J. D. 1968. "How Did Sulla Style His Law *de sicariis*?" *CR,* n.s., 18:140–43.

———. 1969. "The Primary Purpose of the *lex Cornelia de sicariis.*" *ZSS* 86:258–86.

———. 1994. "The Constitution and Public Criminal Law." In *Cambridge Ancient History,* 2d ed., 9:491–530. Cambridge: Cambridge University Press.

Courtney, E. 1961. "The Prosecution of Scaurus in 54 B.C." *Philologus,* n.s., 105:151–56.

Craig, Christopher P. 1981. "The *Accusator* as *Amicus:* An Original Roman Tactic of Ethical Argumentation." *TAPA* 111:31–37.

———. 1990. "Cicero's Strategy of Embarrassment in the Speech for Plancius." *AJP* 111:75–81.

———. 1993. *Form as Argument in Cicero's Speeches: A Study of Dilemma.* American Classical Studies 31. Atlanta: Scholars.

———. 1994–95. "Teaching Cicero's Speech for Caelius: What Enquiring Minds Want to Know." *CJ* 90:407–22.

Crawford, Jane W. 1984. *M. Tullius Cicero: The Lost and Unpublished Orations.* Hypomnemata 80. Göttingen: Vandenhoeck and Ruprecht.

———. 1994. *M. Tullius Cicero, The Fragmentary Speeches: An Edition with Commentary.* 2d ed. American Classical Studies 37. Athens, GA: Scholars.

Crawford, Michael H. 1974. *Roman Republican Coinage.* 2 vols. Cambridge: Cambridge University Press.

———, ed. 1996. *Roman Statutes. Bulletin of the Institute of Classical Studies* Supplement 64. 2 vols. London: Institute of Classical Studies.

Crook, J. A. 1967. *"Patria potestas." CQ,* n.s., 17:113–22.

———. 1995. *Legal Advocacy in the Roman World.* London: Duckworth.

D'Arms, John H. 1970. *Romans on the Bay of Naples: A Social and Cultural Study of the Villas and Their Owners from 150 B.C. to A.D. 400.* Cambridge: Harvard University Press.

David, Jean-Michel. 1983. "Sfida o vendetta, minaccia o ricatto: L'accusa pubblica nelle mani dei giovani romani alla fine della repubblica." In *La paura dei padri nella società antica e medievale,* ed. Ezio Pellizer and Nevio Zorzetti, 99–112. Biblioteca di Cultura Moderna, Laterza, 880. Rome: Laterza.

———. 1992. *Le patronat judiciaire au dernier siècle de la république Romaine.* Bibliothèque des écoles françaises d'Athènes et de Rome 277. Rome: École française de Rome.

David, Jean-Michel, Segolene Demougin, Elizabeth Deniaux, Danielle Ferey, Jean-Marc Flambard, and Claude Nicolet. 1973. "Le 'Commentariolum Petitionis' de Quintus Cicéron: Etat de la question et étude prosopographique." *ANRW* 1.3:239–77.

Dessau, H. 1911. "Gaius Rabirius Postumus." *Hermes* 46:613–20.

———. 1912. "Gaius Rabirius Postumus: Nachtrag zu Bd. XLVI S. 613." *Hermes* 47:320.

Dilke, O. A. W. 1980. "Divided Loyalties in Eastern Sicily under Verres." *Ciceroniana,* n.s., 4:43–51.

Dorey, T. A. 1958. "Cicero, Clodia, and the *Pro Caelio.*" *Greece and Rome* 2, no. 5:175–80.

Douglas, A. E. 1973. "The Intellectual Background of Cicero's Rhetorica: A Study in Method." *ANRW* 1.3:95–138.

———. 1980. Review of Stroh 1975. *JRS* 70:242.

Drexler, Hans. 1944. "Zu Ciceros Rede *pro Caelio.*" *NGG*, phil.-hist. Kl., 1–32.

Drumann, W. 1899–1929. *Geschichte Roms in seinem Übergange von der republikanischen zur monarchischen Verfassung, oder Pompeius, Caesar, Cicero und ihre Zeitgenossen nach Geschlechtern und mit genealogischen Tabellen.* Revised by P. Groebe. 2d ed. 6 vols. Berlin and Leipzig: Gebrüder Borntraeger.

Dyck, Andrew R. 1996. *A Commentary on Cicero,* De officiis. Ann Arbor: University of Michigan Press.

Dyson, Stephen L. 1992. *Community and Society in Roman Italy.* Baltimore: Johns Hopkins University Press.

Ebel, Charles. 1975. "Pompey's Organization of Transalpina." *Phoenix* 29:358–73.

Ennius. 1967. *The Tragedies of Ennius: The Fragments Edited with an Introduction and Commentary.* Ed. H. D. Jocelyn. Cambridge: Cambridge University Press.

Epstein, David F. 1987. *Personal Enmity in Roman Politics, 218–43 B.C.* London: Croom Helm.

Exuperantius, Iulius. 1982. *Opusculum.* Ed. Naevius Zorzetti. Leipzig: Teubner.

Fantham, Elaine. 1973. "Ciceronian *Conciliare* and Aristotelian *Ethos.*" *Phoenix* 27:262–75.

———. 1975. "The Trials of Gabinius in 54 B.C." *Historia* 24:425–43.

———. 1997. "The Contexts and Occasions of Roman Public Rhetoric." In *Roman Eloquence: Rhetoric in Society and Literature,* ed. William J. Dominik, 111–28. London: Routledge.

Fascione, Lorenzo. 1974. "Riflessioni sull'orazione per Rabirio Postumo." *Studi Senesi* 86:335–76.

Ferrary, J.-L. 1991. *"Lex Cornelia de sicariis et veneficiis."* *Athenaeum,* n.s., 79:417–34.

Fortenbaugh, William W. 1988. *"Benevolentiam Conciliare* and *Animos Permovere."* *Rhetorica* 6:259–73.

Frederiksen, M. W. 1966. "Caesar, Cicero, and the Problem of Debt." *JRS* 56:128–41.

Frier, Bruce W. 1985. *The Rise of the Roman Jurists: Studies in Cicero's* Pro Caecina. Princeton: Princeton University Press.

———. 1994. Review of Lintott 1992. *JRS* 84:211–12.

Fuhrmann, Manfred. 1992. *Cicero and the Roman Republic.* Trans. W. E. Yuill. Oxford: Blackwell.

Gabba, Emilio. 1961. "Cicerone e la falsificazione dei senatoconsulti." *SCO* 10:89–96.

———. 1964. "M. Livio Druso et le riforme di Silla." *ASNP* 33:1–15.

———. 1976. *Republican Rome, the Army and the Allies.* Trans. P. J. Cuff. Berkeley: University of California Press.

Gallant, Thomas W. 1991. *Risk and Survival in Ancient Greece: Reconstructing the Rural Domestic Economy.* Stanford: Stanford University Press.

Gamberale, Leopoldo. 1995. "Un probabile errore di latino in Plutarco, *Tib. Gracch.* 13, 6." *RFIC* 123:433–40.

Garnsey, Peter. 1988. *Famine and Food Supply in the Graeco-Roman World: Responses to Risk and Crisis.* Cambridge: Cambridge University Press.

Geffcken, Katherine. 1973. *Comedy in the* Pro Caelio *(with an Appendix on the* In Clodium et Curionem). Leiden: Brill.

Gelzer, Matthias. 1968. *Caesar, Politician and Statesman.* Trans. Peter Needham. Cambridge: Harvard University Press.

————. 1969. *Cicero, ein biographischer Versuch.* Wiesbaden: F. Steiner.

Giuffrè, Vincenzo. 1993. *Imputati, avvocati e giudici nella* "pro Cluentio" *Ciceroniana.* Naples: Jovene.

————. 1994. "'Nominis delatio' e 'nominis receptio.'" *Labeo* 40:359–64.

Gotoff, Harold C. 1986. "Cicero's Analysis of the Prosecution Speeches in the *Pro Caelio:* An Exercise in Practical Criticism." *CP* 81:122–32.

————. 1993. "Oratory: The Art of Illusion." *HSCP* 95:289–13.

Greenidge, A. H. J. 1901. *The Legal Procedure of Cicero's Time.* Oxford: Clarendon.

Griffin, Miriam. 1973a. "The 'leges iudiciariae' of the Pre-Sullan Era." *CQ,* n.s., 23:108–26.

————. 1973b. "The Tribune C. Cornelius." *JRS* 63:196–213.

Gruen, Erich S. 1968a. "Pompey and the Pisones." *CSCA* 1:155–70.

————. 1968b. *Roman Politics and the Criminal Courts, 149–78 B.C.* Cambridge: Harvard University Press.

————. 1969a. "The Consular Elections for 53 B.C." In *Hommages à Marcel Renard,* ed. Jacqueline Bibauw, 2:311–21. Collection Latomus 102. Brussels: Latomus.

————. 1969b. "Pompey, the Roman Aristocracy, and the Conference of Luca." *Historia* 18:71–108.

————. 1971. "Pompey, Metellus Pius, and the Trials of 70–69 B.C.: The Perils of Schematism." *AJP* 92:1–16.

————. 1995. *The Last Generation of the Roman Republic.* 1974. Reprint, with a new introduction, Berkeley: University of California Press.

Guerriero, E. 1936. "Di una supposta 'causa capitale' assunta da Cicerone in favore di Aulo Gabinio, e nuovi dubbi intorno all'autenticità del discorso *Post Reditum ad Quirites." Il Mondo Classico* 6:160–66.

Habinek, Thomas N. 1998. *The Politics of Latin Literature: Writing, Identity, and Empire in Ancient Rome.* Princeton: Princeton University Press.

Hackl, Ursula. 1988. "Die Gründung der Provinz Gallia Narbonensis im Spiegel von Ciceros Rede für Fonteius." *Historia* 37:253–56.

Hall, Ursula. 1964. "Voting Procedure in Roman Assemblies." *Historia* 13:267–306.

Hallett, Judith P. 1984. *Fathers and Daughters in Roman Society: Women and the Elite Family.* Princeton: Princeton University Press.

Hampl, Franz. 1952. "Zur römischen Kolonisation in der Zeit der ausgehenden Republik und des frühen Prinzipats." *RhM,* n.s., 95:52–78.

Harris, Edward M. 1994. "Law and Oratory." In *Persuasion: Greek Rhetoric in Action,* ed. Ian Worthington, 130–50. London: Routledge.

————. 1995. *Aeschines and Athenian Politics.* Oxford: Oxford University Press.

Hayne, Léonie. 1978. "The Valerii Flacci—a Family in Decline." *AncSoc* 9:222–33.

Heinze, R. 1909. "Ciceros politische Anfänge." *Abhandlungen der Königlich Sächsischen Gesellschaft der Wissenschaften,* phil.-hist. Kl., 27:947–1010. Reprinted in *Vom Geist der Römertums,* ed. Erich Burck, 3d ed. (Darmstadt: Wissenschaftliche Buchgesellschaft, 1960), 59–141.

———. 1925. "Ciceros Rede *pro Caelio.*" *Hermes* 60:193–258.

Hermon, Ella. 1993. *Rome et la Gaule Transalpine avant César, 125–59 av. J.-C.* Diáphora 3. Naples: Jovene.

Heurgon, Jacques. 1950. "La lettre de Cicéron à P. Sittius (*Ad fam.*, V,17)." *Latomus* 9:369–77.

Hillard, T. W. 1981. "*In triclinio Coam, in cubiculo Nolam:* Lesbia and the Other Clodia." *LCM* 6:149–54.

Hofmann, J. B. 1965. *Lateinische Syntax und Stilistik.* Revised by Anton Szantyr. Lateinische Grammatik 2. Munich: C. H. Beck.

Hollis, A. S. 1998. "A Tragic Fragment in Cicero, *Pro Caelio* 67?" *CQ,* n.s., 48:561–64.

Horace. 1978. *Odes, Book II.* With commentary by R. G. M. Nisbet and Margaret Hubbard. Oxford: Clarendon.

Hough, John N. 1930. "The *lex Lutatia* and the *lex Plautia de vi.*" *AJP* 51:135–47.

Humbert, Jules. 1925. *Les plaidoyers écrits et les plaidoiries réelles de Cicéron.* Paris: Presses Universitaires.

Husband, Richard W. 1916–17. "The Prosecution of Murena." *CJ* 12:102–18.

Jolliffe, Richard Orlando. 1919. *Phases of Corruption in Roman Administration in the Last Half-Century of the Roman Republic.* Menasha, WI: George Banta.

Jones, A. H. M. 1972. *The Criminal Courts of the Roman Republic and Principate.* Oxford: Blackwell.

Jouanique, Pierre. 1960. "Sur l'interprétation du *Pro Fonteio,* I, 1–2." *REL* 38:107–12.

Kennedy, George. 1963. *The Art of Persuasion in Greece.* Princeton: Princeton University Press.

———. 1968. "The Rhetoric of Advocacy in Greece and Rome." *AJP* 89:419–36.

———. 1972. *The Art of Rhetoric in the Roman World, 300 B.C.–A.D. 300.* Princeton: Princeton University Press.

———. 1994. "Peripatetic Rhetoric as It Appears (and Disappears) in Quintilian." In *Peripatetic Rhetoric after Aristotle,* ed. William W. Fortenbaugh and David C. Mirhady, 174–82. New Brunswick, NJ: Transaction.

Kinsey, T. E. 1966a. "A Dilemma in the *Pro Roscio Amerino.*" *Mnemosyne,* 4th ser., 19:270–71.

———. 1966b. "A *Senatus Consultum* in the *Pro Murena.*" *Mnemosyne,* 4th ser., 19:272–73.

———. 1967. "The Dates of the *Pro Roscio Amerino* and *Pro Quinctio.*" *Mnemosyne,* 4th ser., 20:61–67.

———. 1980. "Cicero's Case against Magnus, Capito and Chrysogonus in the *Pro Sex. Roscio Amerino* and Its Use for the Historian." *AC* 49:173–90.

———. 1981. "A Problem in the *Pro Roscio Amerino.*" *Eranos* 79:149–50.

———. 1982. "The Political Insignificance of Cicero's *Pro Roscio.*" *LCM* 7:39–40.

———. 1985. "The Case against Sextus Roscius of Ameria." *AC* 54:188–96.

———. 1988. "The Sale of the Property of Roscius of Ameria: How Illegal Was It?" *AC* 57:296–97.

Kirby, John T. 1990. *The Rhetoric of Cicero's* Pro Cluentio. London Studies in Classical Philology 23. Amsterdam: Gieben.

———. 1997. "Ciceronian Rhetoric: Theory and Practice." In *Roman Eloquence:*

Rhetoric in Society and Literature, ed. William J. Dominik, 13–31. London: Routledge.

Kroll, W. 1937. "Ciceros Rede für Plancius." *RhM,* n.s., 86:127–39.

Kumaniecki, Kazimierz. 1970. "Les discours égarés de Cicéron 'pro Cornelio.'" *Mededelingen van de Koninklijke Vlaamse Academie voor Wetenschappen, Letteren en Schone Kunsten van België,* Klasse der letteren, 32:3–36.

Kunkel, Wolfgang. 1962. "Untersuchungen zur Entwicklung des römischen Kriminalverfahrens in vorsullanischer Zeit." *AbhMünch,* n.s., 56:1–149.

———. 1963. "Quaestio." *RE* 24:720–86.

———. 1967. *Herkunft und soziale Stellung der römischen Juristen.* 2d ed. Forschungen zum römischen Recht 4. Graz: Böhlau.

Kunkel, Wolfgang, and Roland Wittmann. 1995. *Staatsordnung und Staatspraxis der Römischen Republik.* Section 2: *Die Magistratur.* Handbuch der Altertumswissenschaft 10.3.2. Munich: C. H. Beck.

Kupisch, Berthold. 1974. "Cicero, *pro Flacco* 21,49f. und die *in integrum restitutio* gegen Urteile." *ZSS* 91:126–45.

Kurke, Alexander D. 1989. "Theme and Adversarial Presentation in Cicero's *Pro Flacco.*" Ph.D. diss., University of Michigan.

Laet, Siegfried J. de. 1949. *Portorium: Étude sur l'organisation douanière chez les Romains, surtout à l'époque du haut-empire.* Rijksuniversiteit te Gent, Werken uitgegeven door de Faculteit van de Wijsbegeerte en Letteren 105. Bruges: De Tempel.

Landgraf, Gustav, ed. 1914. *Kommentar zu Ciceros Rede* pro Sex. Roscio Amerino. 2d ed. Leipzig: Teubner.

Laurand, L. 1928. *Études sur le style des discours de Cicéron avec une esquisse de l'histoire du "cursus."* 3d ed. Paris: Les Belles Lettres.

Leeman, A. D. 1982. "The Technique of Persuasion in Cicero's *Pro Murena.*" In *Éloquence et rhétorique chez Cicéron,* ed. W. Ludwig, 193–228. Entretiens sur l'antiquité classique 28. Geneva: Fondation Hardt.

Lendon, J. E. 1997. *Empire of Honour: The Art of Government in the Roman World.* Oxford: Clarendon.

Levick, Barabara. 1990. *Claudius.* London: Batsford.

Levy, Ernst. 1933. "Von den römischen Anklägervergehen." *ZSS* 53:151–233. Reprinted in *Gesammelte Schriften,* vol. 2 (Cologne: Böhlau, 1963), 379–432.

Linderski, Jerzy. 1961a. "Ciceros Rede *pro Caelio* und die Ambitus- und Vereinsgesetzgebung der ausgehenden Republik." *Hermes* 89:106–19. Reprinted in Linderski 1995, 204–17, 647–49.

———. 1961b. "Two Speeches of Q. Hortensius: A Contribution to the Corpus Oratorum of the Roman Republic." *PP* 16:304–11. Reprinted with revisions in Linderski 1995, 328–35, 657–59.

———. 1971. "Three Trials in 54 B.C.: Sufenas, Cato, Procilius, and Cicero, 'Ad Atticum,' 4.15.4." In *Studi in onore di Edoardo Volterra,* 2:281–302. Pubblicazioni della Facoltà di Giurisprudenza dell'Università di Roma. Milan: Giuffrè. Reprinted in Linderski 1995, 115–36, 639–41.

———. 1974. "The Mother of Livia Augusta and the Aufidii Lurcones of the Republic." *Historia* 23:463–80. Reprinted in Linderski 1995, 262–79, 653.

———. 1985. "Buying the Vote: Electoral Corruption in the Late Republic." *Ancient World* 11:87–94. Reprinted in Linderski 1995, 107–14, 638–39.

———. 1995. *Roman Questions: Selected Papers.* Stuttgart: Fritz Steiner.

Lintott, A. W. 1968. *Violence in Republican Rome.* Oxford: Clarendon.

———. 1974. "Cicero and Milo." *JRS* 64:62–78.

———. 1981. "The *leges de repetundis* and Associate Measures under the Republic." *ZSS* 98:162–212.

———. 1990. "Electoral Bribery in the Roman Republic." *JRS* 80:1–16.

———. 1992. *Judicial Reform and Land Reform in the Roman Republic: A New Edition, with Translation and Commentary, of the Laws from Urbino.* Cambridge: Cambridge University Press.

Luraschi, Giorgio. 1983. "Il 'praemium' nell'esperienza giuridica romana." In *Studi in onore di Arnaldo Biscardi* 4:239–83. Milan: La Goliardica.

Magie, David. 1950. *Roman Rule in Asia Minor to the End of the Third Century after Christ.* Princeton: Princeton University Press.

Malcovati, H., ed. 1976. *Oratorum Romanorum Fragmenta Liberae Rei Publicae.* 4th ed. Turin: Paravia.

Marinone, N. 1950. "Cronologia del processo di Verre." In *Quaestiones Verrinae,* 8–14. Pubblicazioni della Facoltà di Lettere e Filosofia, vol. 2, no. 3. Turin: Università di Torino.

———. 1965–66. "I questori e i legati di Verre in Sicilia." *AAT* 100:219–52.

Marquardt, Joachim. 1886. *Das Privatleben der Römer.* Revised by A. Mau. 2d ed. Leipzig: S. Hirzel.

Marshall, Anthony J. 1969. "Romans under Chian Law." *GRBS* 10:255–71.

———. 1975a. "The Case of Valeria: An Inheritance Dispute in Roman Asia." *CQ,* n.s., 25:82–87.

———. 1975b. "Flaccus and the Jews of Asia (Cicero *Pro Flacco* 28.67–69)." *Phoenix* 29:139–54.

Marshall, B. A. 1976. *Crassus: A Political Biography.* Amsterdam: Hakkert.

———. 1976–77. "Catilina: Court Cases and Consular Candidature." *Scripta Classica Israelica* 3:127–37.

———. 1977. "Two Court Cases in the Late Second Century B.C." *AJP* 98:417–23.

———. 1985. *A Historical Commentary on Asconius.* Columbia: University of Missouri Press.

———. 1987. "*Excepta Oratio,* the Other *Pro Milone* and the Question of Shorthand." *Latomus* 46:730–36.

Marshall, B. A., and Robert J. Baker. 1975. "The Aspirations of Q. Arrius." *Historia* 24:220–31.

Mattingly, Harold B. 1970. "The Extortion Law of the *Tabula Bembina.*" *JRS* 60:154–68.

May, James M. 1981. "The Rhetoric of Advocacy and Patron-Client Identification: Variation on a Theme." *AJP* 102:308–15.

———. 1988. *Trials of Character: The Eloquence of Ciceronian Ethos.* Chapel Hill: University of North Carolina Press.

McDermott, William C. 1941. "Varro Murena." *TAPA* 72:255–65.

———. 1970. "The Sisters of P. Clodius." *Phoenix* 24:39–47.

———. 1972. "M. Cicero and M. Tiro." *Historia* 21:259–86.

McDonald, William. 1929. "The Tribunate of Cornelius." *CQ* 23:196–208.

McGushin, P., ed. 1977. *C. Sallustius Crispus, Bellum Catilinae, a Commentary.* *Mnemosyne* Supplement 45. Leiden: Brill.

Mentz, Arthur. 1931. "Die Entstehungsgeschichte der römischen Stenographie." *Hermes* 66:369–86.

Meyer, Eduard. 1919. *Caesars Monarchie und das Principat des Pompejus, Innere Geschichte Roms von 66 bis 44 v. Chr.* 2d ed. Stuttgart: Cotta.

Meyer, Hans D. 1978. "Die Strafklagekonsumption beim Repetundendelikt und die Rechtsregel 'bis de eadem re ne sit actio.'" *ZSS* 95:138–57.

Millar, Fergus. 1964. *A Study of Cassius Dio.* Oxford: Clarendon.

———. 1998. *The Crowd in Rome in the Late Republic.* Jerome Lectures 22. Ann Arbor: University of Michigan Press.

Mitchell, Stephen. 1979. "R.E.C.A.M. Notes and Studies No. 5: A Roman Family in Phrygia." *AS* 29:13–22.

Mitchell, Thomas N. 1969. "Cicero before Luca (September 57–April 56 B.C.)." *TAPA* 100:295–320.

———. 1979. *Cicero, the Ascending Years.* New Haven: Yale University Press.

———. 1991. *Cicero, the Senior Statesman.* New Haven: Yale University Press.

Momigliano, Arnaldo. 1932. *L'opera dell'imperatore Claudio.* Florence: Vallecchi.

Mommsen, Theodor. 1899. *Römisches Strafrecht.* Leipzig: Duncker and Humblot.

Moreau, Philippe. 1980. "Cicéron, Clodius, et la publication du *Pro Murena*." *REL* 58:220–37.

———. 1983. "Structures de parenté et d'alliance à Larinum d'après le *Pro Cluentio*." In *Les "bourgeoisies" municipales italiennes aux IIe et Ier siècles av. J.-C.,* 99—123. Colloques Internationaux du Centre National de la Recherche scientifique 609, Science Humaines. Paris: Centre Jean Bérard.

Münzer, Friedrich. 1909. "Aus dem Leben des M. Caelius Rufus." *Hermes* 44:135–42.

———. 1920. *Römische Adelparteien und Adelsfamilien.* Stuttgart: Metzlersche Verlagsbuchhandlung.

Nardo, Dante. 1970. *Il "Commentariolum Petitionis": La propaganda elettorale nella "ars" di Quinto Cicerone.* Padua: Liviana.

Nicolet, Claude. 1966–74. *L'ordre équestre à l'époque républicaine (312–43 av. J.-C.).* Vol. 1, *Définitions juridiques et structures sociales;* vol. 2, *Prosopographie des chevaliers romains.* Bibliothèques des écoles françaises d'Athènes et de Rome 207. Paris: de Boccard.

Nicols, John. 1981. "The Caecilii Metelli, *Patroni Siciliae?*" *Historia* 30:238–40.

Oost, Steward Irvin. 1956. "The Date of the *lex Iulia de repetundis*." *AJP* 77:19–28.

Pareti, Luigi. 1953. *Storia di Roma e del mondo Romano.* 6 vols. Turin: Unione Tipografico.

Patterson, Jeremy. 1985. "Politics in the Late Republic." In *Roman Political Life, 90 B.C.–A.D. 69,* ed. T. P. Wiseman, 21–43. Exeter Studies in History 7. Exeter: University of Exeter Press.

Peter, Hermann, ed. 1993. *Historicorum Romanorum reliquiae.* 2d ed. 2 vols. Stuttgart: Teubner.

Piazza, Maria Pia. 1987. "La 'lex Valeria' e le 'tabulae dodrantariae et quadrantariae.'" In *Studi in onore di Arnaldo Biscardi* 6:267–91. Milan: La Goliardica.

Picheca, Carmela. 1980. "Un esempio di *moderatio* ciceroniana: La presentazione di L. Sempronius Atratinus nella *Pro Caelio*." *Invigilata Lucernis* 2:41–51.

Pierpaoli, Massimo. 1997. "L'orazione di Servio Sulpicio Rufo nel processo di Murena." *Maia* 49:231–53.

Pina Polo, Francisco. 1996. *Contra arma verbis: Der Redner vor dem Volk in der späten römischen Republik.* Trans. Edda Liess. Heidelberger Althistorische Beiträge und Epigraphische Studien 22. Stuttgart: F. Steiner.

Plutarch. 1954. *Vita Caesaris.* Ed. Albino Garzetti. Florence: La Nuova Italia.

———. 1963. *Vita Ciceronis.* Ed. Domenico Magnino. Florence: La Nuova Italia.

Posidonius. 1989. *Posidonius.* Vol. 1, *The Fragments.* Ed. L. Edelstein and I. G. Kidd. 2d ed. Cambridge: Cambridge University Press.

Pugliese, Giovanni. 1994. "Un nuovo esame della Ciceroniana *Pro Cluentio*." *Labeo* 40:248–55.

Quintilian. 1975–79. *Institution Oratoire.* Ed. Jean Cousin. Vols. 1–6. Paris: Budé.

Ramsey, John T. 1980. "The Prosecution of C. Manilius in 66 B.C. and Cicero's *Pro Manilio*." *Phoenix* 34:323–36.

———. 1982. "Cicero, *Pro Sulla* 68 and Catiline's Candidacy in 66 B.C." *HSCP* 86:121–31.

———. 1999. Review of Cicero 1996. *Gnomon* 71:723–26.

Rauh, Nicholas K. 1993. *The Sacred Bonds of Commerce: Religion, Economy, and Trade Society at Hellenistic Roman Delos, 166–87 B.C.* Amsterdam: Gieben.

Rawson, Elizabeth. 1977. "More on the *Clientelae* of the Patrician Claudii." *Historia* 26:340–57.

Reams, Lee E. 1986–87. "The Strange Case of Sulla's Brother." *CJ* 82:301–5.

Reitzenstein, R. 1925. "Zu Ciceros Rede für Caelius." *NAWG*, pp. 25–32.

Riccobono, Salvatore, ed. 1968–72. *Fontes Iuris Romani Antejustiniani.* 3 vols. Florence: Barbera.

Riggsby, Andrew M. 1995a. "Appropriation and Reversal as a Basis for Oratorical Proof." *CP* 90:245–56.

———. 1995b. "Pliny on Cicero and Oratory: Self-fashioning in the Public Eye." *AJP* 116:123–35.

———. 1997. "Did the Romans Believe in Their Verdicts?" *Rhetorica* 15:235–51.

———. 1999. *Crime and Community in Ciceronian Rome.* Austin: University of Texas Press.

Rivet, A. L. F. 1988. *Gallia Narbonensis: Southern France in Roman Times.* London: B. T. Botsford.

Rosenstein, Nathan. 1995. "Sorting Out the Lot in Republican Rome." *AJP* 116:43–75.

Rutgers, Leonard Victor. 1994. "Roman Policy towards the Jews: Expulsions from the City of Rome during the First Century C.E." *CA* 13:56–74.

Ryan, Francis X. 1994. "Cicero, *Mur.* 47: Text and Meaning." *Gymnasium* 101:481–82.

———. 1996a. "The Quaestorships of Hirtuleius and M. Fonteius." *Hermes* 124:250–53.

———. 1996b. "Some Persons in the *Pro Cluentio*." *Tyche* 11:195–205.

Salzman, Michele Renee. 1982. "Cicero, the *Megalenses,* and the Defense of Caelius." *AJP* 103:299–304.

Santalucia, Bernardo. 1994. *Studi di diritto penale romano.* Rome: "L'Erma" di Bretschneider.

———. 1997. "Cicerone e la 'nominis delatio.'" *Labeo* 43:404–17.

Schanz, Martin. 1927–59. *Geschichte der Römischen Literatur bis zum Gesetzgebungswerk des Kaisers Justinian.* Revised by Carl Hosius. 4th ed. 4 vols. Munich: C. H. Beck.

Schmitz, Dietmar. 1985. *Zeugen des Prozessgegners in Gerichtsreden Ciceros. Prismata* 1. Frankfurt am Main: P. Lang.

———. 1989. "Zeugen im Verres-Prozeß nach Ciceros Darstellung." *Gymnasium* 96:521–31.

Schöll, F. 1896. "Zu Ciceros Rede *pro Flacco.*" *RhM*, n.s., 51:381–400.

Schulze, Wilhelm. 1904. *Zur Geschichte lateinischer Eigennamen.* Abhandlungen der Königlichen Gesellschaft der Wissenschaften zu Göttingen, phil.-hist. Kl., n.s., vol. 5, no. 5. Berlin: Weidmannsche Buchhandlung.

Schütrumpf, Eckart. 1994. "Non-logical Means of Persuasion in Aristotle's *Rhetoric* and Cicero's *De oratore.*" In *Peripatetic Rhetoric after Aristotle,* ed. William W. Fortenbaugh and David C. Mirhady, 95–110. New Brunswick, NJ: Transaction.

Seager, Robin, ed. 1969. *The Crisis of the Roman Republic: Studies in Political and Social History.* Cambridge: Heffer.

Serrao, Feliciano. 1956. "Appunti sui 'patroni' e sulla legittimazione attiva all'accusa nei processi 'repetundarum.'" In *Studi in onore di Pietro de Francisci,* 2:471–511. Milan: Giuffrè.

Settle, James N. 1963. "The Trial of Milo and the Other *Pro Milone.*" *TAPA* 94:269–80.

Shackleton Bailey, D. R. 1961. "On Cicero, *Ad Familiares.*" *Philologus,* n.s., 105:72–89, 263–72.

———. 1970. "The Prosecution of Roman Magistrates-Elect." *Phoenix* 24:162–66.

———. 1979. "On Cicero's Speeches." *HSCP* 83:237–85.

———. 1988. *Onomasticon to Cicero's Speeches.* Norman: University of Oklahoma Press.

———. 1991. *Two Studies in Roman Nomenclature.* 2d ed. American Classical Studies 3. Atlanta: Scholars.

Shatzman, Israel. 1971. "The Egyptian Question in Roman Politics (59–54 B.C.)." *Latomus* 30:363–69.

———. 1975. *Senatorial Wealth and Roman Politics.* Collection Latomus 142. Brussels: Latomus.

Sherwin-White, A. N. 1949. "Poena legis repetundarum." *PBSR,* n.s., 4:5–25.

———. 1972. "The Date of the *lex repetundarum* and Its Consequences." *JRS* 62:83–99.

———. 1982. "The *lex repetundarum* and the Political Ideas of Gaius Gracchus." *JRS* 72:18–31.

———, ed. 1985. *The Letters of Pliny: A Historical and Social Commentary.* 1966. Rev. ed. Oxford: Clarendon.

Siani-Davies, Mary. 1996. "Gaius Rabirius Postumus: A Roman Financier and Caesar's Political Ally." *Arctos* 30:207–40.

Skinner, Marilyn B. 1983. "Clodia Metelli." *TAPA* 113:273–87.

Smallwood, E. Mary. 1976. *The Jews under Roman Rule from Pompey to Diocletian.* Studies in Judaism in Late Antiquity 20. Leiden: Brill.

Smith, R. E. 1966. *Cicero the Statesman.* Cambridge: Cambridge University Press.

Solin, Heikki. 1987. Review of Shackleton Bailey 1991. *Gnomon* 59:595–601.

Solmsen, Friedrich. 1938. "Aristotle and Cicero on the Orator's Playing upon the Feelings." *AJP* 33:390–404.

———. 1941. "The Aristotelian Tradition in Ancient Rhetoric." *AJP* 62:35–50, 169–90.

Starr, Raymond J. 1987. "The Circulation of Literary Texts in the Roman World." *CQ,* n.s., 37:213–23.

Staveley, E. S. 1972. *Greek and Roman Voting and Elections.* Ithaca: Cornell University Press.

Stewart, Roberta. 1995. "Catiline and the Crisis of 63–60 B.C.: The Italian Perspective." *Latomus* 54:62–78.

Stockton, David. 1971. *Cicero: A Political Biography.* Oxford: Oxford University Press.

Stone, A. M. 1980. "*Pro Milone:* Cicero's Second Thoughts." *Antichthon* 14:88–111.

———. 1998. "A House of Notoriety: An Episode in the Campaign for the Consulate in 64 B.C." *CQ,* n.s., 48:487–91.

Strachan-Davidson, James Leigh. 1912. *Problems of the Roman Criminal Law.* 2 vols. Oxford: Clarendon.

Stroh, Wilfried. 1975. *Taxis und Taktik: Die advokatische Dispositionskunst in Ciceros Gerichtsreden.* Stuttgart: Teubner.

Suetonius Tranquillus, C. 1982. *Divus Julius.* Ed. H. E. Butler and M. Cary, with additions by G. B. Townend. Bristol: Bristol Classical Press.

———. 1995. *De grammaticis et rhetoribus.* Ed. Robert A. Kaster. Oxford: Clarendon.

Sumner, G. V. 1965. "The Consular Elections of 66 B.C." *Phoenix* 19:226–31.

———. 1971. "The *lex annalis* under Caesar." *Phoenix* 25:246–71, 357–71.

———. 1973. *The Orators in Cicero's Brutus: Prosopography and Chronology. Phoenix* Supplement 11. Toronto.

———. 1978a. "Governors of Asia in the Nineties B.C." *GRBS* 19:147–53.

———. 1978b. Review of Shackleton Bailey 1991. *CP* 73:159–64.

Swarney, Paul R. 1993. "Social Status and Social Behavior as Criteria in Judicial Proceedings in the Late Republic." In *Law, Politics, and Society in the Ancient Mediterranean World,* ed. Baruch Halpern and Deborah W. Hobson, 137–55. Sheffield: Sheffield University Press.

Świderek, Anna. 1954. "Le Mime Grec en Egypte." *Eos* 47:63–74.

Syme, Ronald. 1939. *The Roman Revolution.* Oxford: Oxford University Press.

———. 1955a. "Missing Senators." *Historia* 4:52–71. Reprinted in *Roman Papers,* vol. 1, ed. E. Badian (Oxford: Clarendon, 1979), 271–91.

———. 1955b. Review of Broughton 1951–52. *CP* 50:127–38.

———. 1964. *Sallust.* Berkeley: University of California Press.

———. 1981. "A Great Orator Mislaid." *CQ,* n.s., 31:421–27.

Tacitus. 1996. *The Annals of Tacitus, Book 3.* Ed. A. J. Woodman and R. H. Martin. Cambridge: Cambridge University Press.

Tatum, W. Jeffrey. 1991a. "Cicero, the Elder Curio, and the Titinia Case." *Mnemosyne,* 4th ser., 44:364–71.

———. 1991b. "The Marriage of Pompey's Son to the Daughter of Ap. Claudius Pulcher." *Klio* 73:122–29.

———. 1997. "Friendship, Politics, and Literature in Catullus: Poems 1, 65 and 66, 116." *CQ,* n.s., 47:482–500.

———. 1999. *The Patrician Tribune: Publius Clodius Pulcher.* Chapel Hill: University of North Carolina Press.

Taylor, Lily Ross. 1949. *Party Politics in the Age of Caesar.* Berkeley: University of California Press.

———. 1950. "The Date and the Meaning of the Vettius Affair." *Historia* 1:45–51.

———. 1964. "Magistrates of 55 B.C. in Cicero's *Pro Plancio* and Catullus 52." *Athenaeum*, n.s., 42:12–28.

———. 1966. *Roman Voting Assemblies from the Hannibalic War to the Dictatorship of Caesar.* Ann Arbor: University of Michigan Press.

Tchernia, André. 1983. "Italian Wine in Gaul at the End of the Republic." In *Trade in the Ancient Economy,* ed. Peter Garnsey, Keith Hopkins, and C. R. Whitaker, 87–104. Berkeley: University of California Press.

Thierfelder, Andreas. 1965. "Über den Wert der Bemerkungen zur eigenen Person in Ciceros Prozeßreden." *Gymnasium* 72:385–414.

Torelli, Marina R. 1973. "Una nuova iscrizione di Silla da Larino." *Athenaeum*, n.s., 51:336–54.

Treggiari, Susan. 1973. "Cicero, Horace, and Mutual Friends: Lamiae and Varrones Murenae." *Phoenix* 27:245–61.

———. 1991. *Roman Marriage: Iusti Coniuges from the Time of Cicero to the Time of Ulpian.* Oxford: Clarendon.

Twyman, Briggs L. 1976. "The Date of Sulla's Abdication and the Chronology of the First Book of Appian's *Civil Wars.*" *Athenaeum*, n.s., 54:77–97, 271–95.

Vasaly, Ann. 1985. "The Masks of Rhetoric: Cicero's *Pro Roscio Amerino.*" *Rhetorica* 3:1–20.

———. 1993. *Representations: Images of the World in Ciceronian Oratory.* Berkeley: University of California Press.

Venturini, Carlo. 1979. *Studi sul "crimen repetundarum" nell'età repubblicana.* Pubblicazioni della Facoltà di Giurisprudenza della Università di Pisa 69; Istituto di diritto Romano e storia del diritto 5. Milan: Giuffrè.

———. 1984. "L'orazione *Pro C. Plancio* e la *lex Licinia de sodaliciis.*" In *Studi in onore di Cesare Sanfilippo* 5:787–804. Università di Catania, Pubblicazioni della Facoltà di Giurisprudenza 96. Milan: Giuffré.

Volpe, Michael. 1977. "The Persuasive Force of Humor: Cicero's Defense of Caelius." *Quarterly Journal of Speech* 63:311–23.

Wallace, Robert W. 1989. *The Areopagus Council to 307 B.C.* Baltimore: Johns Hopkins University Press.

Ward, Allen M. 1968. "Cicero's Support of Pompey in the Trials of M. Fonteius and P. Oppius." *Latomus* 27:802–9.

Wardy, Bilhah. 1979. "Jewish Religion in Pagan Literature during the Late Republic and Early Empire." *ANRW* 2.19 1:592–644.

Watson, Alan. 1967. *The Law of Persons in the Later Roman Republic.* Oxford: Clarendon.

———. 1968. *The Law of Property in the Later Roman Republic.* Oxford: Clarendon.

———. 1975. *Rome of the XII Tables, Persons and Property.* Princeton: Princeton University Press.

———, ed. 1985. *The Digest of Justinian.* Latin text edited by Theodor Mommsen with the aid of Paul Krueger. 4 vols. Philadelphia: University of Pennsylvania Press.

Weinrib, E. J. 1968. "The Prosecution of Roman Magistrates." *Phoenix* 22:32–56.

————. 1970. "The Judiciary Law of M. Livius Drusus (tr. pl. 91 B.C.)." *Historia* 19:414–43.

————. 1971. "The Prosecution of Magistrates-Designate." *Phoenix* 25:145–50.

White, Peter. 1995. "Postumus, Curtius Postumus, and Rabirius Postumus." *CP* 90:151–61.

Williams, Frederick. 1994. "Cercidas, Caelius, and Unsafe Sex: Τυνδαρέοιο γαμβρός (Cerc. fr. 2.28 Livrea)." *ZPE* 102:76–80.

Williams, Margaret H. 1989. "The Expulsion of the Jews from Rome in A.D. 19." *Latomus* 48:765–84.

Wirszubski, Ch. 1954. "Cicero's *Cum dignitate otium:* A Reconsideration." *JRS* 44:1–13. Reprinted in Seager 1969, 183–95.

Wiseman, T. P. 1965. "Mallius." *CR*, n.s., 15:263.

————. 1969. *Catullan Questions.* Leicester: Leicester University Press.

————. 1971. *New Men in the Roman Senate, 139 B.C.–A.D. 14.* Oxford: Oxford University Press.

————. 1974. *Cinna the Poet, and Other Roman Essays.* Leicester: Leicester University Press.

————. 1977. "Cicero, *Pro Sulla* 60–1." *LCM* 2:21–22.

————. 1985. *Catullus and His World: A Reappraisal.* Cambridge: Cambridge University Press.

————. 1994. "Caesar, Pompey, and Rome, 59–50 B.C." In *Cambridge Ancient History,* 2d ed., 9:368–423. Cambridge: Cambridge University Press.

Wlassak, Moriz. 1917. *Anklage und Streitbefestigung im Kriminalrecht der Römer.* Kaiserliche Akademie der Wissenschaften, phil.-hist. Kl., Sitzungsberichte, vol. 184, no. 1. Vienna: A. Hölder.

Wood, Neal. 1988. *Cicero's Social and Political Thought.* Berkeley: University of California Press.

Yakobson, Alexander. 1999. *Elections and Electioneering in Rome: A Study in the Political System of the Late Republic. Historia* Einzelschrift 128. Stuttgart: F. Steiner.

Yaron, Reuven. 1967. "Reflections on Usucapio." *Tijdschrift voor Rechtsgeschiedenis* 35:191–229.

Zehnacker, H. 1979. "La terre et l'argent (Cicéron, *Pro Flacco,* 42–50)." *REL* 57:165–86.

Zetzel, James E. G. 1994. Review of Craig 1993. *BMCR* 94.01.05. <http://ccat.sas.upenn.edu/bmcr/1994/94.01.05.html>.

Zumpt, A. W. 1871. *Der Criminalprocess der Römischen Republik.* Leipzig: Teubner.

Index of Ancient Sources

Peter, *HRRel* 23.365M = frag. 2, vol. 2,
    p. 34: 20

Plato
  Leges (Leg.)
    637E: 277n. 39
Pliny (the Elder) (Plin.)
  Historia Naturales (HN)
    5.3.6: 81
    7.136: 81
    7.139: 1
    7.165: 232
    36.113–15: 289n. 36
Pliny (the Younger) (Plin.)
  Epistulae (Ep.)
    1.20.6–10: 24
    1.20.7: 295n. 7
    1.20.8: 20
    3.9: 211–12
    3.9.17: 293n. 22
    4.9.9: 272n. 116, 279n. 10
    9.13.5: 308n. 4
Plutarch (Plut.)
  Moralia
    Quaestiones convivales
      (Quaest. conv.)
      712e: 294n. 30
  Vitae Parallelae
    Antonius (Ant.)
      3: 291n. 11
    Caesar (Caes.)
      9.1: 287n. 13
      48: 294n. 34
    Cato Minor (Cat. Min.)
      21: 122, 126
      23: 17
      25: 287n. 16
    Cicero (Cic.)
      3: 172, 303n. 6
      14: 313n. 19
      29: 225
      35: 21
    Pompeius (Pomp.)
      53.3: 297n. 2
    Sertorius (Sert.)
      21: 274n. 3

Sulla (Sull.)
  16: 303n. 9
  18: 303n. 9
Polybius (Polyb.)
  2.14.4: 277n. 38
  6.1.4: 264n. 21
  6.14.8: 278n. 53
Posidonius
  no. 67 Edelstein & Kidd: 277n. 38

Quintilian (Quint.)
  Institutio oratoria (Inst.)
    1.5.61: 227, 322n. 43
    1.6.29: 233
    3.6.10: 163, 307n. 38
    3.6.60: 175
    3.6.93: 263n. 4
    3.10.1: 265n. 25
    4.1.1: 266n. 39
    4.1.36: 9, 265n. 25
    4.1.49: 38
    4.2.27: 238, 324n. 68
    4.3.17: 21
    4.5.4: 22
    4.5.13: 163
    4.5.14: 307n. 38
    4.5.19–21: 185
    5.1.1–2: 33
    5.2: 33
    5.5: 33
    5.6: 33
    5.7.1–32: 33, 48
    5.7.3–6: 316n. 10
    5.7.5: 39, 289n. 41
    5.7.9: 210, 271n. 110
    5.7.11: 48
    5.7.13–14: 273n. 127
    5.7.22: 10, 38
    5.7.23: 237
    5.10.69: 306n. 35
    5.13.2–3: 10, 39
    5.13.45–50: 38
    5.13.48: 39
    6.1.9: 10
    6.1.21 265n. 25

Index of Names

This index also covers trials, under the name of the individual on trial.

Index of Topics

For specific trials, see the Index of Names, under the name of the person on trial.